Local Places, Global Processes

*Histories of Environmental Change
in Britain and Beyond*

edited by

Peter Coates, David Moon and Paul Warde

WIND *gather*
PRESS

Windgather Press is an imprint of Oxbow Books

Published in the United Kingdom in 2016 by
OXBOW BOOKS
10 Hythe Bridge Street, Oxford OX1 2EW

and in the United States by
OXBOW BOOKS
1950 Lawrence Road, Havertown, PA 19083

Paperback Edition: ISBN 978-1-909686-93-9
Digital Edition: ISBN 978-1-909686-94-6

A CIP record for this book is available from the British Library

Printed in the United Kingdom by Latimer Trend

For a complete list of Windgather titles, please contact:

United Kingdom
OXBOW BOOKS
Telephone (01865) 241249
Fax (01865) 794449
Email: oxbow@oxbowbooks.com
www.oxbowbooks.com

United States of America
OXBOW BOOKS
Telephone (800) 791-9354
Fax (610) 853-9146
Email: queries@casemateacademic.com
www.casemateacademic.com/oxbow

Oxbow Books is part of the Casemate group

Front cover: *Holme Engine Drain, Whittlesey* © Carry Ackroyd
Back cover: detail from *Woodland Edge* © Jenny Graham

Contents

Art Inserts

Beauty and Aesthetics

Change, Choice and Futures

List of Figures

Abbreviations

ADV	*Archives départementales du Var*
AGM	Annual General Meeting
AHRC	Arts and Humanities Research Council
AMC	*Archives municipales de Comps-sur-Artuby*
AONB	Area of Outstanding Natural Beauty
BBC	British Broadcasting Corporation
BWWC	Birdwatching and Wildlife Club
CPNHV	Committee for National Parks in the Haut Var
CPRE	Campaign to Protect Rural England
CROW	Countryside and Rights of Way Act
DDT	dichlorodiphenyltrichloroethane
DEFRA	Department for Environment, Food and Rural Affairs
EC	European Commission
EDF	Électricité de France
ELC	European Landscape Convention
EPA	Environmental Protection Agency
EU	European Union
FC	Forestry Commission
GIS	Geographical Information System
ICE	Institution of Civil Engineering
ICI	Imperial Chemistry Industries
IMF	International Monetary Fund
IRA	Irish Republican Army
ITE	Institute of Transportation Engineers
IUCN	International Union for the Conservation of Nature and Natural Resources
LCA	Landscape Character Assessment
MAFF	Ministry of Agriculture, Food and Fisheries
MP	Member of Parliament
NAAONB	National Association for Areas of Outstanding Natural Beauty
NCA	National Character Area
NGO	Non-Governmental Organization
NHU	Natural History Unit
NNR	National Nature Reserve
NSIP	Nationally Significant Infrastructure Project

OED	Oxford English Dictionary
RECN	Researching Environmental Change Network
RSPB	Royal Society for the Protection of Birds
SAC	Special Area of Conservation
SDPHV	*Syndicat de défense des proprétaires et habitants du Haut-Var*
SHC	Somerset Heritage Centre
SHD-DAT	*Service historique de la Défense-Département de l'armée de Terre*
SPA	Special Protection Area
SSSI	Sites of Special Scientific Interest
TNA	The National Archives
UK	United Kingdom of Great Britain and Northern Ireland
UNESCO	United Nations Educational, Scientific, and Cultural Organization
US/USA	United States of America

Contributors

Editors

Peter Coates
Professor of American and Environmental History, University of Bristol
   Peter's most recent book is *A Story of Six Rivers: History, Culture and Ecology* (London: Reaktion, 2013)

David Moon
Anniversary Professor in History, University of York
   David's most recent book is *The Plough that Broke the Steppes: Agriculture and Environment on Russia's Grasslands, 1700–1914* (Oxford: Oxford University Press, 2013)

Paul Warde
Lecturer in Environmental History, University of Cambridge
   Paul's most recent books are (with Astrid Kander and Paolo Malanima) *Power to the People: Energy in Europe over the Last Five Centuries* (Princeton: Princeton University Press, 2013) and (with Libby Robin and Sverker Sörlin) *The Future of Nature: Documents of Global Change* (New Haven: Yale University Press, 2013)

Contributors

Carry Akroyd
Painter and Printmaker, Luddington in the Brook, Northamptonshire

Tim Cole
Professor of Social History and Director of the Brigstow Institute, University of Bristol

Marianna Dudley
Lecturer in Environmental Humanities, Department of History, University of Bristol

Graham Gill
Forest Management Director, North England Forest District, Forestry Commission (retired)

Jenny Graham
Artist, Moorlinch, Polden Hills, Somerset

Matt Greenhall
Head of Strategies and Programmes, Archive Sector Development, National Archives, Kew

Jonty Hall
Guest Services Manager (facilities), Northumbrian Water Ltd, Kielder

Duncan Hutt
Head of Land Management, Northumberland Wildlife Trust

Robert A. Lambert
Lecturer in Environmental History and Tourism and Environment, University of Nottingham; Senior Honorary Research Fellow, University of Western Australia

Christine McCulloch
Senior Visiting Research Associate, School of Geography and the Environment, University of Oxford

Richard Oram
Professor of Environmental and Medieval History, University of Stirling

Jill Payne
Research Associate, Department of History, University of Bristol

Chris Pearson
Senior Lecturer in Twentieth-Century History, University of Liverpool

Emma-Jane Preece
Landscape Planning Officer, Quantock Hills Area of Outstanding Natural Beauty Service

Libby Robin
Professor, Fenner School of Environment and Society, Australian National University and Senior Research Fellow, National Museum of Australia

Peter Sharpe
Art and Architecture Curator, Kielder Water and Forest Park

Leona Jayne Skelton
Research Associate, Department of History, University of Bristol

T. C. (Christopher) Smout
Professor Emeritus, School of History, University of St Andrews and Historiographer Royal for Scotland

Petra J. E. M. van Dam
Chair of Water History, VU University Amsterdam

Acknowledgements

We owe our main debt of gratitude to the Arts and Humanities Research Council (AHRC) for funding – under its 'Arts and Humanities Approaches to Researching Environmental Change' initiative, itself part of Research Councils UK's 'Living with Environmental Change' programme – the activities of the research network on which this book is based ('Local Places, Global Processes: Histories of Environmental Change', 2010–11) as well as a follow-on project ('The Places That Speak to Us and the Publics We Talk With', 2011–13). The latter project allowed us to deepen and extend our knowledge and understanding of and engagement with the three places that feature at the heart of this book through the additional activities of an oral history project at Kielder, an orchard mapping project in the Quantock Hills and a re-wilding workshop at Wicken Fen ('Desire for the Wild – Wild Desires?', April 2013). This follow-on award also included provision for a workshop at which early drafts of the various chapters and other contributions to this book were presented and discussed, as well as a subvention for its publisher.

We also thank the core members of the research network for their participation in the three workshops (many, happily, were able to attend all three; a few, just one): Tim Cole, Georgina Endfield, Erin Gill, Robert Lambert, Stephen Mosley, Jan Oosthoek (also our website creator and manager, and podcast interviewer), Richard Oram, Chris Pearson, Ian Rotherham, Sverker Sörlin, Chris Smout and Petra van Dam. In addition, we wish to thank the creative practitioners and others with local expertise who presented and joined in discussion: at Wicken, Carry Akroyd; in the Quantocks, Jenny Graham, Alan Hughes, Gary Penny, Hazel Riley and Denys White; at Kielder, Peter Sharpe; and various others who attended workshops on a guest basis: Bill Adams, Ben Cowell, Marianna Dudley, Andy Flack, Greg Garrard, Matt Greenhall, Clare Hickman, Francine Hughes, Christine McCulloch, Jill Payne, Libby Robin, John Sheail, Leona Jayne Skelton, Anne Marie Smout and Lucy Veale.

Holding our workshops on site would not have been possible without the support, assistance and participation during the events themselves of representatives of our project partners (some of whom gave presentations too): the National Trust (Wicken Fen, November 2010), Quantock Hills Area of Outstanding Natural Beauty (AONB) Service (Quantock Hills, early March 2011) and Northumbrian Water Ltd (Kielder, where the workshop in late March 2011 was also held in conjunction with the Forestry Commission, and Northumberland Wildlife Trust, which are part of the Kielder Development Trust). At Wicken, we thank Stuart Carrington, Carol Laidlaw, Isabel Sedgwick and Chris Soans; in the Quantock Hills, Chris Edwards, Iain Porter, Emma-Jane

Preece and Tim Russell (now the Woodland Trust's site manager for Southwest England); and at Kielder, Margaret Batey, David Hall, Jonty Hall, Andrew Moore, Tonia Reeve and Peter Sharpe. Not least, we would like to thank the staff at the two venues where we stayed on site: Halsway Manor, Crowcombe, Somerset (to which we returned for a book preparation workshop in September 2012), and the Leaplish Waterside Park, Kielder – as well as the proprietors of the Cathedral House Bed and Breakfast in Ely, where, in September 2014, we editors held a write-in to tie up loose ends. Finally, we wish to thank Julie Gardiner, Clare Litt and Tara Evans at Oxbow Books, Nick Nourse for drawing the map, Jamie Carstairs for assistance with image preparation, and Lisa Liddy for her skilful copy-editing of the manuscript prior to submission.

Peter Coates, David Moon and Paul Warde
April 2015

Timeline of Events

November (5–7) 2010:   Wicken Fen Workshop

March (1–3) 2011:   Quantock Hills Workshop

March (25–27) 2011:   Kielder Workshop

June (14) 2011:   'Narrating environmental change' (project presentation at AHRC Landscape and Environment Directorship Impact Fellowship workshop, Royal Geographical Society-Institute of British Geographers, London)

September (30) 2011:   'Socio-cultural issues around woodlands and forests in England' workshop (with the Secretariat to the Independent Panel on Forestry, Nobel House [DEFRA], London)

September (13) 2012:   Researching Environmental Change Network (RECN) award holders meeting (Birmingham)

September 2012:   Book Workshop (Halsway Manor, Crowcombe, Somerset)

October 2012:   Kielder Oral History Project

November (16) 2012:   'Valuing nature: History and Policy environmental forum' (King's College London)

November (17) 2012:   'What's the story?: using journalism to publicize your research' workshop (with 'History and Policy: Connecting History, Policy-Makers and the Media', King's College London)

April (18/19) 2013:   'Desire for the wild – wild desires', Re-wilding workshop (with the AHRC Research Network 'Climate Histories: Communicating Cultural Knowledge of Environmental Change' [University of Cambridge], Wicken Fen/Pembroke College, Cambridge)

October (19) 2013:   Quantock Apple Heritage Day (Fyne Court, Broomfield, Somerset)

January (10) 2014:   'Trees to cherish: Connecting history, policy and future' workshop (with 'History and Policy: Connecting History, Policy-Makers and the Media'/National Trust and Woodland Trust, King's College London)

CHAPTER I

Local Places, Global Processes: In Search of the Environment

Paul Warde, Peter Coates and David Moon

Introduction

This book is the outcome of a project in which a group of environmental historians and specialists in related disciplines left their traditional academic 'environments' and explored a series of places around England, which we selected to represent different aspects of 'the environment' and 'environmental change'.[1] We brought to the project our expertise not just as historians of Britain, but also of different parts of the globe, such as Germany, France, Russia and the United States, which gave a global as well as local context to our work. During our project, we engaged with professionals from the private, public and voluntary sectors who are responsible for managing 'the environment' in our chosen locations. Leaving behind our offices, seminar rooms and libraries, we donned our hiking boots and fleeces, which we normally wear on days off for recreation, and spent as much time walking over fens, up and down hills and through forestry plantations as we did indoors. We crouched in bird hides, toured working wind pumps and dams and observed computerized timber harvesters in action. To add another dimension, we invited artists to talk to us about how they represented our places in their work and an art curator to introduce art works installed in outdoor locations. In crossing disciplinary boundaries, and seeking to bridge the wider divide between the academic sphere and the world beyond, we discussed issues of common interest from a variety of perspectives. In the process, we challenged our very understandings of the words and terms that reside at the heart of our academic endeavours and which, before we embarked on this project, we may have felt we did not need to define.

Perhaps foremost among these notions, in a work of environmental history, is 'the environment'. What do we mean when we talk about 'the environment'? And, by extension, what might we mean when we talk about 'environmental change'? It may seem incredible that we need to raise such questions. Don't we already know all too well that this is a time of unprecedented environmental change? Is it not obvious that 'the environment' is one of the great political issues of our time and arguably the most pressing of current societal concerns? Don't we already know that there are powerful streams of thought called 'environmentalism' and armies of more or less active concerned citizens known as 'environmentalists'? Enter any bookshop, library or university – or go on-line – and you can immerse yourself in environmental science, environmental ethics, environmental economics, environmental justice, environmental law and, most recently, environmental art, eco-criticism, eco-linguistics and eco-performance, not to mention our discipline, environmental history. Is it not entirely self-evident what this 'environment' is?

And yet, it is not entirely clear. At least in its current sense, the meaning of 'the environment' only emerged comparatively recently. As described in the chapter 'The Environment', the word only acquired its modern, authoritative definite article, '*the* environment', around the mid-twentieth century. When the 'state of the environment' became a matter of policy in the UK and around the globe in the 1960s, one of the reasons for using what was seen as a coolly neutral word to brand it was its very unfamiliarity to the general public. 'Environment' did not possess much wider resonance; indeed, people found the word (with its silent 'n') hard to spell. Assuredly, many of those things that we now regard as 'environmental' were there before we named them as such; some of them have been there as long as there has been a planet, or a universe. But the fact that they could be grasped and expressed in a particular way, as a collective entity, 'the environment', is extremely novel. If the meaning *now* seems self-evident, then we must ask: how did this self-evidence arise? Unsettlingly, do we – environmental historians, scientists, artists, conservationists, foresters and other land managers, as well as business people involved in exploiting natural resources – actually all mean the same thing when we refer to 'the environment'? (And do those who are not environmental historians, whether fellow academics or others, assume that environmental history is environmental*ist* history?) Perhaps the proliferation of environmental discourse is not so much because 'the environment' is a clear-cut and easily comprehensible thing, but because it is a fuzzy notion that we are trying, on multiple fronts, to make sense of. It represents an intuition of something important that we have not yet learned how to act in relation to, or to fully comprehend.

An unpicking of the history and sensibilities of 'environment' along these lines follows a well-worn path trod by those who have contemplated the comparably perplexing universality and slipperiness of 'nature' and its shifting meaning over the centuries.[2] Yet the recent proliferation of usage of the term 'environment' suggests that this elision of difference is highly unsatisfactory. As historians, we follow in the footsteps of the American environmental historian, William Cronon, who assembled a team to contemplate the terms 'nature' and 'wilderness' at a residential seminar at the University of California (Irvine) in 1994. Cronon's cohort hammered out seven major ways in which 'nature' was employed (the resultant publication was *Uncommon Ground: Toward Reinventing Nature*).[3] We can hypothesize that one of the reasons for the adoption of 'environment' as a term was precisely to escape the proliferation of meanings and associations (not least social ones, such as 'nature lovers') linked to 'nature'. Using 'environment' instead of 'nature' meant that we could get away from all that awkward, subjective stuff about meaning and feeling (did you ever meet an 'environment lover'?). But it turns out, a short distance down the line, that this is not the case. 'Environment' is no less socially, culturally and historically constructed than 'nature' and 'wilderness', or 'landscape' (if less emotionally gratifying and aesthetically satisfying). We find that 'environment' is a highly elastic concept, yet at the same time, its use is particular, located and related.[4]

As historians (and humanities scholars) working on this project, we set ourselves another task that we think is urgent: to understand processes of environmental change, alongside many others (often natural scientists) absorbed in the same enterprise, and in engagement with those who manage the land, water and air and all its inhabitants, human as well as non-human. Yet, as part of this study, we also need to identify the differing meanings that have been imparted to environmental change in different societies and at different times and in different contexts, whether local, national, international or most likely simultaneously at all levels. How did people perceive change? Indeed, what kind of scientific, experiential, emotional or linguistic resources were available to observe and describe it? How did these possibilities effect *who* described it and the terms in which environmental change becomes understood, and the explanations arrived at?

Explanations of environmental change have fallen into three broad categories. The first is 'environmentalist' narratives of 'degradation' (within which change is usually synonymous with loss). The second is progressive, economic and political narratives of 'improvement' (in which change means gain). And the third is more neutral, complex and subtle narratives of 'transformation' (involving winners and losers among ecosystem members). Talking of 'environmental change' can embrace gradual change unfolding over the longer term as well as extreme change occurring over the short term. It can also concern agency – human and other – while recognizing the inherent dynamism and autonomy of ecosystems and biotopes, even those heavily modified by human activity. In this regard, environment's generosity of meaning can be both useful, drawing attention to the interaction of 'fast' and 'slow' variables, human and non-human agency, but also unhelpful, too slack for us to be sure what is really happening or to pin down what someone is actually getting at. We want to see how the concept has worked in practice, and to help with how we can best think about our changing world now and in the future.

Local and global

Since the mid-nineteenth century, in different parts of the world, conservation initiatives and environmentalist movements have often been localized enterprises to protect particular places, ecosystems or species that were under threat. They have galvanized campaigns to protect such diverse places as Epping Forest near London, Thirlmere in the English Lake District and Snowdonia in North Wales, or Hetch Hetchy Valley in California, an unploughed area of steppe grassland at Askania Nova in Ukraine, wild, 'big game' at Kruger Park in South Africa or, in many cases, individual trees or highly localized green spaces.[5] In Britain, leading conservation organizations, whether independent of government, such as the National Trust, or the governmental body, Natural England, have operated through the purchase and management of particular properties; the country is strewn with thousands of 'nature reserves' and Sites of Special Scientific Interest (cumulatively, the 4,000 so-called SSSIs in England cover 7% of the land surface).[6] Frequently, environmental campaigners in Britain and elsewhere have been suspicious of large infrastructure projects. E. F. Schumacher's book, *Small Is Beautiful*, expressed a widely-held ethic: a suggestion that moderation in scale and ambition would promote a more flexible, intelligent and less destructive relationship with both the rest of nature and fellow human beings.[7] Indeed, the subtitle of Schumacher's work – *economics as if people mattered* – also chimes with an enduring theme of conservationists and 'environmentalists' stretching back to the closely linked arts and crafts movement – that modern methods of production, consumption and development were dehumanizing.

The most ambitious and far-reaching international treaty on environmental problems and sustainable development, the 'Agenda 21' agreed at the Earth Summit in Rio de Janeiro in 1992, was perhaps most notable for explicitly including a 'Local Agenda 21' (albeit a very small part of the overall treaty) among its elements, to be forwarded by local government in partnership with civil society. This initiative connected with a widely-held assumption that people engaged with the environment most profoundly and effectively at the local level. It also reflected an aspiration that 'if all of us acted responsibly locally, global problems would be reduced, if not eliminated.'[8]

At the same time, local experiences and behaviour have been famously expanded since the 1970s by the slogan 'Think Globally, Act Locally'. Recent decades have also been the age of 'global change' and 'globalization'. The local cannot be regarded as an autonomous or autarchic place – if it ever was.[9] We see all parts of the planet being drawn into a global economy (although this is certainly a very ancient process that arguably has continued in fits and spurts for thousands of years)[10] and subject to processes of standardization and administrative 'legibility'.[11] Since 1945, and the establishment of supranational governmental structures through the United Nations, World Bank and IMF – which have their environmental counterparts in organizations such as UNESCO's International Union for the Conservation of Nature (IUCN) and the formulation of global criteria for the evaluation and classification of environments – there has also been a sense that environmental crisis is planetary in scale, undergoing processes of 'global change' that are an interconnected phenomenon, rather than the aggregate of local changes.[12] *Silent Spring* – Rachel Carson's study of the global impact of unregulated chemical pesticides on flora and fauna that introduced millions of readers in the western world to the notions of ecological webs and interdependencies, and helped launch environmentalism as a mass movement –

highlighted this new global order by demonstrating the indiscriminate impact of spraying far beyond target species. And within two years of the book's publication, in 1964 (the year Carson died of cancer), DDT residues were detected even in the fatty tissues and liver of Adelie penguins and crab-eater seals, despite Antarctica being far removed from the nearest points of spraying.[13]

For some, the global environmental crisis demands responses equally epic in scope, whether through international agreement such as the Kyoto protocol on climate change of 1994 or geo-engineering to avert global warming. We are living, a growing cadre of scientists are suggesting, in the 'Anthropocene', a term coined in 2000 by the atmospheric chemist, Paul Crutzen, and the freshwater biologist, Eugene Stoermer, to denote the current geological epoch, in which the impact of human activities is considered to be so extensive that it is tantamount to a fresh geological era meriting its own name to place alongside eras such as the Pliocene.[14]

Another sense in which no place is entirely local is that every protected area, whether in Somerset or the Serengeti, Northumberland or Nova Scotia, has been assigned a place within the IUCN's Protected Areas Categories System, an internationally recognized and applied hierarchy of designation ranging through Category I to Category VI; that is why one of our partners, Iain Porter, included a slide of a cheetah during his presentation at the Quantocks workshop. As well as responding to this international framework, the managers of our sites also operate with reference to pan-European understandings of place, nature and landscape character such as those embodied in the European Landscape Convention (signed by the UK government in February 2006 and binding since March 2007) and EU-generated categories of protected land such as the Special Area of Conservation (SAC), authorized under the Habitats Directive of 1992. Supranational and global processes of landscape classification shape and connect our specific sites as well as ubiquitous forces such as climate change.

Modern globalization has enmeshed the Earth's localities in increasingly extensive and intensive networks, whether economic, cultural, political or environmental and conservationist.[15] However, the overriding of national boundaries equally means finding new ways to speak about, and develop consciousness of, connections that have long been in place, whether of climate, annual bird migrations (that in the late eighteenth century remained such a mystery that Gilbert White noted the belief that swallows hibernated under ponds) or commodity chains bringing 'colonial' goods to European consumers.[16] New forms of engagement have developed from the ready availability of images through the media. The fascination of children with the charismatic megafauna of the African savannah, initially fired by tales of the exploits of white big game hunters in the nineteenth century, has, since the 1960s, become a staple of wildlife documentaries and children's TV programmes that have delivered lions, giraffes and elephants into homes around the world.[17] Television provides access to the riches of the natural world in ways that were inconceivable a few generations ago (see Robert Lambert's contribution in this volume).

Over the same decades as children's localities have narrowed, not least because of risks posed by road traffic, new transportation possibilities, ranging from domestic cars to cheap package holidays by air, mean that many more people have experience of 'environments' quite different from their immediate physical worlds; from a British perspective, taking people to the Mediterranean, Florida, Thailand, the Caribbean and the Maldives ... the list is endless. Iconic images of Planet Earth beamed back to Earth by the Apollo missions to the moon in 1968 and 1972 have been attributed a key role in fostering a global consciousness of Earth as humanity's collective home (and a fragile entity).[18] Most recently, we find important images and understandings of nature that are almost entirely 'virtual' in form, albeit developed out of vast arrays of information assembled from tracking stations, field observation and satellites hung far above us, generating computer models and visions of the Earth's entire surface. As Cronon observed: 'It is well worth remembering that some of the most dramatic environmental problems we appear to be facing ... exist mainly as simulated representations in complex computer models of natural systems.'[19]

Particularly in environmentalist discourse, the experience of globalization is often told as one of loss, degradation and standardization, a 'great acceleration' of pressures; in human society, the experience of alienation, displacement and anomie. Both nature and culture have become subject to irrevocable change by outsiders. 'Invasive' species (usually non-indigenous) and multinational companies such as Starbucks have eroded local identities based on the distinctiveness of local natures, even obliterated the 'real thing' of an original nature or an authentic community.[20] In a globalized world, place can be replaced by placelessness.[21] The 'local' can be imagined as a place of resistance, of mutual obligation, of dialogue. Writing about the remote beauty of Connemara, Tim Robinson argues that, without the 'occasional renewal of memory and regular rehearsal of meaning, place itself flounders into shapelessness, and time, the great amnesiac, forgets all'.[22] The National Trust for England and Wales, a major charitable conservation institution with more than four million members, recently initiated a 'Going local' campaign, accompanied by slogans such as 'Life is local'. 'We may be a national organisation,' explains the Trust's chairman, Simon Jenkins, 'but we want to render our properties, landscapes as well as houses and gardens, individual and distinctive.'[23]

As a counterpoint, however, one can also locate discourses of the 'local' and the particular that are restricting and inflexible – the local degenerating into the parochial[24] – even tyrannical in the pursuit of purism. Moreover, if the deeds of many botanists, anthropologists and environmental historians (among others), who are only too eager to leave their native localities for foreign shores, are to be taken as evidence, a focus on the local can even appear rather tedious and limiting. The situation is further complicated by recent celebration of diversity in all its guises, biological as well as social, cultural and racial. This can assume the form of efforts to protect homogenous localities and species (such as the red squirrels of Kielder Forest, Northumberland, one of our selected locales) in the face of globalizing forces that introduce, at least temporarily, greater heterogeneity to a particular place in terms of the number of resident species. Yet the aim of the defence of local homogeneity is to preserve a greater heterogeneity on a global scale. We see that these values are themselves only relative to the different scales we can imagine them on. Red squirrels range from Portugal across Russia to Japan and Alaska. But the existence of a thriving population in, say, Germany, is of little if any consolation to squirrel defenders in England, where they survive in pockets in more remote areas such as Northumberland in the face of competition from their grey American cousin.

It seems timely, then, to think about place. Thinking about place *right now* also carries a particular set of contemporary and historical resonances that we have begun to outline. This is also a different exercise, as we shall see, than thinking about the history of *places,* of which there is a long, deep and enduring history in Britain, and that has yielded writings that often supply keen insight into wider questions of how location shapes perception (and *vice versa*). But questions of 'environment', a thing at once global, local and immediate – even bodily and internal[25] – pose particular questions about what place is and how we relate to it. 'It is not possible to "think away" the actual geographical location of social life, lives are always grounded,' as Kirsten Hastrup reminds us.[26] But it is not just a question of our idea of 'environment' being a particular, localized perspective that shapes opinion and action (and that non-locals should take into account). It is equally a question of how we locate that sense of *locality* with the knowledge that it has value according to its situation in the shifting dynamics of global processes.

Places

To study locality and 'place' we chose some places to explore. How did the world, and the place, look from the vantage point of particular locations? As a project, the 'Local Places, Global Processes' research network, we wanted to situate ourselves in locations, but not as experts on those places, for we know that this requires years of engagement and situated, 'local knowledge'.[27] Our plan was to move through a trio of carefully chosen places – Wicken Fen in Cambridgeshire, the Quantock Hills in Somerset and Kielder Water and Forest Park in Northumberland – talking with some of those who know them best, investigating themes, feeling the place as a kind of participant-observer – but hardly as insiders (indeed, many of our colleagues in the network group were visiting the places in question for the first time). We also wanted to involve managers on the ground in our conversations, in the hope that they would also benefit, and to engage with their necessarily precise demarcations of space and place, in terms of jurisdictional boundaries, formal relationships with stakeholders, statutory obligations, cartography, production decisions, in their capacity as employers, trustees, conservationists, commoners and 'friends', and their research on the geographical locale, socio-economic origins and 'segmentation' of their sites' various 'user constituencies' (visitors, in plain English).[28] As a research group of historians and related scholars, 'we' represented, if not a global, then nevertheless an increasingly typical movement – in and out, temporarily displaced from our customary environments, but enjoying the experience. In an age of rapid transportation (we travelled by plane, train, bus, car, bicycle and on foot), these acts of 'going places' are not so much a poor substitute for 'going native' as tracing the lines of inquiry and experience we want to pursue. Places are experienced as components of journeys, physical and intellectual, by sojourners.

There was also a more physically practical aspect to going to a place and spending time there. We found that walking together and talking together – raising questions, taking note, being attentive (or non-attentive) to our guides, listening, looking, moving (sometimes as part of the group and sometimes as individuals) and being there at different times of day and at different seasons – made a difference to how we thought about and experienced location. This is not to say that we were replicating the experience of residents (or tourists, for we were fortunate to have some privileged access to sites). There are material benefits to being there (in place); saying is not seeing, and the eye (trained or not), the skin, the mouth, the nose and the ear take in vast amounts of information that a text can never convey. We also found that in motion we had a variety of differently-shaped conversations that would not have been possible amid the habitual place-taking and regimentation of the lecture theatre and seminar room. Importantly, this was a means to learn from people *in situ*, and also share sympathetically experience and perspectives, to learn to speak at least as newly-made friends of the place (friends as in the numerous 'Friends of ...' groups that are so attached to particular places). This kind of site-sensitive engagement beyond the conventional, eminently indoor university environment does not, of course, guarantee a happy ending or lasting amity, and none of it is very surprising in its results.

The employment of the senses, and place as a bodily experience, was also a good reason to try to engage with a wider panoply of ways of relating to place and environment: through the arts, whether painting, photography, plastic arts or installations. These represent and express place, but also are place-makers, becoming characteristic features of a landscape, where in spectacularly influential cases the artistic vision of a landscape ends up defining and even protecting it (and it is of course well-known that the word 'landscape' has its origins in a certain kind of seventeenth-century Dutch painting, the *landschap*). In Cronon's *Uncommon Ground* project, participants were invited to bring 'found objects' that could question or realign views of 'nature' as prompts to discussion. On our project, invited artists brought these objects with them or, as curators, had already installed them in the landscape. But, in another sense, we also set out to find the 'objects' as we walked and explored our locations. This practice could take many forms: a chance remark about the inappropriateness of a certain kind of tree in the skyline; a map of forest management plans; the shape of a nuclear power station; a no-swimming sign; a framed photograph of dogs hunting eels on a pub wall; a Royal Air Force fighter jet flying past on a training exercise; a carving of a folkloric green man on a pew end; and a collection of moths gathered by the Historiographer Royal for Scotland. By being in the same place together, we could, for a moment, see through the eyes of others.

Themes

The three main themes of the project are 'environment', 'beauty' and 'change'. In this book, three keystone essays address the influential themes through which we have understood and discussed questions of the 'state of nature'. They also introduce sections on the closely related issues of 'environment and landscape', 'beauty and aesthetics' and 'change, choice and futures'. 'Places' grounds 'the environment' in specific examples of what the UK government's National Ecosystem Assessment refers to as 'environmental settings'.[29] 'Environment' has frequently come to denote a scientific perspective, conveying an air of neutrality and dispassion. Investigating places through the idiom of environment thus also raises questions of expertise and institutionalization, and why it has risen in prominence in our lexicon over time.

Beauty is a key consideration in the valuation of place. As the example of the Quantock Hills demonstrates, aesthetics have been in the vanguard of informing sensibilities about nature since the Romantic generation. Indeed, the National Trust's full name is the National Trust for Places of Historic Interest or Natural Beauty. In the mid-twentieth century, through the influence of ecological science, notions of beauty in nature attained a certain distance from traditional aesthetic canons associated with the picturesque and sublime, which had privileged mountain environments such as the English Lake District or California's Sierra Nevada.[30] In a much-quoted passage from a book that became one of the key texts of modern environmentalism, the US environmental thinker, Aldo Leopold, blended a land aesthetic with a land ethic. 'A thing is right', he stipulated, 'when it tends to preserve the integrity, stability, and beauty of the biotic community. It is wrong when it tends otherwise.' His objections to the presence of a non-indigenous species within an ecosystem had more to do with the aesthetics of ecology than nativist or xenophobic sentiments. Non-native plants and animals were, above all, 'aesthetically improper'.[31] Dorothy Wordsworth had experienced an identical feeling in the 1790s, when walking in Crowcombe 'dell', a spot immediately adjacent to Halsway, the venue for our Quantock workshop. In a journal entry, she described the dell as 'romantic and beautiful'. Romantic and beautiful, that is, if you overlooked the 'unnaturalized trees' that were 'everywhere planted' (by Thomas Carew when he laid out Crowcombe Court in the early 1700s).[32] These are themselves historical (and value) judgements formed by habit. People in Britain often see the massed ranks of Sitka spruce or Corsican pine in forestry plantations as alien intruders. Yet in parts of East Anglia the Scots pine trees largely introduced during the 1820s and 1830s are now valued landscape features: 'The sea enriches and the pine adorns,' runs the motto of Sheringham on the north Norfolk coast.[33]

The intimacy between notions of beauty and environmental sustainability is particularly vividly expressed by Rachel Carson. The first lines of John Keats' poem, *La Belle Dame Sans Merci* (1819), supplied the inspiration for the actual title: '*Oh what can ail thee, knight at arms, alone and palely loitering, the sedge is withered from the lake, and no birds sing.*'[34] In his preface to the UK edition of *Silent Spring*, the biologist, Julian Huxley, a prominent figure in the international conservationist community from the 1940s to the 1960s, reported a comment of his brother, Aldous, the novelist and writer. After reading Carson's book, Aldous lamented that we risked 'losing half the subject-matter of English poetry'.[35] Nightingales and skylarks were not just important members of ecosystems; they were feathered components of national heritage.

That our appreciation of nature is a thoroughly cultural phenomenon has become a truism. We come to places charged with expectations both of the landscape and the wells of aesthetic feeling within us:

> A sharp change from northern or central Somerset is what one expects, and hopes for, in the romantically challenging terrain of the Quantocks and of the hills towards the Devon border. Nor is expectation denied; the change is so pronounced that a visitor may be forgiven who feels himself no longer in Somerset.[36]

This observation should certainly not be limited to the role of artists or poets in shaping our views of nature, instrumental as these artistic perspectives are. Aesthetic visions permeate all our thoughts. In his influential study of high modernism and planning, James C. Scott noted how;

> the carriers of high modernism tended to see rational order in remarkably visual aesthetic terms. For them, an efficient, rationally organized city, village, or farm was a city, village or farm that *looked* regimented and orderly in a geometrical sense.[37]

Scott devoted considerable attention to dams as a high modernist enterprise and Kielder dam satisfies the criteria of the aesthetic of the 'technological sublime'.[38]

We should not, then, counterpose an aestheticized view of nature to an instrumental one (let alone privilege the visual, overlooking the degree to which the experience and valuation of nature is a multi-sensory phenomenon). What we find are different aesthetic visions and, crucially, visions that seem place 'appropriate'; the rightness of the positioning of certain features or species in the landscape is an aesthetic as much as an ecological judgment.

These observations bring us to the matter of change, and the inevitability of change. The human capacity to transform nature is not in doubt, and we must understand all landscapes – even wildernesses and rewilded environments – as transformed or cultural landscapes. However, to say that 'everything changes' is of course to wish away questions of great complexity: whether a change is part of a recurrent cycle; whether change is short-, medium- or long-term, partial or wholesale; whether there are more winners than losers in terms of individual ecosystem components; and whether change is fundamental or superficial (for which ecological science and resilience theory has attempted to develop a sophisticated language based on ideas of systems that has not, as yet, entered general parlance).[39] When does variation tip from continuity into change? What constitutes fast or slow variables, what drives change; is it reversible? Aside from these more abstract issues, which nevertheless inflect everything we say about real places, many sites clearly designed with human 'artifice' have, unexpectedly, become treasured for their 'natural' populations.[40] Change of one kind has somehow resisted change of another: endangered, indigenous red squirrels find sanctuary in among the introduced Sitka spruce in the Kielder Forest plantation, great crested newts prosper in old clay pits near Peterborough, bryophytes in Cornish tin mines, fairy shrimp in tank track ruts on Salisbury Plain military training area, and water voles in Bristol's Royal Portbury Dock, to take a series of examples in England alone.[41]

The meaning we give to change is closely related to our sense of time (a notion which we as historians are particularly comfortable with), and hence we relate it to our future. Our understanding of change inevitably opens up perspectives on our expectations for future generations, and even the most conservative preservationism remains a statement about how the future should be. A history of environmental change is also, then, a history of environmental futures. We relate our experiences of change to our own life-cycle and lifetimes, to the cultures that have predominated in particular spaces, to our expectations, hopes and needs. We often value accelerated time in terms of, for example, technological advance (which brings the future into the present), while beloved 'natural places' and reserves are frequently highly valued as kinds of 'islands in time' or 'time capsules' resistant to the relentless pace of everyday and especially economic and technological life.[42] These meanings, and actual experiences, often rely on contrasts between 'global' and 'local' phenomena that nevertheless will continue to interact at their own variable temporalities, even when we like to be able to step in and out of what we perceive to be faster or slower streams of time. In previous decades and centuries, the contrast between the timeless country and the frenetic, onrushing pace of life in the city has often been employed to similar effect, without having any necessary close relation, of course, with the reality of life in each juxtaposed place.[43]

Our sense of different places having different 'times', and hence perceiving change differently in those places, again focuses our attention on the question of the limits of a place. In ecological science this might be viewed in a functional way: what permits a discrete ecosystem to operate, which may be relatively easy to define in the case of a lake, a drainage basin or patch of distinct vegetation, becomes harder to define at a 'landscape' scale. Conservation biology, for example, has increasingly recognized that the integrity of certain ecological processes can only be sustained in the long run by protecting extensive areas of land and water – and installing connecting corridors for wildlife movements – that are not interrupted by infrastructure such as roads, pipelines, retail parks and suburban sprawl, or even less visually disturbing changes like 'improved' grasslands. To the human eye, the boundaries of place are even less distinct; does preserving the essential beauty of somewhere like the Quantock Hills require regulation of all of the countryside visible from its heights on the clearest of days?

Places are also linked by flows of commodities and resources, as well as ideas, the experience of our senses and ecological and climatic processes. The reservoir levels of Kielder Water, for example, are determined both by precipitation in the upper North Tyne river's catchment area and the decisions about flow levels in the Tyne and water diverted from the river's lower reaches into a great, hidden pipeline that bores its way southward into Yorkshire to deliver water into other areas of demand (though this facility is rarely used). What happens and what people do outside the three places at the centre of this project – or any other places – matters as much as, if not more than, what occurs and is done inside them. And just as we need to be aware of the inseparability of economy and ecology, place must be spoken or written about, at least if it is to be shared with any sense of precision. So, again, we observe with Tim Robinson 'Without the occasional renewal of memory and regular rehearsal of meaning, place itself founders into shapelessness, and time, the great amnesiac, forgets all.'[44]

Organization of the book

Each of the three themes of environment, beauty and environmental change, which provide this project's organizing principles, is examined by one of the editors, in one case in conjunction with another member of the research network, in essays that were prepared as focal points for each of the three place-based workshops, and amended in the light of subsequent research and discussions both on-site and afterwards. These essays relate to global processes, but also draw on, and were revised to reflect, the lived experience of our places. Paul Warde's essay on 'the environment' is the most global in conception. Peter Coates' essay on 'environmental beauty' is embedded in the Quantock Hills and other places renowned for their aesthetic appeal. David Moon and Leona Jayne Skelton's essay, however, as befits the third of these framing essays, is the most firmly grounded in one of our places, offering a consistently local perspective on global processes of environmental change. In turn, each section contains two to three academic essays that relate these themes to the history of particular environments and places. These essays were produced in dialogue with, but not necessarily about, the places we visited.

However, we also wanted to acknowledge the value of – and provide space for – the often more succinct but influential moments of expression that shape thought and inflect our thinking in a particular direction. One of the issues that emerged in our discussion at Wicken Fen, and in the context of its vision of expansion, was the idea that 'conservation must move from the idea of the conservation of place to the conservation of process.'[45] In our academic practice, we also wanted to move from the idea of 'the finished article' – the product of repeated re-workings, whittled down, winnowed and polished – as the only, or most important, mode of understanding, to one that better reflected and valued process; capturing how we learn from it and work with each other as a 'team' (with a collective aim to learn, rather than a common goal). This orientation also helps to incorporate the approaches and outputs of our project partners and associates (who include representatives of the management bodies responsible for each site), where the report, brochure or artwork might be a rather more important part of their working lives, and reading material. Including edited discussions and other kinds of printed and visual material is a way of including these perspectives without pressing them into an unfamiliar mode of working or expression (or even more likely, not including them at all, or only as objects of academics' observations). The volume therefore mixes a variety of sections and features in among the more 'routine' academic chapters: namely, excerpts from place-related materials of our partners. We found inspiration here in the approach of *Desert Channels,* a book that beautifully and sympathetically pioneered a multi-perspectival approach to thinking about places in a richly-illustrated study of a region of western Queensland.[46]

Thought is often a 'slow variable' that takes time; and respecting and managing places and environments – if we think that place and environment matter – also require a sense of what it is like to arrive, to look around, to have to let go, however fleetingly, of familiar channels of thought and activity. 'Local' and 'global' on their own are both incomplete experiences, and that goes for the experience of anyone, however well-versed or deeply involved in policymaking, management or research. Wherever we go, this is a thought we should always carry with us.

Notes

1. The Research Network 'Local Places, Global Processes: Histories of Environmental Change' (2010–11) was funded by the Arts and Humanities Research Council (AHRC), the statutory UK government research council for the arts and humanities. See the project website: 'Local places, global processes' http://www.environmentalhistories.net/ (accessed 27/10/14). AHRC also funded a follow-on project ('The Places That Speak to Us and the Publics We Talk With') that allowed us to expand the initial work and complete this book.

2. See Peter Coates, *Nature: Western Attitudes since Ancient Times* (Cambridge: Polity Press, 1998); Raymond Williams, *Keywords: A Vocabulary of Culture and Society* (Oxford: Oxford University Press, 1976), pp. 184–6.

3. William Cronon (ed.), *Uncommon Ground: Toward Reinventing Nature* (New York: W. W. Norton, 1995).

4. On issues of language and metaphor, see also Brendon Larson, *Metaphors for Environmental Sustainability. Redefining our Relationship with Nature* (New Haven: Yale University Press, 2011).

5. Harriet Ritvo, *The Dawn of Green: Manchester, Thirlmere, and Modern Environmentalism* (Chicago: University of Chicago Press, 2009); Roderick Nash, *Wilderness and the American Mind* (New Haven: Yale University Press, 1967); John Warfield Simpson, *Dam! Water, Power, Politics and Preservation in Hetch Hetchy and Yosemite National Park* (New York: Pantheon, 2005); Robert W. Righter, *The Battle over Hetch Hetchy: America's Most Controversial Dam and the Birth of Modern Environmentalism* (New York: Oxford University Press, 2006); Vladimir Evgen'evich Boreiko, *Askania-Nova: Tyazhkie versty istorii (1826–1993)* (Kiev: Kievskii ekologo-kul'turnyi tsentr, 1994); Jane Carruthers, *The Kruger National Park: A Social and Political History* (Pietermaritzburg: Natal

University Press, 1995); Robert A. Lambert, *Contested Mountains: Nature, Development and Environment in the Cairngorms Region of Scotland, 1880–1980* (Isle of Harris: White Horse Press, 2001); Thomas Pakenham, *Meetings with Remarkable Trees* (New York: Random House, 1998); T. C. Smout, *Exploring Environmental History: Selected Essays* (Edinburgh: Edinburgh University Press, 2009), pp. 156–60.

6. Natural England, 'Sites of Special Scientific Interest' http://www.sssi.naturalengland. org.uk/Special/sssi/index.cfm (accessed 24/10/14).

7. Ernst F. Schumacher, *Small Is Beautiful: Economics As If People Mattered* (London: Blond and Briggs, 1973).

8. London Borough of Hammersmith and Fulham, 'What is Agenda 21?', to select one from many http://www.lbhf.gov.uk/external/la21/index.htm (accessed 24/10/14).

9. For a sustained critique of this notion in relation to the pre-industrial village and nostalgic views of the countryside, see Raymond Williams, *The Country and the City* (London: Chatto & Windus, 1973).

10. Kevin O'Rourke, and Jeremy G. Williamson, *Globalization and History* (Cambridge, MA: MIT Press, 1999); Ian James, *Why the West Rules – For Now* (London: Profile Books, 2010); Edward B. Barbier, *Scarcities and Frontiers: How Economies have Developed through Natural Resource Exploitation* (Cambridge: Cambridge University Press, 2010); John Richards, *The Unending Frontier* (Oakland: University of California Press, 2003).

11. James C. Scott, *Seeing like a State* (New Haven: Yale University Press, 1996).

12. For early expressions, see: William Vogt, *Road to Survival* (London: Gollancz, 1948); Fairfield Osborn, *Our Plundered Planet* (London, Faber & Faber, 1948); William L. Thomas (ed.), *Man's Role in Changing the Face of the Earth* (Chicago: University of Chicago Press, 1956).

13. 'DDT found in penguins and seal from Antarctic', news release, Bureau of Sport Fisheries and Wildlife, Fish and Wildlife Service, US Department of the Interior (11 February 1965) http://www.fws.gov/contaminants/Documents/historic/19650211a. pdf (accessed 24/10/14); Deborah Zabarenko, 'Pesticide DDT shows up in Antarctic penguins', Reuters (9 May 2008) http://www.reuters.com/article/2008/05/10/us-penguins-ddt-idUSN09335403200805100 (accessed 21/10/14).

14. Paul Crutzen and Eugene Stoermer, 'The Anthropocene', *International Geosphere-Biosphere Programme Newsletter* 41 (2000), pp. 17–18; Jan Zalasiewicz, 'Are We Now Living in the Anthropocene?', *GSA Today* 18/2 (February 2008), pp. 4–8; Jan Zalasiewicz *et al.*, 'The New World of the Anthropocene', *Environmental Science and Technology* 44 (2010), pp. 2228–31.

15. On the complicated meaning of home and the local in globalized world of migration and diaspora, see: J. Edward Chamberlain, *If This is Your Land, Where are Your Stories?: Finding Common Ground* (Toronto: Knopf, 2003).

16. Gilbert White, *A Natural History of Selbourne* (London: Thames & Hudson, 2011[1789]), pp. 35, 43.

17. William Beinart and Katie McKeown, 'Wildlife Media and Representations of Africa, 1950s to the 1970s', *Environmental History* 14 (July 2009), pp. 429–52. The Russian TV show 'V mire zhivotnykh' ('In the Animals' World'), which regularly features African wildlife, has been immensely popular since it was first broadcast in 1968 http://www.worldofanimals.ru/ (accessed 16/08/2012).

18. Neil Maher, 'Gallery: On Shooting the Moon', *Environmental History* 9 (July 2004), pp. 526–31.

19. William Cronon, 'Introduction: In Search of Nature', in Cronon (ed.) *Uncommon Ground*, p. 47.

20. Charles S. Elton, *The Ecology of Invasions by Animals and Plants* (London: Methuen, 1958); Chris Bright, *Life out of Bounds: Bio-invasions in a Borderless World* (London: Earthscan, 1999); Wouter van der Weijden, Rob Leewis and Pieter Bol, *Biological Globalisation: Bio-invasions and their Impacts on Nature, the Economy and Public Health* (Utrecht: KNNV, 2007); Peter Coates, *American Perceptions of Immigrant and Invasive Species: Strangers on the Land* (Berkeley: University of California Press, 2007); Ian D. Rotherham and Robert A. Lambert (eds), *Invasive and Introduced Plants and Animals: Human Perceptions, Attitudes and Approaches to Management* (London: Earthscan, 2011).

21. See Edward Relph, *Place and Placelessness* (London: Pion, 1976).

22. Tim Robinson, *Connemara: A Little Gaelic Kingdom* (Dublin: Penguin Ireland, 2011), p. 69.

23. The National Trust, *Going Local: Fresh Tracks Down Old Roads: Our Strategy for the Next Decade* (Swindon: 2010); Chairman's Statement, *Going Local Annual Report 2009/10* (Swindon: National Trust, 2012), pp. 1, 2.

24. The quality of the parochial also carries more positive connotations. The curate Gilbert White's portrait of the intimacy and detail of the place environing his Hampshire vicarage was not the product of a narrow mind. Nor did White depict a place divorced from the wider world. White, *Natural History.*

25. Kathleen Jamie, *Sightlines* (London: Sort of Books, 2012); Conevery Bolton Valencius, *The Health of the Country: How American Settlers Understood Themselves and Their Land* (New York: Basic Books, 2002); Linda Nash, *Inescapable Ecologies: A History of Environment, Disease, and Knowledge* (Berkeley: University of California Press, 2006); Nancy Langston, *Toxic Bodies: Hormone Disruptors and the Legacy of DES* (New Haven: Yale University Press, 2010); Neil M. Maher, 'Body Counts: Tracking the Human Body through Environmental History', in Douglas C. Sackman (ed.) *A Companion to American Environmental History* (Oxford: Wiley-Blackwell, 2010), pp. 163–80.

26. Kirsten Hastrup, 'Destinies and Decisions: Taking the Life-world Seriously in Environmental History', in Sverker Sörlin and Paul Warde (eds), *Nature's End: History and the Environment* (Basingstoke: Palgrave Macmillan, 2009), p. 334.

27. Clifford Geertz, *Local Knowledge: Further Essays in Interpretive Anthropology* (New York: Basic Books, c.1983).

28. Segmentation is a technique to categorize types of visitor with a likely set of consumption preferences.

29. Andrew Church *et al.*, 'Cultural Services', in *UK National Ecosystem Assessment (2011): Technical Report* (Cambridge: UNEP/WCMC, 2011), pp. 645, 647–52.

30. Robert MacFarlane, *Mountains of the Mind: A History of Imagination* (London: Granta, 2003); Marjorie Hope Nicholson, *Mountain Gloom and Mountain Glory: The Development of the Aesthetics of the Infinite* (Ithaca: Cornell University Press, 1959); Simon Schama, *Landscape and Memory* (London: HarperCollins, 1995).

31. Aldo Leopold, *A Sand County Almanac* (New York: Oxford University Press, 1949), pp. 224–25; Daniel Simberloff, 'Integrity, Stability, and Beauty: Leopold's Evolving View of Nonnative Species', *Environmental History* 17/3 (July 2012), pp. 487–511.

32. 'Dorothy Wordsworth's Journal, Written at Alfoxden in 1798' (entry for 15 April 1798), in W. A. Knight, *Coleridge and Wordsworth in the West Country* (New York: Scribner, 1914), p. 156.

33. The motto was 'granted' to Sheringham in 1953, in the Latin form, '*mare ditat pinusque decorat*': Sheringham, 'Sheringham Town Crest' http://www.at-sheringham-norfolk.co.uk/towncrest.php (accessed 24/10/14). See also: Gerry Barnes and Tom Williamson, *Ancient Trees in the Landscape: Norfolk's Arboreal Heritage* (Oxford: Oxbow Books, 2011), pp. 138–51.

34. Paul Brooks, *The House of Life: Rachel Carson at Work* (London: George Allen & Unwin, 1973), pp. 239, 263.

35. Julian Huxley, 'Preface' to Rachel Carson, *Silent Spring* (London: Penguin, 1962), p. 20.

36. Bryan Little, *Portrait of Somerset* (London: Robert Hale, 1983 [1969]), p. 188; and quoted in Natural England, *National Character Area Profile 144: Quantock Hills* (2013), p. 138.

37. Scott, *Seeing Like a State*, p. 4.

38. Leo Marx, *The Machine in the Garden: Technology and the Pastoral Ideal in America* (New York: Oxford University Press, 2000 [1964]), pp. 195, 217, 222, 230, 294, 375; David E. Nye, *American Technological Sublime* (Cambridge, MA: MIT Press, 1996).

39. David Salt and Brian Walker, *Resilience Thinking: Sustaining Ecosystems and People in a Changing World* (Washington, DC: Island Press, 2006); Marco A. Janssen and Elinor Ostrom, 'Resilience, Vulnerability and Adaptation: A Cross-cutting Theme of the International Human Dimensions Programme on Global Environmental Change', *Global Environmental Change* 16 (2006), pp. 237–39.

40. The notion of a 'designed landscape', hitherto largely confined to gardens and landscaped estates, could benefit from a more elastic application to a whole range of environments 'authored' by individuals other than the likes of Humphry Repton and Capability Brown, or by a less identifiable and renowned group of people. See, for example: Jerry C. Towle, 'Authored Ecosystems: Livingston Stone and the Transformation of California Fisheries', *Environmental History* 5/1 (2000), pp. 54–74.

41. T. C. Smout, 'Regardening and the Rest', in Marcus Hall (ed.), *Restoration and History: The Search for a Usable Environmental Past* (New York and Abingdon: Routledge, 2010), p. 118; Marianna Dudley, 'A Fairy (Shrimp) Tale of Military Environmentalism: The "Greening" of Salisbury Plain', in Chris Pearson, Peter Coates and Tim Cole (eds), *Militarized Landscapes: From Gettysburg to Salisbury Plain* (London: Continuum, 2010), pp. 135–50; BBC News, 'More water voles to live in dock', 30 June 2004 http://news.bbc.co.uk/1/hi/england/bristol/3850765.stm (accessed 21/10/14).

42. This was particularly one of the benefits of nature identified by Henry David Thoreau, who saw the natural world as a refuge from the dependent life of the labourer: 'the laboring man has not leisure for a true integrity day by day; he cannot afford to sustain the manliest relations to men; his labor would be depreciated in the market. He has no time to be any thing but a machine.': Henry D. Thoreau, *Walden* (London: Penguin,1983 [1854]), p. 48.

43. Williams, *The Country and the City*, p. 240 *passim*.

44. Robinson, *Connemara: A Little Gaelic Kingdom*, p. 69.

45. William M. Adams, *Future Nature: A Vision for Conservation* (London: Earthscan, 2003), p. 9.

46. Libby Robin, Chris Dickman and Mandy Martin (eds), *Desert Channels: The Impulse to Conserve* (Collingwood: CSIRO Publishing, 2011). A number of Australia's most imaginative new conservation initiatives are being pursued in the region, including partnerships between private landholders, non-government conservation organizations that buy and manage land and community-based natural resource management groups such as Desert Channels Queensland. Co-editor Libby Robin of Australian National University attended the workshop in the Quantock Hills (March 2011) and published an essay inspired by her involvement with the Network: 'Global Ideas in Local Places: The Humanities in Environmental Management', *Environmental Humanities* 1 (2012), pp. 69–84.

CHAPTER 2

Three Places

Peter Coates, Paul Warde and David Moon

This book is rooted in a series of residential workshops held during 2010–11 at three locations that represent, within the environmental parameters of England, three very different places: Wicken Fen in Cambridgeshire, the Quantock Hills in Somerset, and Kielder Water and Forest Park in Northumberland. We chose them partly for practical reasons (proximity to the project leaders' home institutions) but mainly for their environmental, cultural and historical significance.

Wicken Fen is a survivor, but also a kind of simulacrum – at least, to those who think they are seeing some authentic remnant of the past. It is an area of wetland left over from the Fenland that used to dominate the landscape in large parts of eastern England but that has been progressively drained since the seventeenth century.[1]

Originally exploited by peat diggers, wildfowlers and sedge-cutters, and for summer grazing, the de-watered land was gradually turned over to pasture and the large-scale production of cereals and vegetables. Now, thanks to the shrinkage of dried-out peatlands surrounding it and the 'Fen blow' that has deposited the exposed topsoil elsewhere, Wicken Fen stands proud of the water table and must have water pumped in to sustain its current form. A hectare of Fen was donated to the National Trust in 1899, making it the country's first nature reserve; it has gradually been extended to 320 hectares, 'reclaiming' arable farmland. Wicken Fen is thus the property of a leading national conservation body. This has been a major factor – perhaps the main factor – in shaping the site's current character.

It is also a thoroughly studied site of science, due to its proximity to the University of Cambridge, which lies just 8 miles (12.9 km) to the southwest. Indeed, it was the botanizing and especially entomological field trips conducted by Cambridge scientists that invested this remnant patch of wetland with value in its unimproved form, as distinct from the economic value that agricultural improvement injected, that prompted the Natural Trust's purchase.[2] In 1848, in the Sedge Fen (the least altered part of the Wicken site), university-based naturalists spotted the exceptionally rare Fen orchid, and entomologists soon discovered the richness of its insect life (Wicken Fen was apparently known in scientific circles at the time as 'The Home of Ease for Entomologists'). According to a National Trust article that marked a century of conservation at Wicken Fen, during the nineteenth century, 'a small-scale industry grew up in Wicken village of guides and insect trappers.'[3] Demonstrating how specific locations shape perceptions, including the production of scientific knowledge, Wicken has a long tradition of being highly valued as an outdoor laboratory (indeed, the Trust's original purchase consisted of land bought by entomologist J. C. Moberley in 1893), and more recently as a reservoir of biodiversity; in fact, Wicken Fen has been identified as the place in the UK with the greatest biodiversity.[4] Contingency was an all-important consideration, the site being highly accessible for day-trips to a large pool of naturalists.

Today, the vast majority of day trips to Wicken are undertaken for leisure reasons. By the 1980s, with the disappearance of the traditional Fen economy, large areas of the Fen had become 'overrun' with scrubby, carr woodland, as is typical for abandoned peatlands, blocking vistas and shrinking the sedge and reed beds particularly valued by birdwatchers. Since then, the Fen has been subject to two major managerial transformations: the 're-opening' of the landscape to something resembling its medieval and early modern appearance, combined with, perhaps paradoxically, an ambition to 'rewild' the site. The 'Wicken Vision' of the National Trust anticipates a century of Fenland expansion into available agricultural lands that will eventually cover 53 square km north of the burgeoning city of Cambridge (one of at least 47 such projects underway across Britain). This vision (reproduced in its entirety as Chapter 28), which aligns with the Dutch brand of ecological restoration known as 'nature development', stands the conventional notion of reclamation on its head. What the managers have in mind is the reclamation of former ecological *processes* rather than a specific vision of landscape drawn from a particular historical era. They aim to 'create and restore wildlife habitats'.[5] Key tools for 'nature development' are wild grazing animals, which create and maintain open areas and their floral diversity. The hope is that Highland cattle, which retain primitive bovine traits, and konik ponies (the nearest approximation to the extinct wild horse [tarpan]) will replicate not just the early grazing regime conducted by humans but the regime implemented by herds of herbivores prior to domestication.[6] Some of the ambition to extend the Fen comes from the idea that only relatively large-scale (landscape scale) 'restoration' will allow the autonomous development of ecological processes in which large fauna can survive, thereby permitting the wetlands to flourish.

The presence of these cattle and ponies at Wicken suggests how the neat categories of local, the national and global can be so easily muddied. The herd of Highland cattle is based on stock transplanted in 2005 from an organic farm on the Scottish island of Mull. The konik breed was preferred to natives of Britain's uplands, Exmoor and Dartmoor ponies, because it has a long history

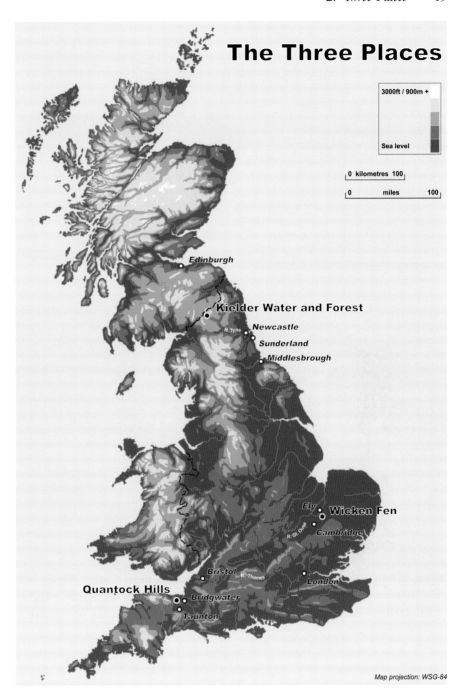

The Three Places

3000ft / 900m +

Sea level

0 kilometres 100

0   miles   100

Edinburgh

Kielder Water and Forest

R. Tyne Newcastle

Sunderland

Middlesbrough

Ely Wicken Fen

R. Gt. Ouse Cambridge

Bristol

R. Thames London

Quantock Hills

Bridgwater

Taunton

Map projection: WSG-84

FIGURE 2.1. Map of the
Three Places.

of successful adaptation to wetland habitats in lowland areas.[7] Koniks arrived
at Wicken in 2001, from wetland conservation grazing schemes in Holland and
Norfolk (Hickling Broad). 'Rewilding' is itself a conceptual import, shaped
extensively by work in the United States but especially by the reclaimed Dutch

FIGURE 2.2. Konik ponies
at Wicken Fen.

polder of Oostvaardersplassen, where since the 1970s rewilders have sought to create an analogue of an allegedly Mesolithic landscape from the sea bed – just half an hour's drive from Amsterdam.[8] The practice of rewilding, which is closely linked to the history of places where it has already been undertaken, has been the subject of fierce debate, criticized by those who argue that it is no more than 'gardening dressed up with jargon to simulate ecology'.[9] Its defenders retort that it is not about a naïve recreation of lost landscapes, but the unleashing of processes and managing the natural world with a lighter touch.

Our second place is the Quantock Hills in the western reaches of Somerset. These hills are a neatly delineated topographical entity, a compact range roughly 10 miles (17 km) long and 4 miles (6 km) wide running on a northwest to southeast axis.[10] They stand out from the surrounding (environing) agricultural lowlands, stretching westward from Taunton and Bridgwater toward the hulking mass of Exmoor and its national park. The Bristol Channel (Severn estuary) lies parallel to and a few miles north of the hills' northern rim. The massif is most readily visible on the right to the southbound traveller on the M5.

The Quantocks' slopes and steep-sided valleys (combes) largely consist of rough pasture and dense copses of semi-natural broadleaf woodland, intermingled with Forestry Commission plantations of ranked conifers. The flat ridge-top plateaus are made up of unenclosed heathland open to common grazing by the livestock (mainly sheep) of right-holding farmers. Once supporting a mixed agricultural and industrial economy (tanneries, textile mills, quarries and charcoal burning sites), the area is now dominated by livestock (pastoral) farming and recreational pursuits (hunting of the area's signature red deer stags as well as rambling, horse riding and mountain biking), its pretty, manicured villages housing retirees and incomers as well as longer-established residents (a total population of just under 3,000 for the AONB area as a whole).[11] The highest point (Wills Neck) is a modest 1,261 ft (381 m), but the hills are still famed for the panoramic views from their scenic heights.[12]

Like Wicken Fen, these hills were also a first. In 1956, under the National Parks and Access to the Countryside Act of 1949, the Quantocks became England's first designated 'Area of Outstanding Natural Beauty' (AONB; confirmed in 1957), shortly preceded by the establishment of the Gower peninsula AONB across the Bristol Channel in Wales. This form of statutory protection in recognition of its scenic values followed a decision not to incorporate it into the newly created (and much larger) Exmoor National Park (1954), and a vigorous local campaign to resist the expansion of conifer plantations in the area after 1945. Although lacking the sublime associations and renown of places like the Lake District and the Wye Valley, the Quantocks contain considerable scenic variety and biodiversity, including eighteenth- and nineteenth-century beech hedgebanks on the gentler eastern slopes that separate upland commons from farmland, parkland and conifer plantation, which, for some, are the area's visual leitmotif, and acid flushes (mires) on the damper parts of the peaty Atlantic heathland, habitat for highly specialist plants such as round-leaved sundew. The hill-top heathland and ancient semi-natural broadleaf (sessile) oak woodland together constitute a single Site of Special Scientific Interest (SSSI) that covers 30% of the AONB area, as well as constituting a Grade 2 Nature Conservation Review site – and is also protected at an international level as part of Exmoor and Quantock Oakwoods Special Area of Conservation (SAC), which is a European designation under the European Commission Habitats and Species Directive. Moreover, 36% of the AONB area is designated Priority Habitat. In terms of birds, the woodlands support the pied flycatcher and redstart (that return here each spring from sub-Saharan Africa) and the heathlands house over 1% of the UK's nightjar population.

They also benefited from association with two of England's most renowned poets, Samuel Taylor Coleridge and William Wordsworth.[13] Through them the Quantocks played a formative part in the emergence of core ideas about the appeal and values of wild nature associated with the Romantic movement in English literature. In the late 1790s, Coleridge spent two years living, envisioning and writing in a ploughman's cottage in the northern foothills village of Nether Stowey (now a National Trust property). Wordsworth joined him in the area for a gloriously productive year, during which much of the landmark collection of romantic poetry, *Lyrical Ballads* (1798), was planned and composed. Roaming the open hills and atmospheric woodlands of the Quantocks in all seasons and weathers (and often at night), the two young poets immersed themselves in the natural world and were inspired to write some of the best known poems in the English language.

FIGURE 2.3. Sheep and deer on the western flanks of the Quantocks (above Bicknoller) in early spring.

PHOTO: PETER COATES

There was plenty of evidence of human presence and activity in the Quantocks at this time, including quarrying, grazing, gorse, heather and peat-cutting, charcoal burning and coppicing (not to mention the traces of relict field systems on the uplands). A silk mill and dye works that harnessed the power of a stream running fast off the hills nestled cheek-by-jowl with the archetypically picturesque waterfall in Holford Glen that was one the poets' favourite meeting points.[14] Coleridge once claimed that he'd always care more for the brook that ran through Nether Stowey than for any stream he might hear while lying in an orange grove in Italy. But Stowey Brook was another river of industry. Tom Poole, his local patron, owned a tannery, and a sluice directed the noxious waste from his tanpits (which used bark stripped from local oaks) into the brook that flowed past the front door of Coleridge's cottage. And at Dodington, not far off the route that the Wordsworths and Coleridge strolled between their respective residences, was a copper mining site.[15] Nonetheless, it was in this far from uncultivated and untrammelled area that Coleridge and Wordsworth pioneered a taste for the uncultivated and untrammelled in nature that still defines many of our responses to Britain's more remote, less intensively farmed and sparsely populated regions.[16]

Today, the hills reside in a mixture of private ownership and common land, but are managed and regulated by the AONB service, which itself is answerable to a Joint Advisory Committee made up of a complex assemblage of stakeholders with an interest in the area, from the local county council and district councils to national governmental bodies such as Natural England. Since 1949, the hills have also been watched over by the Friends of Quantock, a local voluntary campaigning group that closely monitors activities that, in its view, constitute a threat to the long-term integrity and existing values of the hills. The AONB area, 40% of which Natural England classifies as 'publicly accessible', is ranged over by farmers, dog walkers, horse riders, ramblers, mountain bikers and day trippers/picnickers: a comprehensive survey conducted by the AONB service in 2003 indicated that, on a sunny summer day, up to 5,000 visitors can be at large on the hills.[17] These visitors – who are overwhelmingly day trippers rather than 'staying visitors' – come from as far afield as Bristol (45 miles to the northeast), though the majority (73%) of the more than 385,000 'visit days' clocked in 2003 are from residents of Somerset – whose two largest towns, Bridgwater and Taunton, lie just beyond the AONB's boundaries.[18] The reality is in fact more diverse – including extensive Forestry Commission plantations thick with fast-growing conifers from the Pacific Northwest of North America that date back to the early 1920s and are mostly within the designated AONB; and a reservoir (mostly just outside the AONB boundary).[19] But most visitors see the Quantocks as emblematic of the quintessential south-western English territory of deeply-embedded (sunken) and winding country lane, thick hedgerow, copse, green field and hamlet watched over by a sunlit (or mist-enshrouded) heath.

If the Quantock Hills are de-localized by an outsider's perception of them as a symbol of a generic landscape, then the panoramic vistas from the 'smooth Quantock's airy ridge', celebrated by Wordsworth as the poets 'roved unchecked' in the summer of 1797, opens up another link to the world beyond (nine counties, reputedly, are visible on a clear day).[20] This world includes the squat reactor towers of Hinkley Point nuclear power station, on the foreshore of the Bristol Channel. A knowledgeable local author, in the late 1960s, hailed the original twin towers of Hinkley as 'for all the world like the twin keep of some great Norman castle.'[21] But others regard Hinkley (where construction work on a third reactor site began in 2012) as a blemish on the local landscape (according to Natural England, the power station represents 'an incongruous element of a scene otherwise ancient in character'), compromising the Quantocks' viewshed, whose protection is no less important than attractions within the AONB.[22]

Yet if these pieces of infrastructure are inseparable parts of the wider Quantock environment, then Kielder, our third place, *is* infrastructure. One of its key components is a designated Nationally Significant Infrastructure Project (NSIP) under the Planning Act of 2008 (a designation the new reactor planned for Hinkley has applied for). The Kielder area on the upper reaches of the North Tyne river in Northumberland was selected as a study site as it has experienced substantial 'environmental change' over the last century. Kielder is a land of superlatives. The area now hosts the largest artificial lake, by volume, in northern Europe, with a capacity of 200 billion litres (the two reservoirs in the Quantocks region amount to just 950 and 1,050 million litres respectively); the largest hydroelectric plant in England; and Europe's largest artificial forest, which covers nearly 650 square km. In the early twentieth century, however, the area – then part of the estate of the Duke of Northumberland – was mainly moorland, peat bog and rough pasture. It was used for grazing sheep and rearing grouse. A railway ran up the river valley, linking Kielder with industrial Tyneside to the southeast and the Scottish borders to the north. Moreover, Kielder had its own industry: coal mines at Plashetts.

Planting the forest began in 1926. In 1932, the government took over the Duke's estate in lieu of death duties and the land was transferred to the Forestry Commission, which had been charged with creating a strategic timber reserve in Britain in the wake of the First World War. The forest at Kielder was also to supply pit props to the region's coal mines. In the 1930s, unemployed miners and shipyard workers from the industrial centres of North East England were given work planting trees. The forest was greatly enlarged in the decades after the Second World War as the Forestry Commission mechanized its planting operations. Row upon row of imported Sitka spruce were planted. Today, the forest has developed into England's most productive and profitable commercial forestry operation, but mechanization of harvesting has dramatically cut the numbers of foresters employed.[23]

The second major change in the environment at Kielder in the twentieth century was the damming of the North Tyne and formation of the reservoir. In the 1960s, planners foresaw a shortage of water for the burgeoning industries of Teesside by the late 1970s. A location was sought for a large dam to store water. The choice of Kielder provoked much controversy, on account of the impact on the local environment, population and livelihoods. Around 180 people lost their homes. The main dam was constructed between 1975 and 1981. As a concession to local opinion, a smaller dam was also built upstream at Bakethin to regulate water levels and prevent the formation of unsightly mud flats at low water. The Bakethin dam was opened by local schoolboy Jonty Hall in 1979, and three years later, the main dam – which is 1,140 m long and 52 m high – was inaugurated by the Queen.[24]

Kielder is an instructive location for a study of environmental change as it richly illustrates the law of unintended consequences: a heavily engineered environment – an artificial forest with an artificial lake imposed in its midst – is now being marketed successfully as a tourist destination. While the UK no longer needs a strategic timber reserve, and the demand for pit props dried up with the closure of the region's coal mines (Kielder's collieries at Plashetts closed back in 1964), the forest is a profitable operation as well as a leisure amenity. Kielder Water, however, has experienced a different fate. The industries of Teesside declined shortly after water from the reservoir became available. In fact, doubts over its necessity had been expressed earlier and critics branded it a 'white elephant'.[25] The reservoir has become mainly a place for recreation.

The transition from providing a strategic timber reserve and water for

FIGURE 2.4. Forestry Manager Graham Gill explains the history of Kielder Forest.

PHOTO: PETER COATES

industries to tourism and art is not quite as sharp as may be thought, however. The Forestry Commission paid attention to public access and recreation in the interwar years and they are now a significant part of its remit. In recent decades, moreover, as well as promoting public access and providing tourist facilities, the planting policy in Kielder and other Forestry Commission forests has changed to cultivate more diverse species and to design forests that take landscape features into greater account.[26] The dam and reservoir were also designed with regard to creating a pleasing environment and providing for recreation as well as storing water for industry.

Nevertheless, tourism has come to play a far larger role than the water authorities had envisaged in the 1960s and 1970s.[27] Now branded 'Kielder Water and Forest Park', the area is marketed as a single destination for tourists by a Development Trust whose members include the Forestry Commission, Northumbrian Water Limited (since the privatization of the water industry in 1989), the Calvert Trust (which provides activity holidays for the disabled) and Northumberland County Council. Organizations affiliated to the Trust include: the Arts Council England; the Northumberland Wildlife Trust; the Environment Agency; The Scout Association; and local parish councils. The Trust develops and actively promotes a wide range of recreational opportunities offered by the lake in the midst of the forest, such as hiking, biking, watersports and observing wildlife and the night skies. The reservoir has been stocked with brown and rainbow trout for angling.[28]

Kielder has also transmogrified by the installation of a series of striking works of art and architecture, funded in part by the Arts Council, that can be viewed from a lakeside trail.[29] The Development Trust reported that in 2010 the Park had attracted 306,000 visitor-days, with a total spend (direct and indirect) of £15.5 million, and had delivered 397 jobs in the area. In comparison, in 2011, the Forestry Commission had on its payroll 24 people at Kielder and a further 47 at its district headquarters in nearby Bellingham. Contract work and transporting the timber to processing mills generates a further 160 jobs in the immediate area.[30] This is a radical shift from an earlier age when the Forestry Commission had been by far the largest employer at Kielder, in the early 1950s, employing over 300 at Kielder alone.[31] Since 1982, the reservoir has created more jobs in the area, but mostly in tourism. According to Tonia Reeve, the Commercial Manager at Kielder for Northumbrian Water, the company now employs over 50 people in the area, compared with around eight 25 years ago. Most work in the leisure and recreation facilities at Kielder, however, rather than in the water industry.

In a further paradox for a largely artificial environment, Kielder has become an important site for nature conservation. Elements of a 'natural environment' have survived inside the forest. The Kielder Mires, with Sphagnum dominated plant communities, have been designated a Site of Special Scientific Interest (SSSI) and National Nature Reserve (NNR). The location of the mires was enclosed and designated for afforestation in the 1940s. As a result, most have not been affected by burning or grazing, and the Forestry Commission no longer plants trees on them.[32] Most paradoxically, perhaps, an artificial forest of mostly introduced trees has become one of the last holdouts of native red squirrels as they, in contrast to their introduced grey cousins, can thrive in a coniferous forest. The Forestry Commission's planting policy at Kielder now takes account of the needs of the red squirrel population, deliberately excluding broad-leaved trees with larger nuts, such as oak and hazel, that would provide an ideal habitat for grey squirrels, thus retaining a largely coniferous forest where reds can survive. This has been at the same time, moreover, as the species mix in the forest has been diversified to create a more 'natural' appearance for the benefit for visitors.[33]

Most recently, Kielder has also become a desirable place of uncompromised darkness and unpolluted skies for amateur astronomers, hosting 'star camps' and enjoying high visitation rates to its public observatory. A welcome antidote to 'night blight', Kielder Forest came out top in the Campaign for the Protection of Rural England's 'dark skies' survey in 2003. In December 2013, The International Dark Sky Association designated Kielder Water and Forest Park and adjoining Northumberland National Park as an 'International Dark Sky Park'. The status affords protection against light pollution and is a boost to tourism to the area for star gazing. The Kielder Observatory is already popular, attracting 50,000 visitors since it opened in 2008.[34]

Having introduced our three 'places', we should nonetheless make crystal clear that it is not our intention to write new histories *of* these three intriguing, clearly delineated places of incontrovertible historical, cultural and ecological significance. Nor are we in the business of 'deep mapping', however valuable this practice has been for the intensive, fine-grained, deeply-woven understanding of the specificity of particular places (a genre that White's *Natural History of Selborne* and Thoreau's *Walden* arguably pioneered).[35] Rather, we aim to write history *from* these places, examining how being there – and coming and going – shaped our ideas about the environment, the aesthetics of place and environmental change.

Notes

1. H. C. Darby, *The Draining of the Fens* (Cambridge: Cambridge University Press, 1940); Ian D. Rotherham, *The Lost Fens: England's Greatest Ecological Disaster* (Stroud: History Press, 2013).

2. Laurie Friday (ed.), *Wicken Fen: the Making of a Wetland Nature Reserve* (Colchester: Harley Books, 1997).

3. Roger Tabor, 'A Century of Conservation at Wicken Fen', *National Trust Magazine* 86 (Spring 1999), p. 24.

4. Ian Billick and Mary V. Price, *The Ecology of Place: Contributions of Place-Based Research to Ecological Understanding* (Chicago: University of Chicago Press, 2010). Over 250 academic papers have been published on Wicken Fen over the past 50 years. *Wicken Fen Vision*, (National Trust, 1999). See also Friday (ed.), *Wicken Fen*; Natural England, *National Character Area Profile 46: The Fens* (2013), p. 10.

5. *Wicken Fen Vision*, p. 10.

6. For a case study of 'nature development' in a wetland region of coastal Latvia, using herbivores such as the konik pony, see the chapter entitled 'Wild Horses in a European Wilderness', in Katrina Z. S. Schwartz, *Nature and National Identity after Communism: Globalizing the Ethnoscape* (Pittsburgh: University of Pittsburgh Press, 2006), pp. 138–65. On wild horses on the Russian steppes in the eighteenth century, see David Moon, 'The Russian Academy of Sciences Expeditions to the Steppes in the late-Eighteenth Century', *Slavonic and East European Review* 88 (2010), pp. 223–4.

7. Konik ponies enjoy multiple advantages over their domestic cousins: they can foal without assistance, and at an early age; they produce milk of high nutritional value;

they are hardy in terms of ability to withstand cold, rain and snow, not least by building up a layer of subcutaneous fat and fat between the muscles during the growing season, so that, in winter, they don't have to tap into muscle tissue; they are adept at extracting nutrients from poor quality forage, also from foliage and twigs; and, not least, they can effectively fend off predators.

8. Vincent Wigbels, *Oostvaardersplassen: New Nature below Sea Level* (Zwolle, Staatsbosbeheer, 2001).

9. Peter Del Tredici, 'Neocreationism and the Illusion of Ecological Restoration', *Harvard Design Magazine* 20 (Spring/Summer 2004), pp. 87–9), cited in David Lowenthal, 'Reflections on Humpty-Dumpty Ecology', in Marcus Hall (ed.), *Restoration and History: The Search for a Usable Environmental Past* (New York and London: Routledge, 2010), p. 26.

10. This discrete and almost autonomous identity within the larger area is illustrated in terms of Natural England's revised *National Character Area Profiles* (2013). Of our three sites, only the Quantock Hills has its own profile (144); Wicken Fen and Kielder are covered within Profiles 5 (Border Moors and Forests) and 46 (The Fens) respectively.

11. Susan Malmesbury, 'Stag Hunting in Devon and Somerset', *North American Review* 156/435 (February 1893), pp. 187–8.

12. The relatively tame character of the hills is expressed in the final episode of series 6 of Channel 4's *Peep Show* ('Quantocking'). Mark dismisses Jeremy's fears when the two appear to be lost on the hills: 'This isn't the Matterhorn, Jeremy, it's the Quantocks, nobody dies in the Quantocks'. We thank Matt Greenhall for bringing this to our attention.

13. See the chapter entitled 'Among the Quantock Hills', in Henry Van Dyke, *Days Off and Other Digressions* (New York: Charles Scribner's, 1907), pp. 117–39.

14. Hazel Riley, *The Historic Landscape of the Quantock Hills* (London: English Heritage, 2006); J. D. U. Ward, 'The Wordsworths' Waterfall: The Claim of Holford Glen', *Town and Country Planning* 25/3 (March 1957), pp. 132–4; Dorothy Wordsworth, *Journals of Dorothy Wordsworth*, vol. 1, ed. W. Knight (London: Macmillan, 1897), pp. 5, 8.

15. Peter Haggett, *The Quantocks: Biography of an English Region* (Chew Magna: Point Walter Press, 2012), pp. 129, 113, 127.

16. Peter Coates, 'Walking with Coleridge and Wordsworth: Discover Connections between Landscape and Literature in Somerset's Quantock Hills' (2011), 'Discovering Britain', Royal Geographical Society http://www.discoveringbritain.org/walks/region/south-west-england/quantocks.html (accessed 08/12/14).

17. Natural England, *National Character Area Profile 144: Quantock Hills* (2013), p. 11. Natural England is in the process of producing National Character Area (NCA) profile documents for each of the 159 NCAs in England. NCA 144: Quantock Hills encompasses most of the AONB, the exceptions being the coastal zone and some AONB border farmlands that are covered by NCA 146: Vale of Taunton and Quantock Fringes.

18. Quantock Hills Area of Outstanding Natural Beauty, *Draft Management Plan 2014-2019*, p. 39 http://www.quantockhills.com/resources/FINAL_AONB_Management_Plan_18214.pdf (accessed 24/10/14).

19. Though the impoundment of Hawkridge Reservoir (1960–63) required the diversion of some stretches of road, the 32 acre water feature is non-intrusive within the wider landscape. The large broadleaf trees that frame the head of the reservoir, its naturalistic banks and shoreline meadows lend a bucolic air to this particular piece of infrastructure, which has also become a favourite haunt of for fishing (rainbow trout) and sailing: Vincent Waite, *Portrait of the Quantocks* (London: Robert Hale, 1969), pp. 91–2;

Haggett, *The Quantocks*, p. 155; *Civil Engineering and Public Works Review* 56 (1961), p. 1155; *The Surveyor and Municipal and County Engineer* 120 (1961), p. 856; Roger Evans, *Bridgwater with and without the 'E'* (Bridgwater: Roger Evans, 1994).

20. William Wordsworth, *The Prelude* (London: Edward Moxon, 1850), p. 369; Natural England, *National Character Area Profile 144: Quantock Hills* (2013), p. 5.

21. Bryan Little, *Portrait of Somerset* (London: Robert Hale, 1969), p. 189.

22. Natural England, *National Character Area Profile 144: Quantock Hills* (2013), p. 32. There is also, of course – though it is rarely considered – a view southward from Hinkley to the Quantocks. Probably the most unusual of these views is from a window in a corridor within the power station. The visitor is encouraged to gaze southward at the Hills through a window that is framed in a mock, gilt-edged picture frame. As cameras are prohibited throughout the Hinkley site, this view has probably rarely been captured.

23. R. McIntosh, 'The History and Multi-purpose Management of Kielder Forest', *Forest Ecology and Management* 79/1–2 (1995), pp. 1–11; Materials prepared for the 'Visit of the Independent Panel on Forestry to Northumberland (including Kielder) on 26th July 2011', pp. 6, 11–19. We are grateful to Graham Gill, Forest Management Director, North England Forest District, Forestry Commission (retired), for supplying a copy of the file prepared for the visit. For a recent study of forestry across the border in Scotland, see Jan Oosthoek, *Conquering the Highlands: A History of the Afforestation of the Scottish Uplands* (Canberra: Australian National University Press, 2013).

24. On the controversy over the dam, see David Archer, 'Kielder Water: White Elephant or White Knight?', in David Archer (ed.), *Tyne and Tide: A Celebration of the River Tyne* (Ovingham: Daryan Press, 2003), pp. 138–56; Christine S. McCulloch, 'The Kielder Water Scheme: The Last of its Kind?', in Henry Hewlett (ed.), *Improvements in Reservoir Construction, Operation and Maintenance* (London: Thomas Telford Books, 2006), pp. 196–210.

25. Archer, 'Kielder Water', p. 155.

26. T. C. Smout, *Nature Contested: Environmental History in Scotland and Northern England since 1600* (Edinburgh: Edinburgh University Press, 2000), p. 62; 'Public access, recreation and tourism' http://www.forestry.gov.uk/fr/INFD-5VFMB7 (accessed 25/06/13); talk by Graham Gill, Kielder Forest, 26/03/11.

27. Christine McCulloch, 'Kielder Water and Forest Park: The City in the Country', in this volume, pp. **269–78**.

28. See http://www.visitkielder.com/about-us (accessed 29/01/13).

29. http://www.visitkielder.com/tours-tour-guides-courses/kielder-art-architecture (accessed 30/6/13).

30. Materials prepared for the 'Visit of the Independent Panel on Forestry', pp. 6, 7, 19.

31. Gideon Shapiro, 'Varieties of Value: Nature's Value and Variance at the Kielder Water & Forest Park', MA thesis, University of Bristol (September 2012), p. 20.

32. http://www.english-nature.org.uk/citation/citation_photo/2000076.pdf (accessed 25/06/13). Talk by Duncan Hutt, Head of Land Management, Northumberland Wildlife Trust, Kielder, 26/03/11.

33. See 'Transcript of Talk by Graham Gill, Forest Management Director, North England Forest District, Forestry Commission (retired), in Kielder Forest, 26 March 2011' in this volume, pp. **234–39**; Interview with Graham Gill by David Moon and Gideon Shapiro, 3 July 2012; 'Kielder red squirrel buffer zone extended', *The Bellingham Journal*, 14 January 2010 http://bellingham.journallive.co.uk/news/kielder-red-squirrel-buffer-zone-extended.html (accessed 25/06/13); NCA Profile, Border Moors and Forests, pp. 7, 16, 40, 61, 62.

34. http://www.darksky.org/assets/Night_Sky_Conservation/UK_DSP_Press_Release_
      Dec13_FINAL.pdf; http://www.bbc.co.uk/news/uk-england-tyne-25260186 (accessed
      09 05 14); NCA Profile, Border Moors and Forests, p. 17.

35. Mike Pearson and Michael Shanks, *Theatre/Archaeology* (London: Routledge, 2001),
      pp. 64–5; Iain Biggs, '"Deep mapping": A Brief Introduction', in Karen E. Till
      (ed.), *Mapping Spectral Traces 2010* (Blacksburg, Virginia: Virginia Tech College of
      Architecture and Urban Studies, 2010), pp. 5–8; Nigel Cooper, 'Gilbert White and
      the Natural Theology of Selborne', *The Linnean* 23/3 (2007), pp. 29–44.

Environment and Landscape

CHAPTER 3

The Environment

Paul Warde

'Environment', in the sense we are familiar with today, emerged only recently, even though its origins are old. The verb 'to environ', 'to form a ring around, to surround', had its first recorded origins in medieval French but was well established in English usage in the fourteenth century.[1] Given that one's environs encompass, in principle, everything, an 'environment' is potentially a big place. But in both medieval and later forms, the notion was applied with far more discrimination: environs were immediate and neighbourly rather than universal. Today, when we can talk of 'the environment' as a global phenomenon, or Britain's Department of Environment, Food and Rural Affairs (DEFRA) defines the 'natural environment' as 'the whole of the living world', this disjuncture between the word's potential and application often remains. DEFRA does not pretend to take responsibility for the whole of the living world, whether just in the United Kingdom or beyond. Indeed, neither does it limit itself to managing the 'living'.[2] Similarly, the English and Welsh 'Environment Agency', established in 1996, has a mandate 'to protect or enhance the environment, taken as a whole'.[3] In practice, this primarily means the management of waterways and coastal sites, the regulation of waste disposal and the monitoring of air pollution; generally issues to do with safeguarding property (flood prevention), ensuring access and preventing contamination. Thus the vast potential claims of the concept, and political realities, are quite divergent. We cannot assume we know what people mean when they use the term 'environment'. In practice, then, we ask *why* they do so, what associations it evokes, who takes responsibility for it.

Both history and current practice indicate the selectivity that is active when we use 'environment', because it is only one out of a number of ways we can talk about 'the natural world'. Equally, 'the environment' only became synonymous with that natural world during the twentieth century, and probably was only widely recognized as such during the 1960s. A 'Ministry for the Environment' was created in Britain by the incoming Conservative government of 1970, the same year that the American Environmental Protection Agency (EPA) was founded after the signing into law of the National Environmental Policy Act on 1 January by Richard Nixon.[4] It was precisely in 1969–70 that German officials adopted *Umwelt* as a translation of 'environment' in imitation of policy developments in America.[5] In Britain, when it comes to the protection of species in nature reserves, or Sites of Special Scientific Interest (SSSIs), or the power to nominate and manage an 'Area of Outstanding Natural Beauty', we find a different constellation of bodies, with some areas enjoying regulatory protection determined by the European Union, and work being led in England by 'Natural England', a rebranding in 2006 of 'English Nature', then merged with the 'Countryside Agency'.[6] These were the inheritors of changes in 1991, which had seen the amalgamation the Countryside Commission and Nature Conservancy Council, which in turn had their roots in the founding of 'Nature Conservancy' in 1949.[7] There is no mention of the environment in any of these titles and, as we shall see later, 'nature' and 'beauty' figure more prominently in some management agendas than in others.

Thus the common-sensical idea of 'environment' performs many functions, but it soon raises many questions about what it includes, or excludes. In very recent decades, we have developed a singular usage, '*the* environment' that has a rather distinct meaning. We also have a body of study – or at least sets of university departments – dedicated to the 'environmental sciences' (a term probably first employed in 1959).[8] This leads us to ask why this word seemed to have such 'metaphoric resonance', to use Brendon Larson's term, at that historical moment – and what the consequences have been.[9] Why did anyone feel the need to use a term different to 'nature', or talk about 'the Earth'? Why, in turn, do we sometimes persist in talking about 'nature' in certain contexts? Do these choices privilege certain kinds of knowledge, raise the profile of, or even create, new kinds of expert? What kind of power does our understanding of 'the environment' exert?

These are not merely semantic questions. There is a long history of 'nature' being used to demarcate certain areas that are outside what is 'social' and imagined as subject to human steering and agency, and crucially where behaviour can be shaped by argument and choice. 'Nature' in distinction is simply subject to 'natural' laws and where regulation is about compulsion. Of course this boundary is both permeable and can be defined differently by, and relative to, different groups of humans; it is in itself a social artefact that tells us much about the society that produces it.[10] It was a common strategy of colonial writers writing about their indigenous subjects, for example, or those writing about the peasantry, to 'naturalize' their behaviour and make it a function of the environment that they live in. This strategy can aim to render the subordinate group incapable of reflection and progress, legitimizing rule and more 'rational' perceptions of their plight, or, contrastingly, can act as a (usually caricatured) critique of the failings of a 'civilization' that has allegedly forgotten how to live in an organic harmony. Needless to say, these discourses, while hugely influential, have not much to do with actual natural laws, environments or, for that matter, the real workings of society.

And yet – in their way, they do. Deciding that something (or someone) is subject to 'natural laws', or does not influence social processes, is a profound way of allocating responsibility, defining expertise and offering or withdrawing agency to it (or her). Thus the way in which people, by word and deed, assign cause, consequence and consciousness to human or non-human actors becomes a major factor in shaping the 'lifeworld' in which they live. The difficult question of 'what is environment?' can thus be turned into a more productive exercise: examining the shifting boundaries created by a process of 'environing'.[11] This means it really can matter what word gets used, and the wider meanings and associations assigned to that word. What kind of language, for example, is considered to come under the purview of humanists and social scientists, and what gets allotted to other kinds of scientists – who end up taking up managerial responsibilities and shaping policy for things and places so defined? What kind of sense of purpose, fatalism, blame, contrition, indifference or curiosity might result from it?

If we understand categorizations and demarcations as the result of *work* done by our language, whether conscious or unconscious, it becomes clearer how historians and humanities scholars can play an important part in the study of things environmental. 'The environment' is no longer solely conceived as an entirely autonomous realm which we may either damage or protect by our actions. In fact, this is itself a certain kind of story about 'the environment' (and still one that has a lot of truth in it).

This chapter aims to open up, rather speculatively, some ideas of how one might go about writing a history of the 'environment'. It is neither a comprehensive history of the use of the word environment nor even a history of what we call the environment, but some suggestions of what it might mean to think in this idiom. It is also Anglophone, although there are certainly parallels in other languages (for example, as we have already seen with the history of the German *Umwelt*, or the Swedish *miljö*, derived, of course, from the French *milieu,* a word sometimes imported directly into English but to describe a social or cultural context).

Environment before 'the environment'

'Environment' secured a place in the English language thanks to the prolific commentator and biographer Thomas Carlyle, who is recorded as first using it in 1827.[12] The word was well established in French and had occasionally appeared in translations of Francophone works. Carlyle established the idea of writers being shaped by their 'environment': one explained the peculiar genius of Voltaire, Spinoza, Hegel or whoever as the interaction of their own qualities and the environment in which they moved. This use of the term was still going strong a century later when Isaiah Berlin published *Karl Marx: His Life and Environment*, a book that certainly would not be so entitled today.[13] The 1933 classic *Culture and Environment* by F. R. Leavis and Denys Thompson employed 'environment' in this tradition, as the conditions that shaped 'training taste and sensibility', contrasting their own virtuous efforts as scholars with the deleterious cacophony of 'multitudinous counter-influences – films, newspapers, advertising – indeed the whole world outside the classroom'. While they considered the 'wanton and indifferent ugliness ... of the towns, suburbs and houses of modern England' as an affront to the 'natural environment', it is 'ugliness' that they take to be most distinctive of the modern environment, contrasting it with a vanished 'organic community' whose demise has taken with it 'human naturalness or normality'.[14] As a portrayal of the changes attendant on industrialization, this was doubtless little more than lazy stereotyping, of the kind lambasted by Raymond Williams in *The Country and the City*, but it expresses a sensibility frequently found in the twentieth century: that nature can hardly be uttered without evoking some nostalgia, a narrative of loss, while 'environment' is more a statement of fact.[15] In these narratives, 'nature' was increasingly valorized, while 'environment' was purely descriptive.

However, by far the greatest influence on the use of the word came from the English polymath Herbert Spencer, in the context of his evolutionary theories.[16] Such 'evolutionary' works followed the trajectory of Spencer himself, moving easily between biology, psychology and sociology, influencing polymaths and planners such as Patrick Geddes.[17] Spencer first employed the word in writings on psychology in 1855. 'The environment' is simply the source of stimuli that produce sensory effects in the mind: 'those properties of things which we know as tastes, scents, colours, temperatures, sounds, are effects produced in us by forces in the environment.'[18] It was thus imagined not as a thing in itself, but as what a body or mind senses to be 'external circumstances' which act upon it.[19] Hence, in the Spencerian tradition, 'environment' became a key mode of explaining why things were different and how things changed.

In later works, Spencer applied 'environment' more broadly, to the notions he had already formed about the 'universal laws' that drove nature and society. In *The Principles of Sociology*, he wrote 'on ... conditions, inorganic and organic, characterizing the environment, primarily depends the possibility of social evolution.'[20] Anything could have an 'environment' which exerted selective pressure, and which could thus be used to explain the characteristics of species, races, schoolchildren, the insane, and so on. Thus while the term itself was possibly all-embracing, it was only understood relationally; all that mattered about an environment was its effects upon the individual or species of interest. One could talk of 'the environment', but it was 'the environment of ...'. The environment was that part of the exterior world that became interiorized in that it produced lasting effects on physical or mental life: 'Thus it becomes morally certain, that, at last, great, general, permanent, and all-important facts in the environment, will produce in organisms impressions so deep and lasting that they will tend to become intuitive and instantaneous.'[21]

Spencer's influence was wide, and it is probably his legacy that saw the rapid expansion in the use of the term from the 1890s.[22] Among the many authors who used it in direct imitation of Spencer, drawing on his evolutionary thinking, we can note the great Cambridge economist Alfred Marshall, who also employed it to translate the German *Konjunctur*.[23] Another was a writer who straddled the divide between sociology and economics, Thorstein Veblen, who carried the torch for more psychologically-inflected explanation of economic behaviour into the twentieth century. He employed 'environment' frequently in his classic *Theory of the Leisure Class*, a work that sought to refocus economic writing away from preoccupations with production and abstract utility towards a more cultural interpretation of what drove consumers. In his work, 'environment' described the context of the 'struggle for existence' of *social forms* and businesses; institutions and habits were the bearers of evolutionary development, rather than individual people. Veblen concentrated his idea of evolutionary change on institutions which, as a 'social environment', shaped habit, possibly influenced by the British biologist C. L. Morgan.[24] The writings of Marshall, Veblen and the American plant physiologist and later leading sociologist, Lester Frank Ward, indicate the rich conceptual cross-pollination between the social and natural sciences at this time, and the lasting influence of Spencer's terms, if not necessarily his ideas. At the end of Spencer's life, the great British ecologist A. G. Tansley worked for a while as his editor.[25]

In all of these works, 'environment' was not, as it later became, an object subject to assault and being degraded. Rather, it was a thing that shaped us, and generally was only considered in relation to the things it supposedly shaped. This was a strong tradition in geography which also adopted widely the term – particularly found in the New World or dominion geographers, such as Ellen Churchill Semple, Griffith Taylor and Frederick Jackson Turner, advocates of what we now call environmental determinism. The experience of colonial expansion and ethnographic encounter had long raised questions about whether different geographies produced different kinds of people.[26] Environments were not just limiting, but offered challenges and possibilities, exemplified in Taylor's contrasting of the immutable desertlands of Australia with the open frontier of Canada's north.[27] There was some crossover with ecology here, such as in Frederic Clements' *Environment and Life on the Great Plains* (1937) or Griffith Taylor's *Environment and Nation* (1936).[28]

As a word, 'environment' performed a powerfully integrative function in conceptualizing collectively the many influences that shaped a species, a person or a mind. However it was not yet applied as if the wider natural world was itself an integrated system, and thus had a life or dynamic of its own that could change for better or worse. Of course, there *were* essential precursors that had begun to join up the dots of systemic connections in the natural world, notably the biogeographies and studies of climatic zones by Alexander von Humboldt.[29] Yet while geographers and anthropologists had become preoccupied with the degree to which human society might be shaped by its physical environment, the latter was still a category largely impervious to human influence. Nevertheless, there had long been an understanding of risks to parts of what we now consider to be 'the environment'. In that sense, environmental risk is certainly nothing new. In the early nineteenth century, it had been widely recognized that humans could act as agents of soil degradation, deforestation and thereby climate change, but these changes were generally seen as localized and reversible.[30] George Perkins Marsh, author of *Man and Nature* (1864), stands out as an author who took the step from local or regional arguments about the effects of negligent agriculture on the soil to a more general argument that human influence was massively reshaping its physical surroundings, often in negative and unforeseen ways. Writing before 'the environment' was available as a term, Marsh wrote of 'the Earth'. But it was a term that lacked refinement or, as we might say, 'scalability', the capacity to systematically integrate local and global change. The connecting factor was the malign effect of humans, rather than the functioning of 'the Earth'. Similar in conception was the work of Russian scientist Alexander Voeikov, who wrote on 'the influence of man on nature' in 1894.[31]

'The world is sick'

The breakthrough for 'the environment' in its modern sense came in the immediate post-war years. In 1948 both William Vogt's *The Road to Survival* and Fairfield Osborn's *Our Plundered Planet* were published, two works that attacked bitterly the destructive impact of humanity across the entire globe. Diagnoses of crisis in relation to fisheries, soils, resource availability and forests were, of course, nothing new, but it was in the late 1940s and the aftermath of global war that the collective global system gained an identity as an object under possible fatal assault. 'The world is sick,' wrote William Vogt in August 1948 for the British edition. '… We live in one world in an ecological – an environmental – sense.' 'Man has moved into an untenable position', he wrote, 'by protracted and wholesale violation of certain natural laws; to re-establish himself he needs only to bring his behavior into conformity with natural limitations.'[32] Vogt opened up his book with a series of fictional vignettes indicating the varied lives of people living around the globe, not to demonstrate, as might traditionally have been done, how their environments has shaped them, but to lay bare how they were all locked into an enterprise of destruction. The environment was becoming something new: not an explanation, but a victim to which 'man' was bringing 'havoc'. Rather than an independent constellation of forces affecting people, 'today', declared Osborn, 'one cannot think of man as detached from the environment that he himself has created …'. 'Man' was 'becoming for the first time a *large-scale geological force*'.[33]

The new career for 'environment', integrating and describing all those parts of the natural world under assault, proceeded across the 1950s and 1960s, bringing new approaches to policymaking and science. Undoubtedly, World War and then Cold War acted as something of a catalyst, both in highlighting the destructive capacities of humanity, but also calling closer attention to worldwide patterns of development and the scramble for resources with more globalized logistics.[34] The stand-out article for policy was written by American planner Lynton Caldwell in 1963, calling environment 'the complex interrelating reality surrounding us', and arguing that the concept could serve to bring together policy areas previously treated in isolation, and overcoming previous 'failure to see the unifying elements in the complexity'. The world required 'environmental administration'.[35] By the second half of the decade, numerous bills were being submitted to Congress calling for 'environmental policy', culminating in the National Environmental Policy Act signed into law in 1970.[36]

Caldwell used 'the environment' to argue for a wider remit and vision within planning, and others, too, recognized that environmental challenges required new forms of collaboration, across planning, architecture, ecology, medicine and conservation.[37] At the same time, many working in the earth, ocean, atmospheric and biological sciences recognized the need for more integration and collaborative work, exemplified in the International Geophysical Year of 1957–58. These collaborations impressed Solly Zuckermann, the leading British scientific advisor tasked in 1959 by the new Ministry of Science with examining the establishment of a new Research Council focused on what were called 'natural resources'. Seeking a way of naming this range of academic expertise, he came up with 'environmental sciences'. By 1962, this was in print and, in 1964, Britain had a 'Natural Environment Research Council', although 'environment' was actually a compromise among competing disciplines because none of them would accept the more familiar alternatives suggested by others.[38]

Thus, by the end of the 1960s, there was just *the* environment, even if the United Nations Stockholm conference of 1972 still produced a 'Declaration on the *Human* Environment' [my emphasis]. Of course, older uses had not disappeared; but volumes began to crowd the shelves on any variety of topics '... and the environment'. Ecologist Frank Fraser Darling gave the BBC's prestigious Reith Lectures in 1969 and explained to listeners 'the impact of man on his environment'.[39] When, in 1970, organizations such as the Conservative Party or *Fortune* magazine brought out tracts on *The Environment* or *The Environment: a national mission for the seventies*, nobody could be in any doubt what they meant, or what the problem was. Or so it seemed.

A new narrative

There can be little doubt that ecologists were crucial in this transformation of environmental understanding. After all, it was ecology that was, in the words of Darling, 'the science of the organism in relation to its whole environment'.[40] Ecology, emerging as a branch of plant physiology in the 1890s, had enthusiastically adopted the term 'environment' at an early date, often directly from Spencer.[41] 'The environment' was, as we have seen, largely considered as the conditions that shaped evolutionary adaptation. Over time, though, ecologists began to consider these factors in a wider and more integrated manner. Eventually, it was possible to consider the environment, rather than any particular species or even 'community' of species, as the object of study. In turn, for some ecologists preoccupied with population dynamics, it became an easy manoeuvre to attribute the political disasters of the 1930s and 1940s to overpopulation, and make gloomy predictions on a global scale.[42] One influential figure was the renowned American ecologist Aldo Leopold, who argued in 1944 that 'the impending industrialization of the world means that any conservation problems heretofore local will shortly become global.'[43] He, in turn, directly influenced the thinking of William Vogt. It was these years that brought together the previously deterministic social and geographical sense of 'environment', itself the product of the ferment of evolutionary thinking in the second half of the nineteenth century, with the idea that had grown within ecology, of 'environment' as an integrated and mutually sustaining system in its own right.[44] This word, already widely familiar if employed in rather different contexts, was able to capture a systemic global perspective, and also new possibilities for measurement (most notably with radioactivity and toxicology).

The American marine biologist (and best-selling popular science writer) Rachel Carson, in *Silent Spring*, famously described 'the contamination of man's total environment with such substances of incredible potential for harm'. In this, probably the most famous 'environmentalist' work of the twentieth century, Carson found a term that could encompass the astonishing pervasiveness of chemical pollution that she catalogued. Her use of environment was still qualified by 'total', although in other parts of the book, and prefaces to the English edition by Lord Shackleton and Julian Huxley, 'the environment' was used without qualification.[45] Carson was, of course, trained in ecology too: 'The science of ecology teaches us that we have to understand the interaction of all living things in the environment in which we live.' Yet before alighting upon that so memorable a title, *Silent Spring*, she had considered 'The Control of Nature', or 'Man Against the Earth'.[46] We can hear an echo of George Perkins Marsh; also, it might seem as if she was searching for 'environment' as the necessary term to describe what she was pointing to, but it did not yet seem appropriate for a book title.[47] In fact, neither of her early suggested titles – using 'control' or 'against' – were very good descriptions of what she described, as humans were clearly *not* controlling nature in the way that they might desire, while the risks she described were as much to people as to the Earth.

In those post-war years, 'the environment' became embedded in a new kind of story and its status was transformed. Previously, the 'environment' had functioned as context to the real subject of the story (a species, writer, society, race ...), offering a set of unique circumstances, whether limits or opportunities, which might be overpowering, serendipitous, exculpating, promoting adaptation or balance. Now, the environment became a thing with its own essence, and itself the victim of circumstances, a fragile 'web of life' subject to contamination by invisible and uncontainable elements, such as Strontium 90 and Cesium 137, and assault, its 'integrity' subject to 'disturbance', becoming 'corrupt' and threatened by 'engulf[ment]'.[48] There had been a shift from a world where humans were 'moulded by the environment' to a situation in which man [*sic*] was able to 'alter the nature of his world'.[49] This, of course, reflected the experience of transition to an increasingly globalized, urban, industrial and nuclear society. The metaphoric resonance had profoundly shifted. Previously, environmental stories had been told by people considered experts in human societies (or the humanities), often as a way of explaining differences among people. In the post-war story, the environmental expert provided measures and narratives about the state of the world, which itself became the indicator of the wisdom of society. These stories were no less moralized or, in their most striking forms, less literary, but they privileged a different kind of knowledge. In some ways 'environmentalist' stories were structurally akin to the 'Romantic' narratives of people finding the best human values whilst abroad in nature.[50] But the true *measure* of that goodness was now in parts per million or indicators of biodiversity.

A division of labour?

Much has happened since 1962. But the resonance of this history, and the meanings and narratives constructed, endure. What is perhaps surprising news is that discourses of 'environment' in its post-1945 sense did *not* come to dominate thinking about nature, conservation or relations with the 'non-human' to the degree one might expect. Some of the documents produced by this project's partners use the term 'environment' infrequently – if at all – especially those geared towards advertising the attractions of a place to a wider public, rather than listing fulfilment of administrative duties. This is perhaps less surprising if we consider that the modern usage of 'environment' has emerged, above all, in scientific and political contexts, and has been used to evoke, or been embedded within, stories of vulnerability, protection and declension. And why, after all, should such narratives be employed in documents that talk about the character of a landscape or its stirring, romantic beauty, as in the case of the Quantocks? How would an evocation of a narrative of decline and vulnerability make sense in a landscape transformed as utterly as Kielder Water and Forest in the past few decades, when nobody is proposing a restoration of their earlier state?

These observations reflect a division of labour that has existed and endured at the heart of post-war environmental policymaking in Britain, although this division emerged before 'the environment' became an established term, and hence differentiation in language is not always clear-cut. The National Parks and Areas of Outstanding Natural Beauty (AONBs) that were mandated by statute in 1949, were envisaged primarily as areas for recreation and repositories of aesthetic values, albeit ones related to landscape. In contrast, the same act founded the Nature Conservancy which had a remit focused on species protection and ecosystem management.[51] Given its small resources, this body initially began by safeguarding very limited areas of land and securing representative or rare species for posterity. This in fact involved high levels of intervention and the expectation that conservation scientists and ecologists could determine what was good for both the locality and the balance of protected sites across the nation. This was partly in the tradition of Tansley, who had insisted on the 'anthropogenic' reality of the human role in the ecosystems of Britain, a notion partly derived from his own research at Wicken Fen.[52] The surface areas regulated by Nature Conservancy's successor in England, Natural England, are very much larger and extend to large swathes of farmed land via voluntary agreements. Later, the Environment Agency has primarily worked in measuring, regulating and monitoring acceptable levels of risk. While ecologists and environmental scientists are certainly employed across all these agencies, they come to the fore in the work of Natural England and the Environmental Agency, while parks and AONBs use tools such as 'Landscape Character Assessment' and are viewed as part of 'heritage', just as in the 'heritage forests' defined in 2010 as part of government plans for the privatization of the crown forest estate.

These kind of divisions reflect historical developments, firstly, in their fundamentally defensive disposition (one that some agencies are now seeking to overcome): the emergence of 'the environment' in the 1940s as an object in crisis, and the institutional means to confront the crisis at that point in time, alongside fears of the despoliation of the countryside by urban and suburban sprawl and a need to maintain areas for recreation. Indeed, thanks to this legacy, the environment is entrenched in our minds as being in an almost permanent state of crisis, with any policy successes often perceived as local, isolated and possibly temporary at best. Nature is an even more nostalgic idea in many cases, a word we can hardly utter without feeling that we are in the process of losing it: 'heritage'. Natural England may retain 'Nature' in its title, as a holdover from its origins in Nature Conservancy at a time when 'nature' was used to distinguish rural from urban but, subject to the guidance of DEFRA, it undergoes the same triennial review as the Environment Agency and is concerned above all with environmental management as understood in the post-war period.[53] In contrast, the Association of National Parks Authorities do not even mention 'environment' in their website's self-description, instead explaining how they provide, 'Britain's breathing spaces'.[54]

Of course, things change. Efforts at restoration and 'rewilding' may move us beyond a discourse preoccupied with preservation and monitoring to the creation of 'new' nature. The *Wicken Vision*, developed in the late 1990s, is a plan and aspiration to extend the nature reserve over the next century by buying up 53 square km of property to the north of Cambridge, and radically extending a lost landscape of 'fen, reedbed, wet woodland and open water'. This is a project where ecology is clearly fore-grounded, and where the primary aim is 'securing *environmental* benefits'. But such benefits are certainly not to the exclusion of humans: the aim is 'to greatly expand the space for wildlife and people'. Nor is it backward looking – at least, the aim is no longer couched in terms of defence:

we will allow nature to take its course wherever possible and desirable, and will manage positively for this, ... seeking optimum outcomes for nature as an integral part of all land uses ... We accept that some habitats and species will be lost, changed or replaced over time.[55]

This is, rather unusually in modern times, an expansionist view of the environment, of what it could be if it is not being eroded and destroyed. Interestingly, though, it is 'nature' that has agency and that is being liberated; the 'environmental' remains a more passive object of management, even if the managers of the process are not so much guardians or protectors as facilitators. The vision is prescriptive neither for place nor people: it unleashes process, while giving people 'space to breathe ... to think' (The Wicken Vision is reproduced in its entirety as Chapter 28).[56]

Of course, there is much that is old in this new vision. Nature as a place for human self-discovery has been one of the most prominent narratives in western culture for well over two centuries. The idea that we demonstrate our moral sense of purpose in our management of the environment is also well-established, although it has taken radically different forms, from seventeenth-century 'improvement' to contemporary environmentalist ethics that seek to raise the status of non-human species to a level of greater parity with humans.[57] Yet this twenty-first century vision for 'the environment' also, perhaps, represents another turn. If the space for human development is envisaged as being opened up by our management of nature, it is not in the earlier sense of 'environment' as determinant, yet it relates, as earlier thought did, our interior condition to the exterior world we inhabit.[58] At the same time, however, more in the tradition of post-war and ecological thought, the managers and measurers of environmental conditions retain their role as the experts in charge, even if they are not being so closely prescriptive about outcomes (discovering how prescriptive they must be, of course, is part of the experiment itself). The narrative is changing but, as yet, the primary meaning of 'environmental', and those who govern the discourse, are not.[59] Arguably, these facts are themselves true to the vision of generations of managers of, and visitors to, a site like Wicken Fen, and are entirely justifiable – and are indeed in the tradition of Tansley and his influence on UK conservation policy.[60] But these words and processes, set in the longer histories of place and concepts, give us pause to reflect on what kind of discursive resources, systems of knowledge, institutions and politics must operate to make the 'environment' that a place is, in the way we experience, live in and manage it. This work of making and fixing can change quite dramatically over time. And yet, it can become tenacious in the continued life of a place. Past moments of institutionalization (such as changes in property rights, or becoming a destination for university field trips) or becoming a resonant place in the topography of a narrative (peculiarly beautiful, threatened or simply *environmental*) continue to shape change for long periods to come.

Notes

1. *Oxford English Dictionary.*
2. http://www.defra.gov.uk/environment/natural/ (accessed 24/10/14).
3. See http://www.environment-agency.gov.uk/aboutus/default.aspx (accessed 24/10/2014) and http://www.defra.gov.uk/environment/ (accessed 24/08/2012).
4. Internationally, the distribution of responsibilities can be quite varied. In the United States, fish and wildlife and parks are managed by the US Department of the Interior (which also oversees the affairs of Native Americans), while the US Forest Service has always been part of the Department of Agriculture. In Russia we find the Ministry for Natural Resources and the Environment (official English translation, although the Russian word in fact means 'ecology' rather than environment). In being responsible for both exploitation of and protection of nature, it has potentially conflicting interests within it, somewhat like the UK's DEFRA.
5. Sandra Chaney, *Nature of the Miracle Years: Conservation in West Germany, 1945–1975* (Berghahn: New York, 2008), pp. 176–7, 190; Jens Ivo Engels, *Naturpolitik in der Bundes-republik. Ideewelt und politische Verhaltensstile in Naturschutz und Umweltbewegung 1950–1980* (Schöningh: Paderborn, 2006), pp. 275–94.
6. The devolved administrations of Northern Ireland, Scotland and Wales have their own equivalent bodies.
7. John Sheail, *Nature in Trust: A History of Nature Conservation in Britain* (Glasgow: Blackie, 1976); W. M. Adams, *Future Nature: A Vision for Conservation*, 2nd edn (London: Earthscan, 2003).
8. See below, note **38**.
9. Brendon Larson, *Metaphors for Environmental Sustainability: Redefining our Relationship with Nature* (New Haven: Yale University Press, 2011).
10. Paul Warde, 'The Environmental History of Pre-industrial Agriculture', in Sverker Sörlin and Paul Warde (eds), *Nature's End: History and the Environment* (Basingstoke: Palgrave Macmillan, 2009), pp. 70–92; Kirsten Hastrup, 'Destinies and Decisions: Taking the Life-world Seriously in Environmental History', pp. 331–48, in the same collection. Such arguments can also be extended into how social groups are categorized and naturalized, in part in relation to ecological boundaries; between 'civilization' and barbarous lands and people, for example, where 'barbarians' are often seen as incapable of 'cultivation' (in the agricultural and cultural senses of the word), existing in a kind of state of nature; also in the establishment of ethnic identities that are often 'positional' in generating identity through boundary-setting. For a useful discussion, see: James C. Scott, *The Art of Not Being Governed: An Anarchist History of Upland Southeast Asia* (New Haven: Yale University Press, 2009), pp. 256–65.
11. Sverker Sörlin and Paul Warde, 'Introduction', in Sörlin and Warde (eds), *Nature's End*.
12. The following section is extracted from a larger forthcoming work co-authored with Libby Robin and Sverker Sörlin, on *The Environment: A History.*
13. Frank R. Leavis and Denys Thompson, *Culture and Environment: The Training of Critical Awareness* (London: Chatto & Windus, 1933); I. Berlin, *Karl Marx: His Life and Environment* (London: Butterworth, 1939).
14. Leavis and Thompson, *Culture and Environment*, pp. 1, 93.
15. Raymond Williams, *The Country and the City* (London: Chatto & Windus, 1973).
16. Much more so than Darwin. I have only found it fleetingly in *The Descent of Man* (London, 1874) and in *The Effects of Cross and Self-fertilization in the Vegetable Kingdom* (London, 1878), although he used the term more frequently in letters.

17. Patrick Geddes, *Cities in Evolution: An Introduction to the Town Planning Movement and to the Study of Civics* (London: Williams & Norgate, 1915).

18. Herbert Spencer, *Principles of Psychology* (London: Longman, Brown, Green and Longmans, 1855), p. 194.

19. In the words of Lewis A. Selby-Bigge, *The British Moralists, Being Selections from Writers Principally of the Eighteenth Century* (Oxford: Clarendon, 1897), p. lii; who is using a word borrowed from Spencer to describe beliefs about the climate influencing humans held by Henry, Lord Kames.

20. Herbert Spencer, *The Principles of Sociology* (London: Williams & Norgate, 1876), p. 6.

21. Rev. S. R. Calthrop, 'Religion and Science', *Report of the second meeting of the national conference of Unitarian and other Christian churches held in Syracuse, N. Y.* (Boston, 1866), p. 209.

22. One can, for example, trace its usage in *The Times* newspaper expanding rapidly in this decade.

23. Alfred Marshall, *The Principles of Economics* (London: Macmillan, 1890), *passim*.

24. Thorstein Veblen, *Theory of the Leisure Class: An Economic Study in the Evolution of Institution* (New York: Macmillan, 1899); C. Lloyd Morgan, *Habit and Instinct* (London: E. Arnold, 1896), esp. p.340; Geoffrey Hodgshon, 'On the Evolution of Thorstein Veblen's Evolutionary Economics', *Cambridge Journal of Economics* 22 (1998), pp. 415–31.

25. Lester F. Ward, 'The Local Distribution of Plants and the Theory of Adaptation', *Popular Science Monthly* 9 (1876), p. 682.

26. For a useful introductory discussion, see: David Arnold, *The Problem of Nature* (Oxford: Wiley-Blackwell, 1996).

27. Ellen Churchill Semple, *Influences of Geographic Environment* (New York: Holt, 1911); Griffith Taylor, *The Australian Environment* (Melbourne: The Executive Committee of H. A. Hunt, 1918); Griffith Taylor, *Environment and Race* (London: Oxford University Press, 1927); Griffith Taylor, *Canada: A Study of Cool Continental Environments and their Effect on British and French Settlement* (Methuen: Dutton, 1947).

28. Frederic Clements and R. W. Chaney, *Environment and Life on the Great Plains* (Washington: Carnegie Institute of Washington, 1937); Griffith Taylor, *Environment and Nation* (Toronto: University of Toronto Press, 1936).

29. Alexander von Humboldt, *De distributione geographica plantarum* (Paris: Libraria Graeco-Latina-Germanica, 1817).

30. Paul Warde, 'The Invention of Sustainability', *Modern Intellectual History* 8 (2011), pp. 153–70; Ravi S. Rajan, *Modernizing Nature: Forestry and Imperial Eco-development 1800–1950* (Oxford: Clarendon Press, 2006), pp. 24–7; Jean-Baptiste Fressoz, *L'Apocalypse Joyeuse. Une histoire du risque technologique* (Paris: Le Seuil, 2012); Steven Stoll, *Larding the Lean Earth: Soil and Society in Nineteenth-century America* (New York: Hill & Wang, 2002); Benjamin Cohen, *Notes from the Ground: Science, Soil and Society in the American Countryside* (New Haven: Yale University Press, 2009).

31. George Perkins Marsh, *Man and Nature: Or, Physical Geography as Modified by Human Action* (London: Murray, 1864); A. I. Voeikov, 'Vozdeistvie cheloveka na prirodu', in V. V. Pokshishevskii (ed.), *Vozdeistvie cheloveka na prirodu: izbrannye stat'i* (Moscow: Gos. izd. geog. lit, 1949), pp. 40–90; Marsh and Voeikov were later treated as the patron saints of environmental thinking, prominently cited in the introduction to the proceedings of the famous *Man's Role in Changing the Face of the Earth* conference held in Princeton in 1955: William L. Thomas (ed.), *Man's Role in Changing the Face of the Earth* (Chicago: University of Chicago Press, 1956).

32. William Vogt, *Road to Survival* (London: Victor Gollancz, 1948), pp. 14–15, 264.

33. Fairfield Osborn, *Our Plundered Planet* (Boston: Little Brown & Co., 1948), pp. 29–30.

34. Sverker Sörlin and Paul Warde, 'Expertise for the Future: The Emergence of "Relevant Knowledge" in Environmental Predictions and Global Change, *c.*1920–1970', in Jenny Andersson and Egle Rindzeviciute (eds), *Forging the Future: The Struggle for the Long Term in Transnational Science and Politics During the Cold War* (Abingdon: Routledge, forthcoming); Jacob D. Hamblin, *Arming Mother Nature: The Birth of Catastrophic Environmentalism* (Oxford: Oxford University Press, 2013); Thomas Robertson, *The Malthusian Moment: Global Population and the Birth of American Environmentalism* (New Brunswick: Rutgers, 2012); Thomas Robertson, '"This is the American Earth": American Empire, the Cold War, and American environmentalism', *Diplomatic History* 32/4 (2008), p. 565; Thomas Robertson, 'Total War and the Total Environment: Fairfield Osborn, William Vogt and the Birth of Global Ecology", *Environmental History* 17 (2012), pp. 336–64.

35. Lynton K. Caldwell, 'Environment: A New Focus for Public Policy?', *Public Administration Review* 23/3 (September 1963), pp. 132–3.

36. Lynton K. Caldwell, *Environment: A Challenge for Modern Society* (New York: Natural History Press, 1970).

37. Frank Fraser Darling, *Wilderness and Plenty: The Reith Lectures 1969* (London: BBC, 1970), p. 18.

38. John Sheail, *Nature Conservation in Britain: The Formative Years* (London: The Stationary Office, 1998) , pp. 160–6.

39. Darling, *Wilderness and Plenty*, p. 20.

40. Darling, *Wilderness and Plenty*, p. 13.

41. Robert P. McIntosh, *The Background of Ecology: Concept and Theory* (Cambridge: Cambridge University Press, 1985).

42. Robertson, *Malthusian Moment*, pp. 26, 43–6; Robertson, 'American Earth', pp. 572–3; Robertson, 'Total War', pp. 344–5.

43. Robertson, *Malthusian Moment*, p. 34.

44. Of course, as already discussed above, ecology and social thought had been intimately connected in their earlier phases of development.

45. Rachel Carson, *Silent Spring* (London: Penguin, 1962), pp. 23–5, *passim*.

46. Paul Brooks, *The House of Life: Rachel Carson at Work* (London: George Allen & Unwin, 1973), pp. 239, 263. 'Silent Spring' is inspired by the reference to a bleak waterland where 'no birds sing' in John Keats' well-known poem, *La Belle Dame sans Merci*.

47. I am grateful to David Moon for this observation.

48. Carson, *Silent Spring*, pp. 69, 79, 168, 169.

49. Carson, *Silent Spring*, p. 22.

50. And in Wordsworth we find, as Raymond Williams avers, 'a confidence in nature ... which ... was also a broader, more humane confidence in men'; a strong strand in modern environmentalist thinking seems to doubt the capacities of either to endure: Williams, *The Country and the City*, p. 127.

51. Sheail, *Nature in Trust*; Adams, *Future Nature*; Margaret A. Anderson, 'Areas of Outstanding Natural Beauty and the 1949 National Parks Act', *The Town Planning Review* 61 (1990), pp. 311–39.

52. Laura Cameron, 'Resources of Hope: Wicken Fen Stories of Anthropogenic Nature', *Cambridge Anthropology* 31/1, (2013), pp. 105–18.

53. http://www.naturalengland.org.uk/about_us/triennialreviewfeature.aspx (accessed 24/08/12).

54. National Parks, Britain's breathing spaces, 'about us' http://www.nationalparks.gov.uk/aboutus (accessed 24/10/14).

55. *Wicken Fen Vision*, (National Trust, 1999), esp. pp. 7, 9.

56. *Wicken Fen Vision*, p. 1.

57. Paul Warde, 'The Idea of Improvement, *c*.1520–1700', in Richard Hoyle (ed.), *Custom, Improvement and the Landscape in Early Modern Britain* (Farnham: Ashgate, 2011).

58. George Monbiot, *Feral: Searching for Enchantment on the Frontiers of Rewilding* (London: Penguin, 2013).

59. It is, of course, the case that local managers in reserves such as Wicken Fen feel themselves answerable to representatives of local communities, neighbouring landowners, the conditions of bequests, planning authorities, the governing bodies of the National Trust and visitor tastes and opinions.

60. Cameron, 'Resources of Hope', pp. 109–11.

CHAPTER 4

Landscape Character Assessment: A View from the Quantocks

Emma-Jane Preece

The purpose of my talk at the workshop in the Quantocks in March 2011 was to give an overview, in my role as Landscape Planning Officer for the Quantock Hills Area of Outstanding Natural Beauty (AONB) Service, of Landscape Character Assessment (LCA) – what it is and how it works in practice. For a deeper and more detailed understanding of LCA, reference should be made to the current and accepted best practice guidance on the subject – *Landscape Character Assessment: Guidance for England and Scotland*, prepared by Carys Swanwick for The Countryside Agency and Scottish Natural Heritage in 2002.[1] This discussion draws heavily from this guidance document but provides a condensed understanding – one that best reflects the narrative that accompanied my workshop presentation.

As Landscape Planning Officer my role is to help inform planning decisions and planning policy in the best interests of the designated landscape – with the ultimate aim that any decisions for development or change of land use within the AONB are not at the expense of this beautiful and very special landscape. The Landscape Planner's role broadly has two key parts. The first is undertaking the more strategic landscape planning work, which might involve producing guidance documents or responding to planning policy consultations that might effect the AONB, such as housing allocations and minerals policy positions. The second role involves commenting on planning applications within and around the protected landscape.

In September 2012, because of my close involvement in the consultation process for the two new reactors proposed at Hinkley Point nuclear power station – the Hinkley C development – I was asked to speak again to a group that met at Halsway Manor to present and discuss preliminary versions of many of the essays that appear in this collection. This second talk addressed how the AONB Service was involved in the process of consultation and what the predicted implications might be for the nationally designated landscape of

The Quantock Hills AONB. Some of the material from that presentation is reflected on at the end of this paper as an example of how Landscape Character Assessment has been used in practice to underpin our involvement in the Hinkley Point C consultation.

Landscape Character Assessment

Landscape Character Assessment is well established, having been used in landscape professional work since the 1980s. It is perhaps most accurately described as a tool or device – a systematic approach that allows different landscapes to be *identified*, those identified landscapes to be *classified* (mapped and named) and those classified landscapes to be *described*.

Landscape Character Assessment was something of a sea change in how to think and make decisions about the landscape – bucking the historically favoured 'landscape evaluation' approach that was a largely quantitative method of 'scoring' to see 'what makes one area of landscape "better" than another'.[2] Instead, LCA emerged to offer a process that set out clearly 'to separate the classification and description of landscape character (*i.e.* what makes one area "different" or "distinct" from another) from the then more usual approach of landscape evaluation, with its concentration on relative value'.[3]

Landscape Character Assessment sees the landscape as a continuous system – one that does not understand or adhere to administrative boundaries; boundaries that are typically used to identify and separate out the places around us – local authority and parish boundaries being obvious examples. LCA identifies features and elements of the landscape (their combination and expression) in order that the very essence or special 'character' of a particular place can be revealed, explored and understood. Swanwick's *Landscape Character Assessment: Guidance for England and Scotland* states that LCA is the tool that is used to help to understand and articulate the character of the landscape. It helps us 'identify what gives a locality its "sense of place" and makes it different from other areas'.[4] Natural England explains that: 'Appreciation and understanding of our landscapes has increased over time ... often prompted by the need and desire to record, understand, influence and manage change;' and that 'Landscape Character Assessment (LCA) is one tool that helps in that understanding.'[5]

Landscape Character Assessment is now deeply rooted within the planning system. From the national to the local scale there are a wide range of policies, statements and guidance documents aiming to conserve, protect, enhance and positively manage the character of the landscape. In 2006, the UK signed up to the European Council's European Landscape Convention (ELC) – the first international convention specifically focused on landscapes – that promotes landscape protection, management and planning, and European co-operation on landscape issues. The ELC became binding in March 2007.

Landscape Character Assessment can broadly be split into two stages:

Characterization – an objective and relatively value-free process of landscape identification, mapping, classification and description; and

Making Judgements – developing and employing a robust methodology in order that professional judgements about the landscape can be made and which will then assist with decision making.

Characterization

Identification (and mapping)

The identification process is the methodical investigation of the many factors – natural (physical) and human – that have, over time, influenced and shaped the character of a place. These factors include:

- Geology, topography, hydrology;
- Soils and vegetation (land cover) associated with them;
- Historic and current influences of human land use and settlement.

There are many layers of information that can be considered as part of the identification stage.[6] The degree to which each factor influences the character of the landscape will vary from place to place. In one landscape the underlying geology may be such an important influence on the character of a place, being reflected in its use as building material in settlements. In another area, the underlying geology may not be a visually prominent or obvious defining feature. Yet it is the way in which the various factors interact – creating distinct patterns or 'character' in the landscape – that allow the different landscape characters to be identified. The identified landscapes can then be mapped and classified.

Classification

Swanwick explains that 'landscape classification is central to Landscape Character Assessment and is concerned with the process of dividing landscape into areas of distinct, recognisable and consistent common character and grouping areas of similar character together.'[7] In order to classify landscapes, they are typically separated into Landscape Character Types and Landscape Character Areas.

Draft maps are prepared following desk work and these are used in the field where 'ground truthing' ensures amendments can be made and the mapping refined so that the character map is as accurate as is possible. Boundaries typically follow mappable features: some may be visually distinct such as a dramatic change in landform, marking out, for example, a boundary between an escarpment and an open plateau above. Typically, however, landscape character boundaries can be subtle with a gradual change in character being hard to identify and map. In such landscapes there should always be an appreciation that LCA boundaries are transitional and should be treated as such when being used for decision-making purposes.

Landscape Character Types are 'generic in nature in that they may occur in different areas in different parts of the country, but wherever they occur they share broadly similar combinations of geology, topography, drainage patterns, vegetation and historical land use and settlement patterns'.[8] On the Quantock Hills, an example of landscape character type is Open Heathland Summit or Wooded Combe. The Guidance gives examples of landscape types as 'Chalk River Valleys' or 'Rocky Moorland'.

Where landscape character types describe what the overriding character of a landscape is, **Landscape Character Areas** describe the geographical areas where these landscape character types occur. A Landscape Character Area (LCA) is discrete and often has its own nuances and identity yet pertains to the general character (pattern of elements and features) of a landscape type. Using the examples provided in the Guidance, it explains that 'the Itchen Valley, the Test Valley and the Avon Valley (all chalk rivers) would be separate landscape character areas, of the "chalk river valley" landscape character type.'[9]

> *e.g.*   Landscape Type 1: Chalk River Valley.
>   Character Areas: 1A Itchen Chalk River Valley, 1B Test Chalk River Valley, 1C Avon Chalk River Valley.

The names and numbers used will link to the accompanying LCA map.

Description

The guidance is clear that LCA descriptions should be an objective account and that their narrative should 'avoid value-laden judgements, for example, words such as beautiful, bland, attractive, degraded or ordinary'.[10] This is not to suggest that descriptions need be mundane but they should avoid the use of subjective words such as beautiful or attractive and instead focus on qualifying what it is that makes that landscape beautiful – so that the essence, the flavour, the uniqueness of place can be brought to the fore with transparency and robustness. This clear base of evidence then paves the way for practical use of LCA when making judgements.

Making judgements

Most LCAs move beyond the purely descriptive to being a useable resource that informs decision making, for example, decisions for future landscape management, decisions on the location of new housing or renewable energy schemes and even decisions about the types of material to be used on new buildings. The guidance clearly states that 'the main value of having a Landscape Character Assessment is to help in the process of managing change in a particular place. All sorts of change will shape future landscapes, and by applying this tool in an appropriate way, alongside other tools, we can help to ensure that such changes make a "positive" contribution.'[11]

Case Study – LCA and its role in Hinkley Point C

During the period 2009-12, the Quantock Hills AONB Service worked closely with Natural England as consultees on the planning application by EDF Energy for the major infrastructure project to develop two new nuclear power reactors at Hinkley Point (Hinkley Point C). This application entailed the extension of the existing nuclear power site at Hinkley where reactors (Hinkley A and Hinkley B) are already prominent features on the coast at Bridgwater Bay.

For the AONB Service, the concerns regarding Hinkley Point C centred on the landscape and visual impacts of the scheme – if and how the introduction of such a vast infrastructure project into the lowland landscape surrounding the Quantock Hills would affect the perceptual character of the protected landscape (and the quality of views afforded by the hills).

Although the plant is not inside the AONB boundary, the Quantock Hills offer commanding views of Hinkley Point and its hinterland that lies northeast of the nationally designated landscape. Having a nationally significant infrastructure project so close to a nationally protected landscape meant that the AONB Service had a clear duty to engage in consultation on the project. As the Landscape Institute's *Guidelines for Landscape and Visual Impact Assessment* state:

> National designation may be an indication of the potential for significant effects. Accordingly sites within or adjacent to nationally designated landscape require detailed and rigorous examination assessments that are appropriate to the status of the landscape. Particular attention should be given to the special attributes and characteristics that justified the original designation, together with the policy objectives that justified the original designation.[12]

LCAs from the national to the local scale were a key tool used throughout the consultation process. They were a vital source of information that provided a clear picture of baseline (existing) landscape character of the application site and of the protected landscape. Considered alongside the development plans, LCA allowed an understanding of what the changes to the physical landscape would be, specifically, what key features, elements and characteristics making up the landscape pattern would be lost at the site (such as mature woodland, farmland, hedgerow network and natural landform). And, importantly for the AONB Service, LCA helped aid an understanding of how that manifested change in the landscape character might impact upon visual receptors, that is, those people viewing Hinkley Point. Would the perceived change in the character of the landscape around Hinkley Point C, when viewed from within the AONB, affect some of the special qualities that underpin the AONB designation: among them the open hilltops of the Quantock Hills valued for their sense of space, wildness and seclusion; exhilarating views; dark skies at night; tranquillity and quiet enjoyment?[13]

Using LCA to understand existing and predicted changes in character helped the AONB Service to make well informed judgements about the Hinkley C proposals. Those evaluations were fed through at various stages of the consultation process to inform the development of the Landscape and Visual Impact Assessment submitted as part of the final planning application.

This paper has given a brief summary of LCA, with reference to one particular case of how it positively contributes to the work of an AONB Service. AONBs are designated solely for their landscape qualities, for the purpose of conserving and enhancing their natural beauty (which includes landform and geology, plants and animals, landscape features and the rich history of human settlement over the centuries). It is imperative that AONBs continue to develop their understanding of landscape character and make use of landscape character assessments (revising them when and where necessary) so that they can help positively manage change in these living and working landscapes. The Quantock Hills AONB is currently updating its landscape character assessment, which was last produced in the 1990s. The immediate aim is to have an assessment that follows current, accepted best practice and to make information about the character of the landscape more readily accessible via the web. More importantly, perhaps, this exercise will also re-emphasize the importance of LCA in making the case for the continued protection of nationally designated landscapes such as AONBs.

Notes

1. Carys Swanwick, *Landscape Character Assessment: Guidance for England and Scotland* (Cheltenham: Countryside Agency/Scottish Natural Heritage, 2002).
2. Swanwick, *Landscape Character Assessment*, p. 2.
3. Swanwick, *Landscape Character Assessment*, p. 2.
4. Richard Wakeford and Roger Crofts, 'Foreword', in Swanwick, *Landscape Character Assessment*.
5. Christine Tudor, *An Approach to Landscape Character Assessment* (London: Natural England, October 2014), p. 7.
6. It is very rare to undertake landscape character assessment without the use of a Geographical Information System (GIS) that allows computer overlaying of data, to assist in the characterization process. See: *Topic Paper 4: Use of Geographical Information Systems and Other Computer Methods* (*Landscape Character Assessment Guidance for England and Wales*) (London: Scottish Natural Heritage and The Countryside Agency, 2002), pp. 1–16.
7. Swanwick, *Landscape Character Assessment*, p. 37.
8. Swanwick, *Landscape Character Assessment*, p. 9.
9. Swanwick, *Landscape Character Assessment*, p. 9.
10. Swanwick, *Landscape Character Assessment*, p. 51.
11. Swanwick, *Landscape Character Assessment*, p. 52.
12. The Landscape Institute with the Institute for Environmental Management and Assessment, *Guidelines for Landscape and Visual Impact Assessment*, 2nd Edition (London: Spon Press, 2002), p. 27.
13. Quantock Hills Area of Outstanding Natural Beauty, *Draft Management Plan 2014–2019* http://www.quantockhills.com/resources/FINAL_AONB_Management_Plan_18214.pdf (accessed 24/10/14).

CHAPTER 5

The Curious Case
of the Missing History at Kielder

Richard Oram

One thing that struck me most forcefully at Kielder was the almost total disconnection of the locally-based people we met from the deep history of the North Tyne valley. For some, 1982 (the year the main dam was inaugurated) seemed to represent a distinct break-point, with what came before holding little interest. Indeed, there was more than one reference in our discussions with the representatives of the Kielder Development Trust at the workshop at Kielder in March 2011 to how little there was of any historical interest in the valley.[1] When pushed, a very thin sequence of episodes/periods was offered: the dam's construction and the flooding of the upper part of the valley in the late 1970s and early 1980s; from the period after the First World War to the 1960s Forestry Commission management; nineteenth-century coal-mining and building the railway; going further back in time a gap until Border Rievers in the sixteenth century; then a leap straight back to the Romans; before them a vague sense of 'prehistory'; and then straight into geological time.

This lack of awareness of the rich history of this area appears to be compounded by the absence of obvious major archaeological monuments in the landscape. Again, however, some harder questioning revealed that 'history' was something to be equated with large structural remains – castles, parish churches, hillforts, *etc.* – things which were not obvious to the eye in the valley north of Bellingham. But, it was conceded, there were some abandoned post-medieval settlement sites in the afforested areas, some (probably Bronze Age) hut-circles and cairns and some individual standing stones (but, to the disappointment of the representative of the Kielder Development Trust questioned, no major ritual monuments). Yet, especially amongst the Forestry Commission employees, although there was a suggestion of strong awareness of the wider archaeological landscape within the planted areas – expressed in terms of scheduled and unscheduled Ancient Monuments marked on their maps – there was little recognition of the physicality of those monuments except where a line had been drawn around them on an Ordinance Survey map. The system of turf banks between the reservoir and the road just north of Leaplish, for example, marking probably part of an early Improvement era upland farm complex, was clearly not considered even worth mentioning in the literature available at the information centre and passed unremarked upon by our guide.

It was quite shocking to me to hear the upper section of the North Tyne valley described as an area that had no 'real history'. This perception of it by its inhabitants appears to have been reinforced by what is very much a twentieth-century tendency to treat it as a self-contained entity, a closed system that had – and still has – very few dealings with the lower part of the valley from Falstone (just below the dam) down to Hexham (25 miles (*c*.40 km) downstream near the confluence of the North and South Tyne rivers). Indeed, the fact that Falstone represents the southernmost extent of the Kielder Development Trust's territorial range has served to draw an artificial line across the valley and institutionalize the sense of separation between the two halves of what had formerly been the one system. Discussion with representatives of the Trust – especially those who lived in Falstone or Kielder – revealed a perception of difference on their part from the communities lower down the valley: 'people go down the valley for things, never up.' It also revealed a very strong link back to that sense of the area covered by the reservoir and the forest being intrinsically without historical or archaeological interest; all the things that would interest people lay outside the forest boundary (including the closest castles) but really there wasn't that much in any case north of Hadrian's Wall until you were over the Border into Scotland. There was very much a sense conveyed that the Partnership employees were convinced that there was almost no point trying to interest visitors in the history of the district because there wasn't one that merited being talked about; again, there was a powerful view expressed that historic interest was dependent on major stone monuments that could assume an iconic role in the area's promotion. Without such an icon, there was no point in trying. Indeed, there was almost an apology that the whole of the valley was of such obvious lack of historical relevance that we, as historians, had probably been wasting our time coming there!

Ironically, the narrative which we were presented with by way of thumb-nail outline pointed to a much richer and deeper history than the presenters were aware of. The mining history of the valley, for which there is apparently a good photographic record, offers a striking contrast to the large-scale operations in the Northumberland and Durham coastal coalfields. Small in scale, remote and possibly originally serving the needs of the Tynedale communities, it offers a possibility through census records to provide a human-scale link to lost communities in the upper portion of the valley. There was no indication of any link between the mines and the Duke of Northumberland's estate around the head of the valley, much of which now lies under the forest. Passing reference to a grouse moor and shooting interests points to a different economic imperative and perhaps hints at an older importance for the area as part of a much larger, integrated system. Indeed, there are indications of a complex economic network in the upper portion of the valley in the late eighteenth and nineteenth centuries, with mining communities being scattered through a landscape of upland, primarily pastoral farms, which backed onto the high moors and tops which were extensively exploited and used for seasonal grazing and hunting. How old that kind of system was in its origins is unclear, but there are strong grounds for proposing that something of the kind was already in operation in the later twelfth century, when the valley formed part of the lands in England held by the kings of Scots. To understand that system and to present it clearly to the public, however, requires Tynedale to be considered again as a unit and far closer links to be reforged between the section north and west of Falstone and the part to the south and east of the village below the dam.

Perhaps the greatest irony is that many of the historical features which illustrate that former unity are driven past by visitors as they approach Kielder from the southeast. Bellingham is the main community in the lower portion of the valley, a status which it has held since at least the twelfth century when its church became the parish centre for the whole of upper Tynedale. Parishes represent coherent economic and social entities: Bellingham parish stretched from the watershed with the catchment of Liddel Water to Wark and Simonburn. The second major feature is Tarset Castle near Lanehead, which was the principal lordship centre in the upper stretch of the valley from the late twelfth to at least the early fourteenth century. Held by the Comyns, who were amongst the most important vassals of the kings of Scots, this was a major stone-built castle whose construction – and the expenditure on it – underscores the value in real terms which this property held for an important noble family. Now reduced to earthworks (albeit hugely impressive ones) just north of the old railway line, there is not even an information board to draw attention to the existence of the site. Tarset's neglect seems to symbolize the severance of the representatives of the Kielder Development Trust from the richness of their past.[2]

Notes

1. On the Trust, see the 'Three Places' chapter in this volume, pp. 17–30.
2. Awareness of Kielder's pre-twentieth century past is higher among other organizations with a stake in the area. Natural England's *National Character Area Profile* (No. 5. Border Moors and Forests) that includes Kielder refers to the 'widespread archaeological and historical evidence indicating the strategic importance of this border area', most notably Roman marching camps and later defensible farmhouses (bastles), as well as 'the need to conserve these bastles and the remains of shieling settlements that provide signs of the former seasonal occupation of the uplands', pp. 3, 10, 18, 39.

CHAPTER 6

Birds and Squirrels as History

....

T. C. Smout

When we (myself and my wife, that is) were at Kielder, we saw 29 species of birds: they are listed at the end of this piece. Birds are little feathered capsules of history. Each one tells us about our past; each one depends on our present. They underline the extent to which we live in an age of the Anthropocene. What we have done and what we do, and how biota is able to respond, determines the fates of individuals, local populations and entire species.

Take the most distinctive bird of Kielder, the siskin, which was everywhere singing its fizzy little song and swinging from the larch cones, and the crossbill, which uses its twisted mandibles to prize open Sitka cones. They would not have been here unless Germany had come close to winning the First World War by starving Britain of timber, and the government had then decided they needed to listen to the gentlemen of the Royal Scottish Arboricultural Society, who had long been moaning that no-one cared about their views. They held that Britain needed a national forestry service; the Forestry Commission was started, ground was bought at Kielder in the 1920s and 1930s, and the biggest artificial forest in Europe was planted.

The natural habitat for the siskin and crossbill had previously only existed hundreds of miles to the north, in the Highlands of Scotland. The siskins may have visited from time to time the alders along the river banks of England, which provided an alternative winter food, or come to the rather small and mainly ornamental plantations of larch made by gentlemen following the lead of an eighteenth-century Duke of Atholl. The crossbills may, in irruption years when the cone crop failed in Scandinavia, have sought out similar small plantations of pine and fir. But the coming of the Forestry Commission completely transformed the fortunes of both species, especially in Kielder but also across the length and breadth of Britain. Lloyd George made a world fit, if not for heroes, certainly for siskins and crossbills.

Then there were the birds that were easier for us to see, for example at the squirrel hide, and more familiar to most of us from our own gardens: chaffinch, robin, blue tit, great tit and great spotted woodpecker. They would have been common enough here in the absence of the forest, around the farms and houses and in the gardens. But they are familiar and abundant here not only because a Sitka wood is acceptable habitat if it has a bit of an edge and access to alternative places outside, but also because they have adapted to our wish to feed them peanuts and sunflower seeds. Why do we feed them? It is a cultural habit of urban residents that has grown up in the last century and now become a compulsive habit of quite ordinary people (not twitchers or birders or scientists) who seem to want a connection with a wild species that is friendly up to a point, but not a pet like a cat or a dog. It is a cultural development peculiarly British, but certainly not only British – the red peanut bag hangs in Lapland and Oregon as well as in Corby and Liverpool.

Not every bird comes to a feeder as readily as a robin or a chaffinch. The blue tit comes, but not often its congener the marsh tit; the chaffinch but not the linnet. Those that do come thrive better and their populations are generally increasing. Some learn to come. In the last 10 years the long-tailed tit has learned the art of swinging from a peanut holder in Britain, and its numbers do not now crash in bad winters like they used to. Some come in some countries but not in others: the hawfinch has learned to come in Germany, where it is commoner than in England – here it is a declining species. Some never learn and cannot eat the food we provide. The wren is commensal with humans, living in our gardens and barns, but does not digest the food we put out unless we invest in expensive meal worms (which are generally eaten by bigger birds before the wren can get there anyway). So the wren suffers in severe weather. We saw none at Kielder, which had been locked in ice and snow during the worst December on record, though it was an ideal habitat for wrens in other ways.

So it is with every species we encountered, and with some we did not encounter. They all have human cultural and economic history as drivers in their modern story. There was a nuthatch, which would not have been in the forest 20 years ago: they are spreading north with global warming. We failed to encounter the osprey which our hosts were expecting any day to come and boost their visitor attractions. Once upon a time, before the Middle Ages, the osprey is thought to have been widespread in England, but its fearlessness combined with an unfortunate penchant for eating carp from monastic ponds led to it being forced back to the fastness of Highland Scotland. Here it managed well enough until, in the nineteenth century, it was declared an enemy of the salmon fisher and a curio in a cabinet of stuffed raptors, and was wiped out. A pair returned to Speyside in the mid-twentieth century, and in 1959 the RSPB daringly set up a watch point to enable the public to see it, and to guard it from egg-collectors by their very presence. From that point on it became an icon of the conservation movement, a logo for businesses and localities that it blessed by its propinquity, and a factor in the tourist trade.

Ospreys and nuthatches are native species, so more or less everything they do is above reproach. Life is not so easy for an alien species. We were lucky enough to spot on the lake the first breakfast time a pair of mandarin ducks, a bird so curious and beautiful that it looks as if it has swum off a Chinese plate. Indeed, you might readily see them in the parks of Beijing. There is a small population in the south of England brought there by gentlemen in the eighteenth and nineteenth centuries for decoration. They behaved decorously for many years, breeding in the wild, but staying close to Virginia Water and other douce (sober and sedate) places. Recently, they have become more adventurous, and they have begun to breed even in Speyside where they occupy the nesting boxes put out for another duck, the 'native' goldeneye, which in all Britain only nests in Speyside though it spends the winter as a visitor from the Arctic to most reservoirs and gravel pits in the country. The response of some conservationists was to propose, not to put out more boxes, but to kill the mandarins, which was the more bizarre because the goldeneye are no less 'artificially' dependent on humans than the mandarins: neither often nest anywhere except in our nest boxes. And mandarins are not so common in China that they could not do with a bit of conservation in Europe too. But they are *aliens*, and a little microcosm of modern Britain is reflected in the fear and suspicion of them occupying the homes of *our* goldeneye which comes and goes *naturally*.

Even the nest boxes that we put up for wild birds like these two ducks are historical artefacts. A hundred years ago nest boxes were only to provide food for rural communities, in the shape of dove cotes (doo'cots to the Scots) and clay sparrow pots, where the owner could harvest the young when they were nice and fat in the nest. Perhaps the first illustration of a nest box put up for some other reason is in Audubon's great work, *Birds of America* (1827–30), where the purple martin is nesting in a hollowed gourd stuck on a spike in a tree, and the house wren in an old hat similarly impaled. Both would have been welcome around an American homestead to keep the bugs down, and no doubt for the same reason, but much earlier, swallows and house martins in Europe were welcome to stick their own nests round our barns and cottages. It takes a leap of the imagination to realize that these species are so commensal with humans that, without us, they would be reduced to nesting on cliffs and in caves, so until the Neolithic at the earliest must have been of very restricted distribution. Obviously storks, too, have been nesting on churches and farms in mainland Europe for centuries, and they have been tolerated because of their diet of frogs and snakes, creepy-crawlies of the devil. We might wonder when people began to help them along by putting up old cart-wheels to support the nest. The only breeding record of a white stork in Britain is of a pair on the steeple of St Giles in Edinburgh in 1416. A ton or two of storks' nest after a couple of centuries can bring down a roof, so toleration came at a price.

Finally, not a bird but a squirrel. We were all looking out for the red squirrel, and though there are said to be 9,000 in the forest, none of us saw one. Maybe they were asleep in their dreys, confident in the welcome they would receive when they finally leapt down to the feeders, and confident that the nice rangers and foresters would not only shoot their alien grey squirrel rivals, but test their remains for squirrel pox, in an attempt to maintain a quarantine zone around

FIGURE 6.1. Red Squirrel
sculpture at Kielder.

PHOTO: PETER COATES

Kielder. No animal is more beloved in Britain today, and none has had a history more illustrative of the altering foibles of mankind. In the nineteenth century, the red squirrel fell on hard times for rather uncertain reasons. It almost died out in Scotland, probably from disease, as the alternative and commoner explanation of habitat loss due to the over-exploitation of the native Caledonian pinewoods does not seem plausible, partly because it is not restricted naturally to pines and partly because the destruction of the habitat has been overstated. In England it also died out from the London area and much of the south, and here disease is accepted as the cause.

There were still squirrels in the north of England, however, and from here some landowners who rather liked their engaging ways reintroduced them to Scotland. In the London area they were also missed. One landowner brought some European red squirrels in Leadenhall market and released them in Epping Forest, but the first colonist grey squirrels were kindly provided by two Americans sympathetic to the Londoners' loss of squirrel life and aware of their own charming relatives in New Jersey and elsewhere. They released them between 1890 and 1916 in Bushy Park and Kingston Hill, Surrey, assisted by the Duke of Bedford, who brought some from his collection at Woburn to release in Regent's Park. No-one knew then that the newcomer had the ability to drive out the native by a combination of greater strength and by carrying a virus to which it was immune but which was fatal to the red. All this is very well explained by Richard Fitter in *London's Natural History* (1945), an unappreciated masterpiece of urban environmental history.

In Scotland, meanwhile, the new population of reds had made up for lost time and began to multiply beyond expectations. Soon they were declared to be vermin, and the forester's foe. Squirrel clubs were formed to get rid of them, and enormous numbers were shot: 60,000 over fifteen years up to the end of 1917 by the Highland Squirrel Club in Scotland north of the Great Glen; 14,000 in sixteen years on the Cawdor estate in Nairnshire; and 6,600 in one year on the Seafield estate in Speyside. Mark Louden Anderson, from whose *History of Scottish Forestry* (1967) these figures are drawn, said there was not a pine forest north of the border not ruined commercially by the depredations of squirrels, and he plainly regarded their re-introduction as an act of madness. Then the grey squirrel gained ground throughout Britain, reducing the red in England to a few refuges, of which Kielder is the most important, and also driving the red back in Scotland. Now the reds are a conservation icon, and immense sums of charitable and public funds are spent on their preservation. Planning permission is refused for development where it may endanger a population, and tree planting disallowed if the species is judged to encourage the spread of the poxy grey at their expense. At Kielder we were told by the Forest Manager (Graham Gill) that the reds did no harm whatever to his Sitka spruce. Something has changed, but it is in us not in the squirrels.

So this is a plea for species history, not just for what it tells of the history of a species but also for what it can tell us about ourselves.

The 29 birds we met at Kielder (in alphabetical order):

Blackbird	Goldeneye	Pied Wagtail
Blue Tit	Goosander	Redpoll
Buzzard	Great Spotted Woodpecker	Robin
Carrion Crow	Great Tit	Sand Martin
Chaffinch	Greenfinch	Siskin
Coal Tit	Mallard	Song Thrush
Crossbill	Mandarin Duck	Starling
Dunnock (Hedge Sparrow)	Meadow Pipit	Tawny Owl
Fieldfare	Nuthatch	Wood Pigeon
Goldcrest	Oystercatcher	

CHAPTER 7

The 'Nature' of 'Artificial' Forests

Chris Pearson

As an historian of France, visiting Kielder Forest prompted me to think about the Landes forest in southwestern France. If you have ever taken the train south from Bordeaux into Spain, as I once did, you will have undoubtedly passed through it. The Landes forest, at 1,000,000 hectares, is reportedly the largest pine forest in Western Europe. Kielder, meanwhile, is not only England's largest forest, but Europe's largest planted forest. Size clearly matters to the owners of these mega-forests: 'the scale of Kielder Forest is enough to take your breath away!', claims the Forestry Commission's website.[1]

Both these forests are artificial in the sense that humans created them on land deemed largely unpopulated and unproductive. Napoleon III ordered the planting of the Landes forest in the mid-nineteenth century to reclaim supposedly unruly marshlands and dunes, whilst the Forestry Commission oversaw the creation of the Kielder spruce forest from the end of the First World War onwards. National objectives lay behind these schemes. The Second Empire sought to modernize and 'improve' French territory for economic gain and imperial grandeur. As Napoleon III declared:

> we have immense uncultivated territories to clear, roads to open, ports to dig, rivers to render navigable, canals to finish, our network of railways to complete … That is how I understand the empire, of how the empire is to be restored.[2]

Kielder Forest, on the other hand, was to serve as a national strategic timber resource.

Historian Michael Bess has described the Landes forest as 'artifice folded within artifice' and the same would probably apply to Kielder.[3] Of course, all forests that are subject to human use and management are 'artificial' to greater or lesser extents. But if a prize was to be awarded to the most artificial forest in Western Europe (at a kind of sylvan Oscars ceremony with golden tree statuettes for prizes?), it would be a close run thing between the Landes and Kielder forests.

Both these forests are part of history and have their own histories. In the present day, when wildness, sustainability and 'green-ness' are highly praised and prized, the forests' managers have sought to deepen their forests' green credentials. Both authorities portray their forests as spaces of nature protection, alongside sites of recreation and forestry production. Kielder is home to England's largest red squirrel population and the Forestry Commission claims that it is the place to be 'if it is tranquility and wild beauty you are after'.[4] Over in France, the *Parc naturel régional des Landes de Gascogne* (Natural Regional Park of the Landes de Gascogne) manages 315,300 hectares of the forest, with a mission to preserve its natural and cultural heritage. And whilst both authorities are clear that it is the remnants of pre-sylvan habitats that are the most important ecologically-speaking (peat bogs at Kielder, heathland in the Landes), they now seek to manage the forest in more sustainable ways.

The 'greening' of these forests springs from changing social attitudes and attests to their cultural malleability. It also shows a certain amount of slippage between concepts of 'nature' and 'artifice'. Does this matter? Certainly not, it seems, for the red squirrels of Kielder. And I am not sure that it matters too much for us humans. For both Kielder and the Landes are messy hybrids; one is an artificial forest with England's largest remaining native squirrel population; the other an artificial forest that is part of a protected area. We live in a world where nature and culture are all jumbled up, and arguably always have been for as long as humans have lived on this Earth. Both forests question the false separation of 'nature' and 'culture' and for that alone they are worth visiting.

FIGURE 7.1. Harvesting an 'artificial' forest at Kielder.

PHOTO: DAVID MOON

Notes

1. http://www.forestry.gov.uk/forestry/EnglandNorthumberlandKielder (accessed 30/09/14).
2. Matthew Truesdell, *Spectacular Politics: Louis-Napoleon Bonaparte and the Fête Impériale, 1849–1870* (Oxford: Oxford University Press, 1997), p. 82.
3. Michael Bess, *The Light-Green Society: Ecology and Technological Modernity in France, 1966–2000* (Chicago: University of Chicago Press, 2003), p. 262.
4. http://www.forestry.gov.uk/forestry/EnglandNorthumberlandKielder (accessed 30/09/14).

Places

CHAPTER 8

Not All Those Who Wander Are Lost: Walking in the Quantock Hills

Marianna Dudley

There we were, a group of academics atop the Quantock Hills. To the north we could see the Bristol Channel, and to the northeast the geometric forms of Hinkley Point nuclear power plant. To the east lay the Somerset Levels, and rising in the far western distance, the high ground of Exmoor. All around us was heather and the exhilarating openness of unenclosed heathland. Someone mentioned Coleridge, and for the rest of the walk we followed his ghost down through the stream-cut wooded combes that he walked with William and Dorothy Wordsworth at the end of the eighteenth century.

We had walked up to the plateau from Halsway Manor, our base for the second workshop. As a group of predominantly environmental historians, we were naturally predisposed to experiencing the local environment while we explored ways of thinking about and representing the connections between places and processes of historical change. The walk to the top was not a spontaneous jaunt: it had been scheduled into the programme of events, with Tim Russell, ranger for the Quantock Hills Area of Outstanding Natural Beauty (AONB) Service, as our guide. At all three workshops, walks and excursions were an integral ingredient and became important reminders of the omnipresence of place in thought processes, as well as stimulants of the discussions that followed. Of all the activities and discussions at the Halsway workshop, for me the walk connected the themes and purpose of the Research Network like no other. The ideas that came to us in the kind of easy conversation that keeps up with a steady pace drove our sedentary, indoor discussions later that day.

Why was this? What was it about this collective movement of bodies that connected the key considerations of the workshop itself: place, change and beauty? A walk in the Quantocks retraces steps made by Coleridge and Wordsworth, Romantic poets whose ideas have shaped the Western view of nature and beauty. An excursion on foot surrounds the walker with landscape officially designated to be of 'outstanding natural beauty', and protected in law accordingly. Walking is encouraged in this landscape, where other methods of movement (such as driving) are not (as Tim Cole's essay in this volume explores). My reflections on the 'Local Places, Global Processes' workshops were meaningful and lasting, leading to an extended period of research into the possibilities of walking as methodology for historians.[1] The workshops themselves, and the walks they generated, have propelled these reflections on walking in British landscapes, which will start with Coleridge, and wander the Quantock Hills.

Coleridge, Wordsworth and the countryside

In 1797, aged 25, Coleridge walked from Bristol to Racedown, in Dorset, to visit Wordsworth (aged 27) and, 'having persuaded him to move to Somerset, spent much of the next year exploring the Quantocks on foot with him and Dorothy'.[2] In the preface of *Lyrical Ballads*, the joint volume of verse composed with Coleridge during this period, Wordsworth described their work as 'experimental'. Their Quantock creativity could alternatively be described as anarchic, true to the definition of absence from authority and complete individual freedom (a quality captured in Julien Temple's film, *Pandaemonium* [2000]). In 1794 Coleridge had planned, with fellow poet Robert Southey, to found an emigrant communitarian utopia in Pennsylvania called Pantisocracy. That was soon abandoned, but in Nether Stowey he attempted self-sufficiency – with the burden of toil falling largely on his wife Sara's shoulders while he walked. Dorothy and William's close relationship and unconventional behaviour led to local suspicion that they were French spies – this was a time when fear of a French invasion up the Bristol Channel was rife – and their renewal of the Alfoxton tenancy was refused. But during their time together in the Quantocks, Samuel, William and Dorothy explored walking's radical, creative possibilities.

Robin Jarvis ponders the 'possible anticonformist dimension' to Coleridge's walking, 'a kind of extra-parliamentary direct action' that harnessed the 'negative class associations of walking', and through his letters from various tours and walks, concludes that Coleridge discovered 'in movement through space a release from the defining social contexts of his life to date and a realm of physical difference onto which his quest for self-realization could be mapped.'[3] Coleridge's walking mirrored the exuberance and energy of the young radical mind: Wordsworth remembered that when he arrived at Racedown in Dorset, after a 60-mile (96.5 km) walk from Bristol, Coleridge 'did not keep to the high road, but leapt over a gate and bounded down the path-less field, by which he cut off an angle.'[4]

Wordsworth's walking did not express such fervent radicalism. But it was just as bound to his person and ideals, and was sustained over a longer period of time than Coleridge's energetic walking, which ran out of steam by 1804 when he sailed for Malta.[5] Wordsworth undertook a tour of France and Switzerland in 1790, and later played down the political influences of revolutionary France.

Nonetheless, throughout his life, in his own way, he defended and articulated his own vision of democracy and republicanism which that trip had helped shape, and did so often by the act of walking. He was dedicated to the public 'right to roam' and, according to David McCracken, 'championed public footpaths with a spirit that should warm the hearts of modern walkers and conservationists'.[6] An anecdote reported in the *Manchester Guardian* of 7 October 1887, tells of a walk by Wordsworth and John Taylor Coleridge (Samuel's nephew) on a visit to Lowther, in the Lake District, in 1836. When their route ended abruptly at a wall, Wordsworth (aged 66 by this time):

> attacked the wall as if it were a living enemy, crying out, "This is the way, an ancient right of way too", and passed on. That evening after the ladies had left the room, Mr Justice Coleridge said to Sir John Wallace who was a near resident: "Sir John, I fear we committed trespass today; we came over a broken-down wall on your estate". Sir John seemed irate and said that if he could have caught the man who broke it down, he would have horsewhipped him. The grave old bard at the end of the table heard the words, the fire flashed into his face and rising to his feet he answered: "I broke your wall down, Sir John, it was obstructing an ancient right of way, and I will do it again. I am a Tory, but scratch me on the back deep enough and you will find the Whig in me yet."[7]

Wordsworth has been upheld as a 'patron saint' of the National Trust and an originator of the national park concept.[8] But in his vigorous defence of rights of way he also set a precedent for the mass movement of working-class protest walks and trespasses of the people's rambling movement in Britain in the early decades of the twentieth century.

The walking exploits of Coleridge and the Wordsworths caught the attention of their contemporaries and drew comment. Thomas de Quincy estimated that 'Wordsworth must have traversed a distance of 175,000 to 180,000 English miles,' despite having legs that were 'pointedly condemned by all the female connoisseurs on legs that I ever heard lecture on the topic'.[9] The essayist William Hazlitt, avid walker and author of *On Going a Journey*, was a friend of Coleridge and Wordsworth. He stayed with Coleridge at Nether Stowey and described the two men outdoors. Although they were walking companions, Hazlitt describes the two men's different ways of harnessing movement to the creative imagination:

> Coleridge has told me that he himself likes to compose in walking over uneven ground, or breaking through the straggling branches of a copse-wood; whereas Wordsworth always wrote (if he could) walking up and down a straight gravel walk, or in some spot where the continuity of his verse met with no collateral interruption.[10]

The distances that Wordsworth and Coleridge would tackle for a day's walk are still impressive. But their pastime was not exceptional. There was a trend in the eighteenth century for long-distance walking, among 'men from the middling orders of society, and even by the lesser gentry', feats such as that of a certain Captain Barclay who walked 1,000 miles (1,609 km) in 1000 successive hours, on Newmarket Heath in 1809.[11] Walking feats like these made minor celebrities of their exponents, but, Jarvis suggests, remained socially endorsed 'precisely to the extent that it was framed as a sporting spectacle'.[12]

Walking before this period was considered a risky venture. Several writers note the linguistic link between 'travel' and 'travail':[13] in medieval and early-modern England, to move 'abroad' (beyond one's home), particularly on foot, was seen to leave one susceptible to hardship and suffering.[14] Exceptional long-distance walks did little to dispel this perception. But, as Anne Wallace explains, the Romantic period brought a 'dissociation of the idea of travel from the meanings integral to its parent linguistic form "travail"', enabling travel to become 'distinguishable from pain and … regarded as an intellectual pleasure.'[15] Wordsworth and Coleridge set a conspicuous example to both their immediate circles of acquaintances and the nation's wider writing and thinking groups to go walking.

When Coleridge and Wordsworth took to the Quantock Hills they established some cultural paradigms which have resonated with writers – and walkers – ever since. The literature of walking is vast, and speaks of the power of a walk to generate words, thoughts and emotions.[16] And yet despite the breadth of sources, the walk remains 'quintessentially a Romantic image'.[17] In an earlier poem (1795), *Lines on Climbing Brockley Coomb* (a glen to the north of the Quantock Hills in northern Somerset, near Bristol airport), Coleridge affirmed the use of the word 'landscape' in the English language to mean 'inland natural scenery, or its representation in painting'. It had evolved from the seventeenth-century use of the Dutch *landschap* to the eighteenth-century English word Coleridge deployed, and that we still use today. In the poem Coleridge ascends a (modest) summit and takes in the view before him; the landscape is celebrated, the beauty of nature – naked rock, warbling birdsong, spring blossoms – described.

> Ah! What a luxury of landscape meets
> My gaze. Proud towers, and Cots [cottages] more dear to me,
> Elm-shadowed Fields, and prospect-bounding Sea.
> Deep sighs my lonely heart: I drop the tear:
> Enchanting spot! O were my Sara here.[18]

The power of the scene leaves the Romantic heart breathless and sighing, uplifted but yearning. The walk takes the poet out into nature, but his inclination to climb the summit defines his position within the natural world as human, elevated above nature but, in possession of the right sensibilities, moved by its beauty. Nature is both external inspiration, and internal emotion.

When we ascended to the Quantock plateau on the day of the workshop, we too gazed somewhat breathlessly, due I suspect to the steep incline more than our Romantic dispositions, over the Somerset scene. Nonetheless we admired the view, which we saw as picturesque – a way of seeing introduced by Romantic visionaries. Our spirits were lifted by the exercise and the summit we reached. We pondered our response to the landscape at length back at Halsway

Manor, prompted by Peter Coates' paper 'From "the environment" to "an environment (of outstanding natural beauty)"' and Jenny Graham's paintings of the Quantocks landscape (and post-workshop, in blog posts). As Petra van Dam noted, we talked about our 'intuition that high country is more sublime than lowlands'.[19] Was this intuition a learned response to our environment, passed down to us by Coleridge and Wordsworth? Coleridge and Wordsworth linked walking with creative discourse, thinking with the environment. They vaulted over the literary fence to write in and of the landscapes they revered and examined their own use of walking as a rhythmic, experiential route to poetic thought, political act and daily habit. They sought out environments that corresponded with their Romantic vision of nature, sublime and picturesque – landscapes that were subsequently the first to be selected for protection; preserved first in poetry, then protected in law. The places where we can walk freely today are intrinsically tied to the places that they walked at the end of the eighteenth century.

Protecting valued landscapes

In 1951 – six years before the Quantock Hills AONB was made England's first Area of Outstanding Natural Beauty – the Lake District, the Wordsworths' home region, became Britain's first national park. William's wish, expressed in his *A Complete Guide to the Lakes*,[20] for:

> the author [to] be joined by persons of pure taste throughout the whole island, who, by their visits (often repeated) to the Lakes in the North of England, testify that they deem the district a sort of national property, in which every man has a right and interest who has an eye to perceive and a heart to enjoy,

foreshadowed the national parks movement in Britain and became its unofficial, often-quoted slogan.[21] The first organizations to take up his cry, the Commons, Open Spaces and Footpaths Preservation Society (1865), its offspring, the National Trust for Places of Historic Interest or Natural Beauty (1894) and, later, the Council for the Preservation of Rural England (1926), set out in their titles their privileging of certain landscapes (open, natural, rural, beautiful). The emphasis was on preservation and protection of landscape beauty, and their membership was middle-class and well-connected, pursuing the campaign through parliamentary channels.

But the other side of the national parks movement, equally linked to the poets, was about landscape *experience*. These more radical groups (compared to the commons preservation movement) campaigned from a platform of moral and spiritual right to enjoy the countryside, starting with the Hayfield and Kinder Scout Ancient Footpaths Association, in 1876, which sought to establish a freedom to roam across wild upland and open country.[22] This was a class struggle, fighting for the right of the common man against private property. By 1930, when the Ramblers' Federation (later Association) was established, rambling had become a mass sport, with the introduction of paid holidays and availability of mass transport enabling an estimated half a million regular walkers to access the countryside.[23] The uplands close to northern industrial centres were particularly popular. An Access to Mountains Bill had been introduced to parliament in 1884, and rebuffed in the House of Commons regularly since. In 1932, ramblers mobilized in a mass trespass at Kinder Scout in the Peak District. This political walking troubled some preservationists and 'respectable' rambling leaders, but demonstrated a popular will to access, experience and, for some, reclaim for the people the best of the British countryside. It also promoted walking as the universal method for doing so.

Parliament passed the Access to Mountains Bill in 1939. In 1949, it passed the National Parks and Access to the Countryside Act. John Dower, author of the report that helped shape the Act's terms, articulated in 1943 what would become the definition of a national park:

> an extensive area of beautiful and relatively wild country in which for the nation's benefit and by appropriate national decision and action, (i) the characteristic landscape beauty is strictly preserved, (ii) access and facilities for public open-air enjoyment, including particularly cross-country and footpath walking, are amply provided, and (iii) wildlife and places and buildings of historic, architectural and scientific interest are suitably protected.[24]

The provision of national parks united the two sides of the campaign, by protecting natural beauty and providing public access. Whilst the various committees that sat prior to national parks legislation debated whether the two were antagonistic concepts, creating the need for two types of park (one primarily for outdoor recreation, close to urban centres, and another for the preservation of scenery and wildlife), Dower was adamant that the one justified the other.[25] Large numbers of people had to be admitted into the parks to justify the expense of protecting their beauty, he argued; at the same time, public access and recreation would have to be regulated to protect the parks, at times to the cost of the visitor experience, he recognized.[26] For example, maintained footpaths increase safety and keep feet away from rare plants, but also, arguably, create a textural barrier between the walker and the land underfoot and mediate the experience of walking, as well as visually cutting through the landscape. Dower's view prevailed, and national parks protect landscapes by law 'for the preservation and enhancement of natural beauty in England and Wales; and, for encouraging the provision or improvement, for persons resorting to national parks, for facilities for the enjoyment thereof, and for the enjoyment of the opportunities for open air recreation and the study of nature'.[27]

In the uncertainty over the compatibility between landscape protection and outdoor recreation, notions of appropriate use emerged. David Matless identifies a moral geography combining environmental and social concerns that came to inform decisions regarding where to protect, and for whom. In the discourse of 'right' and 'wrong' usages, walkers were favoured, as they physically and spiritually engaged with the landscape. Matless cites the essay 'Walking', by historian and president of the Youth Hostel Association, G. M. Trevelyan, as a 'key wind-and-rain text' which promoted the elemental physicality of walking: 'the fight against fierce wind and snowstorm is among the higher joys of walking, and produces in the shortest time the state of ecstasy.'[28] Motorized vehicles were actively discouraged. The Dartmoor Preservation Association (an organization comparable to Friends of Quantock and other watchdog groups) campaigned unsuccessfully against military road building on the Ministry of Defence training area in Dartmoor National Park, arguing that 'beauty and wilderness are in flight before the invading motor car, and unless action is taken to prevent it, by 1970 Northern Dartmoor will have become a network of crawling vehicles'.[29] On the Quantock Hills in the early 1970s, Friends of Quantock campaigned successfully against a road running along the spine of the high plateau. Driving made remote places too accessible, cheating hikers of the rewards of their robust efforts to experience the landscape directly.

On Dartmoor, the military (mis)use of the moor prompted a comparison to 'playing rugger in the National Gallery and being surprised if paintings got damaged'.[30] Matless collects various caricatures of 'anti-citizens' depicted in open-air movement literature, 'working class charabancers making a racket and leaving their empties', which were deployed, he argues, to define their opposite: the intellectual, physical and spiritual advance of correct outdoors recreation, 'people walking in the country ... seen as part of an orderly movement comparable in self-definition to modern movements of art'.[31] Although those involved in the national parks movement liked to quote Wordsworth as an honourable forefather, the reality is that the wild, off-track walking of 'citizens' William, Dorothy and Samuel on the Quantocks would align them with reckless charabancers as much as responsible citizens.

In the planning for the first round of national park designations, the Quantock Hills were included in the Exmoor proposal. However, the objection of local councils and Friends of Quantock ensured that the Quantocks were omitted from the final designation. The councils were concerned that national park status would create terms of use and planning restrictions that would limit the growth of the local economy, while the Friends feared that it would bring a mass of visitors, 'leading to ice-cream parlours and damage to the land'.[32] When it was pointed out that AONB designation, while offering the same level of landscape protection, did not require amenity provision nor the establishment of a National Park Authority (in effect, a new local authority with statutory duties), the decision to support AONB designation was passed unanimously by the Friends, and supported by the local councils.[33]

The constitution of Friends of Quantock decrees that the objective of the group (a charity) is to 'safeguard the landscape and natural environment' of the area from intrusions such as roads and vehicles. It has no wider political agenda. Alan Hughes and Denys White, two long-serving Friends of Quantock, attended the workshop at Halsway and spoke about their group and their connection to the landscape.[34] They talked – as did artist Jenny Graham – of the special place that the Quantocks occupies in the minds and affections of local people. Residents of Taunton, Bridgwater and the Somerset Levels value the area as 'their' special place, their park for peace and recreation. Hughes told an anecdote about a small but significant Friends' campaign that succeeded in ensuring that the Quantock Hills were not signposted from the M5. Instead, the motoring masses from further afield continue to be directed towards Exmoor National Park, while the Quantocks are reserved for locals, and individual walkers, rather than tour groups and coach loads. (More than two centuries earlier, Wordsworth had amended his *Guide to the Lakes* to voice his concern that its qualities might be spoiled by the numbers following his recommendation to enjoy the area, if brought by the train [rather than bus]-load.) There is a localism at work in the Quantocks to protect its landscape qualities and regional status.

As visiting academics, our efforts to connect the local landscape and its history to wider narratives of landscape appreciation, environmental protection and environmental change might be regarded as an intrusion into this distinctive local quality. But this did not turn out to be the case. We received a warm reception from the Friends, the AONB team, artists who work in the area and others with an expert knowledge of the Hills. This response indicates that, by connecting – and drawing comparisons and contrasts – with other histories and narratives of landscape, environment, beauty and change, it may be possible to inquire more deeply into – and thereby distil more clearly – the qualities that characterize a particular place and strengthen the resonance of the local, both in terms of the environmental and the historical.

Given that it had been judged alongside Exmoor as worthy of national park status, does it then follow that AONB status was a lesser designation, which undervalued the landscape quality of the Quantock Hills? AONBs tend to be smaller than national parks and, at 99 square km, the Quantock Hills are a small AONB – only six are smaller. Proportionately though, the 38 AONBs in England and Wales are a more significant landscape presence than national parks, comprising 18% of national territory. In England, ten national parks make up 9.3% of territory (in Wales, the three national parks cover a more comparable 19.9% of land area).[35] But when it comes to our protected landscapes, it seems that size matters. Our large national parks are known and loved. AONBs on the other hand, as Margaret Anderson contends:

> have never achieved the government or public recognition given to the parks. This does not mean that areas of the countryside with AONB status are not well known – Chilterns, Gower, Forest of Bowland, Cornwall coast and South Downs for example are at least as well loved by the people of England and Wales as are the national parks. It is of their status of AONBs, and implications of that status, that people frequently remain ignorant.[36]

This brings us back to the walk, and workshop papers and discussions. At Halsway we debated at some length our conceptions of landscape beauty, and how it related to lowlands and highlands, and the notion of the natural sublime, tracing an intellectual line from the Wicken Fen workshop that ran through to the final workshop at Kielder.[37] There, a forestry plantation and reservoir combined to create a landscape of shapes and proportions that seem closer to Scandinavian or North American formats than to English environmental settings. We were impressed at the scale of the landscape, yet left feeling disconnected by its known artificiality and commerciality, as well as the absence of visible local history that predates the first tree plantings after the First World War (for more on the absence of earlier local history, see Richard Oram's chapter in this volume). Wicken Fen is no less a human-made aquatic and terrestrial landscape than Kielder, but the lines of its construction have been softened by centuries of time and use.

The Quantocks, too, are a highly worked landscape. Though the summits remain open common land, their edges are farmed and forested (both natural woodland and planted trees) and run seamlessly down to the lowlands. My mapping (in 2012) of the decline of traditional orchards within the AONB and surrounding buffer zone (which are not usually included in definitions of Somerset 'cider country') confirms the strong landscape links between that which is, and which is not, protected as a designated AONB.[38] Agricultural use is a feature of both AONBs and national parks, over 75% of whose lands are used for agricultural purposes (if less intensively farmed than areas of lower altitude in England and Wales). But while an average of 77% of national park land is categorized as 'poor quality', only 25% of AONB land is poor.[39] By contrast, national parks contain virtually no 'good' land and AONBs contain 14%.

'Good' land denotes rich-soiled, productive and easily farmed agricultural land. At the other end of the scale, 'poor' land includes the peaty or stony, nutritionally poor and hard-to-work uplands that have remained open because of their difficulty to cultivate. The openness and emptiness of the high ground in England and Wales drew walkers, from Coleridge in the Quantock Hills and Wordsworth in the Lakes, to the factory operatives of Manchester and Sheffield seeking respite from the working week in the Peak District. The poverty of the soil bears an inverse relationship to our ability to roam unhindered, ascend to high points, take in expansive views and form place attachments with beautiful, recreational landscapes. It is the uplands that have been protected as national parks, and which, from the Romantics onwards, have been labelled as 'sublime'. Meanwhile, AONBs, not given over to recreation (although AONB Services increasingly encourage and provide information/facilities for recreation), stay recognisably 'working' landscapes. For visitors, artists and inhabitants alike, the soft lines of maintained hedgerows, arable fields, mixed uses and visible populations lend their own ingredients of beauty.

In response to conventional notions of beauty, Edmund Burke presented the idea of the sublime in 1757. It was, he suggested, a rush of emotion evoked by 'terrible objects' – things that were uncontrolled and intimidating that, 'in a manner analogous to terror, is a source of the sublime, that is, it is productive of the strongest emotion which the mind is capable of feeling'.[40] Homes, farms and land that was worked and managed were safe places. It was beyond these that the sublime was to be found – the mountain-tops, crags and waterfalls that humans had avoided for centuries previous. Here, the 'wildness' of nature could be encountered and, in doing so, could provoke the feelings of the sublime. There was pleasure to be found in terror, and so it was to the highest peaks that those in search of the sublime trekked. Coleridge was prominent among them, climbing Scafell in the Lake District in 1802. Getting into difficulty, he experienced a 'state of almost prophetic trance and delight' before finding a safe descent.[41]

Robert Macfarlane suggests that altitude was attractive to Romantic artists:

> the mountain-top provided an icon for the Romantic ideal of liberty … and coincided perfectly with the Romantic glorification of the individual. A summit was somewhere where one could stand out – and be outstanding.[42]

We still feel the draw of the summit, and satisfaction on reaching it, as our workshop outing attested. The Romantics left us ways of experiencing and articulating nature that endure. Coleridge tested his mettle on the top of mountains, but he and Wordsworth were equally inspired by the more modest height of the Quantock Hills. Here, in this Area of Outstanding Natural Beauty, we reached the top and felt 'outstanding' too.

The aesthetic of the picturesque trod slightly safer ground, and sat somewhere between the sublime and the beautiful. William Gilpin described the picturesque in his *Essay on Prints* in 1768 and then again in *Three Essays* in 1798. Beauty, as Burke had asserted, was: '*smoothness* … the higher marble is polished, the more silver is rubbed, and the more mahogany shines, the more each is considered an object of beauty: as if the eye delighted in gliding smoothly over a surface.'[43] The picturesque, by contrast, delighted in the visual surprise, the unexpected and non-conforming presence of flora, fauna and human habitation – '*roughness* and *ruggedness* … both are observable in the smaller, as well as the larger, parts of nature – in the outline, and bark of the tree, as in the rude summit, and craggy sides of a mountain.'[44] Gilpin made his initial observations of the picturesque travelling through the Wye Valley, and observing the ruins of Tintern Abbey. The scene was too unordered to be beautiful, and too gentle to be sublime; but it formed a view as perfect as a painting, and the word Gilpin used to describe it – picturesque – is inherently tied to looking at a landscape in the manner of a painter, judging its visual qualities and the pleasing components of a 'scene'.

The Wye Valley was designated as an AONB in 1971. The qualities of beauty that Gilpin observed survive and, as in the late eighteenth century, cannot be categorized as wholly natural. Traces of human use and habitation contributed to the appreciation of nature and landscape: the picturesque placed man (and woman) in his (or her) environment. In this volume, Coates notes the unclear history of the choice of the adjective 'outstanding' to describe the beauty found in AONBs. If the term AONB was not long (and clumsy?) enough, an Area of Picturesque Natural Beauty would also encapsulate many of the qualities found in AONBs, as well as denote the influential history of *viewing* landscape through eyes looking to be pleased by nature.

At the workshops, we explored our own ideas of natural beauty, the 'sublime' and the 'simply beautiful', and generated through experience the undeniable but now-clichéd Romantic sentiments that inevitably come from a good ramble in delightful, invigorating scenery. The walk not only kept 'local places' at the forefront of our discussions of national and global change, but provided a common experience to which we could return. It also spurred me to seriously consider walking as a methodology for historians, who can learn from geographers and anthropologists of the benefits of getting out of the archive and stretching the legs now and then. Notions of beauty are subjective, learned and changeable; but perhaps Coleridge and Wordsworth expressed something universal in their creative discourse of poetry and walking. They and their sentiments have inspired generations of walkers and writers since, and continue to influence the ways we view, experience and talk about landscape. As Jeffrey Cane Robinson has reflected: 'Interested and disinterested, I, walking, think in the face of what attracts and repels me. Furthermore, my thoughts and immediate pleasures belong to me in my solitude but also to me as a part of a historical community.'[45]

Notes

1. I pursued some of the research that informs this paper during a six-month writing fellowship at the Rachel Carson Center for Environment and Society, Munich (2011–12). It is also informed by more recent work that involved mapping orchard decline for the Quantock Hills AONB Service, a project that was funded by the AHRC as a follow-on activity to the 'Local Places, Global Processes' Research Network; and a nine-month AHRC Early Career Fellowship at Bristol University in which I examined the differences between national park and AONB designations (July 2012–March 2013).

2. Robin Jarvis, *Romantic Writing and Pedestrian Travel* (Basingstoke: Macmillan, 1997), p. 127. Wordsworth was born near the Lake District, at Cockermouth, Cumbria, in 1770. He attended grammar school in Hawkshead, near Windermere, and later settled at Grasmere. Coleridge was born in Ottery St Mary, Devon, in 1772.

3. Jarvis, *Romantic Writing*, pp. 33–4, 128–9.

4. Jarvis, *Romantic Writing*, p. 126.

5. According to Robin Jarvis, this event 'effectively marks the end of his remarkable career as a pedestrian': *Romantic Writing*, p. 127.

6. Donna Landry, *The Invention of the Countryside: Hunting, Walking and Ecology in English Literature, 1671–1831* (Basingstoke: Palgrave, 2001), p. 213; David McCracken, *Wordsworth and the Lake District: A Guide to the Poems and their Places* (Oxford: Oxford University Press, 1984), p. 3.

7. Landry, *Invention of the Countryside*, p. 213.

8. John Gaze, *Figures in a Landscape: A History of the National Trust* (London: Barrie & Jenkins in association with the National Trust, 1988), p. 10.

9. Rebecca Solnit, *Wanderlust: A History of Walking* (London: Penguin, 2001), p. 104. In the late eighteenth century, men wore knee breeches and tight stockings, which would have revealed whether legs were shapely (or not).

10. William Hazlitt, quoted in Jonathan Bate, *Romantic Ecology: Wordsworth and the*

Environmental Tradition (London: Routledge, 1991), p. 49.

11. Jarvis, *Romantic Writing*, p. 4; Landry, *Invention of the Countryside*, p. 132.

12. Jarvis, *Romantic Writing*, p. 4.

13. Travail, *n.* 'Bodily or mental labour or toil, especially of a painful or oppressive nature; exertion; trouble; hardship; suffering'. Travel, *n.* '1. Labour, toil; suffering, trouble; labour of childbirth, *etc.* See *OED, TRAVAIL, n.* 2.a. The action of traveling or journeying.

14. Anne Wallace, *Walking, Literature and English Culture: The Origins and Uses of Peripatetic in the Nineteenth Century* (Oxford: Clarendon Press, 1993), p. 19; Solnit, *Wanderlust*, p. 46.

15. Jarvis, *Romantic Writing*, p. 28; Eric J. Leed, quoted in Jarvis, *Romantic Writing*, p. 28.

16. Walking has inspired an extensive literature, both urban and rural. Walter Benjamin, drawing on the poetry of Baudelaire, introduced the flaneur as an object of scholarly attention in the early twentieth century in his *Arcades Project* (published posthumously, Cambridge, MA and London: Belknap Press, 1999), a figure who used walking as a way to negotiate the city (namely, Paris) and modernity. In the late twentieth and early twenty-first centuries, Iain Sinclair and Will Self revitalized the literature of urban walking and relocated it to London, where it revealed new insights to postmodern city life influenced by, and influencing, psychogeography as a practice-based field of study: Iain Sinclair, *London Orbital* (London: Granta, 2002); Iain Sinclair, *Lights Out for the Territory: Nine Excursions in the Secret History of London* (London: Granta, 1997); Will Self, *Psychogeography* (London: Bloomsbury, 2007). The flaneur is a specifically gendered, male figure, and Deborah Parsons, *Streetwalking the Metropolis: Women, the City and Modernity* (Oxford: Oxford University Press, 2000) and Elizabeth Munson, 'Walking on the Periphery: Gender and the Discourse of Modernization', *Journal of Social History* 36/1 (Autumn 2002), pp. 63–75, offer female-focused histories of urban walking. Coleridge's and Wordsworth's association of walking with experiencing nature was expanded on by Henry David Thoreau: 'Walking', in *The Writings of Henry David Thoreau* (Boston: Houghton Mifflin, 1906). For other influential and informative texts on walking and writing, see also: Solnit, *Wanderlust*; John Wylie, 'A Single Day's Walking: Narrating Self and Landscape on the Southwest Coast Path', *Transactions of the Institute of British Geographers* 30/2 (2005), pp. 234–47; Tim Ingold, 'Culture on the Ground: The World Perceived through the Feet', *Journal of Material Culture* 9/3 (2004), pp. 315–40.

17. Jeffrey Cane Robinson, *The Walk: Notes on a Romantic Image* (Norman: University of Oklahoma Press, 1989), p. 6.

18. Excerpt from Samuel Taylor Coleridge, *Brockley Coomb – Lines Composed While Climbing the Left Ascent of Brockley Coomb*, May 1795.

19. See chapters in this volume: Petra van Dam, 'The Beautiful and the Global'; Peter Coates, 'Beauty and the Aesthetics of Place, Nature and Environment'; and Jenny Graham, 'Art Insert'.

20. *Guide to the Lakes* was first written in the form of an introduction and accompanying text for the Rev. Joseph Wilkinson's *Select Views In Cumberland, Westmoreland and Lancashire*, published monthly in 1810. It first appeared under Wordsworth's name in *The River Duddon, A Series of Sonnets: Vadracour & Julia: and Other Poems. To Which is Annexed, A Topographical Description of the Country of the Lakes, in the North of England* in 1820. It first appeared independently as *A Description of the Scenery of the Lakes in the North of England* in 1822. In 1842, it became part of *A Complete Guide to the Lakes, Comprising Minute Directions for the Tourist, With Mr Wordsworth's Description of the Scenery of the Country,* etc. *And Three Letters on the Geology of the Lake District, by the*

Rev. Professor Sedgwick, Edited by the Publisher (*i.e.* John Hudson of Kendal): Jonathan Bate, *Romantic Ecology: Wordsworth and the Environment* (London: Routledge, 1991), pp. 42–3.

21. William Wordsworth, *A Guide to the Lakes: The Fifth Edition (1835)* (Oxford: Oxford University Press, 1984), p. 92; See also, Jonathan Bate, *Romantic Ecology*.

22. John Blunden and Nigel Curry (eds), *A People's Charter? Forty Years of the National Parks and Access to the Countryside Act 1949* (London: HMSO, 1990), p. 29; Melanie Tebbutt, 'Rambling and Manly Identity in Derbyshire's Dark Peak, 1880s–1920s', *The Historical Journal* 49/4 (December 2006), pp. 1125–53.

23. Blunden and Curry, *A People's Charter?*, p. 30.

24. John Sheail, 'The Concept of National Parks in Great Britain 1900–1950', *The Transactions of the Institute of British Geographers* 66 (November 1975), pp. 41–56, 48.

25. Sheail, 'The Concept of National Parks', p. 43.

26. Sheail, 'The Concept of National Parks', p. 43.

27. *The National Parks and Access to the Countryside Act, 1949* (London, 1950), Chapter 97, Part 1, pp. 1–2 http://www.legislation.gov.uk/ukpga/1949/97/pdfs/ukpga_19490097_en.pdf (accessed 20/10/14).

28. David Matless, 'Moral Geographies of English Landscape', *Landscape Research* 22/2 (1997), pp. 141–56, 149.

29. Marianna Dudley, *An Environmental History of the UK Defence Estate 1945–present* (London: Continuum, 2012), p. 49.

30. Dudley, *Environmental History of the UK Defence Estate*, p. 50.

31. Matless, 'Moral Geographies', p. 145.

32. David Worthy, 'The Friends of Quantock: The First Fifty Years' (unpublished, 1999).

33. The purpose of AONB designation is to 'preserve and enhance natural beauty'. In the original 1949 designation there was no remit for the provision of recreation in AONBs. The Countryside and Rights of Way Act (CROW) 2000 enacted new measures to protect AONBs and acknowledged that recreation had become a significant feature. CROW stated that, while recreation would still not be an objective of AONB designation, AONB status should be used to meet the demands of recreation where it does not conflict with the conservation of natural beauty, and the needs of forestry, agriculture and other users: *The Countryside and Rights of Way Act, 2000* (London, 2000), Chapter 37, Part IV, pp. 82–93 http://www.legislation.gov.uk/ukpga/2000/37/pdfs/ukpga_20000037_en.pdf (accessed 20/10/2014).

34. Denys White, 'Views from Friends of Quantock', and Alan Hughes, 'Challenges to the Quantocks', Quantock workshop posts (15 March 2011) www.environmentalhistories.net/?p=369 (accessed 20/10/14).

35. 'An Introduction to Areas of Outstanding Natural Beauty', National Association for AONBs website http://www.aonb.org.uk/wba/naaonb/naaonbpreview.nsf/Web%20Default%20Frameset?OpenFrameSet&Frame=Main&Src=%2Fwba%2Fnaaonb%2Fnaaonbpreview.nsf%2FPublishedContent%2F2.0!OpenDocument%26AutoFramed (accessed 20/10/14); 'National Parks Facts and Figures', National Parks website http://www.nationalparks.gov.uk/press/factsandfigures.htm (accessed 20/10/14).

36. Margaret Anderson, 'Areas of Outstanding Natural Beauty and the 1949 National Parks Act', *The Town Planning Review* 61/3 (July 1990), pp. 311–39, at p. 311.

37. See: Peter Coates, 'Beauty and the Aesthetics of Place, Nature and Environment', in this volume, pp. **150-66**; Paul Warde, 'Aesthetics and the Environment' http://www.environmentalhistories.net/?p=320 (accessed 10/12/14).

38. Marianna Dudley, Nick Nourse and Peter Coates, 'Fallen Fruits and Orchard Roots: Historical Orchard Research in the Quantock Hills', *Proceedings of the Somerset*

Archaeology and Natural History Society 157 (2014), pp. 167–76; Marianna Dudley, 'Quantock Orchard Project', *Exmoor: The Country Magazine* 68 (Autumn 2014), pp. 41–3.

39. The categories were defined and mapped by the MAFF Land Service in 1968. Margaret Anderson, 'The Land Pattern of Areas of Outstanding Natural Beauty in England and Wales', *Landscape Planning* 7 (1980), pp. 1–22, 4.

40. Edmund Burke, *A Philosophical Enquiry into the Origin of Our Ideas of the Sublime and Beautiful* (1757) Part One, Section VII, p. 111.

41. For an entertaining account of Coleridge's tribulations at the summit of Scafell, and the sublime revelation that followed, see: Robert Macfarlane, *Mountains of the Mind: A History of a Fascination* (London: Granta, 2003), pp. 81–4.

42. Macfarlane, *Mountains of the Mind*, pp. 158–9.

43. William Gilpin, 'Essay 1 on Picturesque Beauty', *Three Essays: On Picturesque Beauty, On Picturesque Travel and on Sketching Landscape, to which is Added a Poem, on Landscape Painting* (London: printed for R. Blamire, 1792), p. 4.

44. Gilpin, 'Essay 1', *Three Essays*, p. 7.

45. Robinson, *The Walk*, p. 5.

CHAPTER 9

An Amphibious Culture:
Coping with Floods in the Netherlands

Petra J. E. M. van Dam

Introduction

This paper argues that in the past the low-lying areas of the Netherlands shared an amphibious culture. The essence of this culture is a series of adaptations to a wetland landscape. I want to highlight three features of the distinctive culture that emerged in this watery environmental setting: firstly, the landscape structure as organized into compartments; secondly, the elevation of settlements; and, thirdly, water-based transportation methods, including evacuation of humans and cattle. The adaptations under discussion here involve the capacity to move swiftly and easily between wet and dry parts of the landscape under normal circumstances. At times of disastrous floods, when borders between water and land became obscured, we can see how this amphibious culture operated *in extremo*.

I sketch out this amphibious culture as a heuristic model, using the Netherlands as a case study. I shall also consider whether this model can be applied to other wetland regions, since some of the features of Holland's watery environment are replicated elsewhere in the world, including Wicken Fen, the Philippines and Thailand: the phenomena of sinking soils and increased flooding (due to multiple causes such as [human-induced] sea-level rise); higher precipitation and changes in catchments areas and river deltas; the increasing paving-over of soil with impervious materials; and the shift from water-based to land-based transport ('automotorization'). The central question that this essay addresses is: can knowledge of how human societies have tried to deal with environmental change in the past offer any lessons for today?[1]

My evidence is drawn from the floods of 1675, 1825, 1916 and 1953, for which there are relevant and recent case studies.[2] First, though, some introductory remarks about the physical aspects of flood disasters in the Netherlands and the water authorities are necessary. The typical storm pattern for these floods started with several days of strong southwesterly or westerly winds that pushed water from the ocean into the North Sea Basin. Such weather often included heavy rain, so the dikes, which are basically earthen walls, became soaked. Then the winds developed into a strong northwesterly storm that forced the water from the North Sea into the sea arms, such as the Zuiderzee, for several days.[3] Next, the water spilled over the dikes and eroded them from within, from the landside, which was less protected than the seaward side. Then the dikes collapsed at one or more places.

The second preliminary observation concerns the landscape. In general, since 1500 or so, the difference between sea level and average soil level in the coastal plain has been small, between 0 m and 2 m below sea level, while some exceptional small areas came to lie at between 4 m and 6 m below sea level, due to reclamation of lakes and sinking soils.[4] Soils in the Low Netherlands are often filled-in sea or river beds. No mountains or stone layers come to the surface, only the occasional sand dune. So once the dikes broke, the flood water spread out and did not reach great depths. The level of flooding was counted in metres, not tens of metres. A storm surge in the Netherlands was (and is) not a tsunami. It cannot be compared to a wall of water rolling over the land and destroying everything in its path.[5]

However, some additional detail is needed here. There are three basic causes of floods in the Netherlands: storm surges; high water level in the rivers; and extreme precipitation. A storm surge may cause breaks in the coastal sand dunes and in the human-made dikes. This has led to the flooding of the low-lying coastal plain that stretches for some 400 km along the North Sea coast in the north, the west and the southwest. Another major cause of floods is the breaking of the dikes along the main rivers, the Rhine and the Meuse, and their arms, like the IJssel. This has resulted in flooding of the river basins between Nimwegen and the North Sea coast at Rotterdam, along the Rhine and Meuse, and from Nimwegen up to Kampen, along the IJssel, both stretches of some 100 km. These areas were never all flooded at the same time; if they had been, the water would have covered more than half of the country.[6] Sea flooding happened in different seasons than river floods, apart from a few weeks' overlap. Also, the selection of dikes affected was determined by wind direction so that, for instance, on two sides of a bay, not all dikes broke at the same time.

A further important element of the sea and river floods was the force of the current, though there are major differences between these river and sea currents. Typically, in areas flooded by rivers, the currents might be strong, because the river kept flowing, albeit in a wider bed. Entire villages might be carried off by a river, but it was primarily those villages that were close to the place where the water cut through the dike. Buildings situated further away had greater chances of survival, because as the water spread out, its strength dissipated. Sea floods might also result in strong currents, due to strong winds. But once the storm is over, the only remaining current is the tide, which, by itself, is quite a modest water movement. However, when land was low-lying, large masses of water were involved and forces were stronger.[7]

To complete the picture, a third type of flood needs mentioning, although it only first occurred at the end of the twentieth century. This concerns the flooding after extreme precipitation of built-up areas such as cities, due to the increasing paving-over of soil with impervious materials. Because city soils do not absorb and buffer water, as soon as precipitation increases above the margin set for the city's sewer system, the sewers spill over and the city floods. This is a new, worldwide challenge for many cities built in low-lying coastal areas. Countermeasures involve building subterranean garages and deep-lying squares that can double as water reservoirs, as examples from Rotterdam show.

A statement about specialized water institutions is needed to conclude these introductory comments. In the Dutch historiography of water history, a great deal of attention is devoted to the institutional history of the Local and Regional Water Authorities ('Heemraadschappen'; 'heem' is related to the word 'home'), which are relatively autonomous institutions responsible for water management. Initially, these bodies supervized the work of peasants. After the Middle Ages, however, they developed into boards that raised water levies and contracted out to entrepreneurs the maintenance of dikes and sluices. Meanwhile, the risk of floods was shared by an ever-increasing range of people. One of the main institutional changes in the early modern period took place when more people living further away from the dikes joined the community responsible for maintaining the dikes, increasing the number of the risk-sharing groups and the size of their territory.[8]

Historiography

The history of floods can be approached from at least three important angles: scale; experience; and risk culture. The scale (extent) of flood disasters can be measured in material terms. As Christian Pfister, an expert on the history of natural disasters, has explained, the customary way to evaluate the scale of the material impact of floods is to count the number of casualties and the amount of damage caused (including flooded villages, destroyed buildings, lost cattle and other capital), preferably expressed in monetary terms for purposes of comparability.[9] The historical geographer Elizabeth Gottschalk, in her notable survey of storms and floods, mainly considered the scale of the flooded surface.[10] Others invented longer lists of material and spatial criteria, which included wind force and direction.[11]

For the pre-statistical era and in times of social disruption in particular, reliable figures concerning flooding are rare in the Netherlands (as they are for the whole of Europe). A well-known example is the claim in a chronicle of *c.*1500 that in the St Elizabeth flood of 18–19 November 1421, which affected the area just southeast of Rotterdam, 72 villages were drowned in the Grote Waard, a claim that was repeated again and again in later sources. Yet this area never contained that number of villages.[12] But as seven is a significant figure in the Christian tradition, this number can presumably be taken to mean 'very many' (seven multiplied by ten, plus two). Historian Otto Knotnerus has demonstrated how descriptions of flood disasters in medieval and early modern chronicles often made use of standard fragments of text. The writers copied each other's descriptions of floods and then customized them using figures related to meaningful numbers in the Christian tradition. For instance, 33 villages drowned reflects the 33 years of the life of Jesus.[13] In the same way, the number seven may refer to the seven days when God created the Earth, or to the seven cardinal sins.

Over time, verification of figures becomes possible, particularly after 1800, when more reliable serial sources become available. In her study of the flood of Waterland in 1825, for example, historian Margriet de Roever compared information from a descriptive, contemporary disaster study with administrative records relating date, place and time of death. Although Waterland was entirely flooded and this has been classified by many authors as a major disaster, only 17 casualties were recorded, distributed over five places.[14]

The second approach investigates how contemporaries experienced and perceived a flood. Manfred Jakubowski-Tiessen, Marie-Louise Allemeyer and Franz Mauelshagen, among others, studied perceptions of North Sea Floods. They showed how explanations slowly changed from attributing the causes of floods to supernatural powers (God) to attributing them to natural laws (or secondary causes, as contemporaries formulated explanations which accorded with their religious worldview).[15] Christian Rohr developed cultural history criteria to assess floods. Among these criteria are the availability of aid, the type of explanation for the disaster, the extent to which disasters occur in series, the symbolic connotations of floods and general feelings of crisis. He based these criteria on a series of case-studies of natural disasters in Austria, including river floods.[16] The historians René Favier and Anne-Marie Granet-Abisset approached the discussion of floods from a different angle – that of risk culture. During the Ancien Regime, engineers helped to transform disasters into an object of knowledge, adding the 'control of nature' to the existing responsibilities of public government. One of the results was a slow shift from a *culture of disaster* towards a *culture of risk*.[17]

Rather than seeing a risk culture as the outcome of an historical process in a particular region, Greg Bankoff has made a spatial comparison. He shifts the focus from a general historical process that might operate everywhere to look instead at how one culture might face natural hazards as risks, whereas for another they are disasters. He first studied the Philippines and concluded that Philippine society is characterized by a disaster culture. He then studied the North Sea basin and defined that society as a risk culture. As Bankoff explains:

> A risk society is one whose people have had to adapt to one or more related hazards as a "frequent life experience": one where risk has become deeply embedded in the culture, one where it is very much an integral part of the historical processes of that society, and one that profoundly influences the political structure, economic system and social order of things.[18]

He discerned three 'coping mechanisms' or cultural adaptations for dealing with natural disasters: preventive strategies; strategies that minimize the material influence of disasters; and strategies that reduce psychological stress.[19] In this paper, I examine three variations of the second strategy that involve minimization: the compartmentalization of the landscape structure; the elevation of settlements; and water-based transport.

Compartmentalization

Because of the polder system, the low-lying coastal zone of the Netherlands was divided into compartments with many inland dikes.[20] As a result, flooding often occurred relatively slowly, polder by polder. Consequently, inhabitants had a reasonable amount of time to retreat. In the north of Holland, the sea dike at the Zuiderzee broke on 14 January 1675 at Scharwoude, just south of the city of Hoorn. Initially, only a few polders directly behind the dike were flooded in Frysia. After the dike was closed with great effort, the major sea dike broke twice again at the same place: on 2 December and in the night of 4–5 December. As a result, more and more inland dikes also broke, one after another. Inland dikes are low and weak; they serve to separate polders, they are not meant to stand in seawater for long periods. When these dikes become soaked, they disintegrate like a jelly pudding in the sun. Eventually, the whole of West-Frysia was flooded. However, because the submersion took place so slowly, only four people drowned in this entire area, two who were standing too close to the dike's breach and two during rescue transports. This case provides so much detailed data that historian Diederik Aten was able to draw a map of the phases of the gradual submersion (Fig. 9.1).[21] It was an extreme case. In other cases, dikes would collapse within hours or days. But as even a few hours can provide enough time to evacuate an area, this landscape structure of compartments, established by human agency, ensures favourable conditions for survival during floods.

Living on elevations

Many settlements were situated slightly above the field level, on natural elevations like sandy coastal dunes or river dunes, or on human-made elevations such as dikes, dams or mounds. Concentration of settlement in swampy areas on human-made elevations is an ancient pattern that can be traced back to prehistory. This settlement type applies not just to northern parts along the North Sea and the Zuiderzee, as in Overijssel between Elburg and Kuinre and in Gelre and Utrecht between Bunschoten en Nijkerk, but also to the modern provinces of Noord-Holland and Zuid-Holland. Although many traces of this feature have disappeared through human-induced erosion processes such as ploughing, as well as due to rain and frost, archaeologists continue to find more evidence for this settlement practice.[22] The basic unit is the individual house mound, at an elevation of only 1–2 m, which was just sufficient to keep

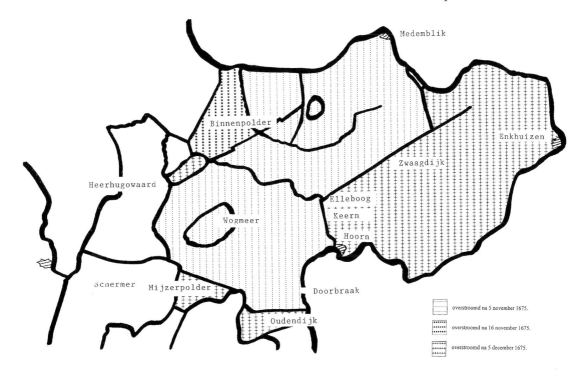

overstroomd na 5 november 1675.

overstroomd na 16 november 1675.

overstroomd na 5 december 1675.

FIGURE 9.1. Schematic map of the flooding of West-Frysia of 1675.

J. DE BRUIN AND D. ATEN *EEN GEMENE DIJK? VERWIKKELINGEN ROND DE DIJKZORG IN WEST-FRIESLAND. DE WATERSNOOD VAN 1675–1676* (2004)

the major part of the house above the water table during floods, securing the survival of its inhabitants. Over time, individual mounds might grow together to form the centre of a village. In some areas, in particular in the provinces of Groningen and Frysia, the mound might develop into a 'terp', a mound some 10 m or more high.[23] But in most areas, the mounds remained low and became inconspicuous over time, only to be rediscovered again by landscape archaeologists in the late twentieth century.

In the Middle Ages, when cities developed, this pattern of living on both human-made and natural elevations continued. Often the settlement took a linear form, as in Amsterdam along both sides of the river Amstel. In the seventeenth century, when the town was extended and new canals ('grachten') were constructed, the excavated earth was used to elevate the ground level of the newly designed quarters.[24] As a result, during a flood, most cities were not destroyed and could even continue to function. Situated on elevations, cities became dry isles standing out in the shallow sea, serving as natural places of refuge for the victims of the submerged countryside. The chronicle writers of the city of Hoorn described how in 1675 the roads (which ran along the top of dikes) and canals were blocked by streams of peasant families. In 1825 the city of Amsterdam accommodated 900 refugees from the inundated adjoining territory of Waterland in and around the Toll House, the city hostel. The hostel was built on other side of the IJ, a sea arm of the Zuiderzee on which Amsterdam was situated. People traveling to Amsterdam who were too late to cross the IJ by ferry and be admitted into city before the gates closed at sunset, could find lodgings at this hostel.[25]

Cities, as reserves of labour and capital, could also provide active aid.[26] In Hoorn in 1675, the fire brigade's warning system was employed. The city burgomaster sounded the trumpet. Six neighbourhoods came to the dike led by their fire brigade commanders. These volunteers worked without payment, but the city provided basic sustenance of bread, cheese and beer. Labour was required to reinforce weak spots along the sea dikes and to raise the height of the dikes. Labour was also needed to guard the scarce dike materials (sails, wood, sand, seaweed and straw) against theft. In 1825 and 1916, military forces stationed in Amsterdam were responsible for guarding both the dikes and the properties left behind by refugees, using boats to survey the submerged. Cities also provided materials for dike repairs and boats for the transportation of such materials; public authorities occasionally seized ships in the harbour for this purpose.

Cities did, of course, suffer to some degree from the effects of flooding. In the major towns of Hoorn, Enkhuizen and Medemblik in 1675, and in Purmerend in 1916, for instance, the streets were inundated, but not by more than a few centimetres above the threshold of the entrance doors.[27] Gardens in and around the city were sometimes also destroyed. Urban trees died too, particularly if salt water remained present for a long time. Buildings were damaged and some even disappeared into the dike as part of strengthening operations. When emergency conditions demanded reinforcement of a dike, buildings close to or on the dike could be buried under the sand.

Essentially, though, the cities were preserved and thus became vital to coping with the consequences of flooding in adjacent rural areas. In addition, the city often functioned as the centre of relief organization. For the city and its immediate surroundings, the city government was an important institution. However other institutions also had offices or even headquarters in the city, the most important being the Regional Water Authorities who maintained the dikes at the regional level. During floods the Water Authorities had to prevent (further) breaches of the dikes. After the floods, they were responsible for carrying out dike repairs as soon as possible, as every delay led to larger breaches and increased the problems (and costs) of closing the dikes again.[28] The offices of Regional Water Authorities were large and prestigious buildings, often lavishly decorated, as the offices in the cities of Edam, Leiden, Rotterdam and Delft demonstrate.

Provincial Councils ('Gecommiteeerde Raden') also had their offices in the cities; this came in handy in 1675 when the Provincial Council of North Holland's headquarters, in the city of Hoorn, was very close to the major dike breach. A Provincial Council, however, was not something peculiar to one city. In fact, in the Republic, such councils consisted of representatives from a range of towns. Thus the Provincial Council of North Holland was a meeting place for the cities of North Holland, including both cities in distress, such as Hoorn, Enkhuizen and Medemblik, and cities not hit by the water, such as Alkmaar. One of the reasons for cooperation between the traditionally competitive cities was to ensure the closure of the inner dikes, so that water did not penetrate further inland and demolish the water infrastructure, which formed part of their trade infrastructure, and included waterways, dams and land roads, often situated on dikes.[29] For cities on the coastal plain, the need to preserve agricultural land was less urgent because they depended on trade, partially based on local output, but for a great share also based on re-exporting imported goods. For instance, by the fourteenth century, cattle raising had already replaced grain growing, forcing cities to become dependent on grain imports from France and the Baltic countries, which were exported to Scandinavia.[30] Cities were of course also interested in preserving the land and protecting agriculture since many of their citizens and institutions owned land in the countryside, but this was an interest for the long-term. The immediate priority was trade. At the risk of simplifying the complexity of the early modern economy, trade was the precondition for agriculture.[31]

Water transportation and evacuation

Transportation by water was the normal mode in the Netherlands' amphibious culture. The land was riddled with waterways such as rivers, canals, ditches and lakes. Most freight was transported by ship, whether sailing ship, rowing boat or a boat towed by horses or men. In the amphibious culture, the farmer was also a shipper. He had to take his dairy products to the city market and return with grain, cloth and other useful products procured there. Every farm owned some kind of boat (Fig. 9.2). Boats were kept in boat houses, which consisted of small roofs, thatched with reeds, standing on piles. These were very similar

FIGURE 9.3. Traditional boat house, Wicken Fen, reconstruction 21st century.

P. J. E. M. VAN DAM

in appearance to the one that has been reconstructed in front of the Wren Building, the visitor centre of Wicken Fen, Cambridgeshire (Fig. 9.3).[32] In the landscape of the twenty-first century, one can identify the mini-harbours situated next to farms as the relics of this amphibious culture, connecting farms to the main water route. And as farms are being bought up by city dwellers, their new owners, consciously or not, reinvent this tradition by building boat houses to house their yachts next to their countryside dwelling.

Many urban residents were merchants. And since merchants were shippers, many kept boats moored at their city houses. The boat symbolizes the ease of movement over water in the amphibious culture. It is the vital condition for amphibious behaviour, moving quickly and securely within the wetland and between wet and dry parts of the landscape. Transportation by water became even more important when large stretches of land were turned into water by flooding. The evacuation of cattle both by land and water deserves special attention. Although transportation and rescue of humans is, of course, a matter of high importance, from the standpoint of the long-term sustainability of an amphibious culture in a flood-prone country, the evacuation of cattle was also a high priority, since livestock represented a valuable, perhaps even the most important, capital good and investment in an agrarian economy.[33] In the low-lying territories of the Netherlands, keeping cattle, both for dairy products and for meat, was a major occupation.

A common practice was to store flood-threatened cattle in the church. Churches were usually built on a large house mound, 1–2 m above the already elevated city level, so they could serve effectively as refuges in times of emergency.[34]

In Waterland, some churches were built explicitly as refuge churches, among them the famously very large church of Edam dating from 1622.[35] Often the cattle had to share a church with humans, and in one particular instance the church at Oostzaan became so crowded that the church windows had to be broken to get sufficient air inside for the bodies of all the creatures sheltering there (Fig. 9.4).[36] During the flood of 1825, the church of Edam contained 500 cows, while Monnickendam's housed more than three times that number (1700).[37]

Having a refuge for cattle is one thing; moving the livestock there is another matter. The majority of the cattle were probably driven to the higher places, simply walking from the low-lying stables to the dikes and then on to the village, as the more detailed accounts for the nineteenth century and later report. Since most of the flooding occurred during winter storms (November–February), collecting the cattle in time was facilitated by the fact that the cows were usually sheltering in byres instead of being dispersed over the meadows. Both textual and pictorial evidence indicate that cattle were also transported by water, both during floods and at other times. Cows in boats, and often in rather small boats, are a famous motif in seventeenth-century landscape paintings. This practice continued into the twentieth century as the classic film *De Fanfare* (1958), by Oscar-winning director Bert Haanstra, vividly demonstrated. Dutch cattle used to be much sportier than their 'industrialized' contemporary successors, jumping with alacrity into and out of flat, but wobbly, boats covered with hay to mimic pastureland.

After the first emergency measures were enacted, such as placing cows in churches, cows were removed to places outside the disaster zone. In 1675, in West-Frysia, where peasants had ample time to act, cattle were simply transferred to the unaffected pastures of more distant villages. By 1916, means of communication

FIGURE 9.4. Evacuated cattle in the Oostzijder Church of Oostzaan during the flood of 1825.

PAINTING BY JAMES DE RIJK, 1830 (PHOTOGRAPH: W. L. DORENBOS)

and transportation had improved so much that the movement of cattle became the object of large scale planning. In the village of Broek in Waterland, all cattle were driven to the church square since there were too many to fit into the church. They were then transported to Amsterdam to make space in the church for human refugees. In Amsterdam, the cattle were concentrated in industrial buildings along the IJ and in the soccer stadium in the south of the city. In the city, shortage of manpower to milk the cows and lack of fodder were serious problems. Subsequently cattle were moved to other places south of the disaster area, in Zuid-Holland; the national railways offered free transportation. The farmers formed special committees to ensure the return of their cattle, while the government issued a special licence to slaughter and export the meat.[38]

How the inhabitants of flood-prone regions dealt with concentrations of cattle in earlier centuries is an important question for further research. Perhaps a substantial amount of hay was available locally, since hay was traditionally stored in the loft of the farms, where it was secure from water damage. Other methods of rescue were also developed, depending upon both water transport and farm adaptations. In the eighteenth century, the frequency of floods increased in the river area for a number of reasons, including weather changes and inadequate human-induced changes to the river.[39] Both farms and stables were situated on elevations. The so-called flood shed ('vloedschuur') stood on top of a mound or was surrounded by (buried into) a mound on three sides. The mound served as a wide ramp leading up to the upper floor, where the cattle were housed during the flood. The roof of the farm contained a special small door, giving residents camping on the upper floor access to their rowing boat, which would transport them to the flood shed so that they could tend the cattle.[40]

An important question for additional research is how successful the cattle rescue operations were. All in all, after the flood of 1916, the number of cows in Waterland had been halved, causing a great deal of misery among the farmers.[41] And yet, in terms of survival and potential for future recovery, this was a reasonably good outcome, for, unlike tractors, cows reproduce.

Conclusion

My preferred term for the long tradition of cultural adaptations to floods in the low-lying Netherlands is an amphibious culture. The landscape features included a relatively slight difference between sea level and average field level, and a land structured in compartments divided by interior dikes. Also, many settlements were situated sufficiently above the field level, both on natural and human-made elevations, ensuring security from flooding when dikes broke. Cities stood out like islands and were indispensable elements of the dry areas. They provided the reserves for the resumption of the more terrestrial life, including refuge for victims, provision of labour and materials for dike repair and the securing of public order. Transport by dikes and waterways made the rescue of both humans and animals possible.

During flood disasters, daily life was very much disrupted. Yet people continued to operate in the half-dry and half-wet environment. As a result, although many peasants were extremely impoverished, the basic conditions required for 'normal' life were maintained. The model of an amphibious culture helps us to understand how human vulnerability differed between groups (cattle raisers and others, for example), according to region (those with deeper and shallower polders) and also over time (with changes in modes of transportation).

The world today

From the nineteenth century, this amphibious culture largely disappeared from the Netherlands. The availability of new technology and materials (concrete and steel) led to the construction of very strong dikes and dams and special storm surge barriers, such as the renowned Delta Works (1954–85) in the southwest and the Closure Dam (1932) in the north. As these new protective infrastructures were installed and were found to be effective, the perception of flooding risk changed considerably.

It became normal to extend cities into the low-lying areas, in river beds and at the bottom of drained lakes and other polders, an important example being the construction of Schiphol Airport at Amsterdam, situated in the drained Harlam Lake, at 4 m below sea level. Highways were built in the polders and boats were replaced by cars. In cities, waterways were neglected and superseded by low-lying streets. In short, large areas of swamp were sealed over by buildings and asphalt. Consequently, for flooding to occur, a storm surge is no longer required. A long period of rain is sufficient for the soil to become unable to absorb the water and for the capacity of the drainage system to become insufficient. River flooding has also become a concern once again, as evidenced by the large river floods of the 1990s, and is related to changes in weather and in the landscape and drainage systems in central Europe.

Since the Dutch live mainly on low-lying lands, the costs of potential floods from the sea and the rivers have risen enormously. For that reason, the potential rise of sea level as a result of climate change has promoted a good deal of government action. The National Ministry of Water Management has started a huge operation to reinforce the coastline with underwater sand supplements. Big dredging ships suck up sand in the North Sea and spit it out at the coastline, underwater, so that the natural forces of wind and water raise it up and unload it upon the beach. The wind then picks up the sand and deposits it on coastal sand dunes, thus reinforcing this natural defence line. At seaside villages, vulnerable (low) parts of the coastal dunes are reinforced by dikes disguised as dunes, with a sand cover and adequate vegetation, so that tourists are not displeased.

Until recently, the main continuity with the age of the amphibious culture seemed to be the use of compartmentalization. For instance, one of the future visions of the government is to introduce the concept of compartmentalized dike rings.[42] Some territories will have a higher security than others, and the ones with the lower security, whose dikes will break more often, will serve as additional flood plains (water reservoirs) in times of flooding.

However, in a recent television documentary, the newest ideas on government flood management were presented.[43] Curiously, policy scientists state that during a flood the government will have very little or no means to exert any control at all, because, due to the destruction of the electricity network, all means of communication will be disrupted, whether digital, radio or telephone. Evacuation by air or over land will be insufficient, because airfields will be flooded and roads totally congested, bringing all traffic to a standstill. Bas Kolen proposes a new government policy, 'vertical evacuation', advising all people to flee to the higher storeys of buildings and to remain there. In my view, this represents a reinvention of one of the traditional coping mechanisms: living on elevations.[44]

In other parts of the world, particularly in river deltas, this transition from a more to a less amphibious culture has also taken place. Thailand provides a prime example. In Bangkok, a transition from water-based transport to land-based transport occurred in the twentieth century, and involved high-wheeled large cars, capable of driving on modestly flooded roads. However the governors of this city realize that this is not the ultimate solution, especially since floods are increasing in frequency, due to weather changes and rising sea levels.[45] Water historians would do well to advise governments all over the globe to also reinvent the third coping mechanism described in this article: water transportation. In the city of Rotterdam, the newest tourist attraction is a sightseeing tour by a coach which doubles as boat on the river Rhine for part of its tour. Learning to 'live with the water', rather than fighting against it, may be the most relevant and urgent message for today's decision-makers based on the historical study of former amphibious cultures.

Notes

1. I would like to thank the organizers of the AHRC Research Network 'Local Places, Global Processes: Histories of Environmental Change', Peter Coates, David Moon and Paul Warde, for the kind invitation to join the network, which became such a vibrant forum for exchanging ideas, and Peter Coates, once more, for his advice on finalizing this text.
2. The floods of 1675, 1825 and 1916 resulted from dike breaches in areas to the west and south of the Zuiderzee (South Sea) so that the events had a fairly comparable geographic situation: the peaty low-lying wetlands. The dike breaches concerned were situated in the territories of the Water Authorities of the West-Frysian dike (north of Amsterdam, near the town of Hoorn), the Water Authorities of the Noorder IJ- en Zeedijk (Waterland, north of Amsterdam, immediately opposite the IJ), the Regional Water Authorities of Rhineland (south of Amsterdam) and the Regional Water Authorities of the Diemer Sea Dike (east of Amsterdam), and in Overijssel, where centralized dike management did not exist. The 1953 flood concerned mainly the province of Zealand, the west of Noord-Brabant and the south of Zuid-Holland and involved many Water Authorities.

3. For the Zuiderzee, see A. Fransen, *Dijk onder spanning. De ecologische, politieke en financiele geschiedenis van de Diemerdijk bij Amsterdam, 1591-1864* (Hilversum: Verloren, 2011), pp. 72, 170, 250.

4. The estimate of 0–2 m is taken from Gerardus Petrus van de Ven (ed.), *Man-made Lowlands: History of Water Management and Land Reclamation in the Netherlands*, 4th rev. ed. (Utrecht: Matrijs, 2004), p. 18 (map); the larger figures refer to the 'droogmakerijen,' the lake reclamations of the sixteenth and seventeenth centuries, like the UNESCO World Heritage monument Lake Beemster http://whc.unesco.org/en/list/899 (accessed 21/10/14).

5. For the phenomenon of the sinking peat lands, see: Petra J. E. M. van Dam, 'Sinking Peat Bogs: Environmental Change in Holland, 1350-1550', *Environmental History* 5/4 (2000), pp. 32–45.

6. For a map of the potentially flooded area, see: van de Ven (ed.), *Man-made Lowlands*, p. 17.

7. The famous flood of 1953 which drowned large parts of the southwestern Netherlands was such a case, when many dikes broke (due to lack of maintenance during and after World War II) and the low-lying land was flooded extensively: Kees Slager, *De ramp. Een reconstructie van de watersnoodramp van 1953* (Amsterdam/Antwerpen: Atlas, 2003).

8. The Dutch term for this is 'gemeenmaking', which translates uncomfortably as 'communalization' or centralization: van deVen (ed.), *Man-made Lowlands*, pp. 116, 150; see for example Milja van Tielhof and Petra J. E. M. van Dam, *Waterstaat in stedenland. Het hoogheemraadschap van Rijnland voor 1857* (Utrecht: Matrijs, 2006), p. 67. Petra J. E. M. van Dam and Milja van Tielhof, 'Losing Land, Gaining Water: Ecological and Financial Aspects of Regional Water Management in Rijnland, 1200-1800', thematic issue: 'Water Management, Communities, and Enviroment: The Low Countries in Comparative Perspective, *c.*1000-*c.*1800', *Jaarboek voor Ecologische Geschiedenis 2005/2006*, (2006), pp. 63–94. This increase in the number of risk-sharing groups did not extend to urban dwellers.

9. Christian Pfister, '"The Monster Swallows You": Disaster Memory and Risk Culture in Western Europe,1500-2000', *Rachel Carson Center Perspectives* (Rachel Carlson Center for Environment and Society, 2011) http://www.environmentandsociety.org/perspective (accessed 21/10/14).

10. M. K. Elisabeth Gottschalk, *Stormvloeden en rivieroverstromingen in Nederland – Storm Surges and River Floods in the Netherlands*, 3 vols (Assen: Van Gorcum & Company, 1971–77).

11. Christian Rohr, *Extreme Naturereignisse im Ostalpenraum. Naturerfahrung im Spätmittelalter und am Beginn der Neuzeit*, Umwelthistorische Forschungen 4 (Cologne/Weimar/Vienna: Böhlau, 2007); Adrian M. J. de Kraker, 'A Method to Assess the Impact of High Tides, Storms and Storm Surges as Vital Elements in Climatic History: The Case of Stormy Weather and Dikes in the Northern Part of Flanders, 1488 to 1609', *Climatic Change* 43/1 (1999), pp. 287–302.

12. A figure of about thirty villages is more likely: Gottschalk, *Stormvloeden en rivieroverstromingen in Nederland*, vol. 2, p. 73. Based on administrative sources such as parish registers, Leenders concluded that there were approximately 2,000 victims: Karel A. H. W. Leenders, 'Die inundacie ende inbreck van onsen Grooten Waert: De verdrinking van de Grote Waard', in Valentine Wikaart *et al.* (eds), *'Nijet dan water ende wolcken' De onderzoekscommissie naar de aanwassen in de Verdronken Waard (1521–1523)* (Tilburg: Stichting Zuidelijk Historisch Contact, 2009), p. 70.

13. Otto S. Knotnerus, 'Dollart geschiedenis(sen) - Mythen en realiteit', Stichting

Verdronken Geschiedenis (2009) http://www.verdrongengeschiedenis.nl/nl/stormvloed/docs/9-%20Knottnerus%20-%20Dollardgeschiedenissen-opmaak-3def.pdf (accessed 21/10/14).

14. Margriet de Roever, 'Watersnood in Waterland. Dijkdoorbraken van de Zuiderzee in 1825 en 1916', *Jaarboek van het Centraal Bureau voor Genealogie* 64 (2010), pp. 85–88.

15. Manfred Jakubowski-Tiessen, *Sturmflut 1717. Die Bewältigung einer Naturkatastrophe in der Frühen Neuzeit*, Ancien Régime, Aufklärung und Revolution 24 (München: R. Oldenbourg Verlag, 1992); Marie L. Allemeyer, *Kein Land ohne Deich...! Lebenswelten einer Küstengesellschaft in der Frühen Neuzeit* (Göttingen: Vandenhoeck & Ruprecht, 2006); Franz Mauelshagen, 'Disaster and Political Culture in Germany since 1500,' in Christof Mauch and Christian Pfister (eds), *Natural Disasters, Cultural Responses: Case Studies Toward a Global Environmental History* (New York etc.: Rowman & Littlefield, 2009), pp. 41–76.

16. Rohr, *Extreme Naturereignisse im Ostalpenraum* , pp. 55–61.

17. René Favier and Anne-Marie Granet-Abisset, 'Society and Natural Risks in France, 1500–2000: Changing Historical Perspectives', in Mauch and Pfister (eds), *Natural Disasters*, pp. 103–36.

18. Greg Bankoff, 'The "English Lowlands" and the North Sea Basin System: A History of Shared Risk', *Environment and History* 19 (2013). p. 19.

19. Greg Bankoff, *Cultures of Disaster: Society and Natural Hazard in the Philippines* (London/New York: Routledge Curzon, 2003); Bankoff, 'Cultures of Disaster, Cultures of Coping: Hazard as a Frequent Life Experience in the Philippines, 1600–2000,' in Mauch and Pfister (eds), *Natural Disasters*, pp. 265–84.

20. There are many maps in van de Ven (ed.), *Man-made Lowlands*. A polder is a territory where the water table is controlled by humans, with the aid of special infrastructure like dikes, small embankments, dams and sluices. The board of such a drainage unit is often also called a polder, although 'polderbestuur' (Local Water Authority) is more accurate.

21. Jan de Bruin and Diederik Aten, *Een gemene dijk? Verwikkelingen rond de dijkzorg in West-Friesland. De watersnood van 1675-1676* 21 (Purmerend: Vrienden van de Hondsbossche, Kring voor Noord-Hollandse waterstaatsgeschiedenis, 2004), p. 33 (map).

22. For evidence for (low) house mounds, see: Juren M. Bos, *Landinrichting en archeologie: het bodemarchief van Waterland*, Nederlandse Archeologische Rapporten 6 (Amersfoort: ROB, 1988); Epko J. Bult, *Midden-Delfland: een archeologische kartering, inventarisatie, waardering en bewoningsgeschiedenis*, Nederlandse Archeologische Rapporten 2 (Amersfoort: ROB, 1983); F. D. Zeiler, 'De "vergeten" watersnood', *Tijdschrift voor Waterstaatsgeschiedenis* 16/1 (2007), p. 23 http://www.stedengeschiedenis.nl/pages/WG/01.html (accessed 03/03/14); Leendert Louwe Kooijmans (ed.), *Nederland in de prehistorie* (Amsterdam: Bert Bakker, 2005).

23. M. Miedema, 'Oost-Fivelingo 250 v.C.–1850 na C., *Palaeohistoria* 32 (1990), pp. 111–245; M. Miedema, 'West-Fivelingo 600 v.C.–1900 na C., *Palaeohistoria* 41–42 (1999/2000), pp. 1237–445.

24. Fred Feddes, *A Millennium of Amsterdam: Spatial History of a Marvellous City* (Bussum: Thoth, 2012), pp. 75-104.

25. De Roever, 'Watersnood in Waterland', p. 78.

26. T. Bosch, 'Nijmegen en zijn "gryze Stroomgod", Hoogwater, strenge vorst en calamiteuze watersnoden, 1781-1861', *Jaarboek Numaga* 56 (2009), pp. 33-53.

27. Gottschalk, *Stormvloeden en rivieroverstromingen in Nederland* 2, pp. 265-7.

28. For an example of a major dike closing project, see Petra J. E. M. van Dam, 'Digging

for a Dike: Holland's Labour Market ca. 1510', in Peter Hoppenbrouwers and Jan Luiten van Zanden (eds), *Peasants into Farmers? The Transformation of Rural Economy and Society in the Low Countries (Middle Ages–19th century) in Light of the Brenner Debate* (Turnhout: Brepols, 2001), pp. 220–55. The history of the relevant Water Authority is described in: van Dam and van Tielhof, 'Losing Land, Gaining Water'.

29. On the infrastructure of cities, taking samples from early sixteenth-century flood disasters, see: Petra J. E. M. van Dam, 'New Orleans aan het IJ? Een waardering van oude en nieuwe dijkdoorbraken', *Tijdschrift voor Waterstaatsgeschiedenis* 16/1 (2007), pp. 11–19 http://www.stedengeschiedenis.nl/pages/WG/01.html (accessed 03/03/14).

30. Van Dam, 'New Orleans aan het IJ?'.

31. Jan de Vries and Ad van der Woude, *The First Modern Economy: Success, Failure, and Perseverance of the Dutch Economy, 1500–1815* (Cambridge: Cambridge University Press, 1997) is the standard survey work for the early modern economic history of the Netherlands, but water management is seen primarily as a source of employment.

32. The Wren Building was the location of one of the workshops of the project that lies at the origin of this paper.

33. Jan Bieleman, *Boeren in Nederland. Geschiedenis van de landbouw 1500–2000* (Amsterdam: Uitgeverij Boom, 2008), pp. 210–33.

34. For illustrations of elevated churches in Zuid-Holland, see: Van Tielhof and van Dam, *Waterstaat in stedenland*, p. 27; for elevated churches in West-Frysia, see: Bruin and Aten, *Een gemene dijk?*, p. 51; for transport of cows and cows in churches in West-Frysia: Bruin and Aten, *Een gemene dijk?*, pp. 32, 34.

35. For instance, for the floods of 1825 and 1916 in Waterland this practice is recorded for the six villages of Ransdorp, Zuiderwoude, Edam, Monnickendam, Broek in Waterland and Oostzaan; in Overijssel this happened everywhere: Zeiler, 'De "vergeten" watersnood', p. 22.

36. Zeiler, 'De "vergeten" watersnood', p. 22.

37. De Roever, 'Watersnood in Waterland', pp. 78–80.

38. De Roever, 'Watersnood in Waterland', p. 81.

39. Gerardus Petrus van de Ven and Anna M. A. J. Driessen, *Niets is bestendig...: de geschiedenis van de rivieroverstromingen in Nederland* (Utrecht: Matrijs, 1995).

40. Judith Toebast, 'Voor als de dijken doorgingen, Maatregelen tegen rivieroverstromingen bij boerderijen, zeventiende-negentiende eeuw', *Tijdschrift voor Waterstaatsgeschiedenis* 21/1/2 (2012), pp. 11–22 http://www.stedengeschiedenis.nl/pages/WG/01.html (accessed 03/03/14).

41. De Roever, 'Watersnood in Waterland', p. 84.

42. *Welvaart en leefomgeving. Een scenariostudie voor Nederland in 2040* (Centraal Planbureau, Milieu- en Natuurplanbureau en Ruimtelijke Planbureau, 2006). The new concern for compartmentalization led to a government-subsidized project of historical research into this phenomenon: Alex van Heezik, *Het voordeel eener dubbele defensie. De discussies rond het compartimenteren van dijkringen n het verleden* ([no place] Deltares publication 2008).

43. Nederland in 7 overstromingen, television documentary broadcasted by Dutch broadcasting companies, NTR and VPRO, December 2013–January 2014 http://www.uitzendinggemist.nl/afleveringen/1384223 (accessed 03/03/14).

44. Leontine van der Stadt, *Nederland in 7 overstromingen* (Zutphen: Walburg Pers, 2013), p. 171.

45. Suwanna Rongwiriyaphanich, 'The Relationships Between Land Use Changes and Flood Risk Management Planning in the Bangkok Delta-Metropolitan Region', unpublished conference paper, Water History Conference, Delft (2010).

CHAPTER 10

Names and Places

Paul Warde

Several of the papers and talks we heard at Wicken Fen were about disappearance and loss: the end of the 'amphibious culture' of the wetlands described by Petra van Dam; or the disappearance of the Fens through drainage traced by Ian Rotherham, a loss so complete in the case of the Yorkshire fens around Hatfield Chase that few people even remember they ever existed. Carry Akroyd spoke about her affinity for John Clare's writings as an inspiration to her, and the man himself as someone who seemed to hold a shared feeling for the environment and the changes that it was subject to, with a common idea to express these feelings in art. Much of Clare's work was of course born of a deep pain at the changes wrought by the enclosure of the Northamptonshire landscape, and then his own dislocation to the Fens.

I was surprised by the degree to which Akroyd's art really was at times a very precise document of places at particular moments; a farmer destroys an actual hedge. The devil is to be found in the detail. Clare's laments were also not just general appeals, but rooted in places and moments. One thing that distressed him was the loss of names as the landscape was torn up, altered and barred to wandering feet. Precious knowledge and folkways were cut adrift from their moorings, so that people no longer had the intimate experience of nature that allowed them to be familiar with the diversity of joys (and dangers) it could offer. Equally, with that link broken, orally-borne and common(s) knowledge vanished, and the names of things become unknown to the great majority of us, now reserved and policed for the large part by scientifically-trained experts. His own words expressed those losses but could not replace them.

The vanishing names include not just the monikers of plants or insects, but places, features, views, prospects. The experience of such things is perhaps, first and foremost, visceral and sensual. But naming them makes a difference, and sometimes alerts us to the fact that they are there. The enclosure of the landscape and urbanization have been associated, to be sure, with long-term processes that have brought us new vocabularies and forms of expression. But they have erased much too: mountains of the mind that have melted into the air. Names and words are, after all, central routes by which we, linguistically-minded creatures, discover, harbour and cherish meaning. We can certainly find meaning in a landscape without names (although most explorers have shown a great enthusiasm for fixing the meanings for subsequent generations by spreading liberally the names of themselves, monarchs and so on), but once named, that landscape enters a new kind of story, develops historical meaning and becomes the vehicle of its unfolding history. The 'linguistic turn' in history famously 'liberated' speech and writing from 'real' things, calling into question categories such as 'class', 'gender', 'race' and 'nation', and demonstrating that real change was as much a matter of how we spoke as anything else. But this discovery did not erase what we currently call 'the environment'. It has demanded that we think anew about our capacity to give meaning to it, and to situate our own lives.

Historians are storytellers, wordsmiths. They are, of course, also a kind of judge (albeit with a rather limited jurisdiction), as well as being archivists, hunters and collectors. They can be guardians of many things, both good and bad. And one thing they are guardians of is names. Place-name provenance is in itself a particular branch of history, and also can serve as evidence of past landscapes, albeit highly disputed. (Does naming a place after the oaks indicate there were many oaks or very few?) But this is generally the province of early medieval history in Britain. Few people pay much attention to place-names after that time. Yet names carry in them the possibility of meaning, and the longevity of a name is in itself a particular meaning. A name is not just a sign of an old meaning, part of the deep historical record of the country, but also the gateway to future meanings, chances for re-articulation, rediscovery and creation. What kind of a relationship do we have with the environment, if the names are gone? How do we speak of what we see, and do we see it at all? It becomes harder to understand how our landscapes have been shaped, and their dynamics, if we cannot put a word to how previous generations spoke of it and located themselves.

Every so often we read or see stories that schoolchildren do not know where milk comes from, or that they do not know the most basic facts about their natural environment. Increasingly, at least in Britain, their mobility is circumscribed. The loss of intimacy with much of the natural world, a bodily and mental disconnection with many natural processes and lives of species (even the ones we exploit most heavily, such as chickens or cows), has been one of the profoundest changes of modern industrial civilization, and is an ongoing process in many parts of the world. It is something that will be difficult, nay impossible, to roll back. But we can still insist on the importance of names, and also that historical names – or simply that names that can allow meaning to thrive – remain in our land and cityscapes. Because without the names, how do we tell stories?

This is a key issue where the global and the local intersect. Increasingly, perhaps, environmental narratives, and environmentalism, have been shaped as a shared public discourse by 'distant' events, or risks that are pervasive but imperceptible, not 'local', even if they are in our locality: chemicals, radiation, oil spills, deforestation, global warming. But how can rage against these things be articulated and embodied on a local level without the tools to make local stories too? Without these, the global stories remain largely shaped by global players, and it is hard to give them local resonance. Repeating the global narratives may be contributing to the oft-observed processes of standardization, reduced diversity and easy substitutability among all of the worlds that we live in. This would be an ironic twist for the many of us who are interested in global (and local) environmental politics and whose engagement in such things was awakened by the thrills and spills of the particular names and places. We're familiar with the injunction to 'think global, act local', but why is the priority assigned in that order – can we also 'think local, act global'?

'Naming' is not that much of a theme in environmental history (as far as I know). The history of names should not simply be an exercise in the exegesis of rather ancient societies (I say that as someone who could happily spend a lifetime in precisely that limited field!). But the challenge of names is also to the future, and to the fashionable idea of 'restoration' (a modish-ness that, of course, is but a re-articulation of many of the ideas of George Perkins Marsh in the 1860s). It is one thing to restore landscapes, or even to set landscape processes going. It is quite another thing to restore or generate meaning. In the case of a project like the Wicken Fen Vision, where will the names come from? How will people articulate what they are seeing and passing over? Will it be 'the cycle-track', 'the big bridge', the 'short walk', that give expression to landscape features as means to a leisure experience that happens to be within convenient driving distance of your house? The individual fens themselves have names, as do the bird hides and bridges. Who will continue to utter them, and why? Will people be aware of historic names and practices that shaped the environment, or will they discover new significance? How will they share that with people who by and large live far from the land, and no longer constitute a resident community? Will the Wicken Fen Vision still be Wicken Fen when it stretches far from those modest origins?

There are projects out there that are starting to think about this (such as the Worcestershire Parish mapping project). The Domesday project back in 1986 turned out to be a one-off, like its precursor (but unlike the original, the 1986 version was stored in machine-readable files for which we no longer have the machines). Akroyd reminded me that these issues were very much the driving force behind Richard Mabey's great *Flora Britannica* (1996). But as with so many other things, I suspect the rate of loss is still much greater than the rate of retention – and even far outpacing the invention of new names in our new urban and suburban landscapes of work and leisure.

CHAPTER 11

Constructing the Kielder Landscape: Plantations, Dams and the Romantic Ideal

Jill Payne

Introduction

The story of recent landscape and environmental change at Kielder is an example of how afforestation, water supply and hydroelectric power schemes brought some of the most visually significant landscape modifications of the twentieth century to the uplands of non-urban Britain. However, the Kielder narrative also serves to emphasize the dynamic nature of interpretations of and responses to particular landscapes. Critically, large-scale twentieth-century resource provision schemes were enterprises that blurred aesthetic and socio-cultural distinctions between developed and undeveloped landscape – between the 'human-made' (and thus, from some perspectives, the 'unnatural') and the 'natural'. Both during and after their physical construction, many of the areas forming backdrops to the schemes were, like Kielder, left with something of an identity crisis. As the editors of this book point out: 'Kielder ... *is* infrastructure'.[1] This 'unnatural-ness' was criticized, yet nevertheless at times enjoyed a measure of acceptability – the price for, and, sometimes, proud symbol of, national standing and domestic resource provision, particularly during the world wars and their aftermath. However, as the significance of plantations and impounded rivers as resource repositories receded, the divisive issue of the utilitarian appearance of these came into increasingly sharp focus. When (and, frequently, because) resource autonomy was de-prioritized, landscape aesthetics became a more viable subject for debate, in a time that was also characterized by broadening public interest in this sphere. In the interests of rationalizing the existence of human-engineered forests and water systems, the primary functions of these were extended to include recreation – amidst an increasingly democratized and variously layered engagement with the outdoors on the part of the British public. Furthermore, the growing multi-dimensional sense of public ownership of landscape and, subsequently, 'the environment' meant that, even where attention to resource provision remained viable, aesthetics and recreation still became part of the list of priorities under consideration. Timber, potable water and energy provision began to share focus with the provision of amenities (both scenic and functional) for visiting outsiders.

During the early years of twentieth-century afforestation, the Kielder uplands, then used by the dukes of Northumberland for shooting and recreation, became more overtly worked land that, particularly with the establishment of Depression-era unemployment camps, also became a landscape of work. There was arguably therefore little disjuncture in the 1960s water engineers' vision for an ambitiously large-scale reservoir and hydroelectric plant within the same setting, designed to meet the needs of potential industrial growth on Teesside. However, even prior to the completion of the controversial damming of the North Tyne Valley, the significance of the Kielder area as a resource repository for timber, water and energy had receded. The priority became the construction of a forest-and-lake landscape more consistent with growing aesthetic requirements for leisure and recreation. It fell to forestry commissioners in particular to buttress Kielder's new identity, a strategy based heavily on the sympathetic integration of the area's regimented conifer plantations within their surroundings.

The Kielder area's present multipurpose role highlights the complexities inherent in reconciling land 'use' and landscape 'delight'.[2] As an engineered landscape that also came to be packaged as a place of recreation, its identity has been subject to a number of reconstructions; its story incorporates useful lessons regarding projects involving long-term, large-scale landscape modification. It highlights just how rapidly resource requirements and priorities can change in the relatively short term, and reminds us that landscape *per se* is a socio-cultural construction, of which landscape protection on aesthetic grounds is an extension. This is not in the least to argue against the validity of landscape protection initiatives – far from it. However, it is important to emphasize the intricacies and, in some instances, the ironies involved in this protection, a point relevant to contemporary instances in which 'environmentalist' proponents of wind and solar energy provision have faced, and continue to face, 'conservationist' opposition on the grounds of impact on landscape aesthetics.

Kielder: (re)creating a worked landscape

Eighteenth- and nineteenth-century British travel and 'discovery' in Asia and Africa operated very much in tandem with the 'internal colonialism' within Britain itself that John MacKenzie referred to as 'the romantic rediscovery of the remoter regions of the British Isles'.[3] 'Remote', of course, is a relative term, but one that continues to underpin some perspectives towards northern England. In the House of Lords in July 2013, Lord Howell of Guildford, Conservative energy secretary between 1979 and 1981, stirred controversy when he referred to the 'large, uninhabited and desolate areas' of the North East as being the most suitable for hydraulic fracturing.[4]

In 1862, the opening of the Border Counties Railway brought new outsider attention to bear on the 'remote' Kielder region, and it is tempting to take the 'internal colonialism' theme a little further in this regard. Resource provision or extraction in the colonial peripheries in the interests of the British metropole was often promoted as making productive use of 'waste' land in marginal territories.[5] It has subsequently become accepted that, prior to development, these places needed to be perceived as undeveloped; before 'frontiers' could be 'tamed', relevant areas had to be constructed as 'untamed'. As Frederik Albritton Jonsson has shown, the construction of 'waste' land was a process that also took place within Britain itself.[6] In the 1860s, much of the Kielder area may have reflected centuries, if not millennia, of modification at the hands of humans, but mid-Victorian commentators were interested in emphasizing its wildest and most remote upland aspects. In August 1863, *Times* readers were reminded of the British Association's forthcoming gathering in Newcastle; its field excursions, including one to Kielder, were to be 'very interesting features of this meeting, as the railways have opened out wild and picturesque districts hitherto almost inaccessible'.[7]

The *Times* contributor's subsequent description of the Association's excursion on the new railway line through Kielder and into Scotland 'through wild and bleak dales at the foot of the far-stretching fells' echoes both earlier narratives of travel within Britain and the more contemporary discourse of imperial mapping, acquisition and resource extraction (much of the latter being facilitated by railway development).[8] In Newcastle in 1863, resonance with ongoing imperial discourses, was, arguably, an of-the-moment reflection of the attention paid to recent exploratory feats in far-flung territories – Speke and Grant's search for the source of the Nile, for instance – which featured prominently in Association discussions that week and which moved the geologist Sir Roderick Murchison, president of the Royal Geographical Society, to speak of the 'remarkable ... race of new travellers that has sprung up of late and is springing up every day'.[9]

In 1889, the *Geological Survey* relating to Kielder and nearby Plashetts noted that 'the entire area is wild and somewhat hilly, and contains very little enclosed ground.'[10] However, rather than demonstrating the existence of 'natural' landscape, the *Survey's* concluding remarks point, as with the Highlands of Scotland, to a developed landscape in decline:

> The cultivated ground is of very small extent and chiefly confined to the river sides. It appears that there was once rather a larger area: this is shown by tradition and also by the old ploughfarrows on what is now moorland, *e.g.*, between Belling Burn foot and the Law. There are also the ruins of an old corn mill and malt kiln up Belling Burn about one-third of a mile above the foot. The Plashetts Colliery no doubt affords, when times are good, work for more persons than the old plough-lands did; but the other smaller collieries and also various limekilns are now abandoned.[11]

Thirty years later, in 1921, the area around Peel Fell could still be described as 'a land of desolation', where '[t]he ground is heavy, with peat hags and clumps of bent[-moss], and the only attraction for the tourist would be the magnificent views to be obtained by various points.'[12] At the same time, as with the Highlands of Scotland, these open stretches of moorland, while potentially daunting to the more incidental traveller, had supported the recreational activities of the Border elite for many years. W. J. Palmer, in his 1882 overview of the Tyne, took pains to point out that Kielder Castle was:

> not one of the ancient Border strongholds, but simply a castellated shooting-box belonging to the Dukes of Northumberland, by one of whom it was built about a century ago. The moors surrounding it abound with grouse, both black and grey, and for the angler there is good sport in the Kielder Burn.[13]

On the national level, landscapes such as Kielder, perceived as 'unused', were seen as logical locations for the new timber plantations that, following the First World War and the publication of the Acland Report and subsequent establishment of the Forestry Commission in 1919, were understood to be vital to domestic self-sufficiency.[14] The focus was on utility and the best economic use of what was then understood to be unproductive moorland. Critically, 'best use' of this land also had associations with the idea, since disproved, that much of northern Britain had been under forest until comparatively recently.[15] The *Geological Survey*, for instance, had recounted earlier descriptions of discoveries at high altitudes of large tree trunks in the Kielder peat, arguing:

> That the whole country was once extensively covered with wood is also shown by tradition. It is stated that, even within the memory of the last generation, as you came up the head of Kielder to cross over into Redesdale you could scarcely see your route for wood, a statement confirmed by the name "Woody Crags", still retained for some scars on the east side of White Kielder. The height of the crags is between 1,250 and 1,500 feet [381–457 m]. The destruction of the woods is attributed to the sheep by many of the shepherds, and it is considered that the small patches of natural wood which still remain will also be gradually destroyed unless fenced in.[16]

During the 1930s and 1940s, then, it was possible for the Forestry Commission's planting achievements at Kielder to be viewed as developmental triumphs that could enjoy a measure of positive coverage in the national press. At this point, resource provision in the 'wild' Kielder area attracted relatively little controversy. In some quarters, the 60,000-acre (*c.*24,288 ha) afforestation project that became Kielder Forest was hailed as a success – a significant chapter in the scientific reclamation of 'former waste lands – sand dunes, peat and heath lands'.[17] In 1944, the *Times* reported on the 'new forest region ... beginning to take shape among the hills and uplands of the Border country', pointing out the technological achievement that the 85,000-plus acres (*c.*34,400+ ha) of the Kielder and Redesdale forests represented:

> The success now attending the afforestation of this bleak and romantic Border country is an encouraging proof of the progress made since the Forestry Commission began its work a quarter of a century ago. It is not easy to persuade trees to grow in peaty and heather-clad soils on hills and moorlands which rise in places to almost 2,000 feet [*c.*610 m] above sea level.[18]

In the Depression years, mirroring Franklin D. Roosevelt's New Deal's Public Works Administration, Kielder had also become something of a showcase location for work camps for unemployed men who participated in forestry, road-building and quarrying activities – an extension of the general effort to deploy afforestation as a means of boosting employment in Special or Depressed Areas.[19] The idea was that the unemployed would undertake 'vigorous work in the open air' in three-month stretches, in the interests of maintaining their 'employability'.[20] In 1934, the *Times* reported in glowing terms on the camps and remarked further that:

> the country in which all that hard work is being carried on [which] has all the allurements of wild beauty, remoteness (for some reason it is easy to imagine the Border as farther away from London than Rome is), historic importance, and romance ... this wild country of moor and fell and forest, of wild birds and beasts of the chase, a country so wild that even forestry cannot be fairly practised in it until roads are made.[21]

Kielder thus assumed, during the interwar years and beyond, a number of the attributes of a newly opened-up frontier environment. It provided a resource understood to be vital to the economic wellbeing of the metropole, and it was also seen as a fresh-air, therapeutic location offering the salvation of labour for the poor and marginalized – as the *Times* put it, for 'relay after relay of enfeebled and objectless men from the depressed areas'.[22] Rather than a symptom of landscape degradation, therefore, afforestation was established as one of the solutions to the problem of how best to reinvigorate depressed regional economies.

At the same time, the socio-economic demands of the Depression, and even fears of another European conflagration, were not sufficient to mitigate growing concern in landscape protection circles about the visual impact of afforestation in England and Wales. In the 1930s, the 'unnatural', blanket-like spectacle presented by large-scale plantations came in for particular criticism and the Forestry Commission began to attract condemnation for failing to show due regard for landscape aesthetics. In Scotland, this demand came later.[23] However, even within England, levels of concern were by no means uniform. Controversy was particularly strong where areas like the Cumbrian Lake District were concerned, and less so regarding Northumberland.[24]

The negative reaction concerning afforestation in the Lake District in particular provides insight into the aesthetic and cultural appreciation of an existing landscape of national significance and invites useful comparison with Kielder.[25] The Lake District was, and continues to be, considered as an exceptionally special case, one in which 'Wordsworth's ghost', as Chris Smout has put it, has loomed large.[26] William Wordsworth, whose early nineteenth-century Lake District *Guide* was so crucial to the subsequent Romantic appreciation of the aesthetics of the region, was unambiguous in his disdain for the 'vegetable manufactory' of larches springing up around him in the 'lovely vales' of his beloved Lakes. He argued that tree-farming on an industrial scale both should and, significantly, could take place elsewhere: 'when there is so much barren and irreclaimable land in the neighbouring moors, and in other parts of the island, which might have been had for this purpose at a far cheaper rate'.[27]

The idea of plantations across the Kielder uplands has never engendered a comparable level of disquiet; responses to Kielder shed light on a more variable attitude to development. With regard to twentieth-century afforestation in the Lake District, the Forestry Commission came under heavy pressure from the then Council for the Preservation of Rural England and the Friends of the Lake District to operate with some caution.[28] Kielder can be placed at the opposite end of the scale: as an area where the emphasis was on production, the plans for its new forests were more utilitarian. A letter from Gilbert Jenkins, president of the Institute of Landscape Architects, to the *Times* in October 1935 illustrates Kielder's position on the Forestry Commission's amenity radar:

> At present, whole sections of the country are being turned into tree slums – places where overcrowding is taking place without imaginative design – thus creating ugly landscapes. No clearer proof of this is needed than a comparison of the plans ... of the New Forest and the Commission's Forest of Kielder. The first has innumerable wide vistas between the plantations, while the second shows miles of solid planting completely filling all the valleys.[29]

The generalized perception of Kielder as a worked landscape had, in effect, rendered it less visible – invisible, even – in an aesthetic sense.

As with afforestation, plans to develop Lake District water systems resulted in significant disagreement and subsequent planning modification.[30] In contrast, as Christine McCulloch has explained, while the flooding of the North Tyne valley's arable pastureland and the construction of the Kielder dam and hydroelectric plant did not go ahead without some measure of protest, Kielder's status, unofficial or otherwise, as a landscape of development was a distinct mitigating factor. Neither the Council for the Protection of Rural England (formerly the Council for the Preservation of Rural England), the Nature Conservancy nor the Countryside Commission objected formally to the plans.[31] What protest there was over Kielder was spearheaded by more localized interests: the North Tyne Valley Preservation Society was presided over by Sir Rupert Speir, a former Conservative MP for Hexham and, as McCulloch has discussed here and elsewhere, a degree of intervention was practised by Geoffrey Rippon, the incumbent Conservative MP for Hexham and also Secretary of State for the Environment.[32]

Critically, supporters of the Kielder Water development made much of the point that the area around Kielder was already developed through afforestation that, to outsiders unaffected by the flooding of the valley, made it 'a dark and forbidding place'.[33] In the Lords, Viscount Ridley, Chairman of the Northumberland County Council, argued: 'Much has been said of the environmental aspects of Kielder, but this valley, I would point out, is poor land, almost entirely in the hands of the Forestry Commission, who are in the process of flooding most of it, anyway, with a green blanket of Sitka Spruce.'[34]

Viscount Ridley's colleague Lord Inglewood added: 'Such an impounding reservoir ought to add to the amenity of the district rather than to detract from it, since it must break into the monotony which a great forest area of this size inevitably creates.'[35]

The need for and relevance of Kielder Water was never entirely resolved. As the reservoir filled up during 1981 and 1982, the *New Scientist* referred to it as a 'prestige project', the 'guilty secret' of Britain's water planners, unnecessarily scarring the landscape and 'the British water industry's most embarrassing white elephant'.[36] Nonetheless, the feat of engineering that it represented was also celebrated in the way that the technological achievement of planting the peatlands was celebrated, but with added emphasis on the degree to which water development had 'improved' the landscape. In 1984, a Civic Trust Award was conferred on the Kielder scheme on the basis that it had augmented the 'quality and appearance of the environment', in what John Sheail described as 'that previously remote and little-visited part of Northumberland'.[37]

Kielder and the integration of aesthetics and industry

During the twentieth century, various factors contributed to the modification of British landscape ideals. However, throughout this time, it is arguable that attitudes as to what constituted aesthetically pleasing landscape remained much informed by Romantic ideals prioritizing varied topography and 'natural' tree lines. In twentieth-century British landscape discourse, there is a clear link, however unconscious by this period, to the reflections that underpinned much of, for instance, Jean-Jacques Rousseau's eighteenth-century engagement with the natural world: 'A flat landscape, however beautiful, has never seemed so to my eye. I need rushing streams, rocks, pine trees, dark woods, mountains, rugged tracks to scramble up and down, precipices on either side to fill me with fear.'[38] Rousseau's ideal landscape, of course, centred broadly on what he referred to as 'that touching beauty which is rarely to be found near the town'.[39] For the most part, it precluded any impingement by overt trappings of contemporary industry, although he was not necessarily opposed to industrial remnants from earlier ages – a contradiction reflected in his admiration of the Pont du Gard (the impressive Roman aqueduct across the Gardon River near Remoulins in the south of France).[40]

In twentieth-century Britain, the artificial tree- and waterscapes produced by early afforestation and damming initiatives stood in direct contravention of still-potent Romantic values. The de-prioritization of domestic resource autonomy in the 1960s and subsequent prioritization of amenity and recreation resulted in a shift in resource provision management towards the integration of aesthetics and industry. Central to this shift were the recommendations of the influential landscape architect Sylvia Crowe, who, during a long career, was associated with a broad swathe of planning issues. Between 1963 and 1976 Crowe acted as landscape consultant to the Forestry Commission. Also consultant to the Central Electricity Generating Board for twenty years, she was involved in projects ranging from the design of the Trawsfynydd and Wylfa nuclear power stations in northern Wales to reservoirs such as Rutland Water. Possibly her central focus, however, was the rehabilitation of developed landscapes. She recognized the difficulties inherent in locating a balance between land-use and landscape protection, but nonetheless made the integration of aesthetics and industry her life's work, at the same time being pragmatic in her acceptance that:

> It is hard to strike a true balance between our needs for electric power, water supply and minerals on the one hand, and on the other our less tangible but perhaps deeper need for the solace of nature. To arrive at this balance means weighing the material against the spiritual, and from that we can expect no exact nor unanimous answer.[41]

As the significance of Kielder as a site of resource provision declined, greater emphasis came to be placed on it as a potential landscape of recreation. For this to be successful, the landscape had to become undeveloped or, in keeping with the ethos of Sylvia Crowe, at least attempt the appearance of non-development. By 1985, the Kielder forestry commissioners could look back on the emergence of a coordinated approach centred on the injection of diversity and undulating lines into its serried ranks of conifers:

> The aim has been to restructure the forest by creating distinct permanent felling coupes with relatively windfirm boundaries conforming to the scale and shape of the landscape. Thereafter the felling sequence for these new compartments has been arranged so far as possible to improve the distribution of age classes within the forest by exploiting any differences in species and rates of development in the present crops at different elevations.[42]

With regard to the reservoir, for all of designer Sir Frederick Gibberd's concern that Kielder not take on, as McCulloch notes, the appearance of a 'municipal park', similarities with recreation-orientated American state parks established alongside large-scale reservoirs are evident.[43] To a certain extent, the Kielder landscape shares the unavoidably 'constructed' appearance of some of the US Army Corps of Engineers' dam projects in the Great Plains – 'flood control' schemes, in many instances, that by the 1970s had to be adapted to take into account a new era of focus on recreation.[44] At the same time, an enthusiastic 1982 *Times* article on the beauties of Kielder's new landscape (dismissed by one opponent of the dam as Northumbrian Water 'propaganda') explained how 'Kielder Water is certainly no bleak-faced concrete banked reservoir.[45] There are bays and promontories, the wooded fells rise gently on three sides and the realigned main road on the southwest bank provides a series of vistas'.[46] Propaganda or not – and improvement or not – Kielder's changing face represented important and hard-won changes in the approach of foresters and water planners, engendered by over six decades of increasing engagement with landscape aesthetics and recreation possibilities.

Conclusion: connecting with integrated landscapes

Kielder is a reminder of how a particular landscape, and responses to it, can change relatively quickly. In the decades since Kielder Forest and Kielder Water were created, the perceived identity of the area has seen a number of shifts. It has variously been viewed as resource repository, 'white elephant' and outdoor recreation hub.[47] Recently, it has regained importance as a flexible water storage capacity able to provide for the North East and, potentially, further afield, in times of drought and other more incidental water supply crises.[48] Its location also means that it now holds a number of appeals over and above the value of its landscape. As its low levels of light pollution attest, the area remains one of the most remote in England. In Kielder, we now have a reserve not only of forest, water and recreational space, but also of dark sky. The Campaign to Protect Rural England designated Kielder as a 'reservoir of the darkest category of sky' – part of the largest remaining expanse in England.[49] Kielder's biodiversity status, long understood to have been disadvantaged by Sitka monoculture, has been enhanced through the Kielderhead NNR (National Nature Reserve) and Kielder Mires NNR and SSSI (Sites of Special Scientific Interest) designations and a range of biodiversity projects, including its red squirrel and osprey programmes.[50] However, the Kielder Water and Forest Park's website first and foremost continues to draw the attention of prospective visitors to its landscape:

> There are many reasons to visit; the most popular being the distinctive scenery. Home to northern Europe's largest human-made lake and England's largest forest, the Park's remoteness and clean air and water offer a fresh outdoor experience.[51]

Actual attitudes towards Kielder *per se* continue to be mixed. As the Bowles Green Kielder Wildlife Tourism Study described in 2010, 'the landscape is wild and threatening to many visitors. It lacks the interesting diversity of competing destinations [although] it undoubtedly has a wild beauty that can be appreciated in all weathers.'[52] Certainly, 'big sky country' has its admirers, but there is no doubt that it remains more of an 'acquired taste' than the more intimate and quintessentially Romantic (and closely protected) landscape of the Lake District; it is arguable that Kielder's popularity continues to suffer from its relative proximity to the latter. To a certain extent, as with much upland British landscape, it continues to be held hostage to Romantic aesthetic ideals, which, in their time, as Peter Coates reminds us in his chapter on aesthetics, were also considered to be an acquired taste – a dramatic reversal, of course, of previously accepted ideas of positive human control over untrammelled nature.

Places like the Lake District and the Highlands of Scotland can be linked to a rich heritage of readily accessible cultural and literary connotations. As landscape 'packages', these areas resonate more generally with what the public expects in terms of visual attributes. Less culturally 'visible' landscapes, like that of Kielder, lack these readily-accessible signifiers and, as a result, do not invite the same level of engagement. These signifiers may be mobilized to engender support for landscape protection movements, as with the various campaigns to protect the Lake District and similarly culturally significant landscapes such as Scotland's Loch Lomond.[53] However, it is also possible that the concerns of protesters regarding despoliation as a result of landscape changes like afforestation or damming can over time be dissipated through the enduring nature of the same cultural connotations; the latter may continue to be associated with these places despite their physical modification. Similarly, it is possible that the cultural connotations of previous eras may be invoked to useful effect where the (re)awakening of interest in post-modification landscapes is seen to be desirable. With regard to the ongoing promotion of the Kielder landscape, it may be that placing, as W. J. Palmer did in the 1880s, a more sustained emphasis on the promotion (and, dare I say it, the creation) of historical and literary signifiers – battles and ballads – could result in outsiders who engage with the area benefitting from a heightened sense of place.[54]

Notes

1. See 'Three Places' in this volume, p. **23**.
2. T. C. Smout, *Nature Contested: Environmental History in Scotland and Northern England since 1600* (Edinburgh: Edinburgh University Press, 2000), pp. 7–36.
3. See, for example, Michael Hechter, *Internal Colonialism: The Celtic Fringe in British National Development* (Berkeley: California University Press, 1975); Linda Colley, *Britons: Forging the Nation* (New Haven: Yale University Press, 1991); John M. MacKenzie, *The Empire of Nature: Hunting, Conservation and British Imperialism* (Manchester: Manchester University Press, 1988), p. 28.
4. House of Lords Debates, 30 July 2013, Col. 1641. David Howell, Lord Howell of Guildford, the father-in-law of the Coalition Chancellor George Osborne, was also the Coalition's Foreign Office minister responsible for international energy policy between 2010 and 2012. According to a government spokesperson, he last advised the Coalition government in April 2013. BBC, 'Fracking OK for "Desolate" North East, says Tory Peer', 30 July 2013 http://www.bbc.co.uk/news/uk-politics-23505723 (accessed 25/08/13).
5. See examples in William Beinart and Lotte Hughes, *Environment and Empire* (Oxford: Oxford University Press, 2006).
6. Frederick Albritton Jonsson, *Enlightenment's Frontier: The Scottish Highlands and the Origins of Environmentalism* (New Haven: Yale University Press, 2013).
7. *The Times*, 24 August 1863, p. 10.
8. *The Times*, 1 September 1863, p. 5. This description as a whole appears to be rather reliant on Thomas Frognall Dibdin's *A Bibliographical, Antiquarian and Picturesque Tour in the Northern Counties of England and in Scotland, Vol I* (London: printed for the author by C Richards, 1838), pp. 299, 416–22.
9. *The Times*, 29 August 1863, p. 8.
10. Charles Thomas Clough, *Memoirs of the Geological Survey, England and Wales, The Geology of Plashetts and Kielder* (London: HMSO, 1889), p. 1.
11. Clough, *Memoirs of the Geological Survey*, p. 53. For the Highlands, see Peter Womack, *Improvement and Romance: Constructing the Myth of the Highlands* (Basingstoke: Macmillan, 1989).
12. 'The Unknown Borders. Tracing the Scottish Boundary. Explorations by Mr J. L.

Mack', *The Times, 20 September 1921, p. 4.*

13. W. J. Palmer, *The Tyne and its Tributaries* (London: George Bell, 1882), p. 11.

14. John Sheail, *An Environmental History of Twentieth-Century Britain* (Basingstoke: Palgrave, 2002), pp. 82–90.

15. Smout, *Nature Contested*, pp. 38–41.

16. Clough, *Memoirs of the Geological Survey*, p. 34.

17. 'Forest Fires, 44 Reported in Three Days, Appeal to the Public', *The Times*, 12 April 1933, p. 17.

18. *The Times*, Tuesday, 5 September 1944, p. 2.

19. Sheail, *An Environmental History of Twentieth-Century Britain*, pp. 29, 97; L. S. Greene, 'State Policy in the British Depressed Areas: An Experiment in Regionalism', *Social Forces* 18/3 (March 1940), pp. 337–50.

20. 'Training Camps for Unemployed: Forestry, Quarry, and Road Work', *The Times*, 10 March 1933, p. 14.

21. 'Forestry in Northumberland', *The Times*, 22 September 1934, p. 13.

22. 'Forestry in Northumberland', *The Times*, 22 September 1934, p. 13.

23. Donald Mackay, *Scotland's Rural Landuse Agencies*, p. 27.

24. John Sheail, *Nature in Trust: The History of Nature Conservation in Britain* (Glasgow & London: Blackie, 1976), pp. 83–5. I am grateful to John Sheail for initially drawing my attention to this.

25. Sheail, *Environmental History of Twentieth-Century Britain*, pp. 95–8.

26. Smout, *Nature Contested*, pp. 61, 112.

27. William Wordsworth, *A Guide Through the District of the Lakes in the North of England*, 5th edn (London: Longman, 1835), p. 279.

28. Forestry Commission, 36th Annual Report, 1955.

29. *The Times*, 2 October 1935, p. 15.

30. Sheail, *Environmental History of Twentieth-Century Britain*, pp. 73–4; Harriet Ritvo, *The Dawn of Green: Manchester, Thirlmere, and Modern Environmentalism* (Chicago: University of Chicago Press, 2009).

31. House of Lords Debates, 20 March 1973, Vol. 340, Col. 710.

32. Christine S. McCulloch, 'Transparency: Aid or Obstacle to Effective Defence of Vulnerable Environments from Reservoir Construction? Dam Decisions and Democracy in North East England', *Area* 38/1 (2006), pp. 24–33, at pp. 30–1.

33. Sheail, *Environmental History of Twentieth-Century Britain*, p. 80; *The Times*, 'Creating a New Beauty Spot as Reservoir Replaces Forest', 12 January 1976, p. 5.

34. House of Lords Debates, 20 March 1973, Vol. 340, Col. 709.

35. House of Lords Debates, 20 March 1973, Vol. 340, Col. 711.

36. 'Water, Water, Everywhere ...', *New Scientist*, 8 October 1981, pp. 90–3; 'Waterlogged', *New Scientist*, 27 May 1982, p. 555.

37. Sheail, *Environmental History of Twentieth-Century Britain*, p. 81.

38. Jean Jacques Rousseau, *Confessions*, trans. A. Scholar (Oxford: Oxford University Press, 2000 [1782–89]), p. 168.

39. Rousseau, *Confessions*, p. 394.

40. Rousseau, *Confessions*, pp. 249–50.

41. Sylvia Crowe, *Tomorrow's Landscape (London: Architectural Press, 1956), p. 38.*

42. B. G. Hibberd, F. C., Kielder Forest District, 'Restructuring of Plantations in Kielder Forest District', *Forestry* 58/2 (1985), pp. 119–29, 1.

43. See Christine McCulloch's chapter in this volume, p. 271.

44. For instance, Colorado's John P. Martin Reservoir, completed by 1949: D. Clayton Brown, *The Southwestern Division: 50 Years of Service* (United States Army Corps of

Engineers, 1987), pp. 25–6. See also Kansas' Melvern Lake, completed by 1975: United States Army Corps of Engineers, Kansas City District, *Heartland Engineers: A Century of Superior Service, 1907–2007* (United States Army Corps of Engineers, 2009), p. 103. J. Siikamäki, 'Contributions of the US State Park System to Nature Recreation', *Proceedings of the National Academy of Sciences of the United States of America* 108/34 (2011), pp. 14031–6, at p. 14032.

45. A. G. Spears, 'Reasons for Kielder', *The Times*, 27 May 1982, p. 13.

46. 'Come On In, the Water's Fine', *The Times*, 21 May 1982, p. viii.

47. 'A Great Lake has Come of Age', *The Northern Echo*, 16 May 2003.

48. 'Water? The North East is Way Better', *The Northern Echo*, 3 February 2006.

49. CPRE cited in Bowles Green Ltd, 'Kielder Wildlife Tourism Study Final Report', January 2010, p. 11. See also 'Three Places' in this volume, p. 27.

50. NNR: Natural England, 'North East NNRs' http://www.naturalengland.org.uk/ourwork/conservation/designations/nnr/regions/northeast.aspx (accessed 15/08/13); Northumberland National Park Biodiversity Action Plan, 2007, p. 8; SSSI: Natural England, 'SSSI units for Kielder Mires' http://www.sssi.naturalengland.org.uk/Special/sssi/unitlist.cfm?sssi_id=2000076 (accessed 15/08/13); Kielder Water and Forest Park, 'Wildlife and Nature' http://www.visitkielder.com/play/discover/wildlife-nature (accessed 15/08/13).

51. Kielder Water and Forest Park, 'Visiting Kielder Water and Forest Park' http://www.visitkielder.com/visit (accessed 18/08/14).

52. Bowles Green Ltd, 'Kielder Wildlife Tourism Study Final Report', January 2010, p. 3.

53. Jill Payne, 'Constructing a "Wild Land" Cultural Heritage for Britain: Water, "Wilderness" and Development in the Highlands of Scotland', in Karen V. Lykke Syse and Terje Oestigaard (eds), *Perceptions of Water in Britain from Early Modern Times to the Present: An Introduction* (Bergen: BRIC Press, 2010), pp. 139–41.

54. Palmer, *The Tyne*, pp. 13–16.

CHAPTER 12

The Kielder Oral History Project: Three Case Studies

Leona Jayne Skelton

Introduction

In October 2012, I undertook an oral history project at Kielder in Northumberland, conducting the interviews at various locations around the village. Kielder, the location of a forestry plantation and artificial lake, was one of the main 'places' in the research project on which this book is based. (See the chapter 'Three Places' elsewhere in this book). The interviewees who participated in the Kielder oral history project, represented a wide and varied cross-section of the local community.[1] These individuals have witnessed successive, deep-seated changes which have taken place in their local environment over several generations, such as planting and expanding the forest, damming the river and creating a tourism infrastructure. The community of Kielder, England's remotest village, has shaped and been shaped by these changes. Planting and expanding the forest, which began in the 1920s and developed intensively after 1945, brought an influx of forestry workers which mechanization halted and then reversed from the 1970s onwards. One interviewee, who moved to Kielder from elsewhere in the North East of England in the 1970s to work in the forest (anonymous C), perhaps took it too far when he remarked: 'everybody's an outsider at Kielder, very few people originate from here because it's a special built village that imported people in.' The construction workers who built the dam in the late 1970s were transient, but the reservoir led to the development of recreational facilities that attracted more people, both to work in the tourism business and simply to live in an environment which they perceive as tranquil, beautiful and even natural. Kielder's past social cohesion has been undermined relatively recently by the decrease in Forestry Commission employment, the Forestry Commission's consequent declining influence in community and social life, and an in-migration of newcomers who are necessarily excluded from the strong sense of forestry history, unified identity and shared memories of what was effectively a Forestry Commission company town with an intense

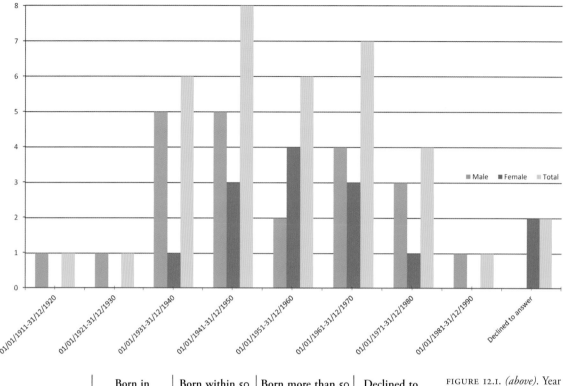

	Born in immediate Kielder area	Born within 50 miles of Kielder	Born more than 50 miles away from Kielder village	Declined to answer
No. of interviewees	9	10	16	1
Percentage	25	28	44	3

FIGURE 12.1. *(above)*. Year of birth and gender.

FIGURE 12.2. *(below)*. Interviewees' birthplaces.

community spirit. There is an unmistakable social dichotomy between the original forestry villagers and the newcomers.[2]

A total of 36 people were interviewed: 22 men and 14 women. They represented a sample of people from different age groups. The oldest was 96 and the youngest was 30. The mean and median ages were both around 61 (Fig. 12.1).

Nine interviewees were born in the immediate area or local maternity hospitals, ten within 50 miles (80.5 km) of Kielder, and 16 further afield (Fig. 12.2). (One declined to answer.) They included 19 long-term residents, *i.e.* those who had lived in the area for more than 20 years, nine relative newcomers, who have lived there for 20 years or less, and eight who have never lived in Kielder, but have worked there or visited regularly for recreational and professional purposes (Fig. 12.3).

Ten of those interviewed were current or retired employees of the Forestry Commission (which caters for tourists as well as managing the forest); four work for Northumbrian Water (which took over the reservoir when the water industry in England and Wales was privatized in 1989, and also runs tourism facilities); four work for the Calvert Trust (which runs activity holidays for

FIGURE 12.3. *(right)*. Length of time interviewees have lived in the area.

FIGURE 12.4. *(below)*. Interviewees' current employment.

	Never lived in the immediate local area	Lived in the immediate local area for 20 years or fewer	Lived in the immediate local area for 21 years or more
No. of interviewees	8	9	19
Percentage	22	25	53

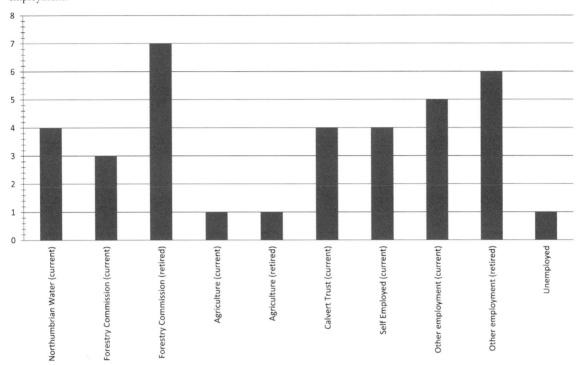

the disabled); two were current or retired farmers, and one works for the Northumberland Wildlife Trust. Three work or worked as teachers. The others mostly work or worked in smaller tourism-based organizations or other services. Five wished to remain anonymous, but gave permission for material from their interviews to be used (Fig. 12.4).

Thus, the subjects were of different ages, from different backgrounds, had different experiences and offered a variety of local perspectives on processes of environmental change. All of the interviews generated a wealth of fascinating insights. This contribution to the book focuses on three individuals' interviews for in-depth analysis.

Case Study A: Billy Steele

Billy Steele was born in 1936 in the neighbouring Scottish border town of Newcastleton, but attended school in Kielder village.[3] He had a varied working life. He maintained a small-holding of over 100 acres (40+ ha) near Kielder, on which he raised 100 breeding ewes and six suckler cows. He also worked for the Forestry Commission, initially as a mechanic in the machinery workshops, repairing wagons and tractors. Then he ploughed the ground with crawler tractors in preparation for planting, before, eventually, he was promoted to Foreman. Billy still lives in Kielder village, where he is enjoying his retirement.

Billy has witnessed dramatic changes in his local landscape and environment over the course of his life, but still feels affection for his physical surroundings. Looking out across the reservoir from The *Boat Inn* at Leaplish Waterside Park, he proudly pointed out 'that you can still see little bits of the railway from here, and whether it goes on to the river or under the lake, up, up past Plashetts there'. Billy remembered the railway, the village of Plashetts and the two coal mines, which were flooded by the reservoir. He recalled that during his childhood, 'most of this was farmland, sheep and cows.' He had witnessed the expansion of the forest, followed by the construction of the dam and subsequent flooding of the valley. His first memory of Kielder is going to Kielder School, the 'very old stone-built school, and just as I started they built another wooden school alongside it, so and the stone one was made into the canteen'. Billy didn't start school until he was six because, as he recalled, 'my father was a shepherd, and I was living at a place called Willowbog which was miles away. And it was thought that I was too young to cycle on my own.'

Billy's memories stretch far back into Kielder's twentieth-century history. But he is also curious about its future, commenting, 'Dunno what the next one'll be like,' by which he meant the next change in Kielder's environment. Perhaps a person such as Billy, who has witnessed successive, dramatic changes in the landscape and environment, has become accustomed to change; indeed, he would not be surprised if there was another dramatic alteration of his environment during his lifetime. Although, initially, he was sceptical about the construction of the dam, he has come to accept it, largely because of the benefits it has brought to the local area. Billy explained:

> well we've got a better access for a start because … I can go back to when … the old C200 road had gates across it and you had to stop and open the gate and so on, so you know, it's nearly a motorway to us now rather than a one track road.

Billy's working life was also peppered with significant changes in both farming and forestry. He recalls living 'in the day when all of the farming work, like making hay, clipping sheep, was all done with the hand, turned the hay with the hand, put it into what we called hay pikes and led it in with a bogey, horse and a bogey'. When Billy began working for the Forestry Commission, trees were still being felled using hand saws, but he noted that 'the machinery (*i.e.* chainsaws) was just coming into its own when I was twenty.' He looked back to the days when the Forestry Commission provided full employment, when Kielder village was home to many more families and its school educated around a hundred pupils. Billy's social and community life has changed dramatically. The improvements to the road enable him to travel to Newcastle relatively quickly to attend football matches 'where it would have been a day's job … in them days'. He recalls being a member of the Kielder Hearts Football Team, but he lamented that it drifted away after a village rugby team was established because there weren't enough men to run two teams. He still organizes a vintage vehicle rally every year in the village, but has noticed a recent decline in village events: 'Sadly, we've got some sad people that's is against all these things and don't want tourism in Kielder and it's a shame because without tourism Kielder can't live. We need … the tourists.' He concluded that community spirit in the village is weaker now than in previous decades. Yet he still feels part of the village community.

Case Study B: Hazel Grimwood

Hazel was born in 1956 at Morpeth, Northumberland, and was brought back to her family's home at Plashetts when she was only two weeks old. Plashetts was flooded after the river was dammed.[4] In Hazel's own words, 'I was just a baby in a drawer, ha ha ha, no cots, just a drawer.' When she was six months old, her family moved to a house in Castle Drive, Kielder, where her father worked as a wood contractor. Later in her childhood, her family moved closer to the school in Kielder, where her father worked as the caretaker. Hazel has positive memories of her childhood in Kielder, where 'we used to have maypole dancing, venison suppers and dances and it was good, that was … cos I was once the May Queen.' Hazel still lives in Kielder, having spent her whole life in the immediate area. She lives with her husband, who works for the Forestry Commission, operating one of the new robotic harvesters, and she works as a Northumbrian Water Housekeeper maintaining the holiday chalets. In her spare time, Hazel enjoys walking her dog, cycling around the dam with her husband and shopping trips to the nearby city of Carlisle.

Although Hazel currently works in the tourism industry, she has numerous and fond memories of her previous employment as a young woman with the Forestry Commission. She recalled working 'out on the hill' where she 'used to have to mark trees ready so they had a count for before … the fellas come in and cut it down' and how 'we used to do a little bit of brashing (*i.e.* removing the lower branches to facilitate felling) and helping out in the castle.' She explained that:

> there used to be two of us, or sometimes three and we used to go about with an axe and we used to take a slither off the tree, y'know a slither of bark, just to count it, and we were classed as markers or tariffers as they're called, I think now.

When asked if this was physically difficult work, Hazel responded, 'No, no, it was quite nice for a woman, y'know, I mean, it sounds daft going about with an axe but we did do.' Hazel's older sister also worked for the Forestry Commission, as did Yvonne Riley, who now runs the village tearoom at Kielder Castle. Hazel sometimes worked at the Working Men's Club, previously situated in Kielder Castle, where she can remember the dam builders drinking after a hard day's work. She recalls 'big machines, clay, [and a] lot of hard spenders in the pub'.

Hazel has the benefit of a lifetime of memories relating to Kielder's dynamically changing landscape. In a similar vein to Billy Steele, Hazel commented on more practical aspects of the changes. She highlighted that the 'roads is better to what they used to be. They used to little twisty, twiney roads, but I mean, it's what y'expect.' When asked if she preferred the landscape before or after the flooding of the valley, she said, 'I think it's better, I think you can see more of it [than] … you could before the reservoir was here.' Reflecting on the changes over the course of her life, she commented on their speed: 'I think it's just like been a slow, a slow change that you just take it in your stride really, all the changes.' Hazel notices the landscape changing when the trees are felled and replanted: 'I've seen it coming down, there seems to be a lot coming down, but they do replant again.' When asked whether the dramatic changes in the landscape have been for the better or the worse, Hazel replied, 'No, I think they've definitely been for the better because it's fetched … work cos I've got work here, and it's fetched tourism as well, which, money, y'know, coming in.' She laments the decline in Forestry Commission jobs: 'the forestry jobs I … thinks nearly zilch (*i.e.* zero)'; but appreciates the new opportunities in tourism brought largely by the reservoir: 'there's always like Calvert Trust takes on people, there's Hawkhirst [*i.e.* the Scout Association Outdoor Centre], which takes on people, here, y'know. There is, there's job opportunities.'

Hazel, who was one of the school governors, was also involved in running a Youth Club, a Badminton Club and a Mothers' and Toddlers' Group at Kielder Community Centre. When asked about her social and community life, Hazel reflected:

> It's a lot quieter now, loads [quieter], at one time you could go to something nearly every night, y'know in the school, in the community centre. There's none of that now, none, and everybody seems to keep theirselves to theirselves and I think there's quite a few holiday homes, which … doesn't do much for village life.

She spends a lot of her time at work and no longer enjoys heavy involvement with village activities and community life. Hazel believes that community spirit has declined, along with the array of community events from which she has benefitted throughout her life: 'Aye that's them days gone by, it's nice. It's good, it was a jolly time … but there's none of that now, all gone.' She believes that community spirit in the village is 'very weak', yet still feels part of the village and 'wouldn't go anywhere else' to live. She finds it 'lovely' to return to Kielder after a busy day out shopping in Carlisle and she is clearly proud of the lesser community spirit which survives, elaborating that 'we're all about the little caring community, we all look out for each other, the older people and things like that.'

Case Study C: Gareth Ramshaw

Gareth Ramshaw was born in Durham in 1982, and grew up in Newcastle-upon-Tyne. He has lived in the Kielder area since 1997.[5] Thus, he is a relative newcomer. He first came to work as an Outdoor Pursuits Instructor at the nearby Scout Association's Hawkhirst Camp, where he lived on site. He now lives in Kielder village with his fiancée and young child and works full-time in the tourism industry, for Northumbrian Water as the Assistant Restaurant Manager at the *Boat Inn*, Leaplish Waterside Park. In his spare time, Gareth enjoys walking his dog in the forest, spending time with his young family and attending village events.

When asked about the changes which have occurred since he moved to Kielder 15 years ago, he focused on the 'new houses in Kielder, [one of] which I was fortunate enough to get'. The partially subsidized construction of several new affordable family homes in the village, a joint venture by Home Housing, the Forestry Commission and Northumbrian Water, was an attempt to retain young families to safeguard the village's future. Gareth is living proof of the scheme's success. He elaborated that 'all six went to young couples that all lived and worked in the area.' He believes:

> you can't find a better place, I don't think, to have a child and raise a child … there's no crime … if there was you'd know about it cos everybody knows everybody and it'll have been sort of round the village quite quickly so and everybody looks out for each other.

Gareth appreciates the environment in which he lives, defining 'nature' as 'everything we're quite fortunate that we're surrounded by' and 'landscape' as 'trees', thus revealing the large extent to which the forest in which he worked as an outdoor instructor has become synonymous with the landscape around him.

Gareth believes that the 'biggest change' he has witnessed in the area since his arrival:

> is when you see them y'know take trees down (*i.e.* fell areas of forest) and things like that, y'know, and it's a bit of a shock, but sometimes it looks quite good … then there's a lot of modern art as well that's been put up.[6]

That Gareth notices the dramatic changes in the landscape as trees are felled and replanted in the working forest reveals his intimate relationship with his environment and his appreciation of how the land is managed. Unsurprisingly, he believes the changes have been for the better and he is passionate about increasing visitor numbers to boost the income generated from tourism. His positive attitude to the reservoir, he admits, is underpinned by the fact that 'without the reservoir, I probably wouldn't be here now.' He is well aware of the scarcity of new employment opportunities in the area, and clearly appreciates his stable, full-time job at the *Boat Inn*.

Gareth was also very upbeat about his current social and community life in Kielder village, which he compares to the far weaker community spirit which he experienced in Newcastle-upon-Tyne rather than to the stronger community spirit that had previously characterized Kielder itself, which he did not witness:

> up here there's more of a community … last year my fiancée gave birth and she was in hospital and I had nigh on [nearly] half the village knock on the door, "is there anything we can do, walking the dog, things like that?", but I know in Newcastle that never happens.

Gareth feels part of the village community and tries to attend village events as much as he can, but he has noted their decline, even in the last 15 years, especially in relation to the once annually-held Kielder Festival, which has ceased. Gareth and his young family provide hope for Kielder's long-term future, yet his story also demonstrates the heavy reliance of that future on the continued success, and expansion, of tourism.

Conclusion

These three selected case studies represent an insightful cross-section of the diverse demographic groups which together form the community currently living in this remotest of English villages. Though some were born in the immediate area, many were born much further afield. Some share long-term memories of working together for the Forestry Commission and of a previously intense and strong community spirit, whereas others arrived much later, drawn to the area to fulfil a desire to live in a landscape that was perceived as tranquil, natural and beautiful. Billy Steele, Hazel Grimwood and Gareth Ramshaw are three vital components of Kielder's history, having arrived at different stages of its eventful story and having witnessed various stages of major environmental change. From farming to forestry, and on to tourism, Kielder has attracted, welcomed and retained a diverse range of inhabitants since its inception in the 1920s. The willingness of these local residents to share their stories and memories will help to ensure that the history of this special place survives to instruct and help shape the identity of the area's future generations.

Notes

1. Oral history has not been widely used by environmental historians in Britain. A notable exception is: Ruth Tittensor, *From Peat Bog to Conifer Forest: An Oral History of Whitelee, its Community and Landscape* (Chichester: Packard, 2009). There has been some use of oral history in environmental history in North America. See, for example: Peter Friederici (ed.), *What Has Passed and What Remains: Oral Histories of Northern Arizona's Changing Landscapes* (Tucson: University of Arizona Press, 2010); 'Ecological Oral Histories', Navigating the Green Road: A Guide to Northern Arizona University's Environmental Resources http://www.greenguide.nau.edu/oral_history.html (accessed 31/01/12); Special Issue: Talking Green: Oral History and Environmental History, *Oral History Forum d'histoire orale* 33 (2013). More typically, however, such oral history research has concentrated on recording the experiences of people who have worked in conservation or forestry over their careers, rather than on attitudes to the environment and environmental change. See, for example: David Todd and David Weisman, *The Texas Legacy Project: Stories of Courage and Conservation* (College Station: Texas A and M University Press, 2010) http://www.texaslegacy.org (accessed 31/01/13).
2. For a study of social relations in the village, see Leona Jayne Skelton, 'The Uncomfortable Path from Forestry to Tourism in Kielder, Northumberland: A Socially Dichotomous Village?', *Oral History* 42/2 (Autumn 2014), pp. 79–89.
3. Interview with Billy Steele, born in Newcastleton, Scotland, 1936, Retired Forestry

Commission Foreman and Smallholder; recorded by Leona Jayne Skelton at the *Boat Inn*, Leaplish Waterside Park, Kielder, 17 October 2012.

4. Interview with Hazel Grimwood, born in Morpeth, Northumberland, 1956, Housekeeper, Northumbrian Water; recorded by Leona Jayne Skelton at the *Boat Inn*, Leaplish Waterside Park, Kielder, 18 October 2012.

5. Interview with Gareth Ramshaw, born in Durham, County Durham, 1982, Assistant Restaurant Manager, Northumbrian Water; recorded by Leona Jayne Skelton at the *Boat Inn*, Leaplish Waterside Park, Kielder, 17 October 2012.

6. On the art works, see 'Three Places' above, pp. 17–30.

CHAPTER 13

Wild Britannia: Environmental History, Wildlife Television and New Publics in Britain

Robert A. Lambert

Writing in 1948 in *The New Naturalist*, alongside some of the heavyweights of British natural history, L. C. Lloyd penned 'Naturalists on Air', in which he bemoaned the fact that just 0.4% of BBC Radio programming was devoted to nature: about four hours per month. Noting the popularity of *Country Questions* and *Nature Parliament* and the wild soundscapes of Ludwig Koch, Lloyd suggested that few BBC officials were naturalists, and that the corporation seemed to think that natural history needed to be 'dressed up' to appeal to the ordinary listener. Part of the problem, he believed, was a dearth of good natural wildlife presenters, people able to blend 'friendliness and authority', suggesting that the radio landscape was bedevilled by 'those who know, but can't broadcast, and those who can broadcast, but don't know'. It was a stinging indictment of talent, but Lloyd did see a way forward, using that great polymath, James Fisher, as an example: a broadcaster and naturalist who was able to conjure up a 'sound mosaic of description, explanation, personal experience and the sounds of nature', to convey a picture which had both 'clarity and coherence'. Lloyd also anticipated what was, in part, to come to fruition in our domestic and global wildlife diet in the later twentieth century, namely, 'the natural history of various characteristic regions or species, presented from the ecological point of view.'[1] We would do well to remember that these words were drafted a decade before the BBC established its influential Natural History Unit (NHU) in Bristol in 1957, founded on the success of pioneering radio endeavours and live outside television broadcasts, such as that from Slimbridge Wildfowl Trust in 1953 (which evolved into the largely studio-based series, *Look*, hosted by Peter Scott in 1955), and longer running radio series on the Home Service like *The Naturalist*; and before the arrival of colour television in 1967 on BBC2.[2]

Although wildlife television in Britain began with the local, much of the output across the later twentieth century, especially from the BBC NHU, was big, co-produced, blue-chip global wildlife series, many of which are hugely profitable when sold on internationally by the commercial wing of the corporation.[3] This has been driven by the fact that the BBC has a duty to the licence payer to get value for money, and the greatest amount of value on screen, and because TV producers liked going abroad! British TV audiences were being captivated, if not overwhelmed, by distant ecosystems and charismatic megafauna that few would ever see in the flesh, despite an emerging eco-tourism industry growing in the 1980s on the back of the so-called 'Attenborough-effect'. Where Sir David went, the tourist followed. Some domestic series were produced about Britain, most notably by Peter Crawford – *The Living Isles* (1986) and *Living Britain* (1999) – but they were often overshadowed by the global landmark series.

According to former BBC NHU producer, Stephen Moss, what changed all that, and re-invigorated the local places/local species British angle was the emergence of the *Springwatch* brand from 2005 onwards, which from the outset sought to be interactive via social media, the 'red button' and webcams, to challenge people to go out and see for themselves, and was often linked to domestic, BBC-led campaigns such as 'Make Space for Nature' (2004), 'Breathing Spaces/Places' (2005–10) and 'Summer of Wildlife' (2013), that urged us to do something to protect nature on our doorstep in the local places we cherish. Moss also maintains that the enduring public popularity of Bill Oddie as a presenter, communicator and 'national institution' has done much to re-assert the value of *our* wildlife and *our* wild places against the blockbuster tide of 'blue' and 'frozen' planets. In the public's eye, Oddie seems to capture the very essence of what a British naturalist should be; an amateur tradition that goes back to Gilbert White in eighteenth-century Selborne.[4] Successful, Oddie-inspired precursors to *Springwatch* were *A Bird in the Nest* (1994), *Wild in Your Garden* (2003), *Birding with Bill Oddie* (1997–2000) and *Britain Goes Wild with Bill Oddie* (2004). The RSPB had set up its own in-house film unit in 1953, with a premiere of *Birds of Britain* being shown in 1956 at the Royal Festival Hall in London; RSPB's most popular film *Osprey* (1979) was seen by 5.7 million, with total person-viewings for all films up to 1988 at 91.75 million in Britain.[5] Many RSPB films were shot on their local nature reserves and focused on specific habitats or individual species.

British ospreys, for example, alongside other returned or 'restored' birds of prey, enjoy a long tradition of media interaction.[6] In 1959 Bob Wade of BBC Radio broadcast live from the Loch Garten nest in Scotland; and with birder and BBC newsreader, Robert Dougall, as President of the RSPB (1970–75) osprey family updates from Loch Garten were a regular feature of summer broadcasts on the evening TV news, which directly brought the cause of nature conservation into living rooms across the country.[7] In 1960 the RSPB awarded their Silver Medal to Desmond Hawkins and the BBC NHU, for 'putting the RSPB on the television map'.[8] British ecologist Frank Fraser Darling, much

influenced by history, delivered the prestigious BBC Reith Lectures in 1969.[9]
Birds, the most visible and accessible aspect of our natural heritage, remain a
potent subject for the British.[10]

Is it possible to estimate the size of the British domestic wildlife family that
environmental history could potentially reach out to in various media formats?
How valuable are the industries associated with it? The current (2013) official
NGO membership figures are impressive; the RSPB has 1.159 million members,
the 47 county Wildlife Trusts have 800,000 members and the Wildfowl and
Wetlands Trust have 206,000 members. But the National Trust dwarfs them
all with 3.7 million members. These figures can be misleading though, as there
is much cross-over, with many (especially middle class folk) being members of
a number of local and national conservation bodies, and often for a variety of
environmental and socio-economic reasons. The doyen of British ornithology,
Ian Wallace, estimated the total British market for bird holidays to be around
£9.5 million to £11 million *per annum*; he valued the entire British birdwatching
sector to be worth around £300 million.[11] Around 25,000 people gather in a
field next to an inland sea in Rutland every August to attend Birdfair ('the
birders' Glastonbury') to connect with people and place, thus raising over
£3 million in direct funding for conservation projects in 25 years.[12] A BBC
audience survey reported in *Natural World* (the magazine of the Wildlife
Trusts) that 30 million of us Brits were engaged somehow somewhere in our
lives with British nature.[13] It refined the findings as follows; that 2 million of
us were the mad keen enthusiasts, the hardcore birders, mammal watchers,
lepidopterists and botanists; but that the other 28 million were a great swathe of
society, unaffiliated and untapped in many ways, but fascinated and connected
with nature and wild places. In part, they are if you like, the *Springwatch* and
Autumnwatch millions, that feed the garden birds, go fox- and badger- and seal-
watching as families, take a walk in the park or on a beach and like to know
that nature is out there doing well.[14]

However, there is a paradox here that Stephen Moss captures: 'sure,
millions of Brits love and cherish nature, but nature is fucked … so how did
we allow this?' This blunt question from a TV producer is fertile ground for
environmental historians to engage with, to give the socio-cultural, economic
and political context to landscape and species change in Britain. And it was
these deeply inter-connected themes that Moss and I explored in the TV series
Birds Britannia, which was, in essence, an environmental history of birds and
people in Britain that consciously sought to appeal to both the established
nature and history-hungry TV audiences, initially on BBC4, then on BBC2.[15]
In that vein, I delivered a piece to camera on red kite history for *Britain's
Big Wildlife Revival* (2013) on BBC1, a series that sought to reinforce public
awareness of the changing plight of certain species, each championed by a
presenter who met with passionate devotees of the animal. Out of necessity,
this series reflected on change over time. The first episode was watched by 2.7
million people.[16]

My own experiences of working in television and radio (with BBC or indies) have been overwhelmingly positive (however clunky and frustrating the process can often be). They have, in part, been founded on established networks and contacts that I already had in the wider British wildlife constituency, and from a long-standing personal desire to reach out beyond the classroom to broader public audiences, be they in living rooms or in village halls or on expedition ships around the British coast. There is an evangelical preacher in me that wants to enthuse the British public with an appreciation of the wonderful biodiversity and ecosystems that we have in Britain (a quality that I also see in many of the wildlife TV producers and presenters that I work with), and then connect them to the NGOs that battle to protect that heritage. But I also need to be wary of that, as it can be perceived as campaigning and un-academic. Television is a fickle, capricious, artificial and blunt instrument, that millions watch, yes, but what are their lasting memories of it? This is a question that all Series Producers and documentary-makers wrestle with. Quite often a finely crafted radio documentary can have far more of a lasting impact. TV does now live on far longer, however, due to its presence on the internet through catch-up and BBC iPlayer, allowing publics to connect at all times (making the unmissable truly unmissable).

At its heart, television is anecdotal and impressionistic, and driven by established celebrity figures. This is why TV gardener Alan Titchmarsh presented and wrote the accompanying books to two landmark domestic series *British Isles: a natural history* and *Nature of Britain*, and David Dimbleby presented *A Picture of Britain* about art, British landscape and identity.[17] However, I have learnt not to treat all television as the same; after all, a 5-minute natural history segment on *The One Show* is very different to a four-part series on BBC2 or a one-hour documentary on BBC4: our publics watch different things at different times. Intellectually, TV history is very different to academic history. It does need to be as rigorous and as scholarly as it can be (and we as environmental historians should demand that ambition, despite the fact that contributors ultimately have very little power over how a programme is edited). But it does work on a far narrower canvas. Executive/Series Producers love an anniversary, quirky stories, anecdotal evidence, eye-witnesses to events, connections and memories, experts and a sort of 'you thought this, but actually this is what happened' ethos that captures audience attentions, however briefly. Television tends to prefer 'things' and events over broad concepts, and it prefers the thematic to the chronological. Much of good TV and radio is actually about telling entertaining stories, and the art of 'storytelling' has fallen out of favour in academic circles, much I think to our loss and to the way we communicate to wider publics.

Besides, the division between traditional TV presenters, camera operators and contributors is far more blurred now that at any time, and this opens up the medium to visionary and skilled academics in disciplines that TV producers want, to take onscreen roles that combine presenting and communicating with established expertise and scholarly script writing or consultancy.[18] My monograph *Contested Mountains* (2001) was born again when it was picked up by BBC Scotland and used as the core text by directors/producers shaping *The Land* programme for *Making Scotland's Landscape* (2010), a series that also featured Scottish environmental historian Chris Smout. And once you're in, you're in. When we sell environmental history ideas to the media (and we can and must do), we need to do it sensibly; we need a story to tell, an angle to take, and we need to understand that our public audiences do not want overwhelmingly doom and gloom stories from our environmental past, a catalogue of one disaster and loss after another. Rather, they accept being taken to the precipice, but then wish to be told that at the eleventh hour, we turned it all around into a positive story or a species comeback; in other words, 'the more we lost, the more we fought to save.' Additionally, wildlife TV producers that I know at the BBC NHU consciously shy away from using the word 'environment' as they feel it puts mass audiences off, preferring instead softer and more publicly digestible words such as 'nature' or 'wildlife'. Similarly, the word 'sustainability' is not yet, and may never be, embedded into the wildlife TV landscape, again because the assumption is from the programme makers that the public do not understand it or connect with it. These are the constraints.

There are, of course, other publics that we can talk to beyond the televisual world. National and local radio, in many ways, is far more suited to the one-off environmental history documentary linked to research project findings. We are often guilty of under-estimating the power of factual radio in reaching wide and new audiences.[19] But I would like to champion other routes to new publics, where I suggest environmental historians will find fertile outreach ground. In 2013, Stephen Moss and I teamed up with Aigas Field Centre near Beauly in Scotland to run a residential 'Wild Histories' course that blended morning environmental history presentations with afternoon field trips out to see iconic Highland wildlife. It worked well and, although commercial in nature, drew in new audiences to our discipline and was rounded off with a well-attended public lecture open to folk from local villages.

Similarly, Moss and I have delivered environmental history (Nature-People themed) talks, using TV clips from our series, directly to places and to audiences that we felt would most connect with them, where they have the most physical relevance, be that at Birdfair, village halls (including my own), town naturalist clubs, staff seminars at NGO headquarters, or accommodation providers such as the Grant Arms Hotel in Grantown-upon-Spey with its pioneering in-house Birdwatching and Wildlife Club (BWWC) open to both residents and locals. At these venues the new publics range from 40 to 400. Environmental historians with ambitions to reach out and connect with new publics can do so in field centres around the UK, at nature reserve visitor centres, at NGO AGMs, in popular membership magazines (note that RSPB *Birds*, now renamed *Nature's Home,* has a readership of 1.2 million), and via the expanding British expedition ship cruising industry (where audiences, I find, are both captive and thirsty for information) and expedition staff teams often feature an historian used to illuminate destinations. Anyone for an environmental history of British islands of the west, in light of the success of the TV series *Hebrides: Islands on the Edge* (2013), which is now being cleverly deployed by VisitScotland as a tourism marketing tool?

Half a century ago, in the early years of television, in *The Second BBC Naturalist* essay collection, the author, editor and radio producer, Desmond Hawkins, mused on how 'nowadays we are all armchair travellers'; adding that:

> at the flick of a switch we can join Armand and Michaela Denis in Africa, or dive beneath the Indian Ocean with Hans and Lotte Haas, or follow in the footsteps of Darwin with Peter Scott and visit remote Galapagos Islands, and on our return to the South American mainland find David Attenborough waiting there to show us new marvels.

The presenters may have changed (bar one) and the fad for married couples gone, but the Hawkins sentiment that 'against the problems and difficulties of our time we must set this wonderful gift of conjuring up the riches of the whole natural world for our enjoyment' remains as valid today in our frantic sound-bite digital age.[20] In the end, television is about entertainment first and foremost, then education and a dose of escapism, themes that Hawkins identified in the very year of the founding of the BBC NHU, in his preface to *The BBC Naturalist*:

> the truth seems to be that very many people, with no specialist knowledge and no undue solemnity in their make-up, find a relief from everyday cares and anxieties in the contemplation of the natural wildlife of the world. The more our human-made perplexities torment and frighten us, the more we seem to find peace and refreshment in looking steadily at the permanent conditions of life and in trying to understand a little more clearly the rules and patterns of animal existence.[21]

Environmental history sheds light on those changing patterns.

Notes

1. James Fisher (ed.), *The New Naturalist: A Journal of British Natural History* (London: Collins, 1948), pp. 214–16.
2. Elspeth Huxley, *Peter Scott: Painter and Naturalist* (London: Faber & Faber, 1993).
3. Michael Bright, *100 Years of Wildlife* (London: BBC Books, 2007); David Attenborough, *Life on Air: Memoirs of a Broadcaster* (London: BBC Books, 2002); Christopher Parsons, *True to Nature: 25 Years of Filming with the BBC Natural History Unit* (Cambridge: Patrick Stephens, 1982); Jeanette Steemers, *Selling Television: British Television in the Global Marketplace* (London: BFI, 2004).
4. Michael Wood, *Gilbert White: The Nature Man*, A Maya Vision International Production (1x60 minutes documentary for BBC4, 2006); Richard Mabey, *Gilbert White: A Biography* (London: Dent, 1986).
5. John Aitchison and A. Blackwell, *The History of the Use of Film and Video by RSPB Film Unit* (Sandy: RSPB, 1988).
6. John A. Love, *A Saga of Sea Eagles* (Dunbeath: Whittles, 2013); Roy Dennis, *A Life of Ospreys* (Dunbeath: Whittles, 2008); Ian Carter, *The Red Kite* (Chelmsford: Arlequin

Press, 2001); Roger Lovegrove, *The Kite's Tale: The Story of the Red Kite in Wales* (Sandy: RSPB, 1990); Philip Brown, *The Scottish Ospreys: From Extinction to Survival* (London: Heinemann, 1979).

7. Robert Dougall, *In and Out of the Box* (Glasgow: Fontana, 1975); Robert Dougall, *A Celebration of Birds* (London: Collins & Harvill, 1978).

8. Robert A. Lambert, *Contested Mountains: Nature, Development and Environment in the Cairngorms Region of Scotland, 1880–1980* (Cambridge: White Horse Press, 2001), p. 83.

9. Frank Fraser Darling, *Wilderness and Plenty: The Reith Lectures 1969* (London: Ballantine, 1970).

10. Mark Cocker and David Tipling, *Birds and People* (London: Jonathan Cape, 2013); Mark Cocker and Richard Mabey, *Birds Britannica* (London: Chatto & Windus, 2005); Stephen Moss, *A Bird in the Bush: A Social History of Birdwatching* (London: Aurum Press, 2004).

11. D. I. M. Wallace, *Beguiled by Birds: Ian Wallace on British Birdwatching* (London: Christopher Helm, 2004), p. 219.

12. Lucy McRobert, 'Once upon a time in a field in Rutland', *Birdwatching* (August, 2013), p. 29.

13. J. Rollins, 'It's official: half the UK loves wildlife', *Natural World* (Spring, 2006), p. 31.

14. Robert A. Lambert, 'Strangers in a Familiar Land: The Return of the Native 'Aliens' and the (Re) Wilding of Britain's Skies, 1850–2010', in Ian D. Rotherham and Robert A. Lambert (eds), *Invasive and Introduced Plants and Animals: Human Perceptions, Attitudes and Approaches to Management* (London: Earthscan, 2011), pp. 169–83, at p. 176.

15. BBC, *Birds Britannia*, 4 × 60 minutes, Series Producer Stephen Moss, BBC NHU, for BBC4 and BBC2 (2010); Stephen Moss, *Birds Britannia: How the British Fell in Love with Birds* (London: Collins, 2011).

16. Stephen Moss, personal comment.

17. Alan Titchmarsh, *British Isles: A Natural History* (London: BBC Books, 2004); A. Titchmarsh, *Nature of Britain* (London: BBC Books, 2007); David Dimbleby, *A Picture of Britain: An Inspirational Journey through Art, Landscape and Identity*, BBC/Tate Series, six episodes for BBC1 (2005).

18. James Gray, *Snarl for the Camera: Tales of a Wildlife Cameraman* (London: Piatkus, 2002); David Hughes, *Himself and Other Animals: A Portrait of Gerald Durrell* (London: Pimlico, 1997); Derek Jones, *Microphones and Muddy Boots: A Journey into Natural History Broadcasting* (Newton Abbot: David & Charles, 1987); Percy Edwards, *The Road I Travelled* (London: Arthur Baker, 1979).

19. David Attenborough, *Life Stories* (London: Collins, 2009); David Attenborough, *New Life Stories* (London: Collins, 2011). See also the huge unexpected success of 'Tweet of the Day' on BBC Radio 4 in 2013.

20. Desmond Hawkins (ed.), *The Second BBC Naturalist* (London: Adprint, 1960), p. 7.

21. Desmond Hawkins (ed.), *The BBC Naturalist* (London: Rathbone Books, 1957), pp. 7–8.

Art Inserts

CHAPTER 14

John Clare, Drainage and Printmaking

Carry Akroyd

Mostly, when printmaking and painting, I am just thinking with colour and composition, but I like it best when an idea for an image has my main fascinations woven into it. These interests are fairly wide-ranging, but the contemporary landscape, wildlife, literature and history are the main threads.

There is a Romantic convention that I am fairly allergic to, of the writer as hero, striding out into the almost unexplored wilderness to sleep under the stars for a profound experience of a specific place, with a garnish of revelatory communion with a certain poet who has trod that way before. Just at that intense moment of connecting through time and space, this character I'm sure hears his mobile phone ring, or pauses to text a pal, check his tweets and worry about charging his gadget. The usual custom is to edit out the modern mundanities of motorways and mini-marts as being no part of the sensational enactment.

With no Romantic inclination or credentials I have nevertheless tried to tread where John Clare trod. John Clare almost disappeared from our literary canon but now has been deservedly brought back, and for chronological simplicity levered into the Romantics grouping with Wordsworth and Coleridge, Keats and Shelley. But there is no grandeur or loftiness about Clare, he just walked from his doorstep to the fields and found his poems 'kicked out of the clods'. And it is almost impossible to tread where he trod, the landscape has changed so dramatically.

Areas of Outstanding Natural Beauty and National Parks followed Wordsworth and Coleridge like confetti, landscapes pickled and preserved despite now lacking the industrial and agricultural basis that first caused those human interventions on the geography. Keats' house can be visited in Hampstead, and his and Shelley's graves in Rome, but they are less attached to place. Keats' places are more imagined, Shelley's more about ideas, whereas Clare was very firmly rooted in his parish, but to go there and try to see it all through his eyes demands an excursion into landscape history.

It is very hard to counter the grip of the Romantic vision. Images that have been given a stamp of approval endure to the extent that they funnel what we see. It is almost as if, as long as there are Areas of Outstanding Natural Beauty marked on the map, then other areas are deemed to have nothing of note and small beauties can be eradicated with impunity. Clare watched this happening under his nose, and two hundred years later I watched the same thing.

There are four principal causes for how the landscape has transformed in 'Clare Country' – the edge of the fens between Peterborough and Stamford. As a young man Clare witnessed the height of the Parliamentary Enclosure movement; in his county of Northamptonshire the intensity of the enclosure acts was such that no common land of any sort remains. The effects, as Clare saw, were not only the rooting up of trees and the ploughing of commons, but a complete reorganization of social order and employment. From that time general access to the landscape was curtailed, reduced to a few paths and roads, the 'rights of way' that we now know. To go to some of his favourite places Clare became a trespasser.

Another alteration to his landscape that Clare witnessed in the planning was the coming of the railway. One day, while visiting his favourite orchid meadow, he found men there pegging out the possible route of the London to Edinburgh line. Like today's motorways, the railway bisects the locality, creating a dividing barrier equal to a river; but, unlike a river, both rail and road transgress customary boundaries, slicing across lanes and paths, sometimes closing them up entirely.

Drainage of the fens created human-made water barriers, in the numerous drains and lodes. Routes that were raised causeways through the marshy land in Clare's time are now roads between intensive arable agriculture. The farmland in the immediate vicinity of his village would be unrecognisable to him.

Any vestigial reminders of former farming practices now have been removed essentially by the intensification of agriculture since the 1980s. The oil age asserts itself in a variety of powerful machines and oil-derived fertilisers and plastics. The flowering meadows that made hay for the former horsepower are dispensed with, either by the plough or through fertilisers and weedicides. The botany that Clare loved is despatched to forgotten history, a mystery to urban dwellers and rural commuters alike. His common flowers can only be seen in nature reserves, requiring a trip out in the car.

Thus a dilemma arises for my printmaking. I am interested in the botany and its attendant insects. I like the birds that prefer the boggy land. But if these things have been removed from the ordinary countryside around where I live, and I have to travel to a nature reserve to see them, when I then make them part of my imagery am I avoiding the truth and telling a lie about the landscape I live in, not recording it as it truly is? Is the idea more important than the fact? Or is imagining nature of equal value to scientific knowledge? Clare doubted that Keats was really listening to a nightingale; he thought it was probably a blackbird. For Clare, accuracy and truth are his essence, and Romantic embroidery exalting his experience would be an anathema. Clare is too close to the mud to quest after the sublime, and too astonished by the miraculous

FIGURE 14.1. *Black Fields* (acrylic). Before raising the water levels: the rich black peat of the arable fenland.

complexity of nature to replace his response to it with just imagination. His observations make him an early ecologist or natural scientist, but expressed with an astonishingly visual and precise and joyful language.

So I sometimes wonder what Clare would write about if he were here now. If he wrote about windmills then, wouldn't he write about turbines now? Is the equivalent of his poem about an old milking shed a nostalgic and affectionate glance at the rusting corrugated iron of an abandoned Dutch barn? He would have to write about the excavators keeping the drains clear, the commuters, the tourists and the traffic, all as part of rural life. So I am constantly being reminded of my own unconscious editing, a failure to be true in the mixed-up mess of the contemporary landscape.

One route is to look at the borderlands between reserves and the 'real' world of agribusiness. I watch where wildlife survives in the margins between arable monocultures. I go for walks with Clare's poetry. Visit places like Wicken that evoke something of the former wet fens he would have known. I try to find the sense of a place by attempting to see and understand the variety of things going on in it, past and present.

FIGURE 14.2 *(right)*. *Holme Engine Drain, Whittlesey* (screenprint). Wheat and potatoes grow where once was the second largest lake in England. Drained, Holme Fen sank to become the lowest place in England, 3 m below sea level. As part of the Great Fen Project, the water level is being allowed to rise, and reedbeds and meres restored.

FIGURE 14.3 *(below)*. *Woodwalton Fen Entire* (acrylic). Painted just before adjacent fields were obtained by the Great Fen Project, this preserved shred of wetland is an island oasis of diversity in a desert of monocultures.

Opposite:

Above: FIGURE 14.5.
Fenscape (screenprint).
Visiting winter swans
feed in arable fields.

Below: FIGURE 14.6.
Swifts and Drain
(screenprint). The drain
divides the reserve
reedbed from crops.

FIGURE 14.4. *Cuckoo* (screenprint). The sedge field and lode at Wicken Fen where cuckoos still breed and parasitize the many reed warbler nests along the dykes and drains. Another example of a tiny patch of preserved wet fen now being expanded by restoration projects.

FIGURE 14.7. *A Fen
Field Full of Swans*
(screenprint). The visiting
winter swans, from
Iceland and Siberia,
roost on Ouse and Nene
washes, where embanked
flood meadows hold
excess water to preserve
surrounding arable land.
Thus uncultivated, these
fields become damp
summer grazing meadows
full of birds and flowers.
By day the swans move
about feeding in the
arable fields.

FIGURE 14.8.
Navigation, Nene Washes
(screenprint). The
whooper swans arrived
overnight from Iceland
without the use of the
Sat Nav employed in the
distant traffic jam on the
A47.

FIGURE 14.9. *Morton's Leam* (acrylic). An early drain and bank from the sixteenth century bounding the washes to the south, while the canalized and embanked River Nene defines the northern side. Birds enjoying the grazing land. Since this was painted, formerly extinct corncrakes have been reintroduced and are now breeding.

CHAPTER 15

Landscape and the Artist in Twenty-First Century Britain

Jenny Graham

Introduction

How should a visual artist in the twenty-first century respond to the British landscape? To be a landscape artist in the twenty-first century is to follow in a long tradition from the luminescent paintings of William Turner to the California-bright Yorkshire paintings and digital prints of David Hockney. But how does each artist fit into that tradition and how does he or she attempt to re-see and reinterpret repeating themes of beauty, structure and change? One way might be for the artist to look for 'new ways of seeing' and new ways of understanding and describing the natural world, to embrace contemporary techniques which can give him or her the means of describing the landscape in new and exciting ways. It has also become increasingly popular for the artist to explore the possibilities of collaborating with the scientific and academic community to come to an integrated truth about the world around us.[1]

By considering the influences of weather, geography, history and location, the artist brings to the interpretation of the natural world an understanding of the forces, both natural and human, which have shaped it. A hawthorn tree that grows on a windy coastline will be very different from one in the heart of a Quantock combe or one wedged in a small block of land on a city roundabout. In this way, science, sociology and art can be linked. All are searching by studying the specific to understand the whole, and by studying the whole to understand the specific.

Processes

To describe a particular place at a particular time while at the same time giving the viewer a sense of the iconography of place is a daunting task. As a painter, I have always created my work by either working on-site or interpreting sketches made on-site. I have worked on a number of photographic projects, but always felt that some form of creative response was missing. My photographs were not what I saw, but what the camera saw, not what I had felt, but what the camera had *not* felt. When I discovered photo-etching a couple of years ago I realized that I had discovered a technique which allowed me to explore the visual complexities of landscape in an accurate, and yet far more interpretative way.

Photo-etching, and more recently digital printmaking, has allowed me to look more carefully at texture, structure of growth patterns and the intricacy of landscape in ways that I was previously unable to capture in either paint or film. The traditional process of etching was first used by the German artist Daniel Hopfer in the fifteenth century, initially to decorate metal armour, subsequently to make pictures, though it is thought that the process may date back to ancient times. This medium, with its rich inks and embossed line and plate mark, lends an aesthetic gravity to the most simple of motifs.

Recently, I have been involved in a project responding to British woodland. Woodlands are difficult to paint, being cluttered, confusing places with lines crossing and intersecting in all directions. It is hard to simplify them and even harder not to resort to some sort of Victorian stereotype. My aim is to use the graphic and aesthetic potential of woodland to make work which asks the viewer to look more closely at the varieties of shape, colour and texture of these unique environments. By using contemporary media and working with these elements, I hope to bring a slightly different way of looking at the landscape which incorporates both the romanticism of the past and the technical precision of the twenty-first century. My inspiration has ranged from the mixed deciduous woodlands of Somerset to the ancient yew forests of West Sussex. (An exhibition of both the photo-etchings and digital work was held at Spike Island, Bristol, in November 2012.)

Photo-etchings are created using an aluminium plate onto which a light sensitive film has been placed. The plate is exposed to ultraviolet light for a few minutes using a photographic transparency which has been translated using the Adobe Photoshop programme into a black and white image using a variety of digital techniques. The image can be changed in a number of ways: contrast altered; details added or deleted; and the image translated into something resembling a pen and ink drawing. After exposure, the plate is washed in a soda and warm water solution to reveal the image, dried with heat and hardened with vinegar. The plate is then etched in a solution of copper sulphate, salt and warm water until the required depth of etch is achieved. Any residual photographic film is washed away using a weak solution of potassium hydroxide. The plate is printed in exactly the same way as a normal etching, coated with etching ink, then the excess ink wiped away, leaving the etched lines and tones to retain the ink. The plate is printed under pressure onto damp paper through an etching press.

Digital prints

Since the advent of graphic programs such as Adobe Photoshop, the possibilities of manipulating photographic images seem to have become never ending. Using

FIGURE 15.1. *Woodland Flight* (photo-etching).

simple techniques, it is possible to transform a relatively ordinary photograph into something much more interesting. This ease of use makes it even more challenging to create a striking image. The idea that anyone with a smart phone can become an artist/photographer has challenged the practicing artist to look for more and more ways to use the technology adventurously and yet with more care.

Conclusion

The world of the visual artist often seems to be ruled by a system more of luck than judgement. After weeks or months of desperate questioning, ideas spring into being unbeckoned. Something is going on in regions of the creative brain that cannot ever be accurately understood or described. A successful image is always greater than the sum of its parts, and that 'eureka' moment is followed by a feeling of exhilaration that must come to all those involved in research in their chosen fields. There is so much potential in these new media, so much possibility for collaboration, that this woodland project seems only the beginning.

Note

1. During a post-prandial session at the Quantock workshop (March 2011), Jenny Graham displayed artwork relevant to the location and gave a talk on 'Painting the Quantock Hills: Images of the Quantock Hills and surrounding countryside'. Her studio is part of the Spring Farm Arts collective at Spring Farm, Moorlinch, the site of a former vineyard on the edge of the Somerset Levels: www.jennygraham.co.uk (accessed 25/10/14).

FIGURE 15.2 *(above). Tree on the Gower Peninsula.*

FIGURE 15.3 *(below). Woodland Clearing, Coombe Woods, Somerset.*

FIGURE 15.4. *Pale Trees, Hampshire* (original photograph and photo-etching).

FIGURE 15.7. *Farm Gate* (oil on canvas).

Opposite:

Above: FIGURE 15.5.
Treeline.

Below: FIGURE 15.6.
Woodland Edge (digital
print).

FIGURE 15.8. *Quantock Spring* (oil on canvas).

FIGURE 15.9. *Towards Wales* (oil on canvas).

CHAPTER 16

Kielder: A Planned Wilderness

Peter Sharpe

There is little of England that can be said to have been purely created by nature. Perhaps the rockier of our coastlines might count, but almost all of our great variety of landscapes has been moulded by human intervention to a greater or lesser extent. While this has usually happened gradually over periods measured in centuries, at Kielder in Northumberland, an entire alternative rural landscape covering 250 square miles (*c.*647 square km) has been 'created' on an industrial scale within a single person's lifespan.

In recent years the area has been developed as a visitor destination – 'Kielder Water and Forest Park' – with tourism growing to counter a decline in job opportunities associated with farming and forestry. Tourism operators at Kielder are using a number of ways to attract people to visit the area such as walking, cycling, fishing and 'ecological tourism', for example, osprey and bat watches, fungal forays and astronomy, with the designation of the area as an internationally recognized Dark Sky Park.

Kielder Art and Architecture programme sits within these public-facing programmes offering artists and architects opportunities to make new work that responds to the environment, and offers visitors and local communities alternative ways to think about and experience this unique place.

Visitors more used to urban and suburban landscapes (more than half the population now) often say they feel disoriented by the scale of the place, the lack of familiar markers, the notion of 'wilderness', the sense they might get lost or encounter some unknown and possibly dangerous creature beyond the visitor centre's strimmed grass edges.

Artists and architects have responded to the challenge of making work for this spacious and sometimes harsh landscape in many different ways, and their efforts are often used as orientation and vantage points as well as being experienced for their creative content. While James Turrell's *Skyspace* seeks to capture the essence of the Northumbrian light, Ryder Architects' *Janus Chairs* provide an adaptable social space on a remote promontory and SIMPARCH's *Silvas Capitalis* references the valley's ancient history and its relatively recent incarnation as forest and lake, while encouraging visitors to ponder on what this landscape might look like in another 500 years or more.

There is much material to draw upon in an environment that has a rich history, extremes of weather and unique communities: at least three within the Park (Stonehaugh, Kielder village and Byrness) were created from scratch 60 years ago by the Forestry Commission. Further, the mixture of operational and recreational usage of the landscape – the fact that this is a manufactured and effectively industrial rural landscape – sits at odds with how many people would prefer to experience and describe the place from the view point of a tourism destination. These differing perspectives are one of the main things that makes Kielder interesting for artists and architects to create installations for.

However, it is easy to forget that this is a place that, despite the perception of Kielder as a vast wilderness in the eyes of most visitors from within the UK, has been and continues to be planned more comprehensively, in finer detail and further into the future than most urban and suburban environments.

Examples of art and architecture at Kielder[1]

Wave Chamber

Chris Drury, 1996
(Fig. 16.1)
Wave Chamber is a camera obscura, projecting an image of the water onto the floor of a small stone structure. Within the dark interior, the walls echo the wave sounds and the floor appears to become liquid. The building takes the form of a dry stone beehive on the shoreline with a small door to allow access. Although the interior initially appears very dark, as your eyes adjust to the low light level, a moving image of waves on the lake appears on the floor as if by magic.

FIGURE 16.1. *Wave Chamber.*

FIGURE 16.2. *Cat Cairn: The Kielder Skyspace.*

Cat Cairn: The Kielder Skyspace

James Turrell, 2000
(Fig. 16.2)
Cat Cairn: The Kielder Skyspace is a sculptural artwork located on a rocky outcrop overlooking Kielder Water and Forest Park created by internationally renowned American artist James Turrell. The artwork consists of a partially buried circular room, a ceiling containing a central circular oculus or opening, and a ring of seats forming the lower part of the inner wall. At dawn and dusk lighting illuminates the interior and creates unexpected experiences of tone and colour.

Mapping

FIGURE 16.3. *Mapping.*

Wolfgang Weileder, 2006
(Fig. 16.3)
The artist developed *Mapping* from old and new maps of Kielder, creating fairways and obstacles from these maps with holes and start points that refer to past and present locations within the valley spread out over the course on a number of levels. Another of the concepts within this work was that there would be no defined 'start' or 'end' points. Players have to choose their own way through, negotiating their passage with other users as they progress.

Silvas Capitalis

SIMPARCH, 2009
(Fig. 16.4)
Silvas Capitalis (a play on the Latin for 'forest head') is a giant timber head located along the Lakeside Way created by American artists' collective SIMPARCH. The head has been conceived as a watcher, an imagined presence who has observed the passing occupation of the landscape over past millennia and how the environment has dramatically changed during the last one hundred years with the coming of the forest and more recently the lake.

Visitors to the head who enter through the mouth and climb upstairs to look out of its eyes literally get inside its head.

FIGURE 16.4. *Silvas Capitalis.*

FIGURE 16.5. *Janus Chairs.*

Janus Chairs

Ryder Architecture, 2009
(Fig. 16.5)
Janus Chairs are three large rotating seats that offer seating, shelter and a view of the open expanse of Kielder Water. Based on the idea of flower petals in different stages of unfolding, the seats can be arranged to face each other, face the sun or the desired view, or turn their backs to inclement weather.

Salmon Cubes

Xsite Architecture, 2009
(Fig. 16.6)
Salmon Cubes are a series of sculptures that reflect on the amazing life cycle of the Atlantic salmon that live in the river Tyne. The four *Salmon Cubes* sited along the Lakeside Way started life as part of the Tyne Salmon Trail, a sculpture project initiated by the Environment Agency to encourage more people to use and enjoy the river Tyne and to raise awareness of the return of a healthy salmon population.

FIGURE 16.6. *Salmon Cubes.*

Note

1. For more information on art and architecture at Kielder, and more installations, see http://kielderartandarchitecture.com/art-architecture.html (accessed 18/09/2014). All photographs © Peter Sharpe.

Beauty and Aesthetics

CHAPTER 17

Beauty and the Aesthetics of Place, Nature and Environment

Peter Coates

Beauty emerged as a major theme at an early stage in our project, which we explored at our second workshop in the Quantock Hills Area of Outstanding Natural Beauty. What, precisely, is it that makes beauty outstanding? If the power of the environment as a concept is linked to the prestige and techniques of science in forming an object of study and political action, then the power of natural beauty as a concept is linked to the prestige and techniques of arts and humanities in forming an object of study and source of political action.

Since our concern with relationships and connections is not limited to material processes of environmental change, but extends to attitudes and perceptions, how tastes in natural beauty differ and have altered over time is a vital element. Another important consideration is how ideas in general circulation shape responses to particular places and arise from particular places. This second keystone essay, which opens the book's second section, therefore begins with a broad discussion of the historical and cultural contingency of notions of beauty. This does not actually inquire about what beauty is (I agree that 'the *diversity* of aesthetic appreciation seems of far less significance than its *existence* in almost all cultures').[1] Instead, it poses the questions: how widely shared are conceptions of beauty; and when does beauty qualify as outstanding? Remaining at the macro-level a while longer, the focus shifts to how understandings of beauty in nature and landscape in the western world have been shaped since the eighteenth century by aesthetic traditions such as the picturesque and the sublime, which have been applied to a spectrum of environmental settings that range from the pastoral and the productive to the rugged, raw and 'unimproved'. In this regard, our project's interest in relationships and links is not restricted to the polarities of the local and the global. It embraces the national scale as well.

Traditionally, natural beauty has been first and foremost an ingredient of scenery: natural beauty and scenic beauty were effectively interchangeable. Moreover, as ideas associated with Romanticism privileged hitherto disparaged upland areas, natural beauty and scenic beauty also became more or less synonymous with mountains. With the spread of ecological ideas since the 1960s, however, understandings of natural beauty have expanded beyond the scenic. They have also opened up to embrace a range of environments beyond the mountainous.

At the same time, beautiful 'human-made' objects have remained a reference point for exponents of natural beauty, even in the United States; taking its cue from landscape painters, novelists and nature writers, the new nation grounded its national cultural identity in a form of nature perceived to be wilder than its 'old world' counterpart. In view of the complexity of understandings of natural beauty – not least debate about the relative contributions of culture and nature to the production of beauty – it is not surprising that efforts to pin down natural beauty have enjoyed little success. Moreover, despite the establishment more than half a century ago of a category of protected land in Britain known as an Area of Outstanding Natural Beauty, no landscape conservationist or environmental manager has ventured a definition of what precisely it is that makes natural beauty more than ordinary.

As the appreciation of wildness, nurtured locally in the Quantock Hills, has grown in popularity in Britain over recent years, discussions of what natural beauty involves have become even more intricate and intriguing. This exploration of beauty as a quality of nature, landscape and place therefore concludes with a discussion of the impact of this growing passion for the wild, including 'rewilding' proposals, on inherited notions of natural beauty. Throughout this chapter, the Quantock Hills serve as a point of departure and return. For, as emphasized in the earlier chapter on 'Places', what these hills lack in height and extent they more than make up for in terms of environmental variety and depth of cultural associations, which renders them eminently serviceable for a discussion that ranges from the global to the local and from the general to the particular.

The nature of beauty: British and American, 'foreign' and 'home'

For many commentators, past and present, beauty is the ultimate subjective quality. The person most widely credited with coining the truism, 'beauty is in the eye of the beholder,' is novelist Margaret Wolfe Hungerford. In her novel, *Molly Bawn* (1878), Marcia offers this comment as a retort to definitive pronouncements of the beauty of another character, Eleanor Massereene.[2] But notions of beauty vary in space and time as well as between individual beholders. The beauty that resides in features associated with non-human nature is no more timeless, universal and trans-historical than these human examples. That not everyone finds a sunrise beautiful, for example, is also suggested in *Molly Bawn* (in which every other reference to beauty, and there are many, is confined to beauty in the human female).[3] The Massereene family is admired, not least, because 'they are not fond of over-early rising; they never bore you with a description of the first faint beams of dawn; they fail to see any beauty in the dew at five o'clock in the morning – they are a very reasonable people.'[4]

For the ancient Greeks and Romans, however, there was science behind beauty. Aristotle (*Metaphysics*) regarded beauty as a property of symmetry. And this property was particularly evident in the mathematical sciences, which exhibited 'order, symmetry, and limitation; and these are the greatest forms of the beautiful.' For Plotinus, beauty resided in the underlying order of natural phenomena; the order and purpose of the cosmos was beautiful.[5]

In the ancient Greek tradition, the utilitarian and the aesthetic were harmonious bedfellows: the useful was beautiful and the beautiful was useful. The aesthetic canon that the Greeks handed down remained essentially in force until the Romantic era dawned in the late eighteenth century. The geometric regularity, angularity and straight lines of the drained fenlands of East Anglia (like the enormous, rectilinear tree farm that was Kielder Forest in its earlier days) were clearly beautiful viewed through the lens bequeathed by the likes of Aristotle, Plotinus and Cicero (resurfacing in the twentieth-century high modernist aesthetic). An environment improved was a more beautiful environment.

Yet through the new aesthetic framework pioneered by the Romantic generation of Coleridge and Wordsworth, landscape features such as mountains were redeemed. In seventeenth-century England, uplands were considered so distasteful to the cultivated palate that travellers and writers described them (and related features such as caverns) as warty, pimply excrescences. 'That which vex'd [the] most', Michael Drayton pointed out in his topographical poem of England and Wales, was the 'Peakish Cave', which, the footnote explains, was popularly known as 'The Devil's Arse' (a reference to the flatulent-like sounds generated within the cave).[6] At the turn of the nineteenth century, regions such as Derbyshire's Peak District that contained such features were elevated to the apex of attractiveness by Romantic ideology, which placed the highest premium on irregularity and unpredictability of shape. The new way of thinking, looking and feeling also prized resistance to cultivation, an intractable quality that frustrated the pre-Romantic connoisseurs of landscape. The metamorphosis from devilish 'mountain gloom' to godly 'mountain glory' created a profound tension between the once congruent values of the useful and the beautiful. 'Use of nature and a delight in nature', according to Chris Smout, were increasingly at loggerheads as the availability of unimproved land shrank.[7]

Across the Atlantic, where uncultivated land remained far more abundant, use and delight were usually still aligned at this time. In the early nineteenth century, the belief that beauty and utility in nature were synonymous flourished particularly among entrepreneurs in North America's frontier regions. Voyaging up the Mohawk, bound for Niagara Falls, the British novelist, Frances Trollope, thrilled to the novelty of scenery of the 'wildest description'. She was amused by a 'Yankee' fellow passenger, who felt the need to apologize for the 'wild state of the country'. He blamed this primitive condition on the fact that it was owned by an Englishman: 'you'll excuse me, ma'am, but when the English gets a spot of wild ground like this here, they have no notions about it like us.' Fortunately, it had recently been sold to an American, so, 'if you was to see it five years hence, you would not know it again; I'll engage there will be by that half a score elegant factories – 'tis a true shame to let such a privilege of water lie idle.'[8]

Nonetheless, as the western frontier line between 'settled' and 'unsettled' country receded apace, the seeds of the veneration of the high and the wild that Coleridge and Wordsworth sowed in the Quantocks were transplanted to increasingly fertile cultural ground.[9] In the receptive soil of places such as Walden Pond, Massachusetts, and Yosemite in California's Sierra Nevada mountains, husbanded by Henry David Thoreau and John Muir, these seeds grew into tall, strong and patriotic plants. The Euro-American love affair with the untamed (idle) in nature, and with wilderness in particular – whose roots in German Romanticism (not least the art of Caspar David Friedrich) should also be acknowledged – partly reflects the depth of antipathy to the city and its status in American culture as a fallen, supremely ugly place. According to historian Gary Wills, 'the city in the American imagination has played roughly the role of hell in Christian theology.' Wills argues that the American location of divinity in wild nature benefitted from the lack of competition from established religious structures. The church as a material entity was never imbued with a sacred quality comparable to the reverence Europeans invested in these buildings.[10] Conversely, Muir's references to the cathedral-like quality of California's redwood and sequoia groves had become standard in the US by the early twentieth century. (And now appear over here too; particularly apposite was the allusion to forests and woods as a 'cathedral for the spiritual' by James Jones, the bishop of Liverpool, who chaired the Independent Panel on Forestry (2011–12) convened in response to public disquiet over proposed changes to the management of England's public forest estate).[11] American cultural nationalists and the first generation of nature conservationists routinely venerated high mountain wilderness as the zenith of environmental beauty.

That is not to say that mountains loosened their hold over British minds as Americans embraced them with increasing warmth. A striking example of a Briton utterly captivated by mountains – and by mountains higher than North America's Sierra Nevada and Rockies – was Francis Younghusband. An army officer based in British India (best known for his 1904 expedition to Tibet), Younghusband was a swashbuckling character who his biographer dubs 'the last great imperial adventurer'. Though he lacked nothing in Victorian 'manly' virtues, Younghusband also propounded the simple life associated with the Russian novelist and thinker, Leo Tolstoy, and dabbled in all kinds of 'New Age' spiritualities, proclaiming, for instance, the power of cosmic rays. No wonder his biographer, Patrick French, also hailed him as a 'premature hippy'.[12]

The mountains dearest to Younghusband were the Himalayas: in the early 1920s, he chaired the Royal Geographical Society's Mount Everest Committee, encouraging climbers such as George Mallory to make the first ascent. In the preface to a collection of essays sub-titled 'The Quest for Natural Beauty', in which the Himalayas loomed large, Younghusband encouraged his readers to take beauty seriously:

The value of Knowledge and Character is duly impressed upon us. Of the value of Freedom we are told so much that we have come to regard it as an end in itself instead of only a means, or necessary condition. But Beauty we are half inclined to connect with the effeminate. Poetry, Music, and Literature are under suspicion with the average English schoolboy … Yet love of Beauty persists in spite of all discouragement, and will not be suppressed.[13]

The first address Younghusband gave as president of the Royal Geographical Society (31 May 1920) was entitled 'Natural Beauty and Geographical Science', and at the Union Society of University College, London, a few months earlier, his talk had been called 'Natural Beauty and Geography'. In this latter talk, he pulled no punches: 'any description of the Earth which excludes a description of its Natural Beauty is incomplete. And personally I would go so far as to say that the description of Natural Beauty is the most important part of Geography.' For him, geography was the science of natural beauty. Nevertheless, beauty was a concept he wanted to refine. He distinguished between the 'austere' beauty of the high Himalaya and the 'voluptuous' beauty of Kashmir. He also drew a distinction between 'foreign' beauty and 'home' beauty – the latter a familiar British-American concept during the interwar era. In fact, he reckoned that home beauty was the most beautiful of the various kinds, especially for those, like him, who had spent most of their adult lives abroad (born in British India, Younghusband spent his childhood and youth in the vicinity of Bath, before returning to imperial fields). Younghusband's notion of home beauty was firmly rooted in southwest England, where he had happy memories of boyhood holidays: 'The Englishman, though he loves the Alps and the Himalaya, is touched by nothing so deeply as by a Devonshire lane with its banks of primroses and violets.' Delving into the recesses of his memory, he recorded that 'almost my earliest recollections are of a Somersetshire village set in a lovely valley, fringed with woods and surrounded by hills.'[14] Though the precise location cannot be pinpointed, he could easily be describing a Quantock foothills village such as Holford or Crowcombe.

The year after his first presidential address, Younghusband and his family settled 30 miles (*c.*48 km) from London, near the village of Westerham, in bucolic Kent, where they lived between 1921 and 1937. Here, he concocted a grandiose plan for a Natural Beauty Association, with branches spread across Britain, Ireland and the Empire, though it remained just a gleam in his eye. He later re-married into a well-to-do family from Dorset, where he is buried in the churchyard at Lytchett Minster, a village nestling in the midst of archetypal 'home beauty'. Younghusband, in French's view, 'belonged in Dorset, not in the Himalayas … It was his last great joy, the place where he found a love and a peace and an understanding that he never reached elsewhere.'[15] It would be rash to conclude that charming 'home' beauty had finally prevailed over the awesome sublime that had once intoxicated Younghusband in foreign climes (what if he had re-married into a family based in the Lake District?). But his attraction to beauty in nature that was both home and foreign, both austere and voluptuous, and both picturesque and sublime, suggests just how complex and multi-layered tastes in landscape and scenery had become by the early twentieth century.[16]

Beauty: artistic and natural

These fondly remembered scenes of English beauty (Younghusband's favourite descriptive term was 'intimate') were patently examples of gently humanized (cultured) nature. Whether beauty is a quality that resides first and foremost in culture or in nature has been a hardy perennial of transatlantic debate for centuries. For many visiting Europeans, the nineteenth-century United States possessed a surfeit of land, but a dearth of landscape. Wild nature, available in profligate quantity (and therefore squandered), was raw, unfinished and impoverished. In the account of her extensive travels from the east coast to the Mississippi Valley in the early 1830s, the generally disapproving Frances Trollope reserved her most favourable comments for the scenery. Yet for all her appreciation of the wild beauty of scenery such as the banks of the Mohawk, she could not help thinking that a bit more human intervention – a generous dose of enriching Europeanism – would be thoroughly beneficial (providing, not least, greater mental stimulation). The Ohio River 'would be perfect', she opined, 'were there occasionally a ruined abbey, or feudal castle, to mix the romance of real life with that of nature'. And Trollope wished that the reflection from evergreens and piles of fantastically shaped rocks, that created the impression of a 'vast gothic castle' on the surface of the Monongahela river, were not just a folly.[17]

Not all Britons felt that cultural interventions enhanced the appeal and value of the natural world, whether in the 'old' or the 'new' world. Walking through the grounds of Crowcombe Court in the Quantocks, Dorothy Wordsworth observed 'quaint waterfalls about, around which Nature was very successfully striving to make beautiful what art had deformed – ruins, hermitages, *etc.*'.[18] Nor is the distinction between nature wild and tame always so sharply drawn. In the second edition of his seminal book, *Landscape into Art* – published in 1956, the year the first AONB was designated on the Gower peninsula in South Wales – British art historian Kenneth Clark wanted it both ways. For him, nature was a broad church: 'Almost every Englishman, if asked what he meant by "beauty", would begin to describe a landscape – perhaps a lake and mountain, perhaps a cottage garden, perhaps a wood with bluebells and silver birches, but, at all events, a landscape.'[19]

That Clark was slightly circumspect – he says *almost every* Englishman – is just as well. One Englishman who was definitely immune to the charms of nature, whether rugged or pastoral, was a character in an Oscar Wilde story (1889), set in the library of a country house in Nottinghamshire. Bursting in from the terrace, Cyril admonishes his friend: 'My dear Vivian, don't coop yourself up all day in the library. It is a perfectly lovely afternoon … Let us go and lie on the grass, and smoke cigarettes, and enjoy Nature.' Unmoved, Vivian retorts: 'My own experience is that the more we study Art, the less we care for Nature. What Art really reveals to us is Nature's lack of design, her curious crudities, her extraordinary monotony, her absolutely unfinished condition.' For nature is 'so uncomfortable. Grass is hard and lumpy and damp, and full of dreadful black insects.'[20]

The hallowed conceptual divide between nature and culture/art engenders amusing stories like this one. But, as is usually the case with dichotomies, if not necessarily false, their binary quality is overstated. The ancient Stoic, Horace, was far more appreciative of grass than Vivian. Anticipating by many centuries the American poet Walt Whitman's paean to the humble and the ordinary in nature (*Leaves of Grass*, 1855), the pastoral poet inquired in *Epistles*, 'Is the grass poorer in fragrance or beauty than Libyan mosaics?'[21]

The movements to preserve the relict monuments of nature and of human creation, both of which industrialization and urbanization jeopardized, converged on both sides of the Atlantic in the latter half of the nineteenth century. The two-fronted crusade was spearheaded by the likes of John Ruskin and William Morris in Britain and by George Perkins Marsh and Charles Eliot Norton in the United States.[22] Norton, Harvard's first professor of fine arts, campaigned in the 1880s to restrict the 'vulgar' commercialization of Niagara Falls, perhaps the most sublime of natural spectacles east of the Mississippi. In American minds, especially, natural and cultural heritage were not just comparable and compatible, and on a par within the enterprise of cultural nationalism; 'green old age' and beauty were superior. A year before Yellowstone National Park was established in 1872, the explorer, scientist and eco-jingoist, Clarence King, echoed Horace. California's giant sequoias were 'monuments of living antiquity' that offered a far more powerful link between past and present than the 'imperishableness' of any 'fragment of human work, broken pillar or sand-worn image half lifted over pathetic desert'.[23]

Outstandingly beautiful artistic treasures remained the reference point for nature conservationists in Britain and the United States alike. Prominent twentieth-century American wilderness preservationists such as Aldo Leopold, Robert Marshall and Edward Abbey continued to employ high cultural reference points. In the penultimate sentence of his essay on 'The Land Ethic' (1949), in which he bemoaned the loss of wild places, Leopold rued that 'we are remodelling the Alhambra [a Moorish palace/fortress complex in Granada, Spain] with a steam-shovel, and we are proud of our yardage.' Marshall, a founder member of the Wilderness Society (1935), when asked how many formally designated wilderness areas were required, counter-attacked by inquiring how many Brahms symphonies were needed. And Abbey, feisty advocate of direct action in defence of untamed Mother Earth, in a 1968 essay entitled 'Industrial Tourism and the National Parks', reminded Americans that 'we have agreed not to drive our automobiles into cathedrals, concert halls, art museums, legislative assemblies, private bedrooms and other sanctums of our culture; we should treat our national parks with the same deference.'[24] In view of the shortage of conventionally prestigious cultural artefacts, nineteenth-century

Americans had been more inclined to locate 'treasures' in the natural world, and invest nature with aesthetic and heritage value. And yet, human artifice remained the gold standard for beauty. A redwood grove was like a cathedral; but a cathedral was never compared to a redwood grove.[25]

Though outstanding beauty was the point of comparison between nature and culture in these American examples, it is not enough, when considering the history of aesthetics in relation to places, to speak only in terms of their beauty. In the eighteenth century, the beautiful was just one of three desirable attributes of nature, landscape and scenery. Two hundred or more years ago, British aestheticians and art theorists fussily distinguished between the beautiful, the picturesque and the sublime.[26] Yet those of us who have never managed to figure out the finer points of difference between the beautiful and the picturesque need not despair. We are in good company. One of Coleridge's notebook entries for December 1803 reads: 'What then is the real Difference & is there a real Difference between the Picturesque and the Beautiful?'[27] For William Gilpin, a leading theoretician of landscape aesthetics, a dell – a narrow, thickly wooded cleft between two rocky walls, usually graced by a tumbling torrent – was the epitome of the picturesque. Yet Gilpin sidestepped the distinction by routinely conflating the beautiful and the picturesque, referring to his 'Observations' on 'Picturesque Beauty' in the titles of books on the Wye Valley, Lake District and Scottish Highlands (1782, 1786, 1789).

The distinction between the (merely) beautiful and the sublime appears to have been much clearer (and more defensible) in the hierarchy of aesthetic experience. In his *Philosophical Enquiry into the Origin of our Ideas of the Sublime and Beautiful*, Edmund Burke based his (thoroughly gendered) notion of beauty in nature on 'a quality that men find attractive in women: smoothness, gentleness, softness'. The sublime, by contrast, was considered more manly, related to grander things like infinity, eternity and the human relationship to the deity. Above all, though, it was related to terror: 'whatever is in any sort terrible … is a source of the *sublime*.' According to Burke, things that precipitated this feeling of terror – 'the strongest emotion which the mind is capable of feeling' – were privation, vastness, magnificence, loudness and suddenness – qualities particularly associated with natural phenomena such as the storm, the cliff-edge, the waterfall and the mountain summit: things and places that make us feel small, helpless and afraid. To feel the sublime – to find the terrible and the threatening strangely attractive – was a multi-sensory experience – a state of consciousness, even – that went far beyond the narrowly visual, painterly (and arguably effete) enjoyment of beauty. This was the 'delightful horror' that thrilled Immanuel Kant; the delicious terror that was largely dependent, of course, on knowing that the danger was imagined rather than real (safely beyond the safety railings).[28]

According to this late eighteenth-century aesthetic schema, the Alps and the Scottish Highlands (not to mention the Sierra Nevada and Rockies) were sublime. The Quantocks, on the other hand, being small-scale, smoothly-rounded and bereft of dizzying heights, would have qualified as no more than beautiful, had

Burke and Gilpin written about them. Observers would undoubtedly derive pleasure from contemplating them, but it would be of a mild rather than powerful sort. Yet whether it labelled a place of nature as picturesque, beautiful or sublime, the Romantic perspective patently deviated from both the pre-modern canon and high modernist aesthetic of the straight and ordered.

What is not as clear cut as the drainage ditches of the Cambridgeshire and Somerset fenlands, though, is where the notion of beauty that is deemed to be outstanding enters the picture. The natural beauty of home that Younghusband so fondly recalled would not have struck him as *outstanding*. In 1935, Vaughan Williams attributed the distinctly English genius of Elgar's compositions not to the 'aloof and unsympathetic beauty of glaciers and coral reefs and tropical forests' but instead to 'the intimate and personal beauty of our own fields and lanes'.[29] The outstanding is something that, well, stands out: and ostentation, in some quarters, is considered unsubtle at best, tasteless at worst.

According to Margaret Anderson, who has studied the politics behind the emergence of the AONB designation under Section 87 of the National Parks and Access to the Countryside Act of 1949, exactly when, where and why the terminology of outstanding natural beauty originated cannot be established with any degree of accuracy: previous talk had been of an 'Area of National Landscape Value' or 'Conservation Area' designation for lands that did not make the grade as national parks.[30] As such, no criteria for the definition, measurement or quantification of natural beauty – whether outstanding or not – have ever been drawn up by a civil servant, government committee or working party.

In 2004, however, the Welsh Assembly, as part of its National Parks Review Action Plan, commissioned the Countryside Commission for Wales to draft a statement that fully considered all meanings and manifestations of the term 'natural beauty'. Following consultation with a wide range of stakeholders (respondents to a written consultation and workshop attendees), the investigators concluded that, however widely applied and inconsistently defined and interpreted – as well as vulnerable to legal challenge – the concept of natural beauty retained considerable cultural authority and relevance, and that it was difficult to avoid, not least because satisfactory alternatives were unavailable. Moreover, the chapter on 'cultural ecosystem services' in the UK National Ecosystem Assessment (2011) flags up not only the aesthetic, emotional, spiritual, inspirational, therapeutic and heritage-related values of natural beauty, but also its financial impact: house prices reflect proximity to environmental settings, such as national parks, characterized by aesthetic beauty. The Independent Panel on Forestry also highlighted beauty as a quality of trees and woodland. Not least, natural beauty was cited as an 'important' 'natural capital asset' in the report of the Natural Capital Committee, an independent body established in May 2012 that advises the Cabinet Office's Economic Affairs Committee on the efficient and sustainable management of England's 'natural wealth'.[31]

There is certainly a case for the adoption of a more watertight definition in law, for this might help rebuff legal challenges to the protection of places based on the criterion of natural beauty. The conservation and enhancement of natural beauty is one of the statutory duties of an AONB authority. But there is no reference to protection and enhancement of cultural heritage. In contrast, national parks have the statutory responsibility to conserve and enhance 'cultural heritage' as well as natural beauty. Whether definitions of natural beauty are strict, or broad enough to include cultural heritage, was a particularly live issue in connection with proposals for new national parks in the New Forest and South Downs. In March 2005, the inclusion of a particular patch of land (Hinton Park) within the newly designated New Forest National Park was challenged (Meyrick case) on the grounds that, since its qualities were more historical and cultural than natural, it did not merit the designation of exceptional natural beauty. Discussions about what constitutes 'natural beauty' and whether this also embraces cultural heritage (as well as flora and fauna) reoccurred during planning for a South Downs National Park (2011) and the Natural Environment and Rural Communities Act of 2006 updated the statutory definition of natural beauty to include wildlife and human influence (in other words, cultural features and heritage).[32]

Designation as outstanding certainly does not imply that the natural beauty within the other protective category of national parks is more (or less) than outstanding. Location and size rather than scenic quality appear to be the critical distinctions between an AONB and a national park. Scenically and topographically, the Quantocks have more in common with a national park such as nearby Exmoor than with a fellow AONB like the (more distant) Cotswolds.[33] Nor does AONB designation suggest that the scenic quality of countryside beyond AONB boundaries is inferior.

Ecology and beauty; and the beauty of the wild

As well as examining when the concept of 'environment' became infused with ecological meaning, we must also consider when the concept of 'natural beauty' became informed by ecological knowledge. The influence of ecological understandings can be seen in two main ways. Firstly, a new layer of appreciation and valuation is added to those that have already accrued (a place, environment or landscape admired, loved and renowned for its scenic beauty and/or the charisma of its wildlife and/or trees and flowers is now cherished even more on account of the richness of its ecological systems). In short, biodiversity renders more beautiful. Secondly, and more spectacularly, knowledge of ecology injects beauty into a place from which it was previously considered absent. For instance, a dismal and ugly swamp is metamorphosed into a precious and beautiful wetland. In other words, beauty resides in biodiversity. Rachel Carson had a hand in both these developments, while Aldo Leopold played a big part too, by underpinning land aesthetics with land ethics.

To move the discussion of natural beauty beyond scenery and visual aesthetics, I refer back to our observation in the introductory chapter that growing ecological awareness has relaxed (but certainly not dissolved) the bond between notions of beauty in nature and traditional aesthetic canons that accorded special status to mountain scenery. The very wet and the very dry – places once characterized as 'dismal' swamps and 'arid' deserts ('arid', after all, is a pejorative term that privileges lush, temperate zones) – have also been redeemed by a land ethic and land aesthetic that are more concerned with the integrity of ecosystems and biodiversity content than with (abiotic) monumental grandeur and the surface-oriented aesthetic derived from landscape painting.[34] Unimproved (un-drained) remnants of swamps such as Wicken and south Florida's Everglades have been reinvented as precious – and beautiful – wetlands. Despite their lowly status – the lowest point in England is Holme Fen National Nature Reserve in Cambridgeshire, about 15 miles (24 km) north of Wicken – lowlands, especially wetlands, are in fact high on the biodiversity scale: higher than more visually arresting, yet often sterile, uplands (though van Dam makes a powerful case for the aesthetic appreciation of watery flatlands elsewhere in this volume – as does Robert Macfarlane in his paean to the mudflats and saltmarshes of Essex's Dengie peninsula, where he first began to appreciate 'the beauty of the lateral').[35]

The threat to natural beauty from environmental change is not a theme included in this chapter's coverage. But the close relationship between beauty as a valued property of place and biotic life was underlined in Carson's discussion of the 'disfigurement of once-beautiful [New England] roadsides by chemical sprays, which substitute a sere expanse of brown, withered vegetation for the beauty of fern and wildflower, of native shrubs adorned with blossom and berry'. As a woman (quoted by Carson) wrote to her local newspaper: 'This is not what the tourists expect, with all the money we are spending advertising the beautiful scenery.' The desire to preserve beauty and to protect the 'intricate web of life whose interwoven strands lead from microbes to man' were increasingly inseparable. With reference to US Supreme Court Justice William O. Douglas' pronouncement that the 'aesthetic values of the wilderness are as much our inheritance as the veins of copper and gold in our hills,' Carson commented that 'there is, of course, more to the wish to preserve our roadside vegetation than even such aesthetic considerations. In the economy of nature the natural vegetation has its essential place. Hedgerows along country roads and bordering fields provide food, cover, and nesting areas for birds and homes for many small animals.'[36]

David Lowenthal is more inclined to distinguish – and perceive a tension – between scenic and other values. Among environmental planners and managers, he recently lamented:

> scenic beauty is now out of vogue … derided as superficial, frivolous, even soulless: to dwell on décor is to scant integral landscape values, notably ecological fitness, residential sustainability, community health and historical authenticity.[37]

It is true that, with the exception of the AONB category, scenic beauty is a less effective rationale for government protection of environments than biodiversity content. However, there is no necessary friction between the values that reside in appearance and content. As the saying goes (attributed, among others, to Aldous

Huxley and Baba Dioum), we can only protect what we love and we can only love what we understand. And what we now know about the Earth's environments extends far beyond visual attributes to their ecological systems and their individual components. Proto-green landscape architects in 1930s Germany believed that the richer the biodiversity, the more beautiful the place. They dismissed Germany's vast swathes of conifer plantations consisting of regular rows of single-species of non-native trees (the template for the original Kielder plantings) as 'neither biologically sound, nor lasting, nor beautiful'.[38] Likewise, Friends of Quantock's battle against Forestry Commission afforestation schemes in the 1950s and 1960s (which brings to mind CPRE's Kielder campaigns in the 1930s, discussed in Payne's chapter) was a stand for beauty in scenery and nature against perceived ugliness and biological sterility. For them and others, rectangular block plantations of non-native conifers would not just obliterate open moorland but also, in the combes, replace the ancient semi-natural woodland that charmed Romantic poets.[39] Knowledge of biodiversity derived from ecological understanding bestows the additional value of beauty. It is not a question of valuing (and loving) a place because of its abundant beauty or its abundant biodiversity. It is beautiful partly because of its biodiversity.

Notions of natural beauty have also been reinforced by a vogue for the wild, expressed, not least, in the growing popularity among land managers of rewilding schemes such as the Wicken Vision and Kielder Wildwood project. Yet this is a relatively recent development. Unpublished data from 1976 cited by Anderson suggested that most people in England and Wales preferred the scenery of AONBs to that housed within national parks. Summarizing the data (what they consist of, or are derived from, is not explained), she reported that:

> the generally rolling countryside of AONBs with their farmland of crops and pasture set off by trees, and with villages and farms nestling in the valleys … is far more to the national taste than the rugged wilder pasture and moorlands of the upland National Parks.[40]

This statement of the enduring grip of the aesthetic of the picturesque confirmed the findings of a study that David Lowenthal and Hugh Prince conducted in 1965: 'the countryside beloved by the great majority is tamed and inhabited, warm, comfortable, humanized.'[41]

'There is no reason to suppose that their conclusions do not remain valid,' remarked Marion Shoard in 2002.[42] Yet over the last decade, British tastes in landscape and natural beauty have shifted considerably. From a North American perspective, the differences between AONBs and national parks appear trivial: the crucial point is that the dominant form of land use in both categories is agricultural, regardless of whether it is extensive or intensive, grazing or arable. Small wonder that all protected areas in the UK fall within Category V of the Protected Areas Categories System formulated by the International Union for the Conservation of Nature and Natural Resources (IUCN), which designates protected landscapes that are essentially cultural rather than natural (Category

I is reserved for 'strict' nature reserves and wilderness areas).[43] Long before the enclosure (fencing in) of common lands gathered steam in the sixteenth century (accelerating with the backing of parliamentary legislation in the late eighteenth and early nineteenth centuries), lands in Britain have been graded with reference to the norm of agriculturally productive cropland or pasture: 'poor', 'unimproved', 'derelict', 'waste', 'abandoned', 'sterilized' and 'difficult'. This is the cultural and linguistic environment entered by British exponents of the wild at a time (the late eighteenth century) when only moorland areas such as the Quantock uplands remained substantially unenclosed, judged to be too high, too rainy and too sour of soil.[44]

Despite the best efforts of the Romantics, British taste has previously not been particularly partial to wild land, let alone wilderness (unless safely located, at a distance, in North America or other former 'settler' colony, and enjoyed as part of the experience of visiting a different country and culture). In a speech on 15 October 1986, Nicholas Ridley, the Environment Minister in the second Thatcher government, accused those who sought to protect the countryside from all forms of development of wanting to return to some kind of wild state of Eden. What this sort of (extremist) conservationist failed to appreciate, he explained, is that 'if you could get through the bogs and the jungles and the thickets [that covered] this country one million years ago, you would say "What a dreadful place this is".'[45] And during the foot and mouth crisis of 2001, many English commentators regarded the removal of livestock from upland areas as a potential disaster from the standpoint of landscape aesthetics as well as the livelihoods of farmers, especially for a treasured national landscape such as the Lake District (reified, like the Quantocks, through association with Coleridge and Wordsworth). For, in the absence of all those nibbling mouths, the place would revert to a scrubby, scruffy and benighted wild state.[46]

Because spontaneous natural processes threaten the particular forms of nature we often cherish for their scenic beauty, flora and fauna, recreational potential and associations with built heritage ('historic environment'), management plans seek to protect these preferred landscapes and ecosystems from nature running wild. In Gower AONB, riotous summertime growth of gorse and bracken not only invades heathland but threatens to obliterate and undermine archaeological sites. In cleared areas, new archaeological treasures have come to light, including prehistoric hut groups and medieval long houses.[47] Bracken bruising with heavy duty machinery is the control mechanism. On the south side of the Bristol Channel, in the Quantocks, a chemical solution has also been tried. This 'pest' (whose native status makes a change from all the non-native invasive species) is subject to airborne assault from helicopters equipped with spray guns.[48]

And yet, over the past five years or so, growing numbers of Britons have been getting more in touch with their wilder sides. Wild places (whether in town or country) are currently fashionable – everything wild, in fact – and, whether implicitly or explicitly, considered more beautiful than their more domesticated counterparts. Wild places, rewilding and pursuits such as wild swimming are the subject of best-selling books.[49] Instead of waxing lyrical about the beauty of the uplands sculpted by grazing animals, environmental commentator George Monbiot bemoans its bleak and biologically parlous, 'sheepwrecked' condition ('bowling greens with contours'; 'aftermath of an ecological disaster') and calls for the repopulation of Britain's countryside with large predators such as wolves and lynx.[50] The John Muir Trust, founded in 1980, is dedicated to the preservation, regeneration and expansion of wild places in England, Scotland, Wales and Northern Ireland; and Scotland celebrated John Muir Day on 21 April 2013, to mark the 175th birthday in Dunbar, East Lothian, of the 'founding father of national parks around the world' – a 'Scot who lived for the wilderness'.[51] Wordsworth and Coleridge would surely approve of this turn to the wild, though they might see it as a *return* to the wild feeling nurtured amid wild Quantock beauty rather than something new. This is the message from the increasingly vociferous advocates of the wild: wild places with fully functioning ecosystems are not just more wondrous, rich and healthy. They are also more beautiful.

Notes

1. Alan Holland and Kate Rawles, 'The Ethics of Conservation: Report prepared for, and submitted to Countryside Council for Wales', *Thingmount Working Paper Series on the Philosophy of Conservation*, TWP 96-01 (Lancaster: Department of Philosophy, Lancaster University, 1996), p. 19.
2. Margaret Wolfe Hungerford, *Molly Bawn* (London: Smith, Elder, 1987), p. 142.
3. The most influential (if inadvertent) publicity that Britain's AONBs have ever received was, arguably, a British tabloid newspaper's jocular campaign for the designation of Australian singer Kylie Minogue's posterior for posterity as an AONB: Grant Rollings, 'It's cheeky butt we love it: *Sun* campaign to put her bum in safe hands', *The Sun*, 9 March 2002, pp. 3–4 ('Across Britain, gently curving landscapes have been protected by designating them Areas of Outstanding Natural Beauty. Our campaign aims to persuade the Countryside Agency to add Kylie's bottom to that prestigious list'); Jon Casimir, 'Kylie's seat of power', *Sydney Morning Herald*, 27 July 2002 http://www.smh.com.au/articles/2002/07/26/1027497413397.html (accessed 18/08/14). I thank Jill Smith, Communications and Events Manager for the National Association for Areas of Outstanding Natural Beauty (NAAONB), for supplying a copy of this article.
4. Hungerford, *Molly Bawn*, p. 14.
5. Carl C. Gaither and Alma E. Cavazos-Gaither (eds), *Gaither's Dictionary of Scientific Quotations* (New York: Springer, 2012), p. 263; Clarence J. Glacken, *Traces on the Rhodian Shore: Nature and Culture in Western Thought from Ancient Times to the End of the Eighteenth Century* (Berkeley: University of California Press, 1967), p. 78. There have been attempts to go beyond the subjective appraisal of taste in place and formulate an evolutionary, trans-cultural basis for the aesthetic preference for open landscape: J. Appleton, *The Experience of Landscape* (London: Wiley, 1975). Well established discussions in philosophy argue that aesthetic judgments may be supported through forms of 'aesthetic testimony' and 'perceptual proof', revealing how aesthetic valuing may have a shared, intersubjective or even more objective foundation: Frank Sibley, 'Aesthetic Concepts', in John Benson, Betty Redfern and Jeremy Roxbee-Cox (eds),

Approach to Aesthetics: Collected Papers on Philosophical Aesthetics (Oxford: Clarendon Press, 2001), pp. 1–23; Aaron Meskin, 'Aesthetic Testimony: What Can We Learn from Others about Beauty and Art?', *Philosophy and Phenomenological Research* 42 (2004), pp. 65–91.

6. Richard Hooper (ed.), *The Complete Works of Michael Drayton, Volume 1, Poly-Olbion* (London: John Russell Smith, 1876 [1612]), p. 74; Thomas Hobbes, *De Mirabilibus Pecci: Being the Wonders of the Peak in Darbyshire, Commonly Called The Devil's Arse of Peak* (London: William Crook, 1678); Roderick Nash, *Wilderness and the American Mind* (New Haven: Yale University Press, 1982 [1967]), p. 45; Marjorie Hope Nicholson, *Mountain Gloom, Mountain Glory: The Development of the Aesthetics of the Infinite* (Ithaca: Cornell University Press, 1959), pp. 63–4.

7. T. C. Smout, *Exploring Environmental History: Selected Essays* (Edinburgh: Edinburgh University Press, 2011), p. 15; T. C. Smout, *Nature Contested: Environmental History in Scotland and Northern England since 1600* (Edinburgh: Edinburgh University Press, 2000), p. 7.

8. Frances Trollope, *Domestic Manners of the Americans II* (London: Whittaker, Treacher, 1832), p. 245.

9. Eco-critics alert to the proto-ecological content of Coleridge's and Wordsworth's literary output, such as James C. McKusick, often overlook the role of the Quantocks as an ideology-shaping crucible, prioritizing their later, better-known period of residence in the Lake District: McKusick, 'Coleridge and the Economy of Nature', *Studies in Romanticism* 35/3 (Fall 1996), pp. 375–6, 383. For greater alertness to the Quantocks' formative role, see: Jonathan Bate, *Romantic Ecology: Wordsworth and the Environmental Tradition* (London: Routledge, 1991), pp. 49, 113, 115.

10. Gary Wills, 'American Adam', *New York Review of Books* (6 March 1997), p. 30.

11. Chairman's Foreword, *Final Report, Independent Panel on Forestry* (London: Defra, 4 July 2012), p. 6.

12. Patrick French, *Younghusband: The Last Great Imperial Adventurer* (London: Penguin, 1994), p. xx.

13. Francis Younghusband, *The Heart of Nature: or, The Quest for Natural Beauty* (London: John Murray, 1921), p. ix.

14. Younghusband, *Heart of Nature*, pp. 204, 100, 106, 121, 123, 223, 227. For the notion of 'home beauty' on the other side of the Atlantic, see Aldo Leopold, 'Farm Arboretum Adds to Home Beauty', *Wisconsin Agriculturist and Farmer* 67, no. 10 (18 May 1940), p. 4.

15. French, *Younghusband*, pp. 361, 397, 405.

16. For a comprehensive discussion of beauty in relation to notions such as awe, wonder and the sublime, see: Emily Brady, *The Sublime in Modern Philosophy: Aesthetics, Ethics, and Nature* (Cambridge: Cambridge University Press, 2013).

17. Frances Trollope, *Domestic Manners of the Americans I* (London: Whittaker, Treacher, 1832), pp. 45, 281.

18. 'Dorothy Wordsworth's Journal, Written at Alfoxden in 1798' (entry for 15 April 1798), in W. A. Knight, *Coleridge and Wordsworth in the West Country* (New York: Scribner, 1914), p. 156.

19. Kenneth Clark, *Landscape into Art* (London: John Murray, 1949), p. 142.

20. Oscar Wilde, 'The Decay of Lying: An Observation', in *Intentions* (New York: Brentano's, 1905 [1891]), pp. 3–4.

21. F. G. Plaistowe and F. P. Shipham (eds), *Horace: The Epistles* (London: W. B. Clive, 1890), p. 87; J. B. Greenough (ed.), *The Satires and Epistles of Horace* (Boston: Ginn, 1888), p. 197; Glacken, *Traces on the Rhodian Shore*, p. 31.

22. David Lowenthal, 'Omens from the Mediterranean: Conservation Nostrums in *Mare Nostrum*', *Studies in Conservation* 55 (2010), pp. 235-6.

23. Charles Eliot Norton, *Letters of Charles Eliot Norton: With Biographical Comments by his Daughter Sara Norton and M. A. DeWolfe Howe* II (Boston: Houghton Mifflin, 1913), pp. 94-6, 135; Clarence King, *Mountaineering in the Sierra Nevada* (New York: Charles Scribner's, 1871), pp. 51-2.

24. Aldo Leopold, *A Sand County Almanac* (New York: Oxford University Press, 1949), p. 226; Nash, *Wilderness and the American Mind*, p. 203; Edward Abbey, *Desert Solitaire* (New York: Random House, 1968), p. 60.

25. I thank Paul Warde for this observation.

26. Anne K. Mellor, 'Coleridge's "This Lime-Tree Bower My Prison" and the Categories of English Landscape', *Studies in Romanticism* 18/2 (Summer 1979), pp. 253-70; Peter Coates, *Nature: Western Attitudes since Ancient Times* (Berkeley: University of California Press, 2005 [1998]), pp. 131-4.

27. Mellor, 'Coleridge's "This Lime-Tree Bower My Prison"', p. 258.

28. Edmund Burke, *Philosophical Enquiry into the Origin of our Ideas of the Sublime and Beautiful* (Philadelphia: S. F. Bradford, 1806 [1757]), pp. 47, 176; Immanuel Kant, *Kant's Critique of Aesthetic Judgement*, James Creed Meredith (trans.) (Oxford: Clarendon Press, 1911 [1790]), p. 131. Mellor distinguishes further between the positive (transcendental) and the negative sublime, the former characterized by joy and awe rather than fear: Mellor, 'Coleridge's "This Lime-Tree Bower My Prison"', pp. 264-5.

29. Quoted in David Lowenthal, 'British National Identity and the English Landscape', *Rural History* 2/2 (1991), p. 215.

30. Margaret A. Anderson, 'The Land Pattern of Areas of Outstanding Natural Beauty in England and Wales', *Landscape Planning* 7 (1980), pp. 3, 18; Margaret A. Anderson, 'Areas of Outstanding Natural Beauty and the 1949 National Parks Act', *The Town Planning Review* 61/3 (July 1990), pp. 316-18, 320-3; Paul Selman and Carys Swanwick, 'On the Meaning of Natural Beauty in Landscape Designation', *Landscape Research* 35/1 (February 2010), p. 11.

31. Selman and Swanwick, 'On the Meaning of Natural Beauty', pp. 3-4, 18-21; Andrew Church, Jacquelin Burgess and Neil Ravenscroft, 'Cultural Services', in *UK National Ecosystem Assessment Technical Report* (Cambridge: Defra/UNEP-WCMC, June 2011), pp. 29, 32, 48, 79; *Final Report, Independent Panel on Forestry*, pp. 16-17, 26; *The State of Natural Capital: Towards a Framework for Measurement and Valuation* (April 2013), p. 45. On the possibility of arriving at an objective description of a landscape's aesthetic rating (with a view to strengthening the case for preservation), see: Luna B. Leopold, 'Landscape Esthetics', in Alfred Meyer (ed.), *Encountering the Environment* (New York: Van Nostrand Reinhold, 1971), pp. 29-45.

32. Selman and Swanwick, 'On the Meaning of Natural Beauty', pp. 16-18.

33. The Hobhouse Report (1947) that informed the 1949 National Parks and Countryside Act recommended (unsuccessfully) the inclusion of the Quantocks in a park centred on Exmoor: E. W. Barnett, *Quantock Hills Management Plan* (Taunton: Planning Department, Somerset County Council, 1990), p. 7.

34. J. Baird Callicott, 'Leopold's Land Aesthetic', in Allen Carlson and Sheila Lintott (eds), *Nature, Aesthetics, and Environmentalism* (New York: Columbia University Press, 2008), pp. 105-18; Allen Carlson, 'Aesthetic Appreciation of the Natural Environment', in Carlson and Lintott (eds), *Nature, Aesthetics, and Environmentalism*, pp. 119-32.

35. Robert Macfarlane, *The Wild Places* (London: Granta, 2007), pp. 285-95; Tim Adams, 'Where the wild things are', *The Observer* (26 August 2007).

36. Rachel Carson, *Silent Spring* (London: Penguin, 2000 [1962]), pp. 74-7.

37. David Lowenthal, 'Living with and Looking at Landscape', *Landscape Research 32* (October 2007), pp. 635-6.

38. Alwin Seifert, 'Reichsautobahn im Wald', *Die Strasse* 5 (1938), p. 419.

39. Vincent Waite, *Portrait of the Quantocks* (London: Robert Hale, 1965), pp. 158-62; Denys White and Alan Hughes, 'Views from Friends of Quantock', in Peter Coates (ed.) 'Local Places: Global Processes: Histories of Environmental Change: Workshop 2: Quantock Hills, Somerset: 1-3 March 2011' (Bristol, 2012), pp. 29-30; also available at 'Views from Friends of Quantock' http://www.environmentalhistories.net/?p=369 (accessed 01/08/14).

40. Study by C. Hall, cited in Margaret A. Anderson, 'The Land Pattern of Areas of Outstanding Natural Beauty', p. 17.

41. David Lowenthal and Hugh Prince, 'English Landscape Tastes', *Geographical Review* 55/2 (1965), p. 190.

42. Marion Shoard, 'Edgelands', in Jennifer Jenkins (ed.), *Remaking the Landscape: The Changing Face of Britain* (London: Profile Books, 2002), p. 120. On alleged British cultural incompatibility with the notion of wilderness, see: Norman Henderson, 'Wilderness and the Nature Conservation Ideal: Britain, Canada, and the United States Contrasted', *Ambio* 21/6 (September 1992), pp. 394-9.

43. IUCN, *Guidelines for Protected Area Management Categories* (Gland, Switzerland: IUCN, 1994).

44. Michael Williams, 'The Enclosure of Waste Land in Somerset, 1700-1900', *Transactions of the Institute of British Geographers* 57 (November 1972), pp. 100-1, 120.

45. Nicholas Ridley, *The Future of the Public Heritage* (London: Cubitt Trust, 1987), p. 92.

46. Recent research in Somerset indicates the important role, however unsightly, of 'small patches of unkempt and weedy areas' within farmlands and farmyards in supporting biodiversity: 'Unkempt, weedy land unintentionally boosts wildlife', University of Bristol press release (20 May 2013); Darren M. Evans, Michael J. O. Pocock and Jane Memmott, 'The robustness of ecological networks to habitat loss', *Ecology Letters* (July 2013), pp. 844-52.

47. English Heritage, *Outstanding Beauty: Outstanding Heritage: AONBs and the Historic Environment* (2005), p. 13.

48. Tim Russell, former head ranger, Quantock Hills AONB Service, in conversation at a patch of sprayed moorland, 1 March 2011.

49. Roger Deakin, *Waterlog: A Swimmer's Journey through Britain* (London: Chatto & Windus, 1999); Macfarlane, *The Wild Places*; Roger Deakin, *Wildwood: A Journey through Trees* (London: Penguin, 2008); Daniel Start, *Wild Swimming* (Bristol: Punk Publishing, 2008); Kate Rew, *Wild Swim* (London: Guardian Books, 2009); Christopher Somerville, *Britain and Ireland's Best Wild Places* (London: Penguin, 2011); George Monbiot, *Feral: Searching for Enchantment on the Frontiers of Rewilding* (London: Allen Lane, 2013). The British Library's exhibition, 'Writing Britain: From Wastelands to Wonderlands' (11 May to 25 September 2012), included writers' relationship with wild places: 'England, My England', *The Economist* (13 May 2012). On urban wildness, see: Bristol City Council's 'Wild City' project (2011-13) http://www.bristol.gov.uk/page/environment/wild-city; 'Wild Capital: Discover Wildlife in London' http://www.wildcapital.co.uk/ (both accessed 18 September 2014).

50. Monbiot, *Feral*; 'Sheepwrecked', *The Spectator* (30 May 2013) http://www.monbiot.com/2013/05/30/sheepwrecked/ (accessed 10/02/14).

51. Susan Wright and Mike Daniels, 'Nature's Way', *John Muir Trust Journal* 56 (Spring 2014), pp. 28-31; Brian Ferguson and Claire Wheelans, 'Conservationist John Muir's Legacy to Sell Scotland Across Worlds', *The Scotsman* (8 January 2013).

CHAPTER 18

Light on Landscape:
An Antipodean View[1]

Libby Robin

So much of beauty is about light. The sunset and the moonlight – classic 'natural beauty' moments – are as much about *trompe d'oeuil*, tricking the eye, as about what is 'out there'. There is also a very physical aspect to light. You can't have light without dust. Evolutionary theorist, Alfred Russel Wallace, alerted his readers to dust in his 1898 essay, 'The Importance of Dust: A Source of Beauty and Essential to Life'. Dust was not only responsible for the 'production of colour and beauty', but also, through its presence 'in the higher atmosphere', we benefit from 'mists, clouds, and gentle beneficial rains, instead of waterspouts and destructive torrents'.[2] Beauty and life itself are intertwined through barely visible particles that create both perception of colour and the quality of soft rain needed for life.

What else is physical about beauty? Psychologists use the widening (dilation) of the pupils of a viewer's eye to measure beauty. Variation in pupil size is a response to the amount of light: dilation when there is less light (pupils contract in bright light).[3] In defining beauty as a physical and independent 'response', they have chosen a measure that is biased by its context in a land of soft lux. More light is not always 'good' or 'bad', but as a measure of beauty, pupil dilation works better in a place where soft light is the norm, and dark shadows trick the eye to observe carefully.

The charm of the Quantocks is the subtlety of the soft browns and greys; even the generosity of the green was muted by the dim light. Coming from Australia, a land of 'pitiless blue skies', I have learned to fear light – and to celebrate the nuances that high latitude English light can draw from landscapes.

High latitudes create situations where the sun lurks near the horizon, rather than overhead, which is also a property of sunset. The appeal of sunsets is that they mark a shift from day into night – a moment in time – and the passing of the sun below the horizon marks this moment. In the tropics, where there is no gloaming, this 'moment' is short and precious. The ten-minute sunset is a moment when all the deck chairs at the Darwin Yacht Club (12° south) face the sea to the west, and the patrons enjoy a celebratory drink. When the blazing disc finally dips below the horizon, everyone claps. The same ritual is observed when the sun sets in Greek islands, although the sun takes a little longer to set there.

Sunrises and sunsets are the only moments when the detail of an Australian desert landscape is drawn out: once the sun is up, it rises rapidly to the overhead position where it beats down mercilessly, bleaching the landscape of colour and interest, and forcing the viewer to squint or cover their eyes from the onslaught of brightly reflective landscape surfaces. Light should 'highlight' beauty – a shaft of sun through storm clouds brings out colours on the opposite hill in the Quantocks, perhaps, and famously in Scotland, but if you have full light everywhere, the landscape is deprived of its shape (shadow) and colour.

The discovery of Kodachrome technologies in the 1960s was the beginning of tourism to Uluru, then known as Ayers Rock. Ayers Rock was an identifiable (black and white) monument in a dead flat landscape that, in the second half of the twentieth century, transformed itself into the colourful and mellifluous Uluru. Uluru is filled with the rich stories of the local Pitjanjarra people, who now manage the place for tourists and encourage them to walk around the rock and photograph its sunsets, rather than to climb it in the 1950s tradition where it was like a Scottish Munro to be 'bagged'. The sunrise and sunset at Uluru play between the orange of the rock and the purple of its secret shadowy places. Such is the view captured by every tourist camera. But you don't see the purple in the middle of the day, unless you are lucky and there is a storm over the rock; you make your pilgrimage when the light is low to the horizon, low like it is all day in the beautiful, softly-lit Quantock country.

As Peter Coates talked about those who detected a feminine beauty in landscape, I wondered how this 'bedroom lighting' in the Quantocks assisted the femininity. The curves and the smoothness of the landscape are drawn by this light. But I am uncomfortable with the preferential treatment of the adult masculine viewer that this implies. Perhaps more primitive is the 'home' beauty that Francis Younghusband identified, which often includes childhood nostalgia.

Looking around the forty-nine Areas of Outstanding Natural Beauty in England, Wales and Northern Ireland, it is clear that we have designated and are celebrating places that people often visit on holidays – not working places, but places of summer contemplation and relaxation. They are often 'small' places, almost islands in a wider landscape, that can be encompassed in a short time frame, human in size. Are they attractive, and therefore places for holiday visits? Or is the beauty itself enhanced by the eyes of holiday consciousness, the step away from working life that a 'break in the country' imbues in adults, and echoes 'limitless summer holidays' of (middle class) childhood? How do the people who work in these landscapes feel about the sojourners? Such issues must be important to the work of the watchdog group, Friends of Quantock.[4]

And what about the generational elements of landscape? It is not just about childhood – before working, and outside school. Sometimes the escape from working life is permanent: where do you choose to retire, for example, if you have the means to make a choice? I wondered where Francis Younghusband finally chose to retire, as Coates talked about his ideas of 'home beauty'.[5] My friend, who regarded Somerset as home, lived in Burma till she was ten, but came 'home' to England to a house in the Quantock foothills for the war years, until she want away to work as a nurse; then, after 1945 she lived the rest of her life in London with an Australian husband also displaced by the war. Somerset was home for her because of those few special years. This was the place chosen by her soldier father for retiring, a place of beauty and peace, after the wilds of life in Asia. It was more an imagined home than a place of dwelling.

People in Australia (of a certain class) still referred to England (not Scotland or Ireland) as Home at the time of Federation in 1901. It was a time of hesitant and anxious Australian patriotism that Dorothea Mackellar captures in her poem *My Country*, written in England in 1904.[6] The six-verse poem, learned by heart by most Australian schoolchildren, is most famous for its lines:

> I love a sunburnt country
> A land of sweeping plains
> Of ragged mountain ranges
> Of droughts and flooding rains
> I love her far horizons
> I love her jewel sea
> Her beauty and her terror
> The wide brown land for me.

This is a vote for the 'sublime' in Coates' terms. Our wide brown land is also famous for its dust storms and its torrential rain. Different dust makes for different light. Indeed the skies of major cities like Sydney and Melbourne can take on an eerie daytime darkness when the topsoil hundreds of kilometres inland blows. Life itself is subject to very different forces in Australia, as Alfred Russel Wallace, who travelled so widely, reflected upon in his biogeographical writings.

In Australia, the sublime comes at a price. The famous 'I love a sunburnt country' verse is in fact the *second* in the poem *My Country*. There was a need first to dismiss the race memory of Old England, the 'home beauty' that makes it harder to love and to see the other beauty of Australia. The first verse of the poem could have been written for the Quantocks. It runs as follows:

> The love of field and coppice
> Of green and shaded lanes
> Of ordered woods and gardens
> Is running in your veins
> Strong love of grey-blue distance
> Brown streams and soft dim skies
> I know but cannot share it
> My love is otherwise.

Notes

1. A piece written in response to Peter Coates' opening (post-sunset) talk at the Quantocks Workshop, 'From the Environment to an Environment (of Outstanding Natural Beauty)', 1 March 2011.

2. Alfred Russel Wallace, 'The Importance of Dust: A Source of Beauty and Essential to Life (1898)', *Alfred Russel Wallace Classic Writings*, Paper 7 (2010), p. 5 http:// digitalcommons.wku.edu/dlps_fac_arw/7 (accessed 25/10/14). Wallace came from a village in Monmouthshire, Wales, a place no more than 60 kilometres north of the Quantocks as the crow flies.

3. For a more sophisticated view of pupillometry, see: Joss Fong, 'The Meaning of Pupil Dilation', *The Scientist: Exploring Life, Inspiring Innovation* (6 December 2012): 'For more than a century, scientists have known that our pupils respond to more than changes in light. They also betray mental and emotional commotion within. In fact, pupil dilation correlates with arousal so consistently that researchers use pupil size, or pupillometry, to investigate a wide range of psychological phenomena.' http:// www.the-scientist.com/?articles.view/articleNo/33563/title/The-Meaning-of-Pupil-Dilation/#sthash.rlKJ9qhm.dpuf (accessed 25/10/14).

4. On the first evening at Halsway, two long-standing Friends of Quantock, Denys White and Alan Hughes, introduced members of the research network to the history and current work of this independent group that has sought to protect and enhance the beauty and other landscape values of the Quantocks since 1949.

5. In 1921, Younghusband settled with his family 30 miles from London in the Kent village of Westerham.

6. Libby Robin, *How a Continent Created a Nation* (Sydney: University of New South Wales Press, 2007), p. 12.

CHAPTER 19

'Beauty and the Motorway – The Problem for All': Motoring through the Quantocks Area of Natural Beauty

Tim Cole

'Beauty and the motorway – the problem for all' was the headline in the local press when the Somerset Planning Authority launched what was described as 'a campaign aimed at preserving the Quantock Hills and at minimising the effects of extra visitors brought by the M5 motorway and other developments' in early February 1973.[1] The 'other developments' included two major issues that had dominated the previous year – plans to build a golf course on the Quantocks and to pave old tracks to create a spine road along the hills. Calls for greater vehicle access to the hills were vigorously discussed in the early 1970s, although the topic was one that pre- and post-dated this high point of debate, fitting into broader questions of how to (and who could) access this designated AONB. The battle over driving onto the Quantocks that I retell in this essay was more than simply a clash between the uneasy bedfellows of preservation and access. It involved a complex mix of class concerns, institutional rivalries and Romantic perceptions of the Quantocks as a landscape most properly explored on foot, rather than experienced through the windscreen of a motor car.

Travel technologies and shifting experiences of the Quantocks

Changing travel technologies have led to new travel practices far beyond the Quantocks. The development of rail travel not only opened up new tourist areas such as seaside resorts in nineteenth-century Britain, but also new ways of seeing the landscape.[2] A similar story can be followed with the beginnings of widespread car ownership in the middle of the twentieth century, which increased access to areas beyond rail routes and led to new ways of seeing through the windscreen.[3] The shifting history of transport technologies – from train to car – can be traced in the pages of guidebooks to the Quantocks published in the first half of the twentieth century. The first edition of Beatrix Cresswell's *Homeland Handbook* to *The Quantock Hills: Their Combes and Villages*, published in 1904, included an appendix extolling the virtues of cycling in the district. That this was a landscape to be accessed by rail and bicycle was made clear in the advertisements that featured the Great Western Railway: shops selling cycling clothing and hotels that met visitors from the train and offered proximity to 'excellent cycling roads'.[4] However, by the time of the guide's fifth edition in 1922, things had changed. Gone was Cresswell's two-page guide to 'Cycling on the Quantocks' and cycling-oriented advertising. Although the text of the handbook itself changed relatively little, the assumption was increasingly that the visitor to the Quantocks would be a motorist whose needs were met by the garages selling petrol and offering car repairs that advertised in the 1922 edition, alongside hotels offering garaging for cars rather than stabling for horses.[5]

The 1922 edition of Cresswell's guide to the Quantocks was published at the very beginning of a period of rapid expansion of car ownership in Great Britain. Between 1919 and 1939 car ownership grew from 109,715 to 2,034,000: a remarkable 20-fold increase in two decades.[6] However, this massive increase in motorists on Britain's roads was largely restricted to the middle classes, with motoring emerging as a key component of inter-war middle class identities.[7] The needs of middle class motorists were central to the concerns of Edward H. Smith, a local reverend, whose *Quantock Life and Rambles* was first published in 1939. Epitomising the shifts in tourist practices associated with changing travel practices, Smith introduced his readers to the Quantocks, in part at least, as if through the windscreen of an interwar roadster. Visitors driving into the Quantocks from Taunton were promised a 'glorious trip', but better was to come.[8] Smith offered up the 6-mile drive from Kingston to Enmore as the finest stretch of road in the whole of England (although it seems that his vision of England was entirely southern). As he explained:

> there are very many stretches of lovely roads in England – that for instance running over Hindhead from Liphook to Godalming – or that from Stowe in the Wold, over the Cotswolds down Fish Hill to Broadway – or the more level road from Evesham to Warwick. But the road from Kingston to Enmore, in the opinion of the writer, has more to offer, in every season of the year, than any of those mentioned.

It was here that Smith assured the motorist that they 'can always find something to charm, and it is all so restful and refreshing', and he advised them to take it slow and make frequent stops at the gateways that offered far-reaching views of the coast, the mountains of South Wales and Glastonbury Tor.[9]

This particular road that pleased Smith so much was one that Cresswell had suggested as one of four possible routes that could be taken by visitors to the Quantocks a few decades earlier. However, while offering 'magnificent and varying views of sea and land', the 'very long and steep hill' meant that Cresswell's cyclists were directed to take the road to Cothelstone Beacon instead of the road to Enmore.[10] Yet while Smith's motorist might find it easier on steep ascents than Cresswell's cyclist, both were restricted by the lack of roads over the hilly ranges. It was here that Cresswell advised that 'the heights of the

Quantocks are best explored on foot,' given that 'the innumerable bridle paths' were 'for the most part too steep and rough for a bicycle' (though this is no bar to today's cyclist equipped with a robust mountain bike).[11]

It was not simply pragmatic concerns that underlay Cresswell's privileging of rambling. Even in the more cultivated southern combes, Cresswell claimed that it was on foot that natural beauty was truly encountered. There was something about both the pace and immediacy of walking this landscape that Cresswell interpreted as affording intimate access. As she advised visitors:

> it is scarcely necessary to add that the number of rambles among the combes are practically inexhaustible. All that we feel after a visit to any of them is that we know something about the hills; we have had a glimpse of their beauties, a taste of their delights. Nature reveals herself slowly, she will not draw aside her veil too soon, we must know her intimately before we can declare that we have seen her, face to face.[12]

There were glimpses of the 'wonderful beauty' of the Quantocks that could be viewed from the road. As Cresswell acknowledged:

> after passing East Quantockshead the road becomes shady and somewhat undulating, and after a sharp decline the scene suddenly opens upon a full view of the beautiful woods that crown the headland and descend to the seashore, with St Audries Church lying in a green hollow close to the way-side. Even after familiarity has taught what to expect, the view never fails to renew the first impression of wonderful beauty, though presently we realise that the secret of its indescribable loveliness lies in the unusual combination of woodland and moorland in sight of the sea, with that additional touch of homeliness and stateliness given by the village church and the mansion.[13]

However, to truly experience the beauties of a nature – to see her 'face to face' – the speed of a cyclist, let alone a motorist, was simply too fast, and the access afforded by metalled roads were too limiting. Cresswell's 'nature' demanded both a more complete immersion and a slowing of pace. She was not alone. As Catherine Brace has suggested, here was a broader issue about driving through interwar Britain where 'a moral geography of speed was … constructed. If haste was considered morally repugnant, the corollary was that a slow, considered, lingering encounter with the countryside was commended.'[14]

Reading Cresswell's and Smith's guides, it is clear that they had different visions of the Quantocks that both shaped, and were informed by, their differing modes and speeds of travelling through and accessing this landscape. For Smith, who adopted the view from the road, this was a landscape on a grand scale – 'a bit of Scotland transplanted into Somersetshire' – to be navigated at speed.[15] In contrast, Cresswell insisted that the Quantocks represented the more intimate landscape of the 'gentle west county' rather than 'the rugged north'.[16] In a striking passage she reassured the prospective visitor that:

> in truth the wildness of the region is but the playfulness of a charming child making pretence to be something extremely terrible, and betraying the jest by its laughter. In the Quantocks there is nothing of that vast wildness which gives almost a touch of terror to some of our English moors. Here Dame Nature is all tenderness. The wind fluttering through the trees seems to fill the leaves with laughter: the wide

views from the healthy summits extend over scenes of culture and prosperity. Only in winter, when the trees are bare, do the hills become grey and saddened, but even then whenever possible they become astir with horse and hounds, and the voices of the streamlets are never silent.[17]

The kind of face-to-face encounter with a benign 'Dame Nature' (impossible through the car windscreen) that Cresswell encouraged was absent from Smith's accessing the Quantocks through the motor car in the 1930s.

However, Cresswell's privileging of accessing the Quantocks on foot did not simply fade away with the ascendancy of the motoring tourist on either side of the Second World War. Rather, this position forcefully reappeared precisely at that moment when car ownership became increasingly widespread. In his *Portrait of the Quantocks*, published in 1964, Vincent Waite reasserted the primacy of rambling as *the* way to access the natural beauty of this place, restating a Romantic tradition of strenuous encounter with nature that arguably begins in the Quantocks, with Coleridge and Wordsworth, in the 1790s (see Marianna Dudley's essay in this volume). For Waite, 'the hills do not need any lengthy description in a book. Their beauty is obvious to anyone whose senses are not blunted by the modern craze for motoring speed and who can still walk, even if their walking is of the gentlest, most unathletic kind.'[18] While the four roads that crossed the Quantocks 'have certainly done much towards revealing glimpses of the beauties of the Quantocks', offering 'even motor-bound week-enders some of the magnificent views which stretch away on all sides below them', there was – for Waite – a better way to experience this landscape.[19] This applied in the particular, with Waite asserting that 'those on foot or bicycle again have the advantage over the motorist in making the journey from Bagborough to Crowcombe, for they can take a narrow road sign-posted to Triscombe at the bottom of Bagborough Hill,' leaving the motorist to take the main road that offered 'some equally fine views' but was 'not quite so picturesque'.[20] But it also applied in the general, with Waite writing that 'it is only the walker who can really appreciate the breath-taking sweep of the distant views – the dipping curves of the sea-coast; the great rise and fall of Exmoor to the west.'[21]

Behind his critique of the limitations of motoring lay a broader set of class-based concerns about a new breed of motorist in post-Second World War Britain. Car ownership tripled between 1949 and 1961, and by 1970 there were 12.2 million cars in Britain.[22] Motoring was no longer the preserve of a middle class elite, something that Waite himself was well aware of. Drawing an analogy with an earlier moment of mass access to the countryside during another transport revolution (1860s), Waite reflected that:

> Some seventy-five years ago the author of Thomas Poole and His Friends wrote of the Quantocks: "Far be it from the present writer not to rejoice, as in a great and signal benefit, that railways have thrown open so much of the beauty of hill and moor and sea to the foot of the cheap excursionist, thus enriching the lives of thousands with new possibilities of enjoyment. Nevertheless there is, and ever must be, a special charm in untroddenness, which we cannot but lose with some regret."

This "present writer" wonders what the "present writer" of that generation would think of the car-cluttered roads of today which have thrown open so much to the wheel of the motorist. If more metalled roads are made over the hills there is no doubt that a great deal of their charm will be lost.[23]

Waite's desire for 'untroddenness' came close to an elitism that sought to keep the Quantocks for the few rather than the many through his privileging of middle class notions of solitary experiences of nature.[24]

As Waite's book suggests, technological change could be, and was, resisted. As I have already suggested at the outset, this battle took place not simply in the pages of guidebooks, but also on the hills themselves where plans for car parking and road improvements were a major source of conflict in the 1960s and 1970s. This conflict was in part a parochial institutional battle between two different interest groups representing different local constituencies. But it also reflected the broader concerns that can be seen in Waite's guidebook. It brought to the fore class-based anxieties about the car bringing too many (and the wrong kind of) visitors to the Quantocks as well as longer-running and broader concerns about how best to (and not just who could) access not only a landscape of natural beauty, but also a cultural landscape trodden by the Romantic poets.

Resisting the 'spine chilling road': battles over preservation and access

The opening skirmishes of what ended up being more than a decade-long battle over driving on to the hills came in 1959 when signs were erected, 'at the request of the Friends of the Quantocks', prohibiting motor vehicles from driving onto the green lanes and bridleways on the Quantocks because of the damage being done to the hills.[25] These restrictions were a local response to the designation of the Quantocks as an AONB in 1957. For the Friends of Quantock, a local pressure group first founded in 1949 to challenge plans for afforestation of swathes of the Quantocks, the priority of preservation necessitated the banning of destructive motoring.[26] However, a counter-argument was offered that also drew on the recent designation of the Quantocks and argued instead from the perspective of access.[27] Over Stowey Parish Council, a local organization that emerged as a powerful proponent of driving onto the hills, claimed that 'invalids and convalescents are … taken on the hills by car to see this outstanding beauty, a beauty which will be deprived by this prohibition.'[28]

Beneath this rhetoric of ensuring that 'invalids and convalescents' could access landscapes of beauty – an argument that would be restated again – lay a set of more self-interested concerns championed by a rival organization to the Friends of Quantock: the relatively short-lived Quantock Rights Association, an organization dominated by landowning interests. The two organizations clashed over the issue of vehicle access to the Quantocks during the 1960s and 1970s based on two very different ways of seeing this landscape as well as the role of the state in preservation.[29] The dual aims of the Friends of Quantock were 'to preserve the natural beauty and amenities' and 'to protect all rights of common and to maintain the freedom of the public to wander at will over the Hills', privileging access on foot.[30] In contrast, the Quantock Rights Association emphasized access over preservation – with dual aims 'to preserve and perpetuate the long-established rights enjoyed by the Public and owners of rights in respect of the Quantock Hills' and 'to resist by all rational means any attempt to restrict freedom of access to or movement over the said hills so that the Public may not be deprived of facilities for enjoying to the full the beauty and amenities of the area' – and were less specific about the mode of access.[31] For the Quantock Rights Association, a constant concern during the 1960s and into the early 1970s was with ensuring continued vehicle access to the Quantock Hills by landowners, hunt followers and the general public alike.

Following the opening skirmishes, the next stage of the battle over accessing the hills came in the mid-1960s when Somerset Council issued plans to invest in car parking facilities on the Quantocks. The Quantock Rights Association played a pivotal role in a newly established Quantock Parishes Action Committee that fought Council plans for a car park at Lydeard Hill.[32] In part, their opposition stemmed from a claim that car parks would be 'a scar on the landscape' and a 'monstrosity', and that it would be preferable if 'cars could be dispersed over the whole area of the hills without affecting their peace or beauty instead of vainly attempting to concentrate them in car parks'.[33] Alongside these aesthetic concerns, there also appear to have been concerns over car parks attracting too many of the wrong kind of people to the Quantocks. Fears were expressed that 'car parks will merely attract greater and greater numbers who will drive anywhere' and, more tellingly, that 'car parks will also attract a noisy element and completely ruin the atmosphere of peace and quiet.'[34]

The assumption that providing facilities would encourage the wrong kind of visitor had been expressed a year earlier, by a representative of the Friends of Quantock who expressed concerns that the provision of open fire places at a proposed picnic site in Quantock Forest (a Forestry Commission plantation) would 'attract an undesirable section of the community'.[35] However the Friends of Quantock were rather non-committal over the issue of building car parks. They were invited to attend the Quantock Parishes Action Committee meeting in March 1965 and did promise to send two representatives, but replied affirming their long-standing belief that 'motorists should somehow or other be confined to the recognized vehicular roads on the hills.' Indeed, it appeared that they were supportive of the original idea.[36] Certainly the scheme meshed with their longer-standing interests in restricting motor access to the hills in order – as the Bridgwater Rural District Council explained to scheme opponents in February 1965 – 'to preserve and enhance the natural beauty of the area by providing ... for properly surfaced Car Parks in order to reduce damage which has been caused by indiscriminate parking and motoring over the area'.[37]

It was this touchstone issue of 'motoring over the area' (and what we might refer to as 'wild parking') that lay at the heart of opposition to permanent car parks by members of the Quantock Rights Association and Quantock Parishes

Action Committee. Ultimately, fundamental issues of self-interest underlay the Quantock Rights Association opposition to plans for permanent car parks which they saw as both threatening commoners' rights and – more importantly – being a waste of public money. As became clear, they had other plans for this money to be 'spent in a variety of ways which would improve the amenities of the Quantock Hills and be of advantage to local inhabitants'. Specifically, they wanted Somerset County Council to use money from the 'Rees Road Fund foundation' to pave the green tracks over the hills rather than build car parks for visitors.[38] What better place to start, suggested the opponents of car parks, than diverting the money earmarked for car parks to make up the track that ran between the Triscombe Stone and Crowcombe Gate which could then be 'further extended in a westerly direction as funds are available'.[39]

Half a decade later, renewed calls for paving the track that ran the full length across the Quantocks by individuals aligned to the Quantock Rights Association, in particular the landowner Major Trollope-Belew, sparked massive debate, bringing the Friends of Quantock once more into the fray. During 1972 and 1973, the dispute rumbled on in the pages of the local press, in parish meetings, planning committees and open meetings – escalating in the process.[40] For proponents of the scheme, the needs of the elderly and invalids were once again articulated, with Alderman Archie Clarke calling for the creation of 'circular routes for the hills with provision for children and the elderly who would arrive by car', allowing drivers to 'picnic on the sunny side of the hill, taking their old people, children and those who cannot walk any distance with them, and have a viewing point'.[41] In the words of Major Trollope-Belew, what was the point of 'having an area of outstanding natural beauty if nobody could see it'?[42]

Proponents of the scheme like Clarke and Trollope-Belew positioned themselves as pragmatists who were ready to accept the need for change. For Clarke, 'the days of walkers in tweeds being the main users of the hills were over, and … the motor would have to be accepted and provided for in future policy' and 'the car has come here to stay and you have got to cater for it. They're catering for cars in the Exmoor National Park but we don't seem to have any idea on the Quantocks. The whole place is bunged up and congested.'[43] Clarke intentionally contrasted his pragmatic stance as an insider who had lived his whole life in the Quantocks with the inflexible, outsider perspective of preservationists in the Council for the Protection of Rural England 'with headquarters in London and composed mostly of commuters, whose ideas on preservation would let our villages and countryside die'.[44] But alongside presenting themselves as forward looking and adaptable modernizers, Clarke and Trollope-Belew also drew on historical precedent. All they wanted, they insisted, was to restore tracks that had been used 3,000 years ago and were in use by horse-drawn coaches in the eighteenth century until 'the parsimony of the Turnpike Trust in the last century allowed it to fall into disrepair.'[45] However, as opponents were quick to point out, 'the pollutant factor of Ancient Britons, or even gigs, is hardly comparable with that of modern motor vehicles.'[46]

Reading through the local press from the period when debate was raging, the voices of opponents to the scheme clearly came through most strongly. Opposition to what was dubbed a 'spine chilling road' brought together the local branch of the Council for the Protection of Rural England and the Friends of Quantock, as well as receiving support from cyclists and ramblers.[47] In part, opponents touched on class-based anxieties that had surfaced during earlier disputes over car parks. While one letter writer agreed that 'Alderman Clarke puts forward a sympathetic plea that the aged and infirm be provided with access to the hills,' they warned readers of the local press that they 'would do well to remember that the same road access will open up the hillsides to noisy group outings, lazy litter droppers and commercial ice-cream sellers', going on to note that it would be impossible to restrict access 'to country lovers like Alderman Clarke. We will have to share our tiny but precious heritage of the Quantocks with friend and foe alike.'[48]

However, far more widely expressed were views that motor cars and roads were quite simply incompatible with the qualities of solitude amongst natural beauty that opponents sought in the Quantocks.[49] Mrs Robin Lewis, Honorary Secretary of the Somerset branch of the Campaign for the Protection of Rural England (CPRE) and a frequent writer of letters to the press on the matter, argued that 'those of us who know and value the peace and comparative seclusion of the Quantocks as a retreat from noise, bustle and urban sprawl' were firmly opposed to the road plans.[50] Another writer to the local press predicted that the road would reduce a 'stretch of country that still retains much of its wild and unspoilt character' to 'a promenade for carborne sightseers'.[51] Auberon Waugh, writing to the *Observer*, agreed that the spine road would turn 'one of the few places in Southern England where people can get away from the motor car in conditions of outstanding natural beauty ... into the sort of Driverama one already sees in Exmoor, where cars are bumper to bumper in summer'.[52]

For opponents of the scheme, it was partly a matter of scale; the 'relatively small Quantock territory' was a landscape to be walked in, and not driven through.[53] As one letter writer put it, 'For God's sake let's have somewhere left where the horse or a pair of legs and a walking stick remain supreme', and another, 'let those who wish to traverse the tops do so on foot or on horseback, whether they be locals or come from up-country.'[54] Moreover, walking the Quantocks was, as a letter writer a couple of years later reminded his readers, a continuation of the Romantic tradition of Coleridge. As he explained: 'I often walk on the Quantocks for the exercise, the views, and that special "something" that Coleridge found and by which he was so inspired.'[55]

By the time that this new Romantic wrote to the press in 1974, plans for improvements to the spine road had long been rejected by the relevant planning committee.[56] Yet concerns rumbled on about vehicles using the green tracks that rang the length of the hills. In 1974 and 1975 Friends of Quantock continued to complain about vehicle tracks on the Quantocks, with hunt followers being identified in the local press as the major culprits.[57] Those who insisted on driving onto the hills revealed 'the worst kind of selfishness. Too lazy to walk, these people still want to enjoy the plum views, and so spoil the pleasure for everybody else.'[58]

As is clear, the first two decades of the designation of the Quantocks as an AONB saw vigorous debate over the place of the motor car in accessing and experiencing the 'natural beauty' of this landscape. Ultimately, repeated calls for greater vehicle access – including plans for a spine road navigating the length of the Quantocks and opening up the vistas to be seen from the car windscreen – were rejected and the supremacy of walking these hills was championed. The opposition to road building in the Quantocks was tinged with class concerns. However, more critical here appears to have been the coming together of perceptions of the Quantocks as simultaneously natural and cultural landscape. The Quantocks was defended against the encroaching motor car not simply on the grounds of a wilderness threatened by an ever expanding modernity.[59] The Quantocks was also defended as cultural landscape of the Romantic poets freighted with ideological assumptions of the moral value of strenuous encounter with the wild. In short, it seems that the Quantocks was not just a place of 'outstanding natural beauty', but a landscape imbued with cultural references that shaped understandings of both this place and the ways to access it. As one letter writer concluded his polemic charge against off-roaders, 'Coleridge composed some of his best poetry whilst walking on the Quantocks. If he were alive now, I wonder how "The Rapacious Motorist" would read? I have a feeling that it would be banned for obscenity.'[60]

The motorists that Smith's guidebook had welcomed into the Quantocks in 1939 were widely seen as problematic intruders into Coleridge's landscape in the 1950s, 1960s and 1970s, both in the pages of Waite's book and on the ground in the battle over plans for a spine road. Indeed, in many ways the Quantocks remains a landscape accessed on foot rather than by car.[61] Driving into the Quantocks from Bristol for the workshop at Halsway Manor, we took one of the few steep, narrow and winding roads that cross the ridge (from Nether Stowey). There were enticing glimpses to left and right at the crown of the hill but then we quickly dropped down to Crowcombe, West Bagborough and, eventually, Halsway, tucked underneath the south side of the Quantocks. Over the next few days that we explored this landscape, we did get the views. But we had to walk for them, firstly up the short ascent of Cothelstone Hill and then, most memorably, along a part of the ridge where the grassy track that had fuelled so much debate in the early 1970s was quietly visible and entirely vehicle free (though off-roading presents an occasional problem for the AONB service's rangers).

In contrast, a few weeks later we headed north to Kielder Water and Forest Park in Northumberland. We did walk at Kielder as well, but Kielder felt more like driving country. Maybe the sporty rental car that a group of workshop participants collected at Newcastle Airport helped frame our experience of this place. But it was not just that we drove a car that was different to our usual vehicles, with powerful acceleration and racing tires. We also drove on very different roads from the steep winding road that we navigated across the

Quantocks. We entered Kielder Water and Forest Park on a road with the sweeping curves of a US national parkway purpose-built for a post-war mass motoring world that cut through a landscape on a far more expansive scale than the intimate Quantocks.[62] Perhaps it was the North American tree species fringing the road as well as the curves of the tarmac, but driving through Kielder awakened echoes of Kerouac rather than Coleridge. If there was 'outstanding natural beauty' in both, then we viewed and accessed it differently both in terms of pace and scale. I am reminded of J. B. Priestly's argument in defence of moving at speed through certain landscapes on the grounds that 'there is a certain kind of pleasant but dullish, rolling country, not very attractive to the walker or the slow traveller, that becomes alive if you go quickly across it, for it is turned into a kind of sculptured landscape.'[63] In short, Priestly hinted at natural 'beauty' as far from static, but potentially constructed at the speed of the moving car in the ever-shifting 'glance' rather than the fixed 'gaze'.[64]

But such notions of speeding through a landscape have been resisted in the Quantocks, where an embodied experience of landscape through walking has been privileged in the pages of guidebooks and the local press. As I have suggested, debates over road building on the Quantocks have been more than simply another local example of battles between modernizers and preservationists. These disputes have been underpinned by a view of the Quantocks as a cultural as well as natural landscape. Viewing the Quantocks as Romantic landscape, this cultural legacy has – at least in part – shaped how this 'area of outstanding natural beauty' has been accessed and seen.

Notes

1.   Somerset Heritage Centre, Taunton (hereafter SHC), A\CVZ/1/1 Newspaper Cuttings (1970s–1980s), 'Beauty and the Motorway – The Problem for All' (2 February 1973); 'Another Warning of Threat to Quantocks' (11 May 1973). Given that this is a press clippings folder, in the majority of cases the title of the newspaper is not recorded. With the coming of the M5, the local press estimated that five million people were now within a three-hour drive time of the Quantocks.

2.   John K. Walton, 'Railways and Resort Development in Victorian England: The Case of Silloth', *Northern History* 15 (1979), pp. 191–209; John K. Walton, 'Transport, Travel, Tourism and Mobility: A Cultural Turn?', *Journal of Transport History* 27 (2006), pp. 129–34; Wolfgang Schivelbusch, *The Railway Journey: The Industrialization of Time and Space in the Nineteenth Century* (Leamington Spa: Berg, 1986), esp. pp. 52–69.

3.   See in particular Jonas Larsen, 'Tourism Mobilities and the Travel Glance: Experiences of Being on the Move', *Scandinavian Journal of Hospitality and Tourism* 1/2 (2001), pp. 80–9; David Louter, *Windshield Wilderness: Cars, Roads, and Nature in Washington's National Parks* (Seattle: University of Washington Press, 2006); Christof Mauch and Thomas Zeller (eds), *The World Beyond the Windshield: Roads and Landscapes in the United States and Europe* (Athens, OH: Ohio University Press, 2008).

4.   Beatrix F. Cresswell, *The Quantock Hills: Their Combes and Villages. The Homeland Handbooks No. 35.* 1st edn (London: Homeland Association, 1904).

5.   Beatrix F. Cresswell, *The Quantock Hills: Their Combes and Villages. The Homeland Handbooks Vol. 35.* 5th edn (London: Homeland Association, 1922). On the growth

of this 'rural entrepreneurship' at the roadside, see: Sean O'Connell, *The Car in British Society. Class, Gender and Motoring 1896–1939* (Manchester: Manchester University Press, 1998), pp. 175–8.

6. Harold Perkin, *The Age of the Automobile* (London: Quartet Books, 1976); O'Connell, *The Car*, p. 19.

7. O' Connell, *The Car*, pp. 8, 19–38; on the broader context see Ross McKibbin, *Classes and Cultures: England 1918–1951* (Oxford: Oxford University Press, 1998).

8. Edward H. Smith, *Quantock Life and Rambles* (Taunton: Wessex Press, 1939), p. 10.

9. Smith, *Quantock Life*, pp. 62–3.

10. Cresswell, *Quantock Hills* (1922), pp. 18–9.

11. Cresswell, *Quantock Hills* (1922), p. 100.

12. Cresswell, *Quantock Hills* (1922), p. 57. This quote is cited in The Countryside Agency, *The Quantock Hills Landscape: An Assessment of the Area of Outstanding Natural Beauty* (Wetherby: Countryside Agency Publications, 2003), p. 50.

13. Cresswell, *Quantock Hills* (1922), pp. 81–2.

14. Catherine Brace, 'A Pleasure Ground for Noisy Herds? Incompatible Encounters with the Cotswolds and England, 1900–1950', *Rural History* 11/1 (2000), p. 87. See also: David Matless, 'Moral Geographies of English Landscape', *Landscape Research* 22/2 (1997).

15. Smith, *Quantock Life*, p. 3.

16. Cresswell, *Quantock Hills* (1922), p. 117.

17. Cresswell, *Quantock Hills* (1922), p. 10.

18. Vincent Waite, *Portrait of the Quantocks* (London: Robert Hale, 1964), p. 9.

19. Waite, *Portrait of the Quantocks*, p. 20.

20. Waite, *Portrait of the Quantocks*, p. 51.

21. Waite, *Portrait of the Quantocks*, p. 20.

22. Trevor Rowley, *The English Landscape in the Twentieth Century* (London: Hambledon Continuum, 2006), p. 36.

23. Waite, *Portrait of the Quantocks*, p. 20. West Somerset was opened up in 1862 by a branch line off the Bristol and Exeter trunk line that ran from the junction at Norton Fitzwarren, near Taunton, in a northwesterly direction up the vale between the Quantocks and the Brendon Hills for 15 miles to Watchet (extended to Minehead in 1874). See Peter Haggett, *The Quantocks: Biography of an English Region* (Chew Magna: The Point Walter Press, 2012), pp. 131–2.

24. On this elitism elsewhere, see: Brace, 'A Pleasure Ground for the Noisy Herds?', pp. 75–94; Elizabeth Baigent, '"God's earth will be sacred": Religion, Theology, and the Open Space Movement in Victorian England', *Rural History* 22/1 (2011), pp. 31–58. For Wordsworth's opposition to the railway in the Lake District, see: James Mulvihill, 'Consuming Nature: Wordsworth and the Kendal and Windermere Railway Controversy', *Modern Language Quarterly* 56/3 (1995), pp. 305–26.

25. SHC, C/GP/HF/852, Concerning Rights of Way and Signage on the Quantocks 8/2/58–16/1/62, Letter from E. S. Rickards, Clerk of Somerset County Council to Clerk of Over Stowey Parish Council (15 September 1959).

26. Friends of Quantock, unlike the more short-lived Quantock Rights Association, is still very much active. See: www.friendsofquantock.com (accessed 25/10/14).

27. While both National Parks and AONBs were to preserve and enhance natural beauty, only National Parks were charged specifically with a mandate to promote public enjoyment. See Margaret A. Anderson, 'Areas of Outstanding Natural Beauty and the 1949 National Parks Act', *The Town Planning Review* 61/3 (1990), pp. 311–39.

28. SHC, C/GP/HF/852, Letter from W. Richards, Clerk to Over Stowey Parish Council to F. A. Goodcliffe, Somerset Association of Parish Councils (14 January 1960).

29. On different (social) groups and their relationship with the environment, see: Alan Taylor, 'Unnatural Inequalities: Social and Environmental Histories', *Environmental History* 1/4 (1996), pp. 6–19. On differing views of the state's role in preservation see David Matless, *Landscape and Englishness* (London: Reaktion Books, 1998).

30. SHC, D\PC\o.sty/5/1/1, Letter from Rex Womack, Honorary Secretary of Friends of Quantock to J. R. Emmett, Clerk to Over Stowey Parish Council (9 March 1965).

31. SHC, D\PC\o.sty/5/1/1, 'Rule and Regulations of the Quantock Right Association' (undated).

32. SHC, D\PC\o.sty/5/1/1, Letter from D. Ferguson, Hon. Secretary of Quantock Parishes Action Committee (23 June 1965); Letter from Clerk of County Council to Mr J. R. Emmett (23 June 1965).

33. SHC, D\PC\o.sty/5/1/1, Letter from Hon. Secretary of Quantock Parishes Action Committee (undated); Letter from Mrs Rita Aherns to the Chairman of Over Stowey Parish Council (undated); Untitled note (undated).

34. SHC, D\PC\o.sty/5/1/1, Untitled handwritten note (undated).

35. SHC, D\PC\o.sty/5/1/1, Bridgwater Rural District Council Notes on Informal Meeting (26 May 1964).

36. SHC, D\PC\o.sty/5/1/1, Letter from Rex Womack, Hon. Secretary of Friends of Quantock to J. R. Emmett, Clerk to Over Stowey Parish Council (9 March 1965).

37. SHC, D\PC\o.sty/5/1/1, Letter from F. J. Bastin, Clerk to Bridgwater Rural District Council to J. R. Emmett, Clerk to Over Stowey Parish Council (25 February 1965).

38. SHC, D\PC\o.sty/5/1/1, Letter from J. R. Emmett, Clerk to Over Stowey Parish Council (18 March 1965); Letter from D. Ferguson, Hon. Secretary of Quantock Parishes Action Committee (23 June 1965).

39. SHC, D\PC\o.sty/5/1/1, Letter from D. Ferguson, Hon. Secretary of Quantock Parishes Action Committee (23 June 1965).

40. SHC, A\CVZ/1/1, 'Misunderstanding Claimed over Quantock Tracks' (26 May 1972).

41. SHC, A\CVZ/1/1, 'Beauty and the Motorway – The Problem for All' (2 February 1973); Letter from Alderman A. W. Clarke (16 June 1972).

42. SHC, A\CVZ/1/1, 'Beauty and the Motorway – The Problem for All' (2 February 1973).

43. SHC, A\CVZ/1/1, 'Beauty and the Motorway – The Problem for All' (2 February 1973); 'Case for Quantock car road. Readers' Letters', Letter from Alderman A. W. Clarke (16 June 1972).

44. SHC, A\CVZ/1/1, 'Case for Quantock car road. Readers' Letters', Letter from Alderman A. W. Clarke (16 June 1972).

45. SHC, A\CVZ/1/1, 'Beauty and the Motorway – The Problem for All' (2 February 1973); 'In steps of the ancient Britons' (16 June 1972).

46. SHC, A\CVZ/1/1, 'Guarding Quantock Peace. Readers' Letters', Letter from Mrs Robin Lewis, Hon. Secretary of Somerset Branch of CPRE (undated).

47. SHC, A\CVZ/1/1, 'Cyclists' Magazine Opposes Quantock Plan' (4 May 1973).

48. SHC, A\CVZ/1/1, 'Guarding Quantock Peace. Readers' Letters', Letter from D. H. S. White, *Somerset County Gazette* (undated).

49. In the United States the 1964 Wilderness Act explicitly prohibited permanent roads in wilderness areas.

50. SHC, A\CVZ/1/1, 'Quantock Spine Road', Letter from Robin Lewis, Hon. Secretary of Somerset Branch of CPRE (9 May 1972).

51. SHC, A\CVZ/1/1, 'Quantocks road', Letter from Martyn Skinner, *Bridgwater Mercury* (27 June 1972).

52. SHC, A\CVZ/1/1, 'Spoiling the Quantocks', Letter from Auberon Waugh, *The Observer* (2 July 1972).

53. SHC, A\CVZ/1/1, 'Curbing Hill-Top Invasion', Editorial, *Bridgwater Mercury* (27 June 1972).

54. SHC, A\CVZ/1/1, 'Guarding Quantock Peace. Readers' Letters', Letter from J. Skeggs, *Somerset County Gazette* (undated).

55. SHC, A\CVZ/1/1, 'Quantock Paths', Letter from Andrew Puckett (22 March 1974).

56. SHC, A\CVZ/1/1, 'Quantock Track Fears Allayed' (2 June 1972); 'Conference on Quantock Track Called' (23 June 1972); 'Hysteria over Spine Road Move' (23 June 1972).

57. SHC, A\CVZ/1/1.

58. SHC, A\CVZ/1/1, 'Quantock Paths', Letter from Andrew Puckett (23 March 1974).

59. Paul Sutter, *Driven Wild: How the Fight against Automobiles Launched the Modern Wilderness Movement* (Seattle: University of Washington Press, 2002).

60. SHC, A\CVZ/1/1, 'Quantock Paths', Letter from Andrew Puckett (22 March 1974).

61. For the development of a 36-mile trail 'in the footsteps' of Coleridge across the Quantocks, see: http://www.coleridgeway.co.uk/ (accessed 25/10/14).

62. On driving and the US national parks, see in particular: Louter, *Windshield Wilderness*; A. Mitchell Whisnant, *Super-Scenic Motorway. A Blue Ridge Parkway History* (Chapel Hill: University of North Carolina Press, 2006).

63. J. B. Priestly, *English Journey* (London: Tauchnitz, 1934), p. 3, cited in Brace, 'A Pleasure Ground for the Noisy Herds?', pp. 88.

64. On the 'glance' from the moving car, see: Larsen, 'Tourism Mobilities and the Travel Glance'.

CHAPTER 20

The Beautiful and the Global

....

Petra J. E. M. van Dam

At the Quantocks workshop we tried to identify the difference between *sublime* and (merely) *beautiful*. Peter Coates argued that beautiful alludes to smooth, soft, gentle and mainly visual dimensions. Sublime has connotations of infinity, deity, delightful horror, terrible cliffs and affects all the senses. An agricultural (working) landscape seems closer to simply beautiful, whereas the (American) idea of pristine wilderness is closer to sublime.

We heard about the English Romantic poets, Coleridge and Wordsworth, who explored the Quantocks as the first 'literary landscape' visitors. They saw the Quantock landscape not as a working landscape, but as a painting, as 'picturesque.' We talked about our intuition (derived from the Romantic poets?) that high country is more sublime than lowlands. We discussed the difference between the (high) Quantock Hills and the (low) Somerset Levels, and considered the bigger mountains in the Scottish Highlands and the north of England as opposed to the gentle hills of southern England. Also, we read in Margaret Anderson's articles (our homework) that, statistically, most national parks are situated in areas of higher altitude than AONBs (Areas of Outstanding Natural Beauty). This seems to express the widely-held belief that hilly areas are more beautiful than flat landscapes, and that very high mountains are closer to sublime than lower peaks.

Now here is a thought experiment I would like to put forward: if in our time (as it was in prehistory, according to archaeologist Hazel Riley),[1] the hilly landscapes had been the *agricultural* landscapes, and the flats the inaccessible *wild* marshes, would this have altered our appreciation of beauty? In short, which is more important to qualify for the label sublime: high or wild?

At this point I would like to quote an important father of Romanticism, the French philosopher Jean-Jacques Rousseau, who was greatly enamoured of the Alps, which was the setting for his best-selling novel, *Julie, or the New Heloise* (1761). In his autobiographical work, *Confessions*, he expresses two different appreciations of natural beauty, the root of the differences we discussed between beauty and the sublime:

Moreover, what I mean by fine scenery must by now be clear. A flat landscape, however beautiful, has never seemed so to my eye. I need rushing streams, rocks, pine trees, dark woods, mountains, rugged tracks to scramble up and down, precipices on either side to fill me with fear.[2]

Rousseau introduces the personal, emotional and physical experience of landscape. That it is difficult, even dangerous, to reach this higher landscape contributes to the greatness of the experience. Emotions of fear enhance the experience. Flat landscapes do not provide these emotions and therefore are not sublime, but, at best, merely beautiful. But apart from that, to me it seems there is also a quality in the landscape which comes from emotions attributed to the landscape, emotions related to speed and dynamics (as in the rushing of the streams) or to natural movements (falling rocks, for example, maybe even avalanches?). I feel that the image of a precipice stands in the border zone; it may act as a connection between the individual and the landscape. For precipices are only dangerous because one imagines one may fall off them. So fear aroused by a precipice is an emotion about the possibility of falling, heightened when one identifies oneself with a falling stone. And where there are falling stones all around (landslide), this might stimulate the imagination further. I like to interpret this text fragment in this way, because I know that fear very well, being a lowlander with lots of experience in highlands.

I continue with a question that follows logically from the previous one, in my opinion: how does our experience with particular landscapes affect our appreciation of and experience with other landscapes? And how did this change over time, or how should we conceive of this in a historical way? Large countries like Great Britain and France contain both highlands and lowlands. My country, the Netherlands, is part of the lowlands of Europe and is so small that it contains only lowlands and some slightly hilly areas, but no highlands whatsoever. Our nearest highlands are the Alps. One finds a surprisingly large number of inhabitants of the lowlands of Europe among Alpine tourists, both Germans and Dutch. I suppose we are all a bit like Rousseau (who was born on the threshold of the Alps, in Geneva, but wrote *Julie* while living near Paris, one of the flattest places in France). We find the Alps sublime and majestic and we appreciate them for the terrific and contrasting landscape experience they provide. We really need to struggle to reach the tops to take in the sublime views. And because we are real lowlanders, this also demands a strong physiological effort: before we can access a real mountain we have to wait a couple of days, after arrival, until our blood has adapted to the thinner air. (That experience has been compromised by the numerous, fossil fuel energized lifts, but that is a different story).

My personal landscape experience was very much influenced by the highlands. I spent long summer holidays in the Alps from age ten. That was beautiful and sublime. In contrast, my own country was only moderately beautiful. It was good enough for a week's cycling tour (a low-budget holiday for a student). Our preference was for the slightly elevated eastern areas, which also contain forests, enclosed fields and old, cut-in country roads with hedges, not unlike the lower parts of the Quantocks and many other agricultural areas in Britain. Only many decades later did I begin to appreciate the beauty of the flat areas of Holland – the famous polder landscape. I cannot say exactly how this happened, but Jenny Graham's remarks made me think about this. She said it took her a long time to appreciate the landscape beauty of the Somerset Levels, where she now lives. I think it has much to do with the light on the water on one hand, and the graphic characteristics of the (reclaimed) wetlands on the other hand (as expressed in rows of trees lining canals, which seems stronger to me in Holland than in England, as my fellow countryman Jan Oosthoek and I both noticed).[3] It may be a rather abstract beauty, and more for the eye than for the other senses. Perhaps it is for this reason that David Moon feels the appreciation of lowlands are an acquired taste, 'in contrast to the more obvious "beauty" of hills and mountains'.[4]

Moon asked Graham how she made the water in her paintings shiny ('by adding white' was her technical answer!), which suggests that the landscape derives its quality from the effect of light on water. A flat wetland landscape without sun is very dreary; the land becomes as grey as the mists that rise from the waters. By contrast, when the sun reflects in the water, everything takes on a new aspect. The water reflects the sky and the clouds. The 'shine' in the landscape is further enhanced when the sun breaks through dark clouds after rain and uncountable drops refract the often fleeting light in all directions.

Finally, moving up to the present, I want to turn to an issue that Iain Porter, development officer (and formerly acting manager) of the AONB team, raised in his presentation at Fyne Court. He told us that the International Union for the Conservation of Nature (IUCN) has developed a set of internationally recognized criteria to categorize the various forms of protected areas across the world. There are six categories in total, arranged in descending order of degree of modification by human action, with Category I divided into two (Ia is a strict nature reserve and Ib is a wilderness area). The Quantock Hills AONB is classified as Category V, which denotes 'a protected area where the interaction of people and nature over time has produced an area of distinct character with significant ecological, biological, cultural and scenic value'. (All other protected areas in Britain, including all nature reserves and national parks, fall into this category of multiple use and multi-purpose – even though IUCN Category II is entitled 'National Parks').[5] If we create institutionalized and internationalized definitions of this kind, we have moved away from the intuitive approach to sublime and outstanding beauty developed by Rousseau, Coleridge and Wordsworth. My impression is that the IUCN standards are strongly influenced by the gold standard of 'real wilderness' in places such as North America, Australasia and Africa. Yet what do these standards say about natural landscape and beauty in our time, in more densely populated and heavily industrialized regions such as western Europe? If the reference point for these IUCN standards is the state of the natural environment outside Britain, how are they relevant for the managers of the Quantock Hills? And what does a change of category imply for a protected area? Is British landscape management policy driven more by global benchmarks than local ones?

Notes

1. Hazel Riley, whose book, *The Historic Landscape of the Quantock Hills* (Swindon: English Heritage, 2006), is based on archaeological fieldwork, transcription of aerial photographs and architectural research, presented her Quantock work during the second day of the workshop, when we met in the Library at Fyne Court, Broomfield, a National Trust property that houses the headquarters of the AONB Service.

2. Jean-Jacques Rousseau, *Confessions*, Angela Scholar (trans.) (Oxford: Oxford University Press, 2000 [1782/1789]), p. 168.

3. Jan Oosthoek created and maintained the research network's website, which can be accessed at: http://www.environmentalhistories.net/ (accessed 25/10/14).

4. Comment (4 March 2011) on Paul Warde, 'The Fens and the Quantocks', at: http://www.environmentalhistories.net/?p=332 (accessed 25/10/14).

5. For the IUCN Protected Areas Categories System, see: http://www.iucn.org/about/work/programmes/gpap_home/gpap_quality/gpap_pacategories/ (accessed 25/10/14).

CHAPTER 21

Reservoirs, Military Bases and Environmental Change: Joining the Dots

Chris Pearson

At first glance, military bases and reservoirs are strikingly dissimilar. The former are used for weapons testing and training soldiers whilst the latter store drinking water and/or produce hydroelectricity. But on closer inspection, connections become apparent. In Northumberland, Kielder Water, completed in the early 1980s to provide water for England's industrial North East, carries no visible traces of militarization, in contrast to the nearby Defence Training Estate Otterburn, established as an artillery range in 1911.[1] But the forest, in the midst of which the reservoir was created in the 1970s, is militarized in subtle ways.[2] After the First World War, the Forestry Commission selected sites, such as Kielder, to create strategic forest reserves for use in wartime. The forest's militarized origins are not detectable in the landscape today, unlike the military communications facilities located on the summit of one of the surrounding hills. And Kielder Dam is now subject to extra security precautions because of its strategic importance. The quasi-militarized environment of Kielder serves as a reminder that the boundary between civilian and militarized environments is often fluid and that environmental militarization is not restricted to battlefields, military bases and other installations.[3]

My visit to Kielder Water and Forest Park sparked further reflections on the relationship between reservoirs and military bases, principally Canjuers Camp, one of the case studies on my project on militarized environments in modern France, and nearby Sainte-Croix Lake (the camp's western border is a few kilometres away from the lake's eastern shore). Both are in the Var *département* of the Provence region in south-eastern France and were created by the French state in the post-war period. Sainte-Croix Lake has now become a tourist attraction, helped by its proximity to the spectacular Gorges de Verdon, and forms part of the Verdon Natural Regional Park. The northern limits of Canjuers Camp run along the park's southern barrier, but it is hardly over-run with tourists. Signs along the roadside declare 'Military Land: No Entry' and official visits to the ruined village of Brovès, whose inhabitants left in 1974 to make way for the military base, are closely monitored by the army. Brovès is visible from the D25 road. This is not the case for Les Salles-sur-Verdon, a village that was dynamited before being submerged by the waters of Sainte-Croix Lake, also in the mid-1970s. In this chapter I use my visit to Kielder Water and Forest Park as a springboard to reflect on the similarities and connections between military bases and reservoirs. In this sense, a visit to a site in northern England has helped me rethink one in southern France, attesting to the transnational analytical connections between these local places.

Both of the post-war state-led projects in Provence transformed these local places; expanses of water, in the case of Sainte-Croix Lake, and firing ranges and military installations, in the case of Canjuers Camp, replaced farmland, pastures, woodlands, houses and villages. They altered human habitations and land uses as well as local ecologies. For instance, the damning of the Verdon River to create the Sainte Croix Lake modified the local fish population as roach and other species were added.[4]

Like Kielder Water, these projects were conceived of and completed during the 1960s, 1970s and 1980s. Regardless of nation state context, all were products of post-war beliefs that centrally planned large-scale projects would bring progress and modernization to economically 'backward' areas and were necessary to meet the demands of modern industrialists, consumers and militaries.[5] Land that central state planners deemed marginal, depopulated and therefore cheap was 'sacrificed' for national interests, determined by the state.

Militarized environments, such as Canjuers Camp, have been overlooked in studies on post-war technological and state projects in France, as they have been more generally within environmental history.[6] In this essay, I make the case that Canjuers Camp needs to be situated within the wider efforts of the French state to modernize France through technological projects to ensure its grandeur and sovereignty. Using the comparison with Sainte-Croix Lake, and within the larger comparative framework provided by Kielder, I argue that local populations have responded to these projects in similar ways. So although militarized environments have distinctive features, such as firing ranges and barracks, and can be particularly secretive and foreboding, they are not disconnected from the wider environmental, political and social context.[7]

Creating the reservoir and military base

The French military used a firing range near Brovès on the Canjuers plateau in the 1930s and plans to create a barrage at Sainte-Croix had circulated around that time without reaching fruition.[8] But it was not until the post-war period that military and civilian officials planned to fundamentally transform and, as they saw it, modernize this remote area of Provence. In part, this was because they articulated more forcibly the need for a military base and reservoir. The

French army argued that it needed more space for training its troops and testing its weapons. Espousing a form of technological determinism, it argued that the increased range of Cold War-era weaponry necessitated larger training camps.[9] Similarly, *Electricité de France* (EDF), a publicly-owned organization formed by the French nationalization law of 8 April 1946, put forward the need for increased water supplies and the production of hydroelectricity. It made a case for creating new reservoirs, such as at Tignes in the Alps, and at the site that would eventually become Sainte-Croix Lake.[10] At Canjuers and Sainte-Croix, as was the case at Kielder, France's perceived national defence and energy needs were placed before local inhabitants' desires to stay in their homes. For although the military base and reservoir would fulfil very different functions and result in very different forms of environmental change (submersion and militarization), both would require the expropriation of land and the forced displacement of people from their homes, farmers from their fields, foresters from their woods and hunters from their hunting grounds.

Historians have persuasively shown how hydroelectrical projects were part and parcel of the French state's wider faith in big technology to secure national sovereignty and grandeur after the humiliation of the Second World War and during the uncertainties of the Cold War.[11] But the army's linking of its Cold War expansion with modernization is less well-known. A report in 1961 by General le Puloch, the army's chief of staff, set out to identify and remedy training and weapons testing deficiencies. It noted that the majority of the army's large camps were located north of the Cherbourg–Lyon Line (which was marked on the map accompanying le Puloch's report) in the most industrial and agriculturally rich part of the country. This geographical distribution was unfortunate in le Puloch's view because the south offered better training conditions due to its light and 'gentle climate'.[12] In short, France's main training grounds were in the wrong place. Le Puloch's report marked a turning point in military geographical thinking. If realized, the army's training centre of gravity would no longer be the plains of Champagne. Instead, it would mobilize heathlands and other economically marginal land in the west and the *midi*. Like its civilian counterpart, the militarized arm of the state stressed the need for territorial balance and rationalization.[13]

The army adopted the language of modernization to justify its territorial ambitions. A preliminary army report on Canjuers argued that only militarization could bring prosperity to a region where 'poor and rocky soils', 'meagre' grasslands and *maquis* inhibited the development of productive agriculture. Militarization would supposedly imbue this depopulating and 'semi-desert' region with national purpose and provide an economic boost through compensation for expropriated land and military personnel's spending power.[14] Colonel Guéneau, head of the military engineering service in Nice, argued that militarization would bring 'certain progress' through its modernization of a region that had some 'beauty' but consisted essentially of a 'dry and difficult nature'.[15] From the military perspective, Canjuers camp was a 'win-win' situation; France would get the training camp it needed and a 'backward' region would reap the benefits of state-led modernization. But this overlooked the fact that by creating the camp the army would produce a space empty of civilians, thereby contributing to rural depopulation.[16]

To better understand the rationale behind the creation of Sainte-Croix Lake and Canjuers Camp, it is helpful to draw on James C. Scott's analysis of high modernist ideology in *Seeing Like a State*. For Scott, high-modernist ideology consists of:

> a strong, one might even say muscle-bound, version of the self-confidence about scientific and technical progress, the expansion of production, the growing satisfaction of human needs, [and] the mastery of nature (including human nature).[17]

In the Var, locals viewed the reservoir and military base schemes as projects imposed upon them by an arrogant central state that would destroy their livelihoods and landscapes. As at Kielder, the state's plans clashed with local attachments to place. These differences are laid bare in two maps of the Canjuers site. Neither map is a realistic representation of the site but they show competing visions of what the site should be like. One is a military map prepared during the camp's creation, which shows how different firing ranges would cover the site. The abstract shapes obscure civilian uses and meanings of the site.[18] The *Syndicat de défense des propriétaires et habitants du Haut-Var* (or SDPHV), a group formed to oppose the creation of Canjuers camp, produced an alternative map that emphasized the economic and social value of the region's woods, pastures, farms, truffles and lavender, as well as the sense of pain and 'complete disorientation' (*dépaysement*) felt by its inhabitants. This map shows a range of human activities that took place in the Haut-Var, including bee-keeping, truffling, shooting, camping, pasturing, tourism, fishing and caving, which would be lost to militarization.[19]

The histories of Sainte-Croix Lake, Canjuers Camp and Kielder do not conform entirely to Scott's argument. For instance, the state did not simply impose its will on local complexity but had to actively engage with local authorities, politicians and populations to achieve its aims. At Canjuers, many local state officials actively opposed the camp's creation. Foresters and others sought to make the army redraw the camp's boundary to protect valued sites. Opposing plans to create a camp in the area in the mid-1950s, Arthur Dugelay, the forestry conservator of the Nice region who had been horrified by the Second World War's impact on Mediterranean forests, feared that this latest form of militarization would upset the region's 'sylvo-pastoral balance' and destroy Châteaudouble forest, a 'splendid ... curiosity of national importance'.[20]

Cries of alarm from other local officials greeted the decision to create Canjuers Camp. At stake, it seemed, was the Var *département*'s economic viability and its geographical survival, especially as two local villages were already due to be lost to submersion during the creation of Sainte-Croix Lake. According to the Var's prefect, locals would see the military camp as yet a further attack on the Var's 'integrity' and a potential threat to its tourism.[21] The council of Bauduen, a commune which was already due to lose 700 ha of its land to the Sainte-Croix Lake and stood to lose another 1,400 ha to Canjuers, raised the spectre of the collapse of the Malpasset dam in 1959 (that had caused 421 casualties) when it suggested that vibrations in the soil from military training might cause a repeat occurrence. Its town council was also concerned that the military base would ruin the town's tourism trade.[22]

Local politicians and experts protested by writing letters, attending public enquiries and pursuing other official channels. Local populations did the same, but also formed protest groups. Their message relied less on an assertion of expertise and knowledge than a display of their passion and producing eye-catching images. Graffiti in the village of Les Salles-sur-Verdon compared EDF with the Nazis. Just as the German occupier had done during the Second World War, EDF was now allegedly pillaging the land.[23]

At Canjuers, protesters employed a protest language rooted in local symbolism. Residents had already formed the SDPHV in 1955 in opposition to earlier military designs on the region. This group of landowners and local mayors organized the campaign against the military camp in the 1960s and 1970s. On 15 September 1963, after a hunt and a barbecue of a whole roast sheep at Brovès village, the group passed a motion declaring that the military camp would 'lead to the pure and simple ruin of this region and the people that live there'. In a defiant tone, they stated that 'we are here because of our ancestors' labour and we'll only leave through the force of bayonets.'[24] This can be compared to the mixed reaction among the residents of Kielder to the decision to dam the North Tyne and flood part of the valley.[25]

The campaign took on an environmentalist hue when the *Comité des parcs naturels du Haut-Var* (CPNHV or Committee for National Parks in the Haut Var, founded in 1967) argued that, instead of a military base, the government should create a national park (no doubt inspired by the creation of alpine Vanoise National Park in 1963). According to its newsletter, military planners, supported by treacherous local politicians, had led a 'policy … against nature', turning the Haut-Var into a 'lost paradise'. Nature and society would lose out to militarization; 'instead of walking and horse-riding routes, we see a nature disfigured by … tanks and canons.'[26]

The Committee mobilized trees as symbols of life, in opposition to the death and destruction entailed by militarization. In November 1972, it organized a tree-planting ceremony on private land bordering the camp and planned to erect competing signs to the military ones that declared 'Forbidden Zone – Danger of Death'. Its sign would read 'Protect the life of these trees – They ensure the survival of humanity.'[27] In April 1973, it held a similar ceremony at Tourtour, producing a poster showing a funerary wreath dedicated to nature. The Committee's environmentalist stance dovetailed with the anti-authoritarian and anti-military sentiments swelling up in post-May 1968 France to create a group that was unafraid to declare its utopian and anti-militarist outlook. It recommended the partial withdrawal of the army from its bases and the replacement of military service with a national service dedicated to the environment and humanity.[28] But the Committee failed to achieve its main aim of securing a national park in the Haut-Var. The most important reason was the army's reluctance to cede any of its land for a national park.

Nonetheless, the promotion of environmental issues shows how the protest against Canjuers Camp was part of the wider emergence of what Michael Bess has termed the 'light-green society', in which the French embraced 'environmentalist concerns' but 'modestly, moderately, without upsetting the existing state of things too much'.[29] Concerns about the loss of wild and domesticated nature at Canjuers were raised, but ultimately the imperatives of national defence trumped environmentalist concerns.

The campaign against Canjuers Camp was only one of many anti-base campaigns in the 1960s and 1970s as Cold War-era militarization reached its peak. The later decade-long protest against the extension of Larzac camp in south-western France was far more successful than the one at Canjuers, as François Mitterrand annulled the decision to extend the camp on securing the presidency in 1981. Environmentalism had been an important part of the Larzac campaign and protesters had mobilized images of the domestic and wild nature of Larzac that would be lost to militarization. Sheep, in particular, became anti-militarist symbols.[30] The Larzac protesters succeeded in forming a wider coalition of protest against the military than the anti-Canjuers Camp campaigners had achieved, as well as benefiting from the wider spirit of protest in post-May 1968 France. Taken together, the Canjuers and Larzac campaigns show how protests against military bases were part of wider environmentalist protests in 1960s and 1970s France, including those against the proposed construction of ski resorts in the Vanoise National Park in 1969, those against nuclear power installations at Plogoff in Brittany (1974–81), as well as those against reservoirs, such as Sainte-Croix Lake. Military bases became part of the network of sites of confrontation in the struggle between the desire to modernize France and protect its environment in the post-war era.

To return to the Var, the campaigns against EDF and the army won some concessions. The villages of Sainte-Croix and Bauduen were saved from flooding by the EDF and the army made some concessions to hunters and foresters.[31] But the projects still went ahead and the state began to expropriate land from local landowners, which met with varying degrees of resistance. Nonetheless, the villages of Brovès and Les Salles-sur-Verdon were evacuated by 1974 and their inhabitants moved to newly-constructed houses nearby, amidst emotionally charged scenes. Les Salles-sur-Verdon was rebuilt on the shores of the new lake, whilst Brovès was attached to the nearby village of Seillans. But whereas the army left Brovès to fall into ruin, EDF dynamited Les Salles-sur-Verdon before it was submerged by the reservoir.[32] Firing ranges and barracks and a barrage and water followed in their respective wakes as Canjuers Camp militarized 35,000 ha and Sainte-Croix Lake submerged 2,000 ha. The camp and lake now form part of France's energy and military complexes.

Similarities are evident between the creation of Sainte-Croix Lake and Canjuers Camp. Both were high-modernist projects that met with local resistance but which went ahead with minor concessions, leading to environmental change and social dislocation. Similarities are also evident in meanings attributed to the sites since the creation of the reservoir and the military base.

At both sites, the contested history of the creation of the reservoir and military base are largely obscured. A handful of websites and blogs present the drowned village of Les Salles-sur-Verdon and the ruined one of Brovès as places of loss where the state muscled out villagers and severed their connection with the land.[33] In this perspective, the deserted villages become symbols of rural depopulation, the central state's arrogance and destroyed ways of life. A website dedicated to the destruction of Les Salles-sur-Verdon describes it as a 'martyred village, victim of the EDF's barrier'.[34] Locals have also created two associations dedicated to preserving the history and memory of the villages: *Mémoire des Salles-sur-Verdon*; and the *Anciens et amis de Brovès*. The latter, created in 2005 after the army threatened to bulldoze the ruins to prevent pillaging of tiles and stones, now campaigns for the village to be restored. But although the army has commissioned reports on the ruins, it possesses neither the inclination nor the funds to restore the village.[35]

Despite their memory work, and in contrast to the ruined villages of Verdun, which were destroyed in combat during the First World War, and Oradour-sur-Glane, a village ransacked by retreating German soldiers in 1944, Les Salles-sur-Verdon and Brovès have not been imbued with national purpose or meaning, even if one journalist describes Brovès as 'kind of "Oradour-en-Provence"'.[36] The official website of the Verdon Natural Regional Park (in which Sainte-Croix Lake now lies) tries to acknowledge the sense of loss created by the evacuation of Les Salles-sur-Verdon and the poignancy of the new village ('a true memorial dedicated to the life of the past') whilst celebrating the turquoise 'calm waters of the lake'.[37] But more commonly, the villages are barely acknowledged sites of local loss or are portrayed as necessary sacrifices to France's modernization. One tourist website, for instance, describes Les Salles-sur-Verdon and other submerged sites, such as Palaeolithic caves, as 'treasures that progress has sacrificed to history'.[38]

In the absence of extensive commemoration, the sites have been given a green gloss as befits a 'light-green society'. Kielder Water and Forest Park is now promoted as a prime recreational destination in the post-industrial North East of England, with its website claiming that the site offers the visitor 'nature on a grander scale'. Without hiding the reservoir and forest's artificial and commercial histories ('we're home to the biggest man-made lake in Northern Europe and, at over 250 square miles [c.650 square km], the largest working forest in England'), the site's promoters highlight the Park's 'distinctive scenery' as the most 'popular' reason to visit. Not only does 'the Park's remoteness and clean air and water offer a fresh outdoor experience', but the visitor can 'enjoy healthy activities in the greenest environment'.[39] Similarly, tourist websites portray Sainte-Croix Lake as a beautiful, clean and peaceful site where tourists can relax, swim, canoe and sail, whilst staying in 'perfectly developed' holiday centres on its shores.[40] Another promises that despite the lake's cold water and 'the large number of bathers, you can find a quiet spot in which to benefit from the calm and the lake's gentleness'.[41] In a 'post-materialist' French society – when basic material security has become assured for the majority of the population – the lake has become a site of repose and recuperation from the stresses of modern and urban life.[42]

The secretive character of military bases means that Canjuers Camp has not become a tourist destination fit for an environmentally aware population. But it has been 'greened' in other ways. In a bid to counter opposition during the camp's creation, the army claimed that its presence would benefit flora and fauna. Since the camp's creation, and in line with the French army's wider attempt to portray itself as a responsible environmental steward, the camp's authorities have joined forces with the *Office Nationale des Forêts and the Conservatoire d'étude des ecosystems de Provence* to preserve the endangered Orsini viper.[43] Similarly, the Forestry Commission claims that its forests, including Kielder Forest, are managed sustainably. In addition to its commercial functions, it portrays the site as 'a valuable home and sanctuary for many species of flora and fauna, including deer, squirrels, birds of prey, border mires with peat bog plant species'. At both sites, the protection of biodiversity is portrayed as a key management aim and justification for the Forestry Commission and French army's ongoing ownership.[44]

The French army's promotion of military environmentalism is problematic in many ways. One of its defining characteristics, however, is its light-green hue. Military imperatives repeatedly trump environmental considerations. Fears that nature protection measures would hinder military activities and sovereignty over its training grounds led the Ministry of Defence to block a convention between Canjuers Camp and the Verdon Natural Regional Nature Park. Moreover, certain military modifications of their land sit at odds with nature protection objectives. At Canjuers Camp, military-sanctioned reforestation and restrictions on pasturing have diminished grasslands, leading to the deterioration of ecologically important habitats.[45] Therefore, like Lake Sainte-Croix, Canjuers Camp plays host to a mixture of contradictory and ambivalent 'light-green' rhetoric and policies.

Conclusion

This essay has tried to tease out some of the similarities between Canjuers Camp and Sainte-Croix Lake to show how both became vectors of environmental and social change. Rather than treat militarized environments as separate from civilian ones, it has underscored their commonalities, even if important differences remain (principally the highly secretive nature of military installations). Three points stand out. The first is that environmental change cannot be divorced from its social context. At Canjuers and Saint-Croix Lake, homes and land were lost, a narrative of tragedy and loss generated and protests formulated against the schemes. Environmental processes in these cases were inseparable from social ones and were understood as such by those affected by them. The second is that environmental change in local places needs to be situated within the wider political and cultural context, in this case, high-modernist post-war planning schemes and the rise of the 'light-green' society. The third and final point is the value of site visits and the utility of a trans-national approach to the study of environmental change. An inspirational visit one early March to a Kielder Water and Forest that was still emerging from the cold northern winter helped me to join the dots between a military camp and reservoir under the more frequently blue skies of a region just over 1,000 miles (1600+ km) to the south.

Notes

1. On Otterburn, see: R. Woodward, *Military Geographies* (Oxford: Blackwell, 2004).
2. J. West, 'Forests and National Security: British and American Forest Policy in the Wake of World War I', *Environmental History* 8/2 (2003), pp. 270–94.
3. On the fluid boundaries between militarized and non-militarized landscapes, see: Edmund Russell, 'Afterword: Militarized Landscapes: Concluding Reflections', in Chris Pearson, Peter Coates and Tim Cole (eds), *Militarized Landscapes: From Gettysburg to Salisbury Plain* (London: Continuum, 2010), pp. 229–37.
4. G. Brun, R. Chappaz, G. Olivari, 'Modification in Habitat Use Patterns and Trophic Interrelationships on the Fish Fauna of an Oligotrophic Artificial Lake: Sainte Croix (Provence, France)', *Hydrobiologica* 207 (1990), pp. 197–207.
5. On the creation of Kielder Water, see: C. S. McCulloch, 'The Kielder Water Scheme: the last of its kind?' www.britishdams.org/2006conf/papers/Paper%2010%20Mcculloch. PDF (accessed 14/03/11).
6. On militarized environments in France, see: C. Pearson, *Mobilizing Nature: The Environmental History of War and Militarization in Modern France* (Manchester: Manchester University Press, 2012). On the modernization of post-war France, see: G. Hecht, *The Radiance of France: Nuclear Power and National Identity after World War II* (Cambridge, MA: MIT Press, 1998); S. B. Pritchard, *Confluence: The Nature of Technology and the Remaking of the Rhône* (Cambridge, MA: Harvard University Press, 2011).
7. For an overview of the environmental history of war, environment and militarized landscapes, see: C. Pearson, 'Researching Militarized Landscapes: A Literature Review on War and the Militarization of the Environment', *Landscape Research* 37/1 (2012), pp. 115–33.
8. Archives départementales du Var (hereafter ADV) 7 PP 68 Colonel Donnio, Commandant les Forces Aériennes du XVᵉ C. A. to Inspecteur des Eaux et Forêts, Draguignan, 15 November 1939; F. Simian, 'Monographie des Salles-sur-Verdon', [n.d.], reproduced at www.lessallessurverdon.com/LSmono.html (accessed 13/08/12).
9. For instance, see Service historique de la Défense-Département de l'armée de Terre (hereafter SHD-DAT) 27 T 117 Secrétaire d'état à la Guerre to Généraux commandant les régions militaires, 'Extension des camps', 28[?] September 1951.
10. R. L. Frost, 'The Flood of "Progress": Technocrats and Peasants at Tignes (Savoy), 1946-1952', *French Historical Studies* 14/1 (1985), pp. 117–40.
11. M. Bess, *The Light-Green Society: Ecology and Technological Modernity in France, 1960-2000* (Chicago: University of Chicago Press, 2003), pp. 18–24. On the wider

twenty-century history of technologically-induced environmental change, see: Paul R. Josephson, *Industrialized Nature: Brute Force Technology and the Transformation of the Natural World* (Washington DC: Island Press, 2002).

12. SHD-DAT 27 T 115 Général le Puloch, Chef d'Etat-major de l'armée, 'Problèmes de l'armée de terre en matière de terrains d'entraînement et d'expérimentations', December 1961.

13. C. Aubert, 'La politique d'installation des camps militaires: Le cas particulier du polygone de tir de Canjuers' (DESS, Université de Nice, 1983–84), p. 19. On territorial balance see S. B. Pritchard, 'Paris et le désert français: Urban and Rural Environments in Post-World War II France', in A. C. Isenberg (ed.), *The Nature of Cities* (Rochester: University of Rochester Press, 2006), pp. 175–91.

14. ADV 1189 W 1 Direction des travaux, Nice, 'Création d'un champ de tir et de manoeuvre dans la région des Plans des Canjuers', [n.d.].

15. ADV 1189 W 1 Colonel Guéneau, letter no. 10.616/D, 8 November 1962.

16. On the military's discourses of emptiness and its displacement of civilians, see: T. Cole, 'Military presences, civilian absences: Battling nature at the Sennybridge Training Area, 1940–2008', *Journal of War and Culture Studies* 3/2 (2010), pp. 215–35.

17. J. C. Scott, *Seeing Like a State: How Certain Schemes to Improve the Human Condition Have Failed* (New Haven, CT: Yale University Press, 1998), p. 4.

18. SHD-DAT 6 T 716 'Monographie' [n.d. 1973?].

19. Archives municipales de Comps-sur-Artuby (hereafter AMC) 1 W 4/3 Syndicat de défense des propriétaires et habitants du Haut-Var, 'Mémoire', 3 November 1964, p. 25.

20. ADV 379 W 510/2 Arthur Dugelay to Directeur des travaux du génie, Nice, 'Champ de tir de Plan de Canjuers (Var)', 24 August 1954; ADV 1790 W 6055 Arthur Dugelay to Directeur des travaux du génie, Nice, 'Champ de tir de Canjuers', 15 November 1954.

21. ADV 1189 W 6 Préfet du Var to Général commandant la 9e Région militaire, 'Grand plan de Canjuers', 28 August 1962.

22. ADV 1189 W 6 Maire de Bauduen, 'Extrait du registre des délibérations du conseil municipal', 19 November 1963.

23. '1974, dernière année de l'ancien village', [n.d], Mémoire des Salles-sur-Verdon website www.lessallessurverdon.com/LSdemol.html (accessed 01/07/13).

24. AMC 1 W 4/2 'Motion', 15 September 1963.

25. See Moon and Skelton's chapter in this volume, pp. **206–223**.

26. Comité des parcs naturels du Haut-Var, Bulletin no. 14 (October 1974). On the rise of environmentalism in France, see: Bess, *Light-Green Society*.

27. Comité des parcs naturels du Haut-Var, Bulletin no. 11 (September 1972).

28. Comité des parcs naturels du Haut-Var, Bulletin no. 14.

29. Bess, *Light-Green Society*, p. 5.

30. Pearson, *Mobilizing Nature*, pp. 254–7.

31. 'Lac de Sainte Croix', [n.d.] Moustiers Sainte-Marie website www.moustiers.eu/?Lac-de-Sainte-Croix&lang=fr (accessed 13/08/12).

32. Simian, 'Monographie des Salles-sur-Verdon'; Pearson, *Mobilizing Nature*.

33. Mémoire des Salles-sur-Verdon website www.e-memoire.com (accessed 13/08/12); 'Le village de Brovès' http://broves.blogspot.co.uk/ (accessed 13/08/12).

34. 'Homepage', [n.d.] Mémoire des Salles-sur-Verdon website www.lessallessurverdon.com/index.html (accessed 13/08/12).

35. J.-B. Malet, 'Brovès, village fantôme humilié et menacé de décrépitude' (9 June 2010) www.rue89.com/marseille/2010/06/09/èè-village-fantome-humilie-et-menace-par-les-

bulldozers-154229 (accessed 13/08/12). For Les Salles-sur-Verdon, see: 'Buts', [n.d.] Mémoire des Salles-sur-Verdon website www.e-memoire.com (accessed 13 August 2012).

36. Malet, 'Brovès'. On Oradour-sur-Glane, see: S. Farmer, *Martyred Village: Commemorating the 1944 Massacre at Oradour-sur-Glane* (Berkeley: University of California Press, 1999).

37. 'Le Lac de Sainte-Croix', [n.d.], Parc naturel régional du Verdon website www.parcduverdon.fr/accueil/un-territoire-7-paysages/les-paysages/lac-de-sainte-croix-10-1.html (accessed 13/08/12).

38. 'Lac de Sainte Croix', [n.d.], Haut-Var website www.haut-var.com/lac-sainte-croix.htm (accessed 13/08/12).

39. 'Welcome to the greater outdoors', Kielder Water & Forest Park website www.visitkielder.com/; 'Visiting Kielder Water & Forest Park', Kielder Water & Forest Park website www.visitkielder.com/visit (both accessed 09/07/14).

40. 'Welcome to the greater outdoors', Kielder Water & Forest Park website; 'Visiting Kielder Water & Forest Park', Kielder Water & Forest Park website; See also: 'Lac de Sainte Croix', [n.d.] Moustiers Sainte-Marie website.

41. 'Le lac de Sainte Croix' (October 2001), Tourisme83 website www.tourisme83.com/lac_saintecroix.htm (accessed 13/08/12).

42. Bess, *Light-Green Society*, pp. 87–8.

43. *Défense et protection de la nature* (Paris: La Documentation française, 2000), p. 20.

44. 'How it all works', Kielder Water & Forest Park website www.visitkielder.com/about-us/how-it-all-works (accessed 09/07/14); 'Managing our forests', Forestry Commission England website http://www.forestry.gov.uk/forestry/infd-6qll9g (accessed 09/07/14).

45. Pearson, *Mobilizing Nature*, p. 291.

CHAPTER 22

Species Conservation at Kielder: Animating Place with Animals

Duncan Hutt

The road from Bellingham twists up the North Tyne valley, passing scattered farms and the small hamlet of Stannersburn with its seventeenth-century inn. Shortly afterwards, the route climbs to emerge at the end of the dam which holds back Britain's largest reservoir. The vista of the valley changes from pastoral to one dominated by the lake and, to the horizon in all directions, conifer forest. This is a twentieth-century landscape, a forest conceived in the aftermath of the First World War and a lake born in a late 1970s world of heavy industry on Tyneside and Teesside.

The two activities, forestry and water supply, cover almost every corner of the landscape for the next 10 miles (16 km) and more. They have blanketed everything of an earlier era, with former fields, farms and tracks buried beneath trees. Farms, the old road, the old school and the relics of a scattered rural community lie under the waters that have been here for the past 30 years.

This is a human-made landscape, from the blocks of trees, growing, felled for timber and replanted, to the water, the dam, the recreation centres and lake-side trail. It is a human-made landscape less than a century old. It is an engineered landscape from the forest roads that splay out across the hillsides, allowing access for trees to be planted and felled, to the large earth dam that holds back the waters of the reservoir. Perhaps it is this large scale engineering that makes it seem so artificial.

If you stand on the dam you can look west to this 'artificial' world or east into the gentle wooded valley of the North Tyne with the fields close by the farms leading out onto areas of open hill beyond. And yet is this fair? The valley below the dam is no less a creation of human endeavours than the one of spruce and water to the west. There is little left of a pre-human world to be seen in either direction; nothing, even, that an iron-age inhabitant would recognize.

The clearance of the wild wood probably occurred quite late up here. Pollen analysis seems to show a sharp increase in grass and decline in tree pollens at around the time of the Roman occupation. While former settlers in these parts may have cleared some woodland glades, it is probably not until about AD 200 that Northumberland was cleared for farming.

This was a hard land in which to live; frontier land, disputed land. It has always been on the edge, the edge of the Roman Empire, the edge of the old Kingdom of Northumbria or the border land between England and Scotland. The result was a landscape born out of human needs, whether for grazing and crops or for shelter or defence. The modern landscape of Kielder is no different, just a more modern manifestation.

This recent artificial landscape is not the most obvious candidate for wildlife conservation, which normally attempts to conserve some of the last vestiges of natural or near natural habitat in more traditional countryside. Here conservation is pursued against a backdrop of commercial afforestation which has swept much away in its march across the countryside. However, there is much of interest within this blanket of conifers, and considerable potential for even greater wildlife benefit.

In wildlife conservation terms, work on species is probably the easiest to understand as there are specialists of this environment. Native red squirrels are perhaps Kielder's most obvious wildlife ambassador; an ideal habitat in which this threatened creature can have a chance against the introduced grey squirrel. Here the conifers provide a food supply for the reds and the lack of large-seeded broadleaved trees, favoured by greys, helps keep the grey squirrels at the edges. Careful management of habitat and species gives a chance of survival for our native squirrel and the chance for visitors to see them.

Ospreys too are doing well. From a collapsed nest of some novice birds in 2008, by 2014 there have been 24 young birds fledged from three nest sites at Kielder. Conservation efforts are simple but effective. Provide a few flat nesting platforms and the birds will come, no cajoling, no re-introducing, just an opportunity to give this magnificent fish hawk somewhere new to live. For years birds had passed through Kielder on the way to their traditional Scottish nests: plenty of food but no ideal nesting trees. The platforms have encouraged three pairs to stop and there is a good chance of even more in the years to come. Wildlife conservation is rarely just about species but also about people appreciating and enjoying them, as it is only by human acceptance that conservation measures will prove successful in the long term. A volunteer-staffed osprey watch has proved to be the perfect introduction for many visitors to this bird, despite the distant views and sometimes challenging conditions.

So what is next in species conservation? Water voles are an ideal candidate. Lost from so much of our countryside, they cling on to survival in some of our remote uplands. They are no longer around Kielder but the conditions are good and the possibilities exist to get them back. Now the attempts at re-introduction are well underway, with the first steps being to ensure that no mink are present to threaten any new arrivals. Once the absence of the North American mink has been established, new voles can be brought in from surviving Northumberland sites in a carefully managed and monitored programme. A step too far for some at this time is the beaver, but perhaps in the future they can return here as well. The discovery of a fourteenth-century beaver-gnawed stick in the area gives some relevance to their return, though they would do so into a very different world to the one that their native cousins left behind.

The very thought of beavers returning indicates that it is not all conifers; beavers would need willow and birch, and perhaps some are right to want to delay the beavers' return until there are more of these broadleaved trees in the mix. It is, ironically, a conifer, however, that drives this native woodland push. In a wild corner of Kielder, in a small steep-sided valley called William's Cleugh, is one of two small outliers of one of Britain's native conifers. Scots pine may not be a rare tree; it has been extensively planted all around Britain including some parts of Kielder Forest. But the interest surrounding these few trees comes from the idea that they may be relics of the former Caledonian pine forests. If so, it is the only English example, though we are unlikely to ever be sure of this, and, as such, it provides a basis for a project that is just beginning to emerge.

The Kielder Wildwood project has its core in the planting of seedling pine from local seed and has evolved into something much larger.[1] The project partners are considering the option to take a couple of isolated valleys and create a large area of replacement native woodland extending up the hillsides into montane scrub. These valleys would have had woodlands of birch, willow and rowan, with other trees such as aspen and hazel also in the mix, and of course they may also have had Scots pine. Indeed the patches of plants such as bluebell, wood sorrel and wood rush are all indicators found across hillsides that point to a former woodland habitat. The proposed area is large, a few hundred hectares, but in the whole scale of Kielder Forest it is just a small corner.

The proposed wildwood would push its way out onto Kielderhead, a vast tract of wilderness, certainly in the English context of such places. It straddles the border into Scotland and at its full extent is about 7,000 ha of heath and bog stretching from the wonderfully evocatively named Deadwater Fell in the south to Carter Pike in the north via hidden places such as Carlin Tooth. The southern segment is part of the Forestry Commission estate, the northern segment a nature reserve managed by Northumberland Wildlife Trust, Whitelee Moor. This is English wilderness where wild goats graze in an environment apparently untouched by human activity. But, of course, it is not. Summer grazing pasture with sheilings, summer shelters, for transhumance agriculture, enclosures and sheep farming and grouse moorland have been amongst the main uses over the last millennium. Somewhere along the line some goats got left behind; our wild herd is in fact more of a feral group of shaggy survivors. Battles were fought here, coal was mined and hill farming survived against many times of adversity. This is far from pristine ground, more a landscape left behind by humans and largely left to its own devices in the last century. Time will change this landscape but it will be beyond the lifetime of those now drawing up the wildwood proposal for it to reach fruition.

Tucked in amongst the tracts of forestry are other wild relics. Possibly the most important of these are the suite of sites that make up the Border Mires. These peatland sites are scattered throughout the forest: flows and mires, mosses and flothers in name, bogs in definition. These are ancient habitats, the slow but steady build-up of peat having taken place over the past 8,000 years or more. Ever since the land emerged from under its icy covering, small pools and hollows have changed from water to fens and eventually to bog. This bog has then continued to grow, layer upon layer of part-decayed plants to give up to 15 m of peat in places. These are perhaps some of our oldest habitats, though the ancient surface may be deep down by now. Locked in these peatlands are thousands of years of history. Small pollen grains give us clues as to the past vegetation cover of the area, and small organisms can allow us to piece together information on climate changes over the centuries.

Drainage of these 'wastelands' is a recent phenomenon in the lifetime of the bog. Most of the drains have been dug in a desperate attempt to plant more and more trees. Some drains date back to older agriculture but most are only about 50 years old. In some cases, the drains worked well enough for trees to be planted, but the deeper, wetter patches defied drainage. These patches survived but other areas were lost to forestry. Forty years of conservation work on these sites has reversed much of the past damage and have left us with a thriving suite of sites which is recognized as being internationally important. From small-scale, humble restoration beginnings in the 1970s to whole scale restoration over the past 10 years, this must be one of Britain's best, if largely unsung, conservation successes of the past half century.

The history of wild Britain is intimately linked to grazing animals, whether that be the wild creatures of the early post-glacial period or the steady domestication and eventual 'industrial grazing' of the most recent two centuries. Wander around Kielder, however, and you are likely to see very few grazing creatures, domestic or wild. Because grazing animals have shaped our land it is not unreasonable for conservation managers to turn to livestock to help mould it again. The old wild creatures have long gone from Britain and re-introduction is a long and complex process, if possible, practical or indeed desirable. Instead, we turn to more modern alternatives, but still to what are termed more traditional breeds – hill ponies, hill sheep and hill cattle – to work on our behalf.

Perhaps in the long term it may be possible for cattle, sheep and ponies to wander through the landscape. For now, though, they are used on smaller patches of ground around the reservoir. Their numbers and location of grazing are carefully controlled to attempt, in some way, to mimic the grazing patterns of long ago and to help provide diversity of plants in areas where single species begin to dominate with the loss of diversity and thus value. This is small scale management of patches of ground within an expansive landscape, but a start nonetheless.

People are often forgotten in the wildlife conservation agenda and yet they are both a part of the natural world and also vital in its conservation into the future. It is nearly always the aim of conservation organizations to ensure that people are involved in the conservation work, either directly through volunteering or in a more general sense of being able to see and appreciate the work that is done. Even in a landscape the size and remoteness of Kielder, conservation cannot be done in isolation. People have to accept and support what is being done so that it survives into the future and also to allow the ideas and actions to be repeated elsewhere. We do not just need isolated pockets of conservation, but a landscape network across the country. Enabling people to see ospreys, red squirrels, animals undertaking conservation grazing, a dam blocking a bog ditch or a tree planted on the hillside is a necessary part of wildlife conservation.

One of the advantages of Kielder is that it is owned by just two organizations, the Forestry Commission and Northumbrian Water Limited. Wildlife conservation around Kielder is dependent on these two parties; it is fair to say that while both provide positive leadership today, it has not always been so positive. Thus the dogged determination of Northumberland Wildlife Trust is also worthy of recognition. In the early days, the Trust pushed hard to achieve conservation in the area; now it is very firmly working in partnership helping to guide, but no longer fighting alone for, the wildlife of the area.

So, far from being just a place of timber production and water supply, Kielder has a lot to offer wildlife: some unique habitats and some unusual species. There is potential for much more, and who knows what might be there to watch from the hides, or on remote cameras in one hundred years: water voles thriving; a wildwood extending from the shores of the reservoir to the boglands on the hill tops; perhaps a beaver adapting their habitat as beavers do best; or, who knows, a European lynx or two?

Note

1. A proposal to plant about 120 ha of native woodland on the edge of Kielderhead National Nature Reserve. Natural England and Forestry Commission are – at time of writing (September 2014) – investigating the potential impact on the adjoining area of blanket bog and heathland, which has been designated a Special Area of Conservation.

Change, Choice and Futures

CHAPTER 23

Environmental Change:
A Local Perspective on Global Processes

David Moon and Leona Jayne Skelton

Introduction: a local perspective

Alf Weir, long retired as Head Forester at Kielder Forest in Northumberland, recalled moving there with his family in 1932. His father Alec 'started Kielder Forest'. 'When I come here', Alf told Leona Jayne Skelton, 'the only trees were round the castle … and the rest was sheep farms …' He explained how experimental planting began in 1926, but the 'big planting' supervised by his father started in 1932. Until the 1940s, when 'they brought in ploughs and tractors', draining and preparing the land and planting the trees was done by hand. Alec Weir had 'fifty odd men to work for him', who planted hundreds of acres. Alf and his father also planted 'one Douglas fir on its own in the junction of Castle Drive and the bypass, that I held while he planted and … a red oak and further on … a sitka spruce'. Alf left the area, but came back in the 1970s when he heard 'that they were gonna make a dam in Kielder', and was elected to the Parish Council. He explained to Skelton how they had 'told the reservoir, the water authority, if they were going wrong with locals … and the big dam was our business because we didn't want mudflats at the top [of the lake].' Indeed, subsequent research in The National Archives at Kew uncovered a letter from Kielder Parish Council to the Kielder Scheme inquiry in July 1971. They expressed their views to the Secretary of State for the Environment:

> 'The Parish Council is concerned about the appearance of the dams themselves, especially the main dam viewed from Falstone, and about the shore line which will leave a variable width of mud round the perimeter of the reservoir.'[1]

The protest was successful: a smaller dam was built upstream at Bakethin to prevent mudflats forming when the water level was low.[2] Thus, while Alf spent his career as a forester exploiting timber grown in a plantation, he was also concerned about the appearance of his local 'environment' and took steps to protect it.

Skelton pressed Alf, asking him whether he preferred 'the landscape before or after the reservoir'. 'Now you're telling,' he replied, 'now I'm not gonna commit maself.' He continued – mindful of the controversy that had accompanied the decision to dam the North Tyne – that before 'it was nice, and there was farms and there was houses … and people living up and down the valley.' 'Now', there was 'nothing' between Falstone and Kielder villages (the area flooded by the reservoir), apart from Leaplish (the location of *The Boat Inn* restaurant, holiday chalets and other tourist facilities run by Northumbrian Water Ltd), the scout centre and the Calvert Trust (which runs activity holidays for the disabled). Alf noted that these developments had 'come as a result of the reservoir'. He continued: 'Well, it was nice before and it's even nice now and it's more attractive to the people coming in, visitors, holiday makers … the Forest[ry Commission] has built cycle tracks and all sorts of things so that holiday makers can enjoy themselves.' He noted that 'tourism has put money into the place' – there is now a pub and cafe – and tourism and the reservoir have provided 'other work' that has partly compensated for the loss of jobs in forestry as a result of mechanization.

The Kielder area is striking from the perspective of environmental change: there has been quite a lot of it. Since the 1920s, the area has experienced the planting and managing of a vast forest on former farm land, the construction of a dam that flooded the valley and created a large reservoir and the development of facilities for tourism.[3] Many of the changes have taken place in the lifetimes of longer-established and older inhabitants. The forest, reservoir and growth of tourism, moreover, all attracted people from outside. Thus, Kielder provided very fertile ground for the Kielder Oral History Project conducted by researcher Leona Jayne Skelton in October 2012.[4]

Global processes

The changes in the environment in the relatively small area at Kielder over the last century, and the attitudes to them revealed by the oral history project, can serve as microcosm for much broader, indeed global, processes of environmental change. The changes at Kielder, as elsewhere in the world, have been driven by economic and political considerations, and utilized various, and changing, technologies.[5] In changing their environments, moreover, human societies around the globe have changed themselves.

One of the major global changes in the environment over the last century has been accelerating deforestation.[6] Inside this story of loss of forest cover, however, there is also a narrative of planting trees, indeed forests, that dates back at least as far as the seventeenth century in parts of Europe, European colonies and, later, in North America. Trees were planted for economic, strategic (naval timber) and also for environmental reasons, to prevent erosion and desiccation of the climate.[7] Kielder Forest was conceived as part of the UK government's policy of creating a strategic timber reserve after the First World War.[8] As in parts of southwestern France from the mid-nineteenth century, and the USA, such as the Nebraska sand hills and Appalachia more recently, at Kielder trees were planted on land considered marginal for other forms of land use.[9] Afforestation has prompted various responses. The regimented rows of introduced, fast-growing Sitka spruce planted by the Forestry Commission in Britain until the late twentieth century provoked much opposition on aesthetic grounds from people who wished to use the countryside for recreation, and wanted forests to look more 'natural': less geometric shapes and more native species, including broad-leaved trees. This raises questions over what is 'natural'?[10]

A more drastic change in land use is drowning valleys by damming rivers. Rivers have been dammed and water diverted for irrigation since ancient times. In the late nineteenth century, urbanization and industrialization led to a growth in demand for water, and for hydroelectric power. The combination of this demand and the development of appropriate technologies unimaginable less than a century earlier ushered in what Joachim Radkau has called: 'The great era of the gigantic dams … in Germany, France, and the United States'. The fashion for building enormous dams spread to the Soviet Union in the 1920s, and later to Egypt, India, China and elsewhere.[11] Decisions to build dams have been highly politicized and controversial. They have led to narratives of the dispossessed among those who lost their homes and livelihoods under artificial lakes. The Siberian writer Valentin Rasputin produced a highly evocative depiction of loss in his novel *Farewell to Matyora* (1979), which echoed his personal experience of the drowning of his native village when the Angara river was dammed.[12] Closer to home, as Harriet Ritvo has demonstrated, the damming of Thirlmere, in the much-loved Lake District in the late nineteenth century, to provide water for the burgeoning industrial city of Manchester, aroused passions among those who wanted to preserve the existing environment.[13] The first hydroelectric power station in the world, and the first house to be powered and lit by electricity generated by water power, was the home of industrialist and inventor Lord William Armstrong. Starting in 1868, he installed the equipment at his house at Cragside in Northumberland, 40 miles (*c*.64 km) northeast of the larger dam and power station built at Kielder around a century later.[14]

Radical changes in land use, such as planting forests on farm land, damming rivers to flood valleys, designing landscapes and providing facilities for tourists, have all, moreover, had an impact on the appearance of landscapes. Thus, this chapter touches on the theme of 'environmental beauty' analyzed by Peter Coates elsewhere in this book. Keith Thomas dated appreciation of nature for its own sake in England back to the early modern period, correcting a common assumption that this began with the Romantic Movement.[15] In England, the work of poets such as Wordsworth and Coleridge celebrated the Lake District, the Quantock Hills and other 'wild' landscapes. During the nineteenth century, around the globe, particular landscapes became associated with national identities: the forests of Germany, mountains of Switzerland, wilderness areas of the United States.[16] This association of certain landscapes with particular nations creates a paradox at

Kielder. For many visitors, including Duncan Hutt, the Northumberland Wildlife Trust's Head of Land Management, the lake and coniferous forest are reminiscent of Scandinavia or North America. Nevertheless, as the interviews demonstrated, local inhabitants express affection for their local, albeit artificial, landscape.

Artificial forests and lakes around the globe, even if constructed primarily for economic and political motives, have often also become amenities for leisure and recreation. In the United States, forests planted on marginal land in Appalachia in the New Deal period were also intended to become centres for leisure and tourism. A well known example is the Shenandoah National Park and Skyline Drive in Virginia.[17] Graham Gill, the regional director of the Forestry Commission in the north of England, spoke about the Appalachian hiking trails as an example of the US Forest Service's involvement in providing for recreation. Indeed, from its early days in the 1920s and 1930s, elements in the Forestry Commission in Britain promoted public access and amenity as well as timber production. Forest Parks, which catered for hikers, were established.[18] Artificial lakes created to store water and generate electricity have also become amenities for recreation. Also in the United States, the great dams of the New Deal era were anticipated by the Bagnell Dam on the Osage River in Missouri, built in 1929–31. As well as providing electricity, the dam created the Lake of the Ozarks, which became a major recreation centre.[19] Kielder Water and Forest Park, run jointly by a trust including Northumbrian Water Limited and the Forestry Commission, is another example of this phenomenon.[20]

The changes at Kielder and elsewhere have altered the lives and livelihoods of the local population, some of whom have actively taken part in the changes. Others have been dispossessed and either left or found new ways to live. Thus, the story of environmental change is also a story of the people who live in a changing environment. This takes us back to the key issues addressed by Warde in this book in his chapter on 'the environment' and how we use and understand the term. Analyzing perspectives on environmental change raises the issue of the relationship between the human and non-human worlds. In 1935, Arthur Tansley, the pioneering British ecologist who carried out research at Wicken Fen, asked: 'Is man part of "nature" or not?' His answer was:

> Regarded as an exceptionally powerful biotic factor which increasingly upsets the equilibrium of pre-existing ecosystems and eventually destroys them, at the same time forming new ones of very different nature, human activity finds its proper place in ecology.[21]

Thus, in his concept, the population of Kielder are part of 'nature'. Environmental historians increasingly consider human history as part of environmental history, and environmental history as part of human history. Some, however, have emphasized the idea of 'care' for the environment and the need to avoid 'misuse' of nature.[22]

The perspectives of all those who took part in the Kielder Oral History Project, although often highly local and focused on their community and its environment, can serve as examples of those of people who have lived through, participated in, benefitted from and lost out to such global processes of environmental change.

Local understandings of 'environment', 'nature' and 'landscape'

The interviewees were asked to define the terms 'environment', 'nature' and 'landscape', questions which some perceived as rather academic. Nevertheless, several offered striking views regarding their relationship with Kielder. Others contributed insightful observations on the concept of 'nature' in the context of the largely artificial world and how they conceptualize 'landscape'.

Many interviewees defined the 'environment' as being 'around us', 'around you' or simply the 'surroundings'. These words feature in 14 of 22 responses. Jonty Hall, who was born in 1970 and has lived in the area all his life and worked in various capacities for Northumbrian Water Limited, said that the environment was 'the surroundings *etc.*, which are around us'. Thomas Grimwood, who was born in the area in 1948 and has spent his whole working life in the forest, said: 'Well we live in it, it's all around us.' The words 'everything' (five times), 'whole' (three times) and 'the world' (once) recurred in the definitions of the 'environment'. Yvonne Riley, born in Kielder in 1960, termed it: 'everything that's around you, the scenery'. Notions of 'lifestyle' or 'living' occurred seven times. One respondent used the phrase 'where we inhabit'. Some definitions located their understanding of the term in Kielder. In an interview conducted in *The Boat Inn* at Leaplish Waterside Park, overlooking the reservoir, Tonia Reeve, Northumbrian Water's commercial manager at Kielder, said 'environment … means the trees, water, the place that we're looking out over today, it means the nice clean air and the very dark skies.' Steve Webb, who moved to Kielder with his wife Julie and their two boys six years earlier and runs the village store, personalized and localized the term: 'Environment means here, in my environment here for me, it means all around here, all around Kielder.'

Several responses featured the words 'people', 'community', 'social', 'manmade' or the notion of people 'caring for' or 'looking after' the environment. Ken Gaskin, who was born in 1941, worked in schools in Northumberland and visits Kielder regularly, expressed this idea clearly: 'The environment's the whole of the area what you're living in and breathing, the whole structure of the community *etc.*' Kathy Wylie, who was born in Kielder in 1947 and worked variously as a teacher, for the Forestry Commission and for the Calvert Trust, replied: 'It means the area around us and the people around as well in that they help the environment type of thing, you know?'. Terry Gregg, who has worked in Kielder tourism businesses for nine years, said 'the environment is everything around us, the air, the water, the trees, the land, people, buildings, … it's the world.'

The definitions suggest that the interviewees envisage the 'environment' as all-encompassing; they see themselves not only living in the environment, but as the central point around which their 'environment' is arranged.

Several definitions of 'environment' included such words as 'nature', 'natural', 'air', 'water', 'flora and fauna' and 'wildlife'. Peter Cockerill, Chief Executive of Kielder's Calvert Trust, stated: '[Nature] means countryside, ... all the natural cycles of nature and the flora and fauna.' He defined 'nature' as the 'separation between human interests and those of the natural world around us'. The words respondents used most frequently in their definitions of 'nature' concerned wildlife. Yvonne said: 'Nature means all the wildlife that I see every day from squirrels, rabbits, ducks playing out in the water, birds on the feeder.' Ken included mosses and trees as well as animals. Steve, again, personalized and localized the term: 'because of the close contact we have with nature, I consider Kielder as...that link to nature.' Four people used 'everything' when defining 'nature'. Two foresters, Stevie Temple and Simon Banks, used 'surroundings' or 'whole surroundings' in their definitions of 'nature', leaving open whether they included the forest. Terry pushed the notion further: 'Nature is the natural environment, I suppose, it's water, air, trees, animals, birds, ourselves.'

The emphasis on wildlife is unsurprising, but the word 'everything', and Terry's specific use of 'ourselves', suggests that some local inhabitants, though possibly not the foresters, define both themselves and the whole of Kielder – including its artificial forest and lake – as 'natural'.

The interviewees' definitions of 'landscape' were similarly insightful. 'Look' and 'looking' were most commonly used, suggesting that the interviewees envisage the landscape as what they see and what it looks like. The words 'views' and 'hills' were also used three times respectively, thus revealing the extent to which landscape means a beautiful view including hills. The word 'trees' was used three times, suggesting that this particular local feature is prominent in local definitions of the entire concept of landscape. The sense of local place is clearly strong.

Local residents' understandings of the ideas of 'environment', 'nature' and 'landscape' informed how they thought about changes in Kielder's environment. In the oral history project, interviewees' perceptions of change were addressed by asking them both about environmental change and their first memories of Kielder.

First memories of Kielder

Interviewees who were born in the area and/or are long-established residents had first memories connected with school, the community and the local environment: farms and the forest. Jonty recalled going to school. So did Stevie, who moved to Kielder from Swansea aged six in 1964. Yvonne remembered the community spirit during her childhood in the 1960s:

> I can remember everybody coming in and out of their house and me mam going in and out to other people's houses, having coffee and chatting, ... that real community spirit where everybody just knew everybody, everybody's business and socialized all the time cos there wasn't anything else here really, wasn't even a shop.

Others remembered playing on farms as small children. Susan Riley, born in 1957:

> just always loved playing down at ma first home at Bewshaugh, … I can maybes remember being outside playing in the … fields and the hay fields …, when the hay's been baled and getting told off for climbing on the stacks …

Jacqueline Wylie, born in 1975, said her first memory was 'just the village walks and the trees around you, and I just love that and like a frosty morning, just going for a walk in the trees, it's lovely.'

Other long-established residents, however, offered first memories that anticipated a major change in the local environment. Simon, born in nearby Falstone in 1962, who made a career in forestry, remembered: 'me very first bike ride to Kielder village and cycle under the viaduct…cos I wasn't allowed till I was a certain age … seven mile up the valley … just the vastness of the … big viaduct.' What he did not say was that part of this road was later drowned by the reservoir.[23] Tonia, who has always lived in nearby Bellingham, remembered visiting Kielder with her father and a friend in the late 1970s:

> we stopped off for our bait … our snack … and just admired the view … knowing that it was to change radically … with the construction of the reservoir, so … just seeing the massive trees and the different farms and then trying to envisage how it would look once construction and all the … machinery came in and this reservoir was gonna be created and it was very difficult to picture that at that stage, but I was obviously very very young then …

Interviewees who moved to Kielder before the dam also had first memories connected with the work that brought them there. A retired forestry worker who moved to Kielder in the early 1960s (anonymous B), said: 'Me first memory of Kielder was all the trees.' Tom Bowbeer, who first came to Kielder as a trainee forester in 1968, remembered 'the impression of … the place I was put to live in, which was in fact a bothy … which housed all the single guys who worked in the forest at the time, which was … a glorified shed at the back of cottages at Kielder Castle'.

In contrast with the varied first memories of long-established inhabitants, almost half of people who first came to Kielder after 1982 have first memories of the dam and reservoir. Most are similar. Peter, on moving from London to the North Tyne valley in 1987, described 'coming up over the hill just before the dam and then suddenly seeing the lake before me, an absolutely stunning experience'. Dennis Crowe, who retired to Kielder with his wife in 1992, remembered:

> Firstly the … road from Bellingham coming into Kielder. Margaret was always keen and happy with trees and water and as we approached Kielder and the vision opened up and all of Kielder, all the trees and the water became obvious she … and I [were] absolutely staggered at the beauty of it.

Duncan, who has been visiting Kielder for 15 years, recalled his first memory as:

driving up in our Wildlife Trust minibus … over up and to the dam and looking out across the lake, … which was something completely different from anything I'd ever been working in before so it was just that view, I believe it was a sunny day as well, … looking out across the reservoir.

Terry remembered:

where you drive up the little road from Falstone until you reach the dam, on a hot summer's day, you've just got this huge expanse of water. I think that's the point … when you follow a tourist up the valley, that everybody slows down by 20 miles [32 km] an hour … that view when you first come over the ridge and…you see the land, see the water on the right and the trees round it and the blue sky.

Linda Squire, employed by the Calvert Trust since 2010, put it more succinctly: 'it was the wow factor when I saw the lake.'

Not all newcomers and visitors recalled the view of the lake. Steve and Julie Webb moved to Kielder in 2006. Steve remembered the 'rugged, wide and open' landscape. Julie said 'it was just wandering around and seeing the place … taking [their young boys] on picnics and to the park and thinking yeah this is …[the] right place to be.'

Changes in the environment

When asked specifically about changes they had witnessed in the environment, many longer-established residents spoke about the forest and the reservoir. Alf's comment at the start of this chapter was echoed by farmer Jim Hall (Jonty's father). Born in 1938, he has lived all his life in the area. The family farm at Deadwater, three miles (4.8 km) upstream from Kielder Village, offers a perspective over the valley, but partly obscured by large blocks of coniferous trees. Asked how the area had changed, Jim replied: 'Oh, dramatically. First of all it was trees, and they changed the whole, and then the railway closing down and the forestry coming in, taking over, and then the water board joining them.'

The forest

Foresters commented on how the forest had changed. Thomas Grimwood has witnessed changes in technology and planting policy since he started working for the Forestry Commission in 1966. At first, he worked with a chainsaw, but now operates mechanical harvesters part time. On planting policy, he noted:

when I … started, [the forest] was a blanket of trees, now it's … just like a patchwork quilt …, and you've got blocks of trees that have been cut and replanted and then there's blocks … that haven't been cut.

Tom Bowbeer, a trainee at Kielder in the late 1960s, who returned in 1987 and went on to manage harvesting operations, expanded on this point:

[M]ost of the area that was hill farm when I first came here, or was … being transformed from hill farm into forest is now at … pole stage, more mature forest, so there's open areas within the forest itself …, but the way the forest has been managed has also meant that the regular block … structure has disappeared and the restructuring of the forest has led to management in … less rigid geometrical shapes … to comply with the landscape.

He approved of the changes.

Stevie, who has worked for the Forestry Commission at Kielder since 1978, emphasized continuity as well as change:

[the forest] hasn't changed a great deal apart from … you fell a block off, you replant it, fell a different block off, replant it. The forest's changing all the time, but it's not changing, if you know what I mean, it's still forest. There has been more broad leaf areas planted than previously. It's not just a commercial forest now, it's more designed for wildlife and recreational facilities.

He thought the changes were 'probably for the better' and that they enabled more people to use the forest.

Other interviewees, mostly newcomers, also commented on changes. Pamela Dove, a retired secretary and librarian who moved to Kielder in 1987, noted that the forest:

changes a lot because it depends what part of the forest is being harvested, so sometimes you go along and they've suddenly done something and you think good grief, it's quite different …

A member of staff (anonymous D) at the Calvert Trust, who has lived in Kielder for sixteen years, remarked:

when they've clear felled …, they have planted native trees like rowans, cherry and opened bits of the blocks throughout the forest for the native wildlife, the birds *etc.* and that's been a good thing.

Duncan commented:

the whole landscape around Kielder … is constantly in a state of change, tree felling, large areas of trees are removed and replanted …, it's … a bit like arable agriculture on a very very slow scale, you suddenly see large areas cleared … and then you see areas replanted, and indeed some areas are not replanted so we've seen some areas that have been cleared for the protection of natural habitats and … peat land sites … so they've been…left open. So we've seen a change away even in the last 15 years … from very much tree production to a much more integrated approach with habitats and wildlife being taken into consideration.

A longer term perspective was offered by retired farmer Jim Hall. Skelton asked him if he had 'affection' for the local landscape. He replied: 'Well the forestry finished that didn't it? … you've just got these great expanse of conifers [*i.e.* soft wood].' She then asked him if he thought it had 'ruined the landscape'. His response was measured: 'Well it has up to a point …, but [growing] hardwood's such a long-term thing. Oh I wouldn't run the forestry down like. Some people may, but …'

The reservoir and tourism

For later generations, the reservoir was the biggest change at Kielder. Several newcomers, when asked about changes in the environment in their experiences, mentioned that they had not seen the area before the dam was built. Peter concluded that, since 1987, the environment had 'changed very little because most of the tree planting and the flooding of the reservoir and those major projects had all been completed before I arrived.'

On the other hand, some long-established residents described what it had been like before the reservoir. Ken remarked:

> when I first lived in the area, of course the dam wasn't built, and, when you went … from Falstone up to Kielder [village] you were driving virtually through a forest, which, cos the trees came right down to the road, with an occasional opening where there was a farmhouse …, it was a very twisty, dark road to travel along.

His description of the road contrasts with the exclamations of delight – the wow factor – on seeing the reservoir offered by several whose first memories were after 1982.

The answers interviewees gave to questions on first memories and changes in the environment indicate the importance of the damming of the river and the creation of the reservoir in the collective memory of both long-established and newer Kielder residents as well as visitors. In the 1970s, in contrast to the later positive descriptions by newcomers, the decision to dam the North Tyne aroused great controversy. Concerns were raised over the impact on the local environment, the population and their livelihoods. The reservoir drowned parts of the road from Falstone to Kielder village, three farms, the colliery village of Plashetts and a school. Around 180 people lost their homes and were relocated. The reservoir also drowned areas of forest. Questions were raised at the time over whether such a large reservoir was needed. The critics, to some extent, were proved right. The industries on Teesside it was designed to supply went into decline and so the water lost its intended customers.[24] Writing in 2003, however, David Archer, in an essay entitled 'white elephant or white knight?', concluded: 'It would appear that most residents of the North Tyne are not only reconciled to Kielder Water, but positively welcome the contribution which it made to amenity and employment.'[25] The project allowed us to gauge local attitudes to the reservoir over a generation after the Queen officially opened the main dam at Kielder in 1982.

Skelton asked Jonty how the area around Kielder had changed:

> Over the course of my life? [he replied] well, really when the construction work [on the dam] began I was pretty young, and I was at Kielder First School … and back in those days … I was pretty much stuck up the top end of the valley … but I can … remember … seeing all the big machines *etc.* working on the dam, … and obviously when I was nine [in 1979], I pushed the button which opened [the] Bakethin [dam], what closed the sluice gate which started the … backing up of the water, … and I can remember that well because obviously that was a big day in me life …

Jonty is a local celebrity and has regularly commented on his experiences. Three years before he spoke to Skelton, he told a local journalist:

> It was such an exciting time, especially when the diggers and bulldozers moved in ... I do remember some of the grown ups getting upset about all the changes, but I didn't really understand why.[26]

Other local residents recalled the construction of the dam. Raymond Terry, a forestry worker who has lived most of his life in Kielder, remembered the construction workers drinking in the Working Men's pub at Kielder Castle at weekends. He recalled that there had been 'no trouble ... because they were working hard and getting up early'. It took them six years to complete the main dam, from 1975 to 1981. Hazel Grimwood recalled the valley flooding 'very very slowly I think, ... it was a big change from what we were used to.'

Several people recalled the impact of the reservoir on the landscape. During a group interview, while looking through the window at the reservoir, Simon said: 'the dam's starting to fit in and just look the part now,' adding: 'The lakeshore side is just starting to come round.' Tom Bowbeer recalled, however, that 'it was pretty stark around the edges when it was first flooded.' Susan commented that the local environment had:

> changed quite ... obviously now it's nice cos everything's established, but there was a period where it looked pretty grim when obviously the reservoir was being built, cos ... they took all the nice trees down from around the river, but now obviously thirty years on everything's established again along the new road and around the lake.

Are local residents, as Archer suggested, now reconciled to Kielder Water? Interviewees who had witnessed the whole story of the reservoir – from conception, arguments, planning and construction to it becoming an established part of the landscape – offered various views. Some, like Alf's quote at the start of this chapter, preferred to weigh up the consequences. Tom Bowbeer remarked:

> makes a big difference to the number of people that come even though it isn't fulfilling the purpose it was put there for in the first instance, but it does attract a lot of people. For instance ... how many people were in that marathon?

Simon replied that a thousand people took part in the marathon (which had taken place shortly before the interviews were held). 'And they wouldn't be here if ... the lakeside way wasn't there,' Tom continued, 'and the lakeside way wouldn't be there [if the reservoir had not been built]'. Another forestry worker (anonymous B), interviewed in full view of the reservoir, indicated how local views had evolved over time:

> The reservoir, aye, changed the whole place altogether. In fact when it ... first ... came out in 1969, that they were gonna flood the dam [*sic*], I thought oh dear me, but, it's absolutely put Kielder on the map like. It brings a lot of tourists in, everything.

Likewise, Kathy Wylie, when Skelton asked her directly if she thought the reservoir had been a good thing, replied:

> It has brought employment *etc.*, but for a lot of years it was a big white elephant. They built it to provide water and it was gonna be such a wonderful thing and, I mean yes the water is being used, but these days it's providing employment ... and tourist attraction.

In response to the same question, Yvonne, who runs the Tea Room at Kielder Castle, replied:

> It's hard to say because it's a bit like you dunno what the valley would've been like had the lake not happened. I know it's brought tourism and ... the lake's stunning, but Kielder before the lake was extremely stunning, the ride down the valley was beautiful, so it might have been really busy and people still flooding into the area to enjoy the beauty of it, being like a national park type thing, so it's hard to say.

Some interviewees commented on residents losing their homes when the valley was flooded, and whether it was worthwhile. Anne Spottiswood, who works at the Bellingham Heritage Centre, had direct contact with some of them. She remembered, 'going to Kielder with ma father who did the valuations of the people that were coming out of the farms that were gonna be flooded ...' On balance, she felt that the changes had been for the better: 'For me yes, I think ... so, to look on those black trees, it's opened the valley up and it's made it much lighter.' An interviewee born in the 1930s who has spent her whole life in Northumberland (anonymous A), remarked that the reservoir:

> wasn't particularly wanted in the first place. It did take away a few houses and a school, but it has made a tremendous difference. It opened the whole area out, it's wonderful for tourists. It's the biggest manmade lake, it's got so many facilities now. It must have brought a tremendous amount of income to that whole area.

Asked whether she thought the changes had been for the better, she replied: 'Oh definitely, because I think the whole place would've died. People wouldn't have been able to get their livelihood because even the forestry's cutting back so it's made tremendous advantage for people.' Clearly there is a widespread appreciation of how integral the growth of tourism is to the local economy of the Kielder area now and in the future.

However, not all villagers share similar levels of enthusiasm for encouraging the growth of tourism. Simon commented:

> The forestry encourage events, the water authority encourage events, but some people that come into the village ... have a tendency not to support them ... which is a little bit disappointing, cos they came into the area knowing what it was like originally so they shouldn't be trying to change it.

Tourism is a significant source of income in the local area and it employs many residents. Some interviewees are well aware of the large extent to which the reservoir underpins tourism, which clearly shapes some of the more positive opinions. However, a lot of the work is seasonal and many people hold multiple jobs to make ends meet. Carl Garsman, a Falstone resident, works as a barman, a cleaner and a waiter. Terry manages a bed and breakfast, a tearoom and teaches Nordic Walking.

Thomas Grimwood described the dramatic changes: 'Now we have a great big lake, which wasn't here when I … first started working.' Did he think the changes had been for the better or worse? 'Argh, definitely for the better.' To contextualize this remark, we should consider that at the start of the interview he said: 'I was born in a little place called Bewshaugh, which is now under the Bakethin reservoir.'

His neighbours included Susan Riley's family. Asked if she could remember the valley before the reservoir, she replied:

> Oh yes, I can, … we lived originally in a little farm called Bewshaugh, which is now under the lake, just down from the viaduct. And I remember from about six or seven years old people coming and asking ma mam and dad their opinions, I can remember them setting up all the big drills to explore into the ground and then we moved from Bewshaugh up to Gowanburn because obviously it was going to be flooded, so yes.

Asked whether she thought building the dam was a good thing, she measured her words:

> Well that's a catch 22 isn't it? If it stayed the way it was, I mean you can't tell, I mean, it's good, I like it, it's created employment, it's brought some new faces to the area, but then it's also had a detrimental effect on the school, because the forestry moved their workshops and offices to Bellingham, … therefore, the children … moved, … [and] went to either Greenhaugh or Bellingham, and some of them even moved to Hexham [35 miles/56 km away], so … it did have a bad affect on the school, certainly.

Ken's first reaction to the flooding of the valley was to buy a boat, on impulse, while on a routine shopping trip to buy some potatoes in Carlisle:

> the second time we went out with it, we took … one of the local farmers on the lake, sailing down and he lived near Bull Crag … and he says, "oh … I recognize that, I recognize the fields from here", he says, "we must be about the top of my farm at the moment" and he … thought it was great and I said "well what d'ya think, are you pleased you're out of it?" "Oh", he says, "yes, it was a hard life."

Jonty, who has evidently thought a lot about it over the years since he started the whole process of flooding the valley in 1979, shared his thoughts:

> For maself, and ma family, I would probably say for the best, maybe for some of my ancestors *etc.* and other parts like more distant family, probably I would say to the detriment, but for me, personally, I would probably … have moved away for work, so for me … if it wasn't here, there'd only be forestry commission or farming … Me dad and brother's farmers and I just didn't want to go into farming at all; it wasn't for me, and that's why I wanted to go into graphic design, but with the reservoir being here, obviously not just for maself but for other people it has … created … a lot of employment so, from that point of view it's a good thing.

On balance, therefore, longer established residents have accepted the reservoir, recognize its contribution to the development of tourism, and the jobs it has brought to the area, but remain aware of its contested history.

Conclusion: use and delight

Kielder serves as a compelling example of what Chris Smout has called 'the twin considerations of use and delight' that have always shaped 'human attitudes to the environment'.[27] It could be added that they have also shaped attitudes to environmental change. Many of the people interviewed work or worked at Kielder, making use of the resources afforded by the environment. Not all were delighted, however, especially in the early days (before the forest, reservoir and tourist facilities). Alf first arrived with his family in 1932. His first memory of Kielder was:

> coming up in the train from South Wales with ma mother and father and sister ... the dog barked all the way ... I remember getting out of the train here and ma mother says, "where the God have I got to?" ... because all you could see was Ravenshill, the church and the station and ... the coach house, which was just a shed really and that was it.

Seventy years later, Skelton asked Alf: 'Do you enjoy living here?' 'I've lived here most of me life, lass,' he replied. 'And do you like it?' 'Course I do. I wouldn't stop here if I didn't.'

In contrast to the Quantock Hills and other Areas of Outstanding Natural Beauty or National Parks, Kielder is not delightful to all its residents. When Anthony Dove, who has lived in the area for twenty-five years, was asked if he had affection for landscape, he replied: 'A bit strong really, ... I don't mind it at all, it's ... no sort of Lake District as it were, ... but it's ... nice if you exclude the [RAF] jets that fly over ... They used to almost knock the chimney pots off.' His wife Pamela was also a little reticent: 'I like the landscape, yes, I think it's beautiful, but when I go back to Sussex or Hampshire, I feel more of a draw there than I do here.'

Others, including long-established residents, newcomers and visitors, were less restrained. A selection of their comments when asked if they liked the environment or had affection for it gives an indication of the feelings of most of the interviewees: 'I think it's beautiful;' 'Absolutely love it;' 'Yes, I think it's wonderful. Visually it's fantastic;' 'I think [living in this environment is] the best thing I've ever done in my life;' 'I thoroughly enjoy [it] yeah, I've a real deep affection for it, nice;' 'the openness, the freedom of it, I think it [is] just ... lovely;' 'Definitely, definitely, yeah.' The strongest views were expressed, perhaps not surprisingly, by people who chose to move to the area from elsewhere:

> Yeah, it's fantastic, ... I love seeing the ... ducks and the squirrels ... I think especially for the kids ... so for them to be in this environment is fantastic, but we still try to introduce them into the towns and city life so that they realise that ... there are cars and things like that ... but I mean it's a lovely place to live. (Julie)

> I love the forest, I love the fells, I love the lakes, they're inspirational, they're uplifting, they're great for the soul and the heart and coming up to Kielder when the sun is setting on a beautiful evening, nothing can beat it in terms of the quality of life, tranquillity and peace, so in that respect it's greatly enhanced my life. (Peter)

Even some who lost their homes to the reservoir, such as Thomas Grimwood, offered positive comments. When asked if he enjoyed living in this environment, replied: 'I do, yes, aye, ... I didn't think I would want to live anywhere else.'

The environment at Kielder, for which many of its residents have affection, has been shaped by the people who have lived and worked there, planting and harvesting the forest, watching the reservoir form, building and managing tourist facilities. While the interviewees shed light on these processes of change, we did not need to conduct an oral history project to find out that people had changed the environment, and certainly not at Kielder. What we did learn, and could not perhaps have found out in any other way, was the extent to which both long-established residents and newcomers had come so greatly to appreciate the largely artificial environment. A few clearly articulated its artificiality. Anonymous A, who has lived in the area for half her life, remarked: 'I think it's beautiful, whether it's summer or winter, I think it's been designed very well and I think the way they're now managing all the tree plantations and they've opened it out such a lot.'

We also learned from the oral history project, and again probably could not have done so in any other way, that members of the local community see themselves as part of the environment. This had an intriguing implication which we did not anticipate.

Some of the interviewees, unprompted by the interviewer, considered whether the artificial environment was somehow 'natural'. Those who did so, however, were newcomers or longer-established residents who worked in tourism or for Northumbrian Water. Foresters, it seems, did not conflate the 'artificial' and 'natural' worlds at Kielder. Thus, Terry, who runs the Bed and Breakfast where Skelton stayed while conducting the interviews, agreed that he had an affection for the landscape. He continued: 'I'm very into maps and land shapes and forms and nature and the outdoors, and things not manmade, so it's, yeah anything natural, environmental, clean, I'm really into.'

Two people most clearly articulated the 'naturalness' of the artificial environment. Tonia said:

> it's a beautiful area this time of year [October], you can see the different colours of the trees ..., winter can become very picturesque with the very frosty white ..., and it's just very peaceful and it's picturesque, ... it gets you away from it all and ... it's a nice area of outstanding, you can't say natural beauty because neither the forest or the water's natural, but to me it does look quite natural in comparison and as good as the Lake District but in a much different way.

Jonty expressed this very clearly:

> for my grandparents or ma great grandparents, ... the forest being planted and the outlook of the whole valley changing would have been a massive thing ... and then ... for me ... looking at the reservoir, it's natural because I can't really remember

the valley before, and for … my daughter, this again will be completely natural to her, whereas looking back to ma parents and ma grandparents … it was very alien to them whereas for us, it's, it's natural.

Tonia's use of the words 'beautiful', 'picturesque' and 'outstanding' are insightful because they refer specifically to her positive visual perception of the landscape. Tonia is fully aware that Kielder's landscape is not natural and her appreciation of it does not result from the intentional emulation of a typically natural environment at Kielder. Rather, she appreciates it in its own right despite, and perhaps even because of, its non-natural origins. Jonty's comments that his parents and grandparents found Kielder's environmental innovations 'alien' are also revealing in the context of the dichotomy between natural and non-natural; native and alien. Perhaps by 'alien', Jonty meant 'non-natural', whereas his parents and grandparents might have perceived their native environment as natural. In the context of Duncan's comments about the landscape's foreignness, comparing Kielder to North American and Scandinavian landscapes, this confirms Kielder's non-natural, non-native and ultimately changed characteristics in the minds of some, if not all, of those who live and work in the area.

Moving from the local to the global, 'from a very early time', Radkau has reminded us, 'water and forests have been leitmotifs of environmental history. If we leave aside air, these are the two most important resources that were always used in tandem by many people.'[28] Smout, another leading environmental historian, in line with recent thinking in the field, has argued that 'people are part of nature … Once we recognize …[this], we can see our choices more clearly … We can respect nature, intervene lightly.'[29] And yet, what we found at Kielder was indeed a community that used its forests and water in tandem, but one that was part of a wider society that had intervened radically to utterly transform its environment, and where those people who stayed or chose to move there have come to like their engineered environment, even to the extent of considering that which they had made natural. To the extent that they are part of nature and their 'environment', of course, they are right.

Notes

1. TNA HLG 127/1280: Documents submitted to the Kielder Scheme Inquiry, 1971, Item 91: Letter from Kielder Parish Council to the Secretary of State for the Environment, Mr Rippon, received 22 July 1971.
2. On the decision to build the Bakethin reservoir, see: TNA MAF 135/775, Item 23a: Local Inquiry into Applications Concerning the Kielder Water Scheme by the Northumbrian River Authority, 3 February 1972 to 15 March 1972, p. 26.
3. For more detail on the location, see 'Three Places' and the chapters by Jill Payne and Christine McCulloch in this volume, pp. 17–30, 97–108, 269–78. The moorlands of England have been modified by people since prehistoric times. See: Ian G. Simmons, *The Moorlands of England and Wales: An Environmental History 8000 BC to AD 2000* (Edinburgh: Edinburgh University Press, 2004).
4. See Leona Jayne Skelton's chapter in this volume, pp. 109–17.
5. See, for example: Paul R. Josephson, *Industrialized Nature: Brute Force Technology and*

the Transformation of the Natural World (Washington, DC and London: Island Press, 2002).

6. See: Michael Williams, *Deforesting the Earth: From Prehistory to Global Crisis* (Chicago: University of Chicago Press, 2003).

7. See, for example: Joachim Radkau, *Nature and Power: A Global History of the Environment*, Thomas Dunlap (trans.) (New York: Cambridge University Press, 2008), pp. 190-2, 216-18; Richard Grove, *Green Imperialism: Colonial Expansion, Tropical Island Edens and the Origins of Environmentalism, 1600-1860* (Cambridge: Cambridge University Press, 1995), pp. 120, 273-84; Robert Gardner, 'Constructing a Technological Forest: Nature, Culture, and Tree-Planting in the Nebraska Sand Hills', *Environmental History* 14/2 (2009), pp. 275-97.

8. For a wider perspective, see: A. Joshua West, 'Forests and National Security: British and American Forestry Policy in the Wake of World War I', *Environmental History* 8/2 (2003), pp. 270-93.

9. Samuel Temple, 'Forestation and Its Discontents: The Invention of an Uncertain Landscape in Southwestern France, 1850–Present', *Environment and History* 17 (2011), pp. 13–34; Sara M. Gregg, *Managing the Mountains: Land Use Planning, the New Deal, and the Creation of a Federal Landscape in Appalachia* (New Haven: Yale University Press, 2010); Gardner, 'Constructing a Technological Forest'.

10. T. C. Smout, *Nature Contested: Environmental History in Scotland and Northern England since 1600* (Edinburgh: Edinburgh University Press, 2000), pp. 58-63. On non-native species, see: Ian D. Rotherham and Robert A. Lambert (eds), *Invasive and Introduced Plants and Animals: Human Perceptions, Attitudes and Approaches to Management* (Washington, DC: Earthscan, 2011).

11. Radkau, *Nature and Power*, pp. 181-2, 256-8; Josephson, *Industrialized Nature*, pp. 18-38.

12. Valentin Rasputin, *Farewell to Matyora: A Novel*, Antonina W. Bouis (trans.) (Evanston: Northwestern University Press, 1995).

13. Harriet Ritvo, *The Dawn of Green: Manchester, Thirlmere, and Modern Environmentalism* (Chicago: University of Chicago Press, 2009).

14. Geoffrey A. Irlam, 'Electricity Supply at Cragside', *Industrial Archaeology Review* 11/2 (1989), pp. 187-95.

15. Keith Thomas, *Man and the Natural World: Changing Attitudes in England 1500-1800* (London: Allen Lane, 1983).

16. See: Berhard Gissibl, Sabine Hohler and Patrick Kupper (eds), *Civilizing Nature: National Parks in Global Historical Perspective* (New York and Oxford: Berghahn Books, 2012). On the less well known case of Russia, see: Christopher Ely, *This Meagre Nature: Landscape and National Identity in Imperial Russia* (DeKalb: Northern Illinois University Press, 2002).

17. Gregg, *Managing the Mountains*.

18. Smout, *Nature Contested*, p. 62.

19. Robert M. Crislera and Mahlon S. Hunta, 'Recreation Regions of Missouri', *Journal of Geography* 51/1 (1952), pp. 30-9.

20. http://www.visitkielder.com/ (accessed 01/06/13).

21. A. G. Tansley, 'The Use and Abuse of Vegetational Concepts and Terms', *Ecology* 16/3 (July 1935), pp. 284-307, at p. 303.

22. See: Sverker Sörlin and Paul Warde (eds), *Nature's End: History and the Environment* (Houndmills: Palgrave Macmillan, 2009), p. vii; Smout, *Nature Contested*, p. 2.

23. See the overlaid maps, before and after the construction of the dam, at: http://www.environmentalhistories.net/?page_id=39 (accessed 11/02/13).

24. On the controversy over the dam, see: David Archer, 'Kielder Water: white elephant or white knight?', in David Archer (ed.), *Tyne and Tide: A Celebration of the River Tyne* (Ovingham: Daryan Press, 2003), pp. 138–56; C. S. McCulloch, 'The Kielder Water Scheme: the last of its kind?', in Henry Hewlett (ed.), *Improvements in reservoir construction, operation and maintenance* (London: Thomas Telford Books, 2006), pp. 196–210.

25. Archer, 'Kielder Water', p. 155.

26. 'This is my Kielder', *Hexham Courant*, Thursday, 29 October 2009 http://www.hexhamcourant.co.uk/tourism/this-is-my-kielder-1.629803?referrerPath=/ (accessed 12/02/13).

27. Smout, *Nature Contested*, p. 7.

28. Radkau, *Nature and Power*, p. 86.

29. Smout, *Nature Contested*, p. 2.

CHAPTER 24

Hidden History: Kielder's Early Modern Landscape

Matt Greenhall

The present-day landscape of Kielder Water and Forest Park is a far cry from its early modern predecessor and shows little sign of its place within the turbulent history of the Anglo-Scottish borders. Lying in the English 'Middle March', the inhabitants of sixteenth- and seventeenth-century Kielder were often vulnerable to the raiding of quasi-kin groups, known locally as surnames, from either side of the border. As a reflection of such socio-economic turbulence, the Kielder area was pebble-dashed with defensive homesteads, or bastles, used for the protection of both the landscape's human inhabitants and their livestock.[1] Made of rough-hewn stone, bastles were notable for their defensive construction and for making the greatest use of the landscape for their own protection. Often clustered amongst surname groupings such as Armstrong and Hall, they were strategically placed within sight of one another. In addition to these features, they had thick stone walls (sometimes up to a metre in width), narrow windows and a slate roof (to increase fire protection). The defining feature of a bastle was its floor design: the ground floor was reserved for livestock, whereas the first floor was for its human inhabitants. The latter was accessible via a removable ladder which could be withdrawn at night or during attack. In offering a family protection, bastles were defensive structures designed to withstand aggression and therefore lacked offensive elements. Built throughout the fifteenth, sixteenth and early seventeenth centuries, it was during the gradual pacification of the borderlands in the mid-1600s that bastles began to fall from use as defensive structures and were gradually abandoned or transformed into semi-gentrified farmhouses. Many can still be seen throughout Northumberland on farm estates or as ruins.

In offering protection to humans and livestock, bastles were an integral element of the pastoral landscape of the borders and were largely built along the valley sides of Kielder rather than on high moorland. This reflected their wider role in the pastoral economy in the process of transhumance. They were accompanied by other constructions, notably sheilings, which had no defensive purpose but were rectangular buildings for the housing of livestock during their summer pasturing. The largely flooded undulations of the Kielder landscape now obscure the geographical relationship between both of these buildings, although the ruins of at least three sheilings and seven bastles can still be seen around the water's edge. Kielder's ruined bastles no longer enjoy their defensive position within the landscape and are now nestled amongst non-native species of conifers or along the banks of its reservoir. As a result, they occupy a very alien landscape to that originally intended, something which obscures their original setting and purpose.

Kielder's bastles and sheilings are also accompanied by a number of pele towers. The latter formed a gentrified counterpart to the more humble bastle and were multi-stored rectangular structures for the protection of families (but not livestock). At least seven pele towers can still be seen in the Kielder area. It should be noted that bastles, sheilings and pele towers are constructions synonymous with borderlands and can also be spotted in the Pale of Ireland and the Balkans.

Note

1. Natural England, *National Character Area Profile 5: Border Moors and Forests* (2013), pp. 10, 18, 39, 40.

CHAPTER 25

Waterlands to Wonderlands

....

Paul Warde

In travelling up to Kielder Water, I traced a direct the path from the beginning to the end of our workshops: from my house, a few miles from the National Trust reserve at Wicken Fen, to what are now the shores of the Upper Tyne Valley. I travelled from the 'Waterland', famously evoked in Graham Swift's novel of that name, to the site of the popular 'Winter Wonderland' laid on for the seasonal enjoyment of Tynesiders amid what might be a pastiche of a snowbound landscape on the Canadian Shield, all wooden cabins, looming conifers and the sky in the lake. And after all, Northumbrian Water was owned, at the time of our visit, by Canadian pensioners. We missed the loons. Alternatively, with more rocks it might have been Lapland. But the wonderland I was also reminded of was what Hans Dominick, writing about dams in 1922, evoked as being 'In the Wonderland of Technology: Masterpieces and New Achievements that Our Youth Should Know'. I suspect that nearly all of us felt some of this wonder (what David Nye called parochially 'the American Technological Sublime') as we strode through the strangely arid tunnels beneath the lake (Fig. 25.1), or watched the power and exactitude of computer-controlled twenty-first century tree-felling in close-up.

When Graham Swift wrote *Waterland*, he had, in fact, never encountered the Fens save through a train window. Reflecting on the work, he wondered if he had chosen the Fens as 'the ideal non-setting, the ideal flat, bare platform for my human drama'. In his eyes, '*Waterland* is set where we're all set, inside our own heads.' Given that the novel is now viewed more widely as an evocation of the almost timeless properties of a place, *Waterland* is testament both to the power of the imagination and to the power of the text that seems to link us to the past. Yet the widespread misinterpretation of Swift's own backstory that he has encountered since writing the novel, the assumption that he was umbilically linked to the Fens, also indicates that stories *take place*. Our own heads are always somewhere and, like the salmon, the stories we tell find their way back towards that particular niche from which they seemed to rove out. A non-setting becomes a setting. The wonderland takes its place in history.

In our discussions Petra van Dam expressed some bemusement at the British preoccupation with distinguishing the 'natural' and the 'artificial'. At Kielder she saw a polder, just a polder. I expect British environmental historians could indeed exhaust themselves discussing the naturalness (or not) of polders. In Kielder Polder, the water is hemmed in; in the Fens, of course, that really are polders, it is drained out, except at Wicken, where the wetland has to be maintained by pumping water into land now standing proud above the water table. In this regard, Wicken Fen has more kinship with Kielder: they are islands of water, anti-polders. Every polder and anti-polder is a little utopian vision, perhaps, a kind of wonderland that seeks to transcend the time and space that we inherited. In this regard, nature reserves are no different from engineering projects. But every utopia turns out to be in some place; it comes back to the spawning ground. And every scrap of land and stretch of water we see, and give love, hate, character and numbers to, was once somebody else's wonderland, their leap into the cascade of time, something that seemed wholly novel.

Thus, while we talk a lot about the past of landscapes and their organic or their designed qualities, what shaped these landscapes, of any kind, has been a certain orientation towards the future. They are the products of what past imaginations made of the clays they found in their hands, whether texts, soils, water, technologies, training, visions, feelings (all with their different qualities and effects), and what elements they expected to shape these into in the henceforth. A quivering sense of anticipation, and perhaps disappointment, resonates through the Fens, Wicken Fen and Kielder Water and Forest Park. These were the products of certain kinds of *anticipatory knowledge* and the expertise allied with it. They are both formed of projects and predictions. In the case of the Fens, the age of 'projecting' that was the seventeenth century (in fact viewed with a high degree of contemporary scepticism) great scheme for draining marshes, registering populations, establishing new industries and technological quick-fixes to poverty, idleness and ignorance; all too often hand-in-hand with arrogance, venality, deceit and, in the language of the time, covetousness, but also with a zeal that ingenious and knowledgeable men could restore Eden, could make a better world. With the enormous drains and waterworks the seventeenth-century engineers did indeed propel the Fens towards its modern, angular, intensively-farmed and somewhat desiccated form.

Kielder Forest and Kielder Water equally belong to an age of projection and prediction, especially in the age of 'technical development' with the high esteem for technocrats and the white heat of technology in the decades after World War Two. The astonishing rapidity of post-war reconstruction and economic growth was closely bound up with fears of resource exhaustion: the setting up of the Natural Resources Council of America and the Presidential Materials Policy Commission in America; and the reports of the committee on Political and Economic Planning in Britain in the late 1940s and 1950s. Water demand was predicted to outstrip the rate of economic growth. The risks of development were highlighted in the massive collection *Man's Role in Changing the Face of the Earth*, published in 1956; the famous 'Club of Rome' report of 1972, albeit a first prominent outing for computer modelling, was the sum, rather than the beginning, of these fears. This, to some extent, was also the intellectual hinterland of the dam-builders of the 1960s and 1970s, and those who saw the water demand of the North East racing ahead of capacity to the end of the century. The problems were big and the solutions were envisaged as being big too.

As we know with hindsight, the problems brought about by the solutions were frequently also big. As a reaction, we were told that 'small is beautiful' by E. F. Schumacher – a man who cut his economic teeth working with John Maynard Keynes and later as a planner for the National Coal Board. By the time Kielder was completed, the mega-project was falling out of fashion, whether in engineering discourse, economics or the rising political mood on both left and right (but by no means everywhere – some still celebrated the London Stock Exchange's 'Big bang' of October 1986, leading to the market crash of 1987, and subsequent booms and busts). A different kind of anticipation was emerging – perhaps one that did not look, in many cases, too far into the future, and did not base decisions on projections far ahead in time. This shouldn't, certainly, be confused with the actual proliferation of 'smallness' in the economy, which has tended to become ever-more concentrated.

The writing of Christine McCulloch and her paper delivered at Kielder seem to fit well into this micro-age and its scepticism towards the grand narrative and the grand design as the outcome of the grand projection. It belongs to the age of white elephants and unintended consequences. The North East of England was left with a waterland designed with the projected demand of industry in mind – but as it turned out, that wonderland did not come to be. Kielder did not perhaps involve the kinds of brutal expropriations and suffering found, and continuing, with so many mega-dam projects around the world. Indeed, one could conjecture that the local population is rather larger now than it would have been without the forest and the dam. But I find myself in sympathy with Christine's scepticism. I enjoy the spectacle of dams, but I doubt that I would be very enthusiastic if somebody presented me with an upland valley and asked me whether I wanted it to be 'drowned'.

Yet now we find ourselves in a new age of anticipatory knowledge and (often highly uncertain) prediction. Our future-orientation is changing again. We are coming to value 'resilience', the capacity to withstand shocks and the unanticipated – which itself requires a certain kind of anticipation. Resilience can be 'small-scale', avoiding overdependence on big networks and distant expertise and resources. It encourages diversity. But a diverse world is also one that embraces both the big and the small. If we move to a world less preoccupied with short-term efficiency and optimization, then big spaces and big capacities may yet come back into fashion – even if much of the time they lie redundant. I find myself thinking that the Wicken Vision, expanding the ecological capacity and scale of the Fen reserve, and hoping for a grander scale of freedom from the utilitarian framing of the landscape, has some kind of kinship with the big thinking of engineers and post-war resource planners. Certainly it shares uncertainty about outcome – it is providing capacity in an ongoing process. Understanding this kinship can perhaps help our lines of communication, informed debate and articulation of needs (including emotional). Big reservoir capacity may come in useful again (although climate change may make us wetter, it may not distribute the rain where we need it, so storage may be become more of an issue, as with the electricity network). That projects are wiser if strongly grounded in clear evidence of need (build dams only according to demonstrable demand) might seem a good bet now, but a new age of resilience and uncertainty may come to see things differently. Perhaps diversity will require the full colour-range of elephants, as well as a good biodiverse mix of all kinds of species.

Examining the future-orientation of landscapes, and our imaginings of what they might be, is one framework by which we can understand the history and future of places, and how local and global processes, and those at all other scales, become intertwined. Giving credit to the wonderings that shaped the land and water enables a more historically-informed debate on landscape change, and how that landscape is linked to values and stories. We can help demonstrate how certain visions of the future may include or exclude other visions, and other species, or 'segments', of humanity. We can demonstrate that how far we wish to look ahead is always linked to how far we wish to look back. We discover much in common, a kind of shared language, while never erasing profound differences.

CHAPTER 26

Kielder Dam and Reservoir

Jonty Hall

Transcript of talk by Jonty Hall, Guest Services Manager (facilities),
Northumbrian Water Limited, Kielder, on Kielder Dam,
inside the Dam, 26 March 2011[1]

JONTY HALL: So, [I'm going to talk about] reasons why Kielder Water was actually built here, and why it was chosen to be built at Kielder, a bit about the dimensions, a bit about the Kielder transfer scheme, and what it's meant to Kielder and the people of Kielder as a whole.

So one reason [why it was built here] is we have a hell of a lot of rain, twice the national average. I think the most the reservoir's ever risen in one day was about 1.7 metres. When you think that the surface area's about 3,000 acres [*c.*1214 ha], that's a hell of a lot of water to fall here in one day. And that's a mix of melting snow as well as a deluge of rain at the same time. Another reason, the valley is very narrow, so it meant that when they came to build the dam itself, it wasn't having to go over a massive, wide area of the valley. A lot of the materials which they needed to build the dam were actually already on site. Most of the materials were here to be quarried and brought down and used here, all the clay, whinstone, sandstone *etc.* You would've seen on your drive up [from Newcastle to Kielder] that the road isn't particularly good, so it would've meant that they would've had to build a road north and south to get all those materials in. The valley itself had a very flat gradient, so it meant that there was a huge area of storage [for a large] volume of water. Where they looked at the other areas, there wasn't really a valley which had such a flat gradient and had the capacity to store as much water. And another reason, the area where they were going to be building the dam was very sparsely populated compared to a lot of the other places that they were studying. So it meant they weren't going to have to relocate as many people, and pay as much compensation.

I think the biggest community which was underneath the reservoir now would be Plashetts Village, a small coal-mining village, which had gradually got smaller and smaller because the mine had closed in the '50s. There were small hamlets and houses dotted around, so there wasn't a great many people to move on. They did build some houses in Falstone [just below the dam], and as part of their compensation, they were given the opportunity to buy those houses for about £1,000 at the time. Those houses are going for nearly £200,000 now.

…

After two lengthy enquiries, they decided on Kielder [as the location for the dam]. It turned out to be a record-breaking achievement. I believe it's still the largest engineering project within the water industry [in Britain] to this day. It cost around about £160,000,000 to £170,000,000 in total to build both Kielder Reservoir and the transfer system [to take water to the Wear and the Tees], digging through the hills to put the pipelines in. When you think these days you can win 50 or 60 million on the Euro Lottery on a weekend, so in terms of money looking at it now, it wasn't massive amounts of money when you think of this huge expanse of water and the fact that the North East have never known or been anywhere near having a hosepipe ban or a water shortage. And the fact that through the whole of the transfer system, and the water grid, we can provide water to pretty much around about 80% of the North East. So, it's pretty good. There is some areas up in North Northumberland, where they have the smaller reservoirs or boreholes which provide their water supply.

It was [built by] a consortium. The project was too big to be undertaken by any one company. It was an Anglo-Scottish consortium of Balfour Beatty and Fairclough, and those two companies combined to undertake the project. And on 21 May 1974, Kielder Water came into operation, and the very next day they started cutting down the trees, knocking down the buildings *etc.*, making way for all of what was to come. There is talks of church steeples and certain buildings which poke out of the water when the level goes down. That simply isn't the case at Kielder, everything was bulldozed, knocked down and all the wood was burnt *etc.*, so we didn't have all the spoil coming to the surface and ending up on the dam wall and washing up on the lakesides.

…

The dam itself is about a quarter of a mile long ... and we're roughly at full capacity. We're roughly at above 52 metres of water here [looking out over the reservoir from inside the Valve Tower, just behind the dam]. It holds 44 billion gallons, which is 200 billion litres. It has a surface area of about 3,000 acres [*c*.1214 ha] and in a day we can yield from a single source about 200 million gallons [*c*.910 million litres]. It's said there's enough water at Kielder that everyone in the world could have 32 litres or 7 gallons and they still think there would be a little bit left at the bottom.

LEONA JAYNE SKELTON: Everyone in the world?

JONTY HALL: Yeah, everyone in the world could have roughly 32 litres. Who made that up, I don't know. [laughter]

...

MARIANNA DUDLEY: Was there much local protest to the dam or was it quite accepted?

JONTY HALL: There was a few protests, that it was a white elephant, that it wasn't needed.

ERIN GILL: And they were right.

JONTY HALL: I suppose looking at it now, yeah, the industry on Teesside which it was primarily built for, isn't certainly anywhere near as big as what it was.

MARIANNA DUDLEY: Was it active protests?

JONTY HALL: Yeah it was. There were banners, saying it'd be a white elephant. But I think there was something like 180 objections, something like that, and, you know, looking at that now, you'd probably expect that coming in in a day, I would imagine. So, as far as objections are concerned, there wasn't a massive amount but there were protests.

MARIANNA DUDLEY: Other organizations didn't take it up as a cause, like Greenpeace or more organized?

JONTY HALL: No, I don't think so. It was more local.

IAN ROTHERHAM: Presumably, with Kielder coming on in strength, did Cow Green [reservoir in Teesdale] need to be built? Because Cow Green ecologically was the very damaging one.

CHRISTINE MCCULLOCH: No, you wouldn't have had to have Cow Green, if you'd had Kielder.

JONTY HALL: But, they looked at all the reservoirs that they had. But they needed to have one source which would pretty much double the water resources in the region with the way the water projections were going.

ERIN GILL: Why was Cow Green turned down?

CHRISTINE MCCULLOCH: Because it's on a site of scientific interest, alpine vegetation.

IAN ROTHERHAM: It's one of the only wild areas in England and there was a very successful campaign to stop it and that pre-dates, that's 1960s, '70s wasn't it? Late '60s. [Cow Green reservoir was eventually built.[2]]

ERIN GILL: You mentioned that your father's a farmer, and did he lose land?

JONTY HALL: He didn't, no. Fortunately all of his land was on the other side.

	Some of his land was actually right on the water's edge, it didn't actually become flooded, but that land he actually rented anyway.
ERIN GILL:	And so, were there farmers who did lose land?
JONTY HALL:	Oh yeah there was. I mean, Otterstone Lee, which was just over under this area here, that was, I believe, the largest sheep farm of its kind at one stage. Yeah, so there was a lot of land lost on that one.
ERIN GILL:	And what sort of compensation? Was it a good lump of compensation?
JONTY HALL:	I'm not sure what the compensation was, but it would vary from person to person, I would imagine. I mean, a few of my family actually did live on what is flooded now, and I mean if you put yourself in their shoes, and think that the place where they were born and grew up, you know, we would want to go back and visit at some stage, wouldn't you? But for these people that was never, never going to happen, and for them it must have been a horrible, horrible situation to be in.

Notes

1. Transcribed by Leona Jayne Skelton, edited by David Moon.
2. See Roy Gregory, 'The Cow Green Reservoir', in Peter J. Smith (ed.), *The Politics of Physical Resources* (Harmondsworth: Penguin, 1974), pp. 144–201.

CHAPTER 27

Kielder Forest

Graham Gill

Transcript of talk by Graham Gill, Forest Management Director,
North England Forest District, in Kielder Forest, 26 March 2011[1]

GRAHAM GILL: Usually when I'm doing the talk about forestry, I talk about the
history of forestry because that helps put it in context and I'm just
a bit nervous of doing that with Chris Smout here. [laughing] But
if I give my perception of history then you'll see where I'm coming
from, and what I usually say to people is that if you go back 12,000
years ago, Britain was mostly covered with ice and de-vegetated. So,
as the ice age came to the end and the ice retreated, we were still
joined to the continent, and the country re-vegetated mainly from
the south to north and a wave of forest invaded. To begin with, it
was more pioneer species like Scots pine and birch and then heavier
seeded trees like oak and ash and later beech. Following the ice age
we moved into the Boreal period, which was very good for tree
growth. At that time, the country wouldn't have been completely
covered with natural forest, but almost. Around 6,000 years ago,
the climate changed again from the Boreal to the Atlantic period,
became cooler and wetter, and peat bogs started to form on the
higher ground. Trees didn't regenerate, so larger openings started
to develop on the higher ground. At about the same time, humans
beings were turning from hunter gatherers to agriculture and were
beginning to clear the forest, not to use the timber particularly,
just to make space for living, grazing animals and growing crops.
The forest clearance was fairly steady and by 2,000 years ago, the
time of the Romans, we think that the forest cover in Britain was
down to something like 20%. The Romans talk about standing
on Hadrian's Wall and seeing 'the great wood of Caledon', but
I think by 2,000 years ago, an awful lot of tree clearance would
have happened in Scotland as well, so it wasn't as if you got to
Hadrian's Wall and then there was solid forest north of that.

Over the next 2,000 years there was further clearance of forest. By 1900, we were down to about 4% of forest cover. Britain was a big trading nation and imported all the timber it needed so there was no requirement to grow timber in this country. During the First World War, the blockade meant we were unable to import timber, but we needed timber for the war effort. But in this country there were no forestry skills, no logging skills, no saw milling skills. So, Canadians and Newfoundlanders came over and set up logging camps and saw mills and produced wood for war time. From the 4% of forest that there was in the country, there had been some planting in the nineteenth century, but not very much. At the end of the war, the government decided that we needed a strategic reserve of timber. The Forestry Commission was created with that single purpose in 1919. It was asked to do the job in two ways: one was by encouraging through grants and incentives private owners to replant some of the forest that had been cleared for the war and the second was to plant new forests. The Forestry Commission was given powers to acquire land and create new strategic reserve forests. It was not to use good land for agriculture, but to look for poorer land which tends to be in the north and west of the country. If you look at a map of Britain now, the forests are mainly in the north and west of the country. There are some exceptions, like Thetford Forest in East Anglia, but it's on quite poor agricultural soil.

The Forestry Commission would buy land and plant trees and that's how Kielder came into being. It was the same for much of the upland forest in Britain. The first acquisition at Kielder was in 1925 from the Duke of Northumberland, but the hills here hadn't carried trees for quite a long time, as they had been grazed by sheep, quite low density sheep grazing, and used for grouse shooting. So, the tree planting was all quite experimental and there was quite a lot of work done to test out different species from around the world to find out what would grow on what were quite wet, cold soils in this part of the country. Quite quickly it was discovered that Sitka spruce from northwest America grew very well and seemed quite well adapted to the climate. It needed a raised planting spot, which was done first with hand turves and later on with plough furrows, and large areas were planted. Northumberland's owned in quite big chunks, so the Forestry Commission was able to acquire land in quite big chunks. In 1932, there was a huge acquisition from the Duke of Northumberland, about 20,000 hectares, which included Kielder Castle, which had been his shooting lodge. That was planted over the following 10 or 15 years. When the Second World War came along, the new forests still weren't producing much timber, and the blockade meant we couldn't import timber again, so the Canadians came back and set up more logging camps. The Second World War just reinforced the need for a strategic reserve. During the 20 years after the war there was the real expansion of Kielder. About half the current area was planted just in that 20-year period.

By the 1950s, the thought of strategic reserve had really gone and thoughts of Third World Wars were pretty horrendous, so timber wasn't on anyone's mind for wartime by then. The justification for state involvement in forestry was much more about creating rural employment and raw material for industry. But, by the late 1960s, government economists started looking at forestry and saying you only make a 3% return from investment and we would expect six from other nationalized industries like coal or steel. The foresters' response then was, well it's not just about timber, it's about lots of other things, such as the environment. When you looked at what had been created, quite often, these strategic reserve forests were square blocks on hillsides and didn't fit well to the landscape. They were very densely planted, so who would want to go there for a picnic? And very often the wildlife value of the open moorland before was thought to be greater than that of the new forests. I think that during the late '60s and early '70s there was a lot of work done to make forests better for visitors. It wasn't a completely new idea because forest parks had been thought up back in the 1930s, a good 10 years before there was any National Parks. So, public recreation around forests was certainly in people's minds before. But it was in the '70s that really the Forestry Commission started to develop forest walks and trails and more picnic sites and so on. And it also started employing landscape architects to advise on the design of new forests and the redesign of existing ones. At that time, those other objectives were known as secondary objectives, but they've increased in importance since. At the Rio conference, there was an internationally agreed statement of forestry principles, which stated that forests should be managed for a whole range of public benefits, multi-purpose forestry.

That's very much the policy we apply now: forests are capable of delivering a range of benefits, and timber is one of these, but public recreation, landscape, water supplies, bio-diversity, protecting heritage and engaging with communities as well are all functions that forests can deliver. It doesn't mean every forest has to try and do everything. In different parts of the country and in different parts of the forest, you'll be able to deliver more on some of these objectives than others, but overall we're about trying to deliver multiple benefits from the public forest estate.

CHRISTINE MCCULLOCH: What do you use your trees for?

GRAHAM GILL: About half the timber we produce goes to saw mills, so it's cut into construction timber, fencing, pallets, packages, but the main one we try to grow for is the construction timber element, because that's the most valuable market. And then the other half, it's a bit less than half now because the trees are getting older, is what we call small round wood – that's the smaller trees and the tops of the bigger trees – that goes to make chipboard, which would be turned into kitchen worktops and chipboard flooring, and also to a pulp mill to make carton board, and a little bit now goes to a power station and is burned to generate electricity.

...

GRAHAM GILL: Trees at Kielder all grow at about the same rate. We call it yield class 12, which means it's putting on 12 cubic metres per hectare per year, averaged over the time to its maximum growth rate. That's reasonably fast for north temperate. Scandinavia would be around 4 to 6 and Canada is 2 to 4 in their forests. There are a lot faster areas, Ireland would tend to be 18 to 20, and Radiata pine in New Zealand is more like yield class 30, and some of the southern pines in the United States. But here, it's yield class 12. By the time trees reach about 45 to 50 years old (they would grow older, but by then their growth's beginning to slow up) in economic terms that's the time to replace them.

If we were just to grow for maximum timber production, we would pretty well just fell and replant in the same sequence as the forest had been planted, but if you're a red squirrel living in this bit of the forest, then where do you go when that's been felled? And in terms of the landscape, it's not the best way to manage a forest, and in terms of public recreation as well or even water supplies because you get a big change in a big catchment. So what we would rather do, or what our plans are, is to diversify the age structure a lot more. And these different colours [points to map of forest] are the felling decades for that area. What we're trying to do is break up these even age patches by felling some bits earlier and, where we can, hold some bits later, to break up the age structure. We try to relate the areas of the felling coups to the landscape, so in the valley bottoms, where it's more human-scale landscape, smaller sizes, and on the plateaus, larger areas. As far as we know, that's really driven by landscape, but it also works quite well for different species of wildlife to have that diversity of felling coup size.

CHRIS SMOUT: Can I ask about the broadleaf woodland corridors?

GRAHAM GILL: Yes, I was just coming to them.

CHRIS SMOUT: Sorry.

GRAHAM GILL: That's alright.

GRAHAM GILL: That's a very good point. These felling coups: the idea is that we get that area felled and replanted so it's growing up before we're felling the next area. The other change are these corridors through it. And, on the first rotation's strategic reserve, we planted spruce right up to the edge of the streams and that was the objective. Strategic reserve: so you planted every square metre. But when you plant up to stream sides, the spruce casts a lot of shade, so you lose the ground vegetation and then the stream banks would erode and the streams went wide and shallow, and were poor habitat for fish. Really, what you want for stream sides is lots of vegetation tumbling over the bank to protect it, and also we reckon if you can get part of the stream in shade and part of it open to sunlight, then the fish can find the right temperature environment whatever the weather conditions are. Broadleaves in that corridor help because they provide feeding for the fish and the other is that the stream sides are where the richest soils are in the forest. That meant they've grown really good trees, so we do lose production by not planting [conifers in] these areas, but it's also where you get the more diverse vegetation. So, what we're looking for in the new forest are stream sides that are open to sunlight with broadleaf planting through it. It was a very good point about the grey squirrels, because what we were doing was looking at the vegetation and trying to match that to the NVC (National Vegetation Classification) class to try to work out what types of native trees to put into these areas. Some of it is oak and on some of the soil it's ash. And then we thought, well what about grey squirrels? Well those trees won't be producing acorns [good food for grey squirrels] for a long time. Eventually they will and that wouldn't be good news [for the red squirrels].

CHRISTINE MCCULLOCH: Do you try to control them?

GRAHAM GILL: Well, what we thought was, is Kielder important for native woodland or is it important for red squirrels? And red squirrels, we don't have greys here, it's only red and red is the important species. So, on the broadleaf planting we've said we're not going to plant any large seeded broadleaves in Kielder now. We'll still plant rowan and willows and alder, hawthorn, and on the better sites, aspen, where there's suitable conditions, but not oak or ash or sycamore.

IAN ROTHERHAM: Do you have any relic hazel?

GRAHAM GILL: Is there any relic here? There's relic, yeah, tiny bits, yes. We haven't been planting hazel, but people are in two minds about how much that encourages greys. We've done a lot of squirrel modelling with Newcastle University on how much energy is there in the seed crops and is there enough. And we reckon there's enough energy in the spruce to support red populations, but not enough to maintain a grey population. We do get greys occasionally appearing now in the valley and our rangers are pretty hot on getting rid of them. Our main concern with squirrels is not greys coming in on their own, but bringing in the pox disease. Actually, we think this felling pattern is helping with that because it's breaking up the forest. While our red squirrel from one year to the next is quite happy to cross a felling area, it won't day to day, it stays in the same stand, so we have sort of sub-populations of squirrels, and they will move right across the forest, but from day to day they tend to be in a single stand. Pox disease is quite bad for reds and once they've caught it they die within about two weeks and for a lot of that time they won't be moving around, so we think if we did get a disease into the forest, it would burn out in a section of the forest, disappear, and then reds could re-invade. But we don't have much information on these models, so it's a bit see what happens, but we thought we'd avoid planting the large-seeded broadleaves. Some of the greys have had antibodies, but that doesn't necessarily mean they were infectious.

Note

1. Transcribed by Leona Jayne Skelton, edited by David Moon.

CHAPTER 28

Wicken Fen Vision

National Trust

The National Trust's 'Wicken Vision', launched in 1999, envisages a century-long process of Fenland expansion into agricultural lands that become available. Wild grazing animals play a key role in this habitat restoration and creation scheme, which is intended, eventually, to cover 53 square kilometres to the north of the rapidly growing city of Cambridge.

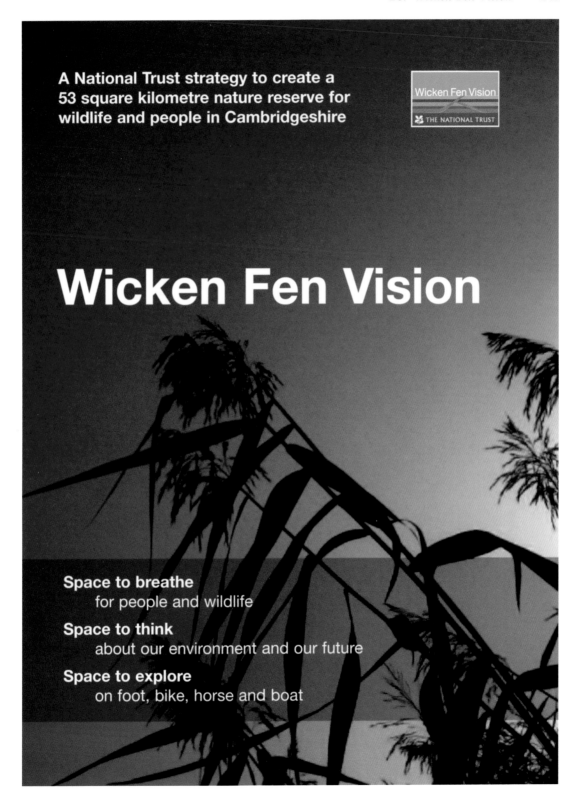

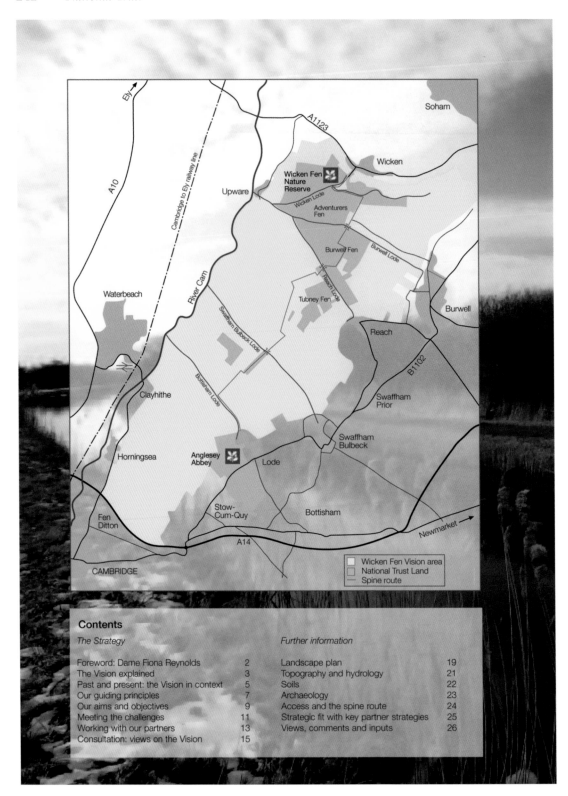

Wicken Fen Vision area
National Trust Land
Spine route

Contents

Working together for this very special place

Wicken Fen was the very first nature reserve to be owned by the National Trust and has been in our care since 1899. It remains one of the most important wetlands in Europe – an iconic habitat, supporting thousands of plants, insects, birds and mammals, but at the heart of an area facing major pressure for new development.

We have worked hard for more than a hundred years to protect the rare species here through the intensive management of the fen habitats. However, this became increasingly difficult and by the late twentieth century it had become clear that we could not protect this unique place because the wetland nature reserve was just too small and too isolated. The concept of extending the reserve was conceived.

In 1999, we launched the Wicken Fen Vision. The 100 year Vision aims to extend the reserve to a maximum of 5,300 hectares by purchasing land to the south and east of Wicken, restoring its fen and wetland habitats and creating a landscape-scale space for wildlife and people.

Already we have acquired sufficient land to more than double the size of the reserve to its current 758 hectares. We are now working with individuals and organisations at community, regional and national levels to create a unique series of habitats and a huge public open space for people to explore and enjoy.

This document lays out our ideas and aspirations and we welcome comments and inputs from everyone: please read it and tell us what you think, and how you can help.

Dame Fiona Reynolds
Director General
National Trust
May 2009

2

The Vision explained

Where we are now

Wicken Fen has developed a superb range of wetland habitats – fen, reedbed, wet woodland and open water, on a deep, peat soil which is kept wet by rainfall and clean, chalky river water. The reserve's rich habitats and species are protected by national, European and international law, but legislation alone will not conserve wildlife. Active management, such as cutting, has been required to maintain the fen and reed bed habitats. Even at 255 hectares in area, the designated National Nature Reserve is too small to guarantee the long-term survival of all of its numerous rare and special species. Wicken Fen is vulnerable to damaging influences from the surrounding more intensive land uses and is isolated and quite some distance from other wetland reserves.

The best strategy to protect and enhance the wildlife of Wicken Fen is to make the nature reserve much bigger and to bring much more adjacent land into conservation management.

Pioneering fenland restoration

In 1999, the National Trust launched the Wicken Fen Vision with the long-term aim of a massive increase in the reserve's size to a maximum of 5,300 hectares, expanding southwards towards the edge of Cambridge. The National Trust plans to use ecological restoration techniques to create and restore wildlife habitats on a landscape scale and to provide visitors with new access to nature and green space. The aim is to create a mosaic of wetland habitats: wet grasslands, reed beds, marsh, fen and shallow ponds and ditches, as well as establishing chalk grassland and woodlands where soil and topography dictate.

The Wicken Fen Vision, along with the related Great Fen Project near Peterborough, are exciting, pioneering projects to put wildlife back into heavily managed fenland countryside. They will have international significance for the ecological transformation of landscapes and will form part of a new network of wetland habitats across the East of England. This in turn is helping conserve species at risk from the loss of freshwater coastal habitats and from climate change. These projects recognise that to deliver this kind of conservation vision requires integrating the requirements of wildlife with the needs of local people, the economy and tourism. New opportunities to gain access to the countryside on foot, bike, horse and boat are an essential part of these projects. It is this holistic approach that is promoting such widespread support.

Conventional approaches to land restoration are highly prescriptive and intensive in their approach. They are costly both in their creation and subsequent management. The Wicken Fen Vision approach is planned on a sufficiently large scale that it provides an opportunity to create self-regenerating habitats which can be managed less intensively. Species assemblages will change over time, creating a dynamic habitat mosaic. The exact composition of this mosaic is less predictable but will be more responsive and adaptable to long term environmental change. The added benefit of this extensive approach is that we believe it is less costly and more sustainable both in the short and longer term.

Hydrology – water levels in ditches and soil – across the Vision area will be controlled appropriately,

Wicken Fen is one of the few remaining fragments of fenland wilderness in East Anglia. Its biodiversity is exceptional but it is too small and isolated to support sustainable populations of its special and rare species.

This unique place is at the heart of an area experiencing considerable pressure for new housing and other developments and in a county containing very limited open spaces with public access.

We want to create a massive new area open to the public covering 53 square kilometres between Wicken Fen and Cambridge, an inspirational place for people and a sustainable home for wildlife.

and there will be free-roaming, self-reliant herds of large herbivores such as cattle, horses and deer. Grazing animals are critical for adding a vital element of dynamism to that created by the variations in water levels. Large herbivores influence rather than manage vegetation, but the National Trust is deliberately aiming for a 'lighter touch' for the Vision land, which will be more maintainable in the long term. Animal welfare will be paramount. We will consider meat production as a secondary product from land grazed with domestic stock.

It is important to acknowledge that, although the National Trust has identified 53 square kilometres of land that could form part of the Wicken Fen Vision, there is no necessity to acquire all the land in order for the Vision to meet its objectives. In some areas, management agreements with landowners might form a sensible approach, and this is being actively investigated.

The 100 year timescale has been deliberately chosen to allow as much flexibility of approach as possible. Conservation priorities, farming practices and demand for access to public open space will all change over time: this very long-term approach will ensure that the Vision can evolve to meet these changes while holding true to the underlying principles of the project.

The next 100 years – looking after special places, for ever for everyone

The National Trust has the experience, expertise and capacity to make this long-term vision a reality. Founded in 1895, we are the largest environmental charity in Europe and have landholdings totalling over 250,000 hectares in England, Wales and Northern Ireland. We have 3.6 million members, an annual turnover in excess of £160 million per annum and endowed assets exceeding £70 million. Every year we attract over 12 million paying visitors and a further 50

A VERY SPECIAL PLACE

Wicken Fen has the following designations:

• National Nature Reserve under the National Parks and Access to the Countryside Act, 1949.

• Site of Special Scientific Interest under the Wildlife and Countryside Act, 1981.

• Special Area of Conservation under the EU Habitats Directive.

• Wetland protected under the International Convention on Wetlands of International Importance, 1971 (Ramsar Convention).

million enjoy access to our free countryside properties. We pride ourselves on our holistic approach to the work of helping to look after the nation's cultural and natural heritage and helping people to access and benefit from it.

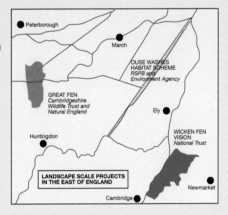

4

Past and present: the Wicken Fen Vision in context

From Roman transport to post-war restoration

The origin of the Lodes

The straight, raised waterways, known as Lodes, which cross the area to the south of Wicken have been considered by some to be of Roman origin. They were probably constructed as a transport system, taking products and goods from villages on the southern extremity of the Fen across to the River Cam and from there up to the coast at King's Lynn. Through the early medieval period the landscape, crossed by slow moving rivers, was an impenetrable 'wild undrained fen'.

Drainage begins

The later medieval period saw some localised drainage which produced grazing land but this was restricted to the fen edge. It was not until the 17th century that more extensive drainage plans were initiated. The Adventurers – venture capitalists who provided the funding to drain the land – transformed the landscape from the 17th century, producing the intensively farmed countryside that is now characteristic of the Fens running from Cambridge up to the Wash.

The area known as Wicken Fen remained undrained. It was used for peat digging and sedge

harvesting by local villagers. It became well known from 1850 onwards to Victorian naturalists who came to the Fen to collect moths and butterflies. In the 1890s the peat and sedge economies collapsed being replaced by coal and roof tiles. As a result there were major concerns that Wicken Fen would be drained as had happened elsewhere. A number of the early entomologists (particularly G.H. Verrall and The Hon N.C. Rothschild) played a vital role in ensuring Wicken's survival by acquiring parts of the Fen and donating them to the National Trust.

Safeguarding a unique landscape

Wicken Fen was the first nature reserve to be owned by The National Trust and has been in the Trust's care since 1899 when the first parcel of land on the Ancient Fen was purchased. In the hundred years since this first purchase, there have been a further 53 land conveyances and the reserve had grown to 255 hectares. However there have been some diversions from this steady expansion of wildlife habitats in the intervening years.

During the Second World War the land known as Adventurers Fen was requisitioned by the War Office, drained again by Alan Bloom and converted to arable cultivation. The Ancient Fen at Wicken however remained undrained and protected by the National Trust, 'an island in a sea of intensive agriculture'.

In 1946 the adjacent and most recently drained land was handed back to the National Trust and the extensive areas of mere, reed beds and wet meadows took shape. It is from this experience and the capacity to restore fen habitats from previously drained and farmed land in more recent years that we can draw confidence in the ongoing expansion of the Wicken Fen Vision.

Wicken Fen is a product of thousands of years of man's interaction with the landscape. From the earliest drainage, possibly in Roman times, to today's pressure for new homes, the landscape has been continuously evolving, along with the wildlife which it supports.

However, this small corner of Cambridgeshire is unique because some areas of Wicken Fen have never been drained, making this whole landscape internationally important for biodiversity and for conservation.

Our 100 year vision is to protect and safeguard this valuable resource not just to help rare species survive and thrive, but so that people can enjoy the space and solitude so rare in today's world.

Today's picture – a shared Vision

The Wicken Fen Vision is a very long-term project, but in the first few years significant progress has been made in bringing the Vision to life.

Land acquisition
Since 1999 the National Trust has acquired several new areas of land, and we now own more than 800 hectares in the area, including land around Anglesey Abbey in . We have received support from a wide range of partners in helping us purchase land, as well as using our own funds.

Conservation
We have created 422 hectares of new habitat over the past few years. We begin the process by stopping infield drainage and allowing permanent vegetation to develop. In some places we allow the land to become much wetter which encourages birds, wildflowers and insects. We have introduced Highland cattle and Konik ponies to help manage some of the new areas, creating a mosaic of different habitats which are providing a home to a wide range of species. These new areas all help to protect the existing Wicken Fen National Nature Reserve, which is one of the most important in Europe.

Public access
Helping people enjoy the Wicken Fen Vision area is one of our biggest priorities, and we have made major progress towards creating a spine route that crosses the area from north to south. The spine route also links into the network of quiet lanes and footpaths which crosses the Vision area.

Bridging the gap
In early 2008 a new bridge was installed over Swaffham Bulbeck Lode opening up new routes for

walkers, cyclists and horse-riders and linking with new paths on land recently purchased by the National Trust. We are planning another bridge over Reach Lode, and we hope to improve public access over Burwell Lode which will complete the north-south link across the Vision area.

Working with local people
We have held hundreds of meetings with local people and organisations, and in spring 2008 we undertook a major public consultation exercise to seek local people's views on the Vision and how it should grow in the future. A series of drop-in sessions took place in early autumn 2008 to get views from specific groups about what they would like to see in the future. An on-going programme of working with local communities is at the heart of the Wicken Fen Vision.

Our guiding principles

Guiding Principle 1

We will manage the land to enhance its nature conservation value, protect the depleting peat soils, secure sufficient water resources and preserve and interpret the cultural heritage.

We are guided here by the management principles set out in 'Nature and the National Trust', our nature conservation policy (2005). These principles are:

• We will strive for an abundance and diversity of species appropriate to local climate, geology and soils.
• We will allow nature to take its course wherever possible and desirable, and will manage positively for this.
• Where a habitat is of intrinsic significant cultural and/or ecological importance, the Trust will promote active management to maintain it as far as this is sustainable.
• We will respect and promote the intimate relationship between natural and cultural heritage.
• We will plan and manage on a landscape scale to create a network of large, high-quality habitats, working in partnership with others as required.
• We acknowledge that the effective conservation of

water resources, soils and a host of wetland habitats can only be achieved by working at a catchment or river basin level.
• We will manage for wildlife in the context of sustainable land use seeking optimum outcomes for nature as an integral part of all land uses.
• We will manage for the long term, in the context of predicted climate change and other environmental influences. We accept that some habitats and species will be lost, changed or replaced over time.
• We will adopt land management techniques that work with natural processes rather than attempt to impose habitat creation plans or manage land based on narrow species-driven goals. We will use low-input management such as extensive grazing to achieve our conservation and habitat creation goals.

- Enhancing nature conservation, protecting the depleting peat soils, managing water resources and preserving cultural heritage.
- Ensuring a sustainable financial future and supporting the local economy.
- Working with local people, landowners, businesses, government agencies and voluntary and conservation organisations.
- Encouraging public access and recreation, scientific research, volunteering, community engagement and learning.

Guiding Principle 2
We will ensure that the Vision has a sustainable financial future and supports the local economy

We are guided by the principles of sustainable development enshrined in the accounting technique of the Triple Bottom Line, where the *financial* costs and *social* benefits will be evaluated alongside our primary aim of securing *environmental* benefits.

In addition, we will:
- Encourage new business ventures that are appropriate to the aims of our overall vision.
- Build strategic funding partnerships in the public, private and voluntary sectors.
- Explore opportunities for financial support for peat soil protection and carbon fixing as well as realising wider social benefits of providing for flood storage, aquifer recharge, and water quality enhancement.
- Investigate and adopt innovative income streams to sustain the financial future of the project.
- Ensure that there are sufficient appropriately skilled, valued and respected staff and volunteers to achieve the Vision's purpose.

Guiding Principle 3
We will work in partnership with local people, landowners, businesses, government agencies and voluntary and conservation organisations.

We are guided here again by our nature conservation policy (2005) which states:
- The Trust will use its experience to influence policy, working with partner organisations and public campaigns.
- The Trust will seek to contribute to nature conservation by learning from what it does, and by sharing this knowledge and experience with others.
- We will seek to integrate our work with other policies and strategies at local, regional and national levels, with councils, regional government, statutory agencies and other Non-Governmental Organisations.

Guiding Principle 4
We will provide expanding opportunities for public access and recreation, scientific research, volunteering, engagement and learning.

- We will encourage access to the expanding Nature Reserve to act as a source of inspiration, enjoyment and learning for members, visitors, volunteers, enthusiasts and scholars.
- We will extend educational and community outreach activities across the expanding Vision area.
- We will provide a uniquely valuable large open space within the Cambridge Growth Area, with public access corridors linking to other areas beyond the boundaries of the Wicken Fen Vision.
- We will encourage community involvement across all our activities.
- We will engage with the Health and Wellbeing agenda.
- We will facilitate scientific research which will inform our ongoing management.

8

Our aims and objectives

WILDLIFE
To greatly expand the space for wildlife and people.
We will increase the area of accessible nature reserve around Wicken Fen to a sustainable and adaptable landscape, extending towards Cambridge over an area of 53 square kilometres.

Objectives
1.1 Prioritise which areas of land we would wish to purchase on the basis of their potential for habitat creation, public access and ongoing sustainable management.
1.2 Sensitively negotiate purchase of land from local landowners.
1.3 Develop and maintain our relationships with individual landowners and farmers across the Vision area, where they are not at this juncture selling their land.

HABITATS
To create a mosaic of habitats, securing the essential resource of water and protecting peat soils.
Farmland to the south of Wicken Fen is being gradually converted into a nature reserve, with a fascinating mosaic of habitats, and a wealth of cultural and historical features and where the careful management of water levels and subsequent adoption of extensive grazing regimes will provide for sustainable future land management.

Objectives
2.1 Increase control of water availability and retention, whilst maintaining the integrity of the drainage function of the Internal Drainage Board (IDB) system.
2.2 Increase control over water quality by working with statutory authorities and local landowners.
2.3 Develop land management processes for restoration after farmland is acquired according

to soils, hydrology, size of land parcel and proximity to other Wicken Fen Vision land.
2.4 Develop extensive grazing management systems with self-reliant herds of herbivores to create a mobile mosaic of self-regenerating wildlife habitats.
2.5 Work closely with the Environment Agency, who are responsible for the Lodes, to find the best way to secure the long-term future of these historic waterways.
2.6 Monitor hydrological and ecological processes across restored areas.
2.7 Promote land management agreements with farmers that encourage sympathetic management for wildlife.
2.8 Investigate use of suitable areas for flood alleviation.

PEOPLE
To provide opportunities for visitors, tourists and local residents to benefit from access to the Vision area and engage supporters in our work.

The extensive nature reserve will provide access routes from Cambridge and surrounding towns and villages by foot, cycle, on horseback and by boat and will create recreational opportunities across a unique and developing area of countryside. The Vision area will also provide extensive opportunities for volunteering, education and interpretation.

We want to ensure that the National Trust engages with local communities and that local people can develop a sense of ownership of the Vision.

Objectives
3.1 Engage with all local stakeholders, especially people living within the Vision area and in

In all our activities we will take full account of the requirements of the Disability Discrimination Act.

- **To greatly expand the space for wildlife and people.**

- **To encourage habitats that benefit wildlife.**

- **To provide access to the Vision area and encourage local people to become involved in our work.**

- **To learn continually from our experience and influence policy development at a national and international level.**

- **To ensure a secure financial future**

neighbouring villages.

3.2 Promote sustainable transport, growing in scope with the Vision, and encourage public transport to, from and within the Vision area.

3.3 Promote and encourage a wide range of community activities and engagement.

3.4 Work with partners to maximise opportunities to address the Health and Wellbeing agenda.

3.5 Develop an access forum to involve local stakeholders in access management decisions.

3.6 Provide recreational and tourism facilities appropriate to the landscape and the integrity of the National Nature Reserve.

3.7 Provide appropriate educational opportunities to help engage the public with nature conservation, climate change issues and the developing landscape.

3.8 Provide a wealth of opportunities for volunteering.

3.9 Continuously improve interpretation of the area's landscape, wildlife and cultural heritage.

LEARNING
To learn continually from our experience and influence wider policy development on landscape-scale conservation at a national and international level.

The Wicken Fen Vision and the Great Fen Project are pioneering landscape-scale projects in the UK. Experiences from both these projects will be shared in the future to influence policy development and practice in sustainable land management, habitat restoration and community engagement. Over the past 50 years, more than 250 academic papers have been published on various aspects of Wicken Fen.

Objectives
4.1 Encourage research into and monitoring of ecological restoration, and the wider socio-economic aspects of the project.

4.2 Encourage research looking at responses to climate change afforded by the project, particularly in respect of 'ecosystem services' (e.g. carbon sequestration, flood control and ground-water replenishment).

4.3 Contribute to policy development on landscape-scale conservation at national and international levels.

4.4 Record, interpret and conserve important archaeological, historical, cultural and landscape features.

RESOURCES
To ensure a sustainable financial future for the management of the expanding nature reserve.

Better management of a wider range of income streams – from Higher Level Stewardship payments to 'green' businesses like cycle hire – is a central part of our financial future, in the context of a potential reduction of visitors paying to access the nature reserve.

5.1 Develop our capacity for fund raising for land purchase by building strong partnerships with a wide variety of partners across the public, private, community and voluntary sectors.

5.2 Develop new initiatives to ensure funding is sustained for ongoing management of land being restored and opened up for public access.

5.3 Investigate land uses and business activities that can provide additional income sympathetic to the biodiversity aims and the visual landscape.

5.4 Produce a Financial Plan for the next five years that identifies expected costs and revenues to address all agreed aims and objectives.

5.5 Reduce overall energy usage by the National Trust and promote energy efficiency measures.

10

Meeting the challenges

Managing landscape, water resources and soils
There are four major challenges:
- creating a mosaic of wetland and other wildlife habitats, using control of water levels and extensive grazing
- re-wetting peat soils to avoid their loss without recourse to major engineering solutions
- maintaining the internal drainage function for land that will continue to be farmed
- re-wetting peat soils to avoid their loss and to create a wider range of habitats.

In eastern England, climate change is likely to cause milder winters and warmer summers, with an overall increase in rainfall. This may result in greater quantities of water being present in winter but warmer summers will increase evaporation and water take-up by plants, causing a more rapid drawdown of the water table. Securing winter water supply should enable suitable areas of the new Vision land to be maintained as wetland with year-round higher water tables even with future climate change.

The Wicken Fen Vision area offers valuable potential for storing flood water and to allow water to percolate into the soils and replenish groundwater resources. A full hydrological resources plan, taking account of climate change scenarios, and covering the whole Vision area has been commissioned: details are available on our website.

Historically, peat soils have been some of the richest for food production. However, decades of intensive cultivation and hundreds of years of drainage have significantly reduced the extent of peat soils, as they have oxidised and eroded away, in places at a rate of more than two centimetres a year.

The 2,000 hectares of remaining peat soils to the south of Wicken Fen are in an important location. Re-wetting these soils will have the significant benefits of

reversing centuries of soil loss and greatly expanding the nature reserve. The area required to support sustainable wildlife varies from species to species but, in general, the larger the area of suitable habitat, the more sustainable the wildlife populations can become.

Research into the soils, hydrology and habitats will guide the project and help to inform the management of this, and other, landscape-scale projects.

Working as part of the community
How does the Vision interact with existing land use and with the area's heritage? How do plans for the Vision fit with our partner's policies? How can local people and visitors benefit from the Wicken Fen Vision and shape its future?

Landownership, landscape and settlements: there are over 120 land owners in the Vision area ranging from large farm businesses to small equestrian holdings and hobby farms. We need to maintain close relationships with landowners and land managers to understand the pressures faced by all types of farming. We also need to:
- establish a clear policy for vermin control
- deal with invasive and noxious weeds
- avoid disturbance to the drainage of adjacent land

There are existing dwellings, roads and rights of way across the Vision area. Our plans for creating new habitats will take account of all existing rights of way and in relation to private property, drainage infrastructure and all land not in our ownership, we will not undertake work that will have any potentially deleterious effect in their vicinity.

Fitting in with other plans: the Wicken Fen Vision fits very closely with the plans and policies of a broad spectrum of agencies, central government departments and local and regional government. We will continue to work with our partners to ensure that

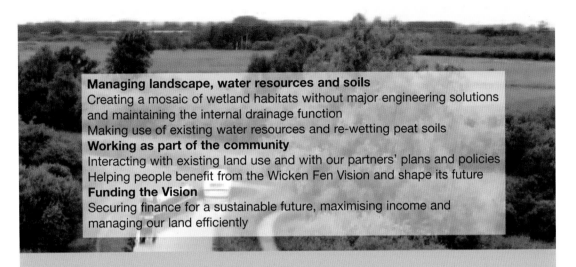

Managing landscape, water resources and soils
Creating a mosaic of wetland habitats without major engineering solutions and maintaining the internal drainage function
Making use of existing water resources and re-wetting peat soils
Working as part of the community
Interacting with existing land use and with our partners' plans and policies
Helping people benefit from the Wicken Fen Vision and shape its future
Funding the Vision
Securing finance for a sustainable future, maximising income and managing our land efficiently

our plans reflect both the needs of local people through working with local authorities, and the national development pressures which are affecting Cambridgeshire (see page 25 for more information).

Getting to the Vision area: we need to plan for a significant number of additional visitors to the Vision area, but we will not encourage car travel within the Vision area. We will need to assess suitability of existing car parking on the periphery of the Vision area and the impact on local communities. Public transport to the Vision area is currently limited and we will encourage the expansion of public transport routes: a transport and access strategy has been commissioned.

New access: increased access for local people and visitors is a key aim of the Wicken Fen Vision. We will achieve this by enhancing the existing public rights of way, providing bridges across water courses and completing missing links in the existing network. More information on the new spine route and other access improvements is on page 24. Grazing by cattle and ponies is an important way of managing land in the Vision area: it will be important to manage grazing to avoid conflict with users of new and established rights of way running across the grazed areas.

History and cultural heritage: there is a rich cultural heritage across the Wicken Fen Vision area with more than 400 archaeological sites including three Scheduled Ancient Monuments and 44 listed buildings (see page 23 for more information). To protect and interpret these sites we need to:
- make sure that habitat creation and water management is preceded by field-walking and metal-detecting surveys
- undertake palaeo-environmental sampling or other investigation whenever appropriate
- carry out research and oral history recording of the cultural history of the area.

Funding the Vision
What will the Vision cost to achieve? Where will the money come from to fund land purchases and for ongoing management?

The National Trust has sound financial disciplines and clear rules for acquiring land: as well as raising the purchase price of any land that we buy, we must also create an endowment to pay for managing the land, for ever. We use a formula to work out the size of the endowment we need, taking into account any income that the land will generate.

We need to build relationships with partners and funders to ensure long term sustainable support both for land purchases and for other projects. We need to maximise income from our enterprises (shops, cafés, education service and visitor centres) as well as establishing new environmentally appropriate businesses such as cycle and canoe hire and camping. We need to make our land management as efficient and low-cost as possible and we need to encourage volunteers to help achieve this.

The scale of the overall funding challenge is set out below, based on the prevailing assumptions in autumn 2008. To date we have secured £4 million in grant between 2003 and 2009 and established an endowment reserve of £900,000.

THE OVERALL FUNDING CHALLENGE
- To buy a further 4,600 hectares at today's prices (autumn 2008) will cost £55 million.
- Investment in new infrastructure is expected to cost £10 million.
- Creating the endowment we need for ongoing management will cost £18 million.
- Total investment would be £83 million.

Working with our partners

There has been enormous support for the Wicken Fen Vision since its launch in 1999. The National Trust is committed to working with all stakeholders, listening to their concerns, interpreting their needs and, most importantly, securing on-going support and involvement as the Vision area expands.

Developing strong working partnerships will widen our knowledge base and support amongst key partners, including potential users of the expanding Vision area. We believe this approach will produce more sustainable results.

Who are the key stakeholders in the project and how will we involve them?

Local stakeholders: landowners, local businesses, local communities, Cambridge residents, recreational visitors, Swaffham Internal Drainage Board, donors

National Trust internal stakeholders: Local Committee, National Trust Regional Committee, Wicken Fen staff and volunteers, National Trust regional staff, National Trust head office staff

Local authorities: Parish Councils, East Cambridgeshire District Council, South Cambridgeshire District Council, Cambridge City Council, Cambridgeshire County Council

Government agencies: East of England Development Agency, Environment Agency, Natural England, DEFRA, GO-East, English Heritage, Swaffham Internal Drainage Board

Universities and other research bodies: University of Cambridge, Anglia Ruskin University, Cranfield University, Centre for Ecology and Hydrology

Non-governmental organisations and conservation bodies: Wildlife Trust, Great Fen Project, RSPB, Wet Fens Partnership, National Farmers Union

Utility Companies: Anglia Water, EDF Energy, National Grid.

Fundamental to our success to date has been the active support of the **Wicken Fen Local Committee**. This Local Committee has been in existence for 90 years and has throughout this time provided the National Trust with a wealth of scientific knowledge and experience of nature conservation management and provided links with the local community.

The Local Committee helped launch the Vision in 1999 and will continue to provide invaluable advice on all aspects of nature conservation management of the existing National Nature Reserve as well as advising on the interpretation of monitoring, recording and interpreting the ecological development of land being restored to wetlands in the Vision area.

The National Trust, with the Local Committee's support, recognises the value of key partnership working in furthering the aims of the Vision and that we will need to extend the range of consultation, advice and particularly investigations into long term funding. At a strategic level, a **Vision Partnership Panel** has been established.

Membership of the Panel includes the following external organisations: Environment Agency, Natural England, DEFRA, Cambridgeshire Horizons, EEDA, Cambridgeshire County Council, South Cambs, East Cambs and Cambridge City Council, Greater Cambridge Partnership, Swaffham IDB, Cambridge University, Anglia Ruskin University, Sustrans and local business representatives. The Partnership Panel:

- Provides guidance and advice to further the Vision's aims and objectives and immediate input into the development of this Strategy
- Provides a forward look at sources of financial support for acquisition and management of new land

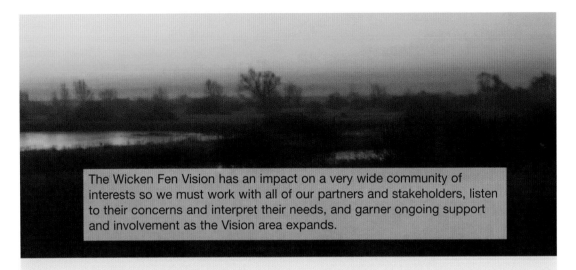

The Wicken Fen Vision has an impact on a very wide community of interests so we must work with all of our partners and stakeholders, listen to their concerns and interpret their needs, and garner ongoing support and involvement as the Vision area expands.

- Considers and advises upon the wider context of the Vision when considered against their own organisation's forward strategies and the opportunities for cross working
- Considers and advises upon the longer term issues and their impact on our project e.g. green infrastructure developments in the sub-region, biodiversity and climate change, flood defence management, CAP reform, carbon sequestration and public engagement
- Considers and advises upon risk management as the land area of the Vision expands.

We also wish to engage more directly with users of the Fen and Vision area. In order to help this engagement we have set up a **Wicken Fen Parish Liaison Group** and a **Wicken Fen User Forum**. This informal forum brings together interested parties from the local area to consider specific topics, providing a sounding board for the concerns and aspirations of all local users. The Forum discusses and considers topics such as:

- Public access, footpaths, bridleways and cycle routes
- Boating and navigation issues
- Community engagement, interpretation, wider site management, recording, volunteer opportunities and events
- Education and wider environmental studies
- Healthy living initiatives.

Forum members represent the interests of their communities or specific interest groups with the topic to be considered, e.g. Parish Councils, ramblers, disabled access representatives, horse riders and cycling organisations, local National Trust members, boating organisations, Fenland By-Ways Users, Volunteer Bureau, teachers, etc.

We have also set up a **Grazing Forum** to consider and advise upon all aspects of our free-ranging grazing regimes and in particular:

- Management of large free-ranging herbivores (cattle, horses, deer) for the long term sustainable management of a dynamic landscape
- Shorter term, seasonal traditional grazing management, using domestic cattle and sheep, during conversion from arable cropping
- Operating within the parameters of animal welfare and cross compliance with subsidy regimes
- The management challenge of the interaction between free-ranging grazing herbivores and visitors
- The effect of grazing on biodiversity and habitat development.

The Local Committee, the Partnership Panel, the Parish Liaison group, the User Forum and the Grazing Forum are all advisory in function. Decisions on the management of Wicken Fen are taken by the National Trust through its own governance structure at property, regional and national level in the light of the advice provided by these advisory panels.

If you would like to participate in one of these advisory groups, please contact National Trust staff at Wicken Fen. See page 26 for contact details.

Consultation: views on the Vision

The 2008 consultation process for the Wicken Fen Vision centred on a series of public meetings in Swaffham Bulbeck, Wicken, Waterbeach, Fen Ditton, Lode and Burwell, with special events and drop-in sessions in Soham, Ely, Newmarket and Cambridge.

The exercise elicited over 550 responses covering overall views on the Vision as well as comments on how and why people enjoy the countryside, what sort of facilities and developments they would and would not like to see, and what is important to them when visiting new places.

Most of the responses were from the local area, but some were received from further afield, reflecting the fact that people from all over the world are interested in Wicken Fen.

What aspects of the countryside are important?
Nine out ten said that peace and quiet and the chance to get away from it all were important. Other high scoring areas were the chance to see wildlife, getting some health and exercise and discovering and enjoying your local area. When asked which aspect was most important, peace and quiet came out strongly on top, scoring twice as strongly as its next nearest response.

Are there any problems with the countryside from the visitor's perspective?
Too much traffic was the biggest complaint, closely followed by too much litter. Two of the biggest problems involved access to the countryside with 30 per cent saying that there were too few footpaths and public open space and 25 per cent saying that they weren't sure where they could and couldn't go in the countryside.

How could a visitor's experience of the countryside be improved?
Responses reflected the huge variety of visitors that places like Wicken Fen attracts. Some wanted the area to be left as it is, while others said that board

walks, lavatories and visitor centres were important. Some wanted to plan their own visits and some wanted guided trails and children's facilities.

What specific facilities in the countryside are most important?
The most frequent response was a desire for well signposted paths and trails. Getting to the countryside is an important issue too, with car parking and road signage both scoring highly. Further down the list but still important were good interpretation and visitor information, easy-to-use paths like boardwalks. Lowest scores went to countryside being close to home and good public transport links.

The final question sought views on the Wicken Fen Vision.
Around 70 per cent think that the Wicken Fen Vision is an excellent idea, 13 per cent think it's a good idea on the whole, 11 per cent have some reservations about the project and six per cent are opposed to it.

Continuing consultation activities
During September and October 2008 a series of drop-in sessions were conducted at Wicken Fen aimed at specific groups of users including walkers, horse-riders, cyclists, anglers, bird-watchers, naturalists, dog-walkers and boaters. The intention was to identify specific needs amongst these groups of users and to create an ongoing series of forums for public consultation.

A newsletter is being published on a regular basis and around 20,000 copies are distributed extensively across the area.

The Wicken Fen website includes a wide range of information on the Vision as well as contact details to enable interested members of the public to participate in the development of future plans.

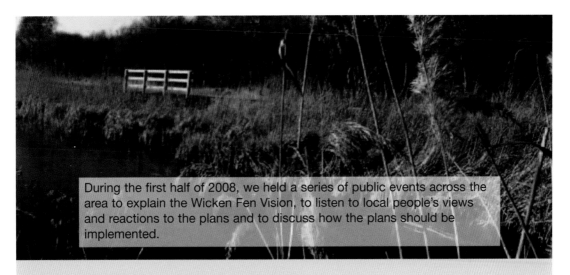

During the first half of 2008, we held a series of public events across the area to explain the Wicken Fen Vision, to listen to local people's views and reactions to the plans and to discuss how the plans should be implemented.

❝ Despite having large areas of open farmland around Burwell access is very limited so greater access to a larger area for walking would be wonderful! •

• I think it's an excellent idea, and hope that the vision can be achieved as soon as possible so that the residents of Cambridge can enjoy it. •

• Go for it – but try not to forget the original Vision for wildlife and wild landscape – leave some bits without way-marked trails, facilities and amenities. •

• Vital for wildlife and us, to keep biodiversity and varied habitats, to balance all the new housing increases. •

• There must be a balance between accessibility for people and too much disruption to the wildlife. •

• I already enjoy walking and cycling in the area. I am looking forward to the new paths opening up and being under NT management. This is a great Vision! •

• I live in Cambridge and welcome the idea of being able to access new areas on foot or by bike. There is a real need to balance the urban environment with green spaces. •

• Fenland area needs to be better managed for wildlife – currently farming is too intensive. More interesting areas for walking are also needed, even if there aren't any hills! ❞

CHAPTER 29

Kielder Water and Forest Park:
The City in the Country

Christine McCulloch

Kielder Water and Forest Park in Northumberland is a human-made lake in a human-made forest, a simplified, industrialized nature which may be described as 'the city in the country'. Starting in the 1920s, much of the area has been planted with fast-growing coniferous trees to form the most extensive forest in England (and the second biggest in the UK). In 1982, the North Tyne was dammed to form a large artificial lake set within the forest. The initial purposes of both were utilitarian and economic. The forestry plantation has become a profitable commercial enterprise but decline of major water-consuming industries on Teesside meant that the reservoir lost its *raison d'etre* at around the time it was created. It is a paradox that Kielder Water and Forest Park has become a major destination for recreation and tourism, attracting visitors from the towns and cities of the post-industrial North East of England, as well as further afield. Thus 'the city in the country' has become 'countryside for the city'.

The change is not as abrupt as this might suggest. Since the interwar years, the Forestry Commission envisaged its plantations also serving as venues for recreation. Kielder Water, moreover, was deliberately designed with aesthetic as well as utilitarian considerations in mind. This essay explores the design of the lake, the current use of the area as a leisure facility, and the prospects for the future, before returning to the central paradox of the juxtaposition of the rural and the urban at Kielder.

Design of the Kielder Water landscape

Kielder Water took almost two years to fill and, because its level is rarely drawn down, it has many of the attributes of a large lake, 6½ miles (10.5 km) long from dam to toe. Yet its shape differs from that of natural lakes extolled by poets in the nearby Lake District: rather than the streamlined shores of lakes gouged out by moving ice during the Pleistocene, this young, artificial lake, raised high above the natural river level, has a very indented shoreline following contours formed mainly by pre-glacial, sub-aerial erosion, because here, the ice sheets moved too slowly to excavate hollows for lakes. The current landscape of open water bordered by complex inlets was envisioned, and its use for recreation planned, before the great reservoir submergence by an outside expert, Sir Frederick Gibberd, who likened its planned form to a Chinese dragon.[1]

Before he brought his experience to Northumberland, Gibberd had earned a reputation as one of the most eminent architects and town planners of post-war Britain. He is well known for designing Harlow New Town, Terminal One at Heathrow Airport, Liverpool Metropolitan Cathedral and Hinkley Point A nuclear power station (near the Quantock Hills AONB). He had been hired to landscape several reservoirs before he became involved in the design of Kielder Water in the 1970s. According to his biographer: 'He was particularly concerned with a sense of place and sought in his work to respect and, if possible, enhance it.'[2]

Gibberd gave telling testimony to the two Public Inquiries considering the case for creation of Kielder Water in 1972–73. His claims were persuasive. He made a case for 'thinking big' and explained how his work in shaping the dam, planning vistas, designing a new road and other artefacts would produce a landscape of beauty. The Planning Inspector welcomed such promises to add to his report on the engineering case for the dam, which threatened to place the arbitrating Minister, the Right Honourable Geoffrey Rippon, the Conservative Member of Parliament for nearby Hexham, in an uncomfortable position. By a curious twist of fate, the opposition to the dam included not only local people's testimony to the harm they would suffer by displacement from their homes, but was magnified by the backing of the former Conservative MP and Rippon's predecessor, Sir Rupert Spier. When economic pressures on the Minister to accede to the building of a large reservoir prevailed after the first Public Inquiry into the Kielder Water Scheme in 1972, Rippon's reluctance to sacrifice a valley in his own constituency was reflected in his calling for investigation of the valley of the Irthing, a tributary of the River Eden in nearby Cumbria (then Cumberland) as a possible alternative. Yet, following a second Public Inquiry in 1973, the North Tyne was selected. Fear of subsequent political damage led to investment in the palliatives offered by Gibberd, who gained an unusually large budget to design the dam and reservoir in order to make them objects of pride and recreational value.[3]

Gibberd was allowed to hold sway over the engineers in particulars of the design. On previous occasions, when engaged on dam schemes such as Treweryn in Snowdonia, Derwent and Cow Green in Durham, it was difficult to detect any difference introduced by him. But, at Kielder, significant expenditure was authorized to prevent unsightly and smelly mud flats being exposed when the water was drawn down for long periods. The danger of such exposure was greatest in the reservoir's shallow upper reaches. To avoid lowering of the water level in this area, permission was granted to build a second, minor dam to restrain the water at the same level all year.[4] Construction of this dam,

FIGURE 29.1. Kielder dam.

PHOTO: CHRISTINE MCCULLOCH

the Bakethin, purely for amenity, angling and wildlife habitats, was a rare concession. This smaller reservoir has been designated a nature conservation area, stocked with brown trout for angling and, in 1993, artificial islands and bird hides were introduced.

The photograph of the dam (Fig. 29.1) shows some other features introduced by Gibberd: the curvature of the dam to emulate natural slopes; local grasses used on the embankment; and local (and very expensive) masonry, rather than concrete, for walls and permanent buildings. Gibberd stipulated that the embankment dam's downstream wall should not to be mown so as to appear more natural by blending in with nearby unplanted grassland. As can be seen in the photograph, this instruction has not been followed because the engineers needed to instrument the slope with piezometers to detect any land slippage or water leaks.

Gibberd was fastidious, not to say snobbish. His philosophy for the design of reservoirs was to 'avoid like the plague anything redolent of a municipal park'.[5] A road was planned around the south shore of the reservoir to replace the submerged road linking Falstone downstream of the dam with Kielder village upstream of the reservoir, but he decided to leave the north shore inaccessible to the public. Cuttings in the forest on the south shore would allow vistas over the reservoir at intervals, and discrete visitor centres and lodges were planned. The aim was for quiet enjoyment of the reservoir and forest which Gibberd felt incompatible with active recreation: 'The glint of the sun on a motorcar shatters the illusion of natural solitude. The beauty of nature does not cross the consciousness when travelling on water skis at 30 mph [48 km per hour].'[6] Yet planning for solitude did not survive commercial pressures later when Kielder became increasingly like an urban park.

Kielder Water and Forest Park today

As in many other places across the world, transition to urban modernity has prevailed over rural continuity. Since Gibberd's time, the memory of his exclusive ambition for restrained public access has faded in favour of a move to cater for city dwellers travelling to the area by road. The versatility of the British post-industrial economy and society has precipitated a change from extracting natural resources from Kielder towards attracting tourists to the location. The Forestry Commission and Northumbrian Water Limited (who took over the lake when the water industry in England and Wales was privatized in 1989) have combined resources to develop tourism and invested £5.4 million in 2007–11. Plans are being laid for great expansion in the future.[7]

Realization of the economic potential of tourism has not only stimulated the development of boating, bird watching, camping, cycling and other activities in and around the reservoir, but has also altered the nature of the forest. Forestry itself has changed from single-purpose productivity to embracing recently-acknowledged ecological imperatives to diversify the coniferous forest by introducing deciduous trees along the streams and by working towards a mosaic of forest zones of felling and planting. This reconstruction of diversity has been shown to be appreciated by visitors.[8] Amenity considerations and conservation of attractive wildlife, especially the native red squirrel, now play a part in forest management, although the Sitka spruce remains the dominant commercial product.[9] New markets have been found in saw mills, chipboard manufacturing and even use of the timber as biofuel in power stations. Whether or not forestry remains a good investment once subsidies and tax breaks are removed, is a matter for future government policy. In 2011, the British government proposed to privatize public forests in England. The resulting outcry from members of the public concerned about the threat to public access prompted a rethink. An Independent Panel on Forestry, chaired by the Right Reverend James Jones, Bishop of Liverpool, was set up. It recommended against privatization and the government endorsed its conclusion.[10]

The remote Kielder village has survived despite concerns about depopulation, partly with the help of Government subsidies. Concentration of ownership means that the tenants and homeowners work mainly for Northumbrian Water Ltd and its outsourced companies as well as for the Forestry Commission. This planned settlement, originally designed for foresters and their families, was built to a higher standard than previous tied cottages, which were built by the Forestry Commission elsewhere during the 1920s and 1930s, that lacked

FIGURE 29.2. Kielder
Observatory.

PHOTO: PETER COATES

bathrooms and had only outside toilets. Today, the regularity of this settlement and the uniformity of the houses painted in white or pastel colours give an outward appearance of attractive harmony. Oral history studies reveal a more divided community, the majority being incomers and an 'unmistakable social dichotomy of original forestry villagers and newcomers'.[11]

Despite Gibberd's aims, Kielder Water and Forest Park has indeed become akin to a municipal park; a playground for people from all social groups from post-industrial Tyneside and elsewhere in Britain. The meeting and movement, which Raymond Williams thought distinguished the city from the country, are experienced here too.[12] Two and a half million pounds has been invested in a cycleway, the Lakeside Way, around the northern perimeter of the reservoir to make a 26-mile (42 km) circuit suitable for marathons and cycle races. Wildlife has been converted into a spectacle by artificially feeding birds and red squirrels. Bird hides (constructed from wood imported from Scandinavia!) have been added, birds of prey have been caged for display in a commercial aviary and play zones have been equipped for children. The reservoir is regularly stocked with favoured species of fish (brown and rainbow trout) to encourage sale of fishing permits.[13] Even the night sky, little polluted by artificial light, has been harnessed for tourism with the building of the Kielder Observatory, which opened in 2008 (Fig. 29.2).[14]

Kielder Water and Forest Park is parkland on a grand scale, despite its remoteness, 1,400 mm of annual rainfall and a low permanent population. Nature is controlled, improved and made safe and thought to require embellishment. Urban parks frequently have statues of prominent historic figures to encourage gratitude and respect, often funded by public subscription. Kielder Water and

Forest Park lacks such links with the past. There is no plaque to commemorate Gibberd's work or any personal tribute to the engineers and labourers who created the dams and planted the forest. All reference to the more distant past is contained in Bellingham's 'heritage' centre and an exhibition in Tower Knowe Visitor Centre. Instead of historic totems, the monotony of the planted forest has been relieved by the insertion of works of imaginative contemporary art.[15] As John Ruskin observed, in nature both 'monotony' and 'change' have their use: 'like darkness and light, and the one incapable of being enjoyed without the other: change being most delightful, after some prolongation of monotony, as light appears most brilliant after the eyes have been for some time closed.'[16]

Art installed in the Forest Park is truly modern yet with pagan references, inspired by artists' reactions to the forest.[17] The large, conspicuous pieces are set on the perimeter path to inspire views over the reservoir and to provide 'points of interest' to tempt people to circumnavigate the reservoir. Some of the art pieces function not just for their intrinsic merits but for the utilitarian purpose of providing shelter from the frequent rain. Addition of the art spectacle contravenes Gibberd's recommendation that the landscape should remain free of 'the equipment of civilization' likely to shatter 'the illusion of natural solitude'.[18]

Recently, the Park has made a profit for the first time.[19] The arrival of the tourist trade has brought a new, subtle form of domination to Kielder. As well as regarding incomers as citizens exercising their rights of access to the publicly-owned reservoir perimeter, the public-private consortium running the site now treats them as consumers as well as citizens. Indeed, the transformation of Kielder into a destination for tourism has had the consequence of bringing consumers of the products of Kielder – in particular water – to the place of extraction, drawing visitors' attention to the dual purpose of the location. The management of the Park classifies tourists into various categories based on their spending potential for marketing purposes as well as for planning future amenity. Those who spend little or no money at Kielder are defined as 'functionals', whereas the more desirable, from the management's perspective, higher spending and more demanding visitors are categorized as 'cosmopolitans' or 'discoverers'.[20]

These visitors, mostly from urban and suburban areas, further add to the idea that Kielder Water and Forest Park is essentially a city landscape even though inserted into a remote countryside. Rather than a palimpsest in which the inscription of earlier landscapes can be read, the past has been largely, but not totally, erased from the Park.[21]

In common with many other landscapes around the world, the commercial forest and the recreational reservoir testify to modernity and domination by global capitalism. The Park liberates visitors from the noise and pollution of city streets and allows them the opportunity for vigorous exercise amongst plantation and reservoir. At Kielder, as in national parks around the world, nature has been produced as a spectacle, simplified and only sustainable by continual intervention by humanity.

Future visits

The transition from local relationships to regional and national interdependencies began as European capital investment was augmented by national funds to pay for the Kielder Water Scheme. Dependence on outside capital has now become global, as the private owners of Northumbrian Water Ltd seek capital investment on world markets. Publicly owned before 1989, ownership transferred firstly to a French water company and then passed to Hong Kong-based Cheung Kong Infrastructure Holdings Limited.[22] Such external pressures to finance the borrowing of capital will continue to influence the commercial ambitions of water supply and tourism.

Forest management practices are likely to continue to follow a commercial timber production paradigm in an attempt to reduce subsidies to the Forestry Commission.[23] Yet the growing importance of tourism has led to appreciation of amenity and ecological benefits. Whilst unsightly clear cutting of mature timber is often a necessity in Kielder because of the danger of windthrow in thinned stands on shallow soils, biodiversity and amenity concerns are driving introduction of a mosaic of varied forest with deciduous trees along stream channels and conservation of blanket bog.

The Park is a large area managed by the Development Trust, which does not allow unplanned initiatives, such as funfairs, roadside ice cream stalls or campsites, without permission. Tourism is likely to remain the main economic activity, but tourism is fickle and influenced by the weather and economic changes, including the cost of transport to the remote valley, 50 miles (80 km) from the nearest large centre of population on Tyneside. Northumberland has low wage rates and any increases in the cost of fuel may deter local visitors, as it did in 1973, when petroleum prices rose rapidly.[24] The current (2013–14) annual figure of around 345,000 visitors will need continuous investment to compete with other attractions, making the Park increasingly urban.[25]

The initial high cost of construction of the dam and tunnels, and the high operating costs of pumping to take Kielder water to the Wear and Tees basins, makes Kielder water expensive.[26] The barriers to its greater use in future are economic, rather than physical, feasibility. Water from the Upper Tyne, regulated by the reservoir, could be taken south via the Kielder Water Scheme tunnel to the Tees, and from the Tees via a pipeline into the Wyske in Yorkshire, and so to the whole Ouse basin. Alternatively, a feasibility study conducted for Thames Water, when its Resource Management Plan was under scrutiny at a Public Inquiry in 2010, has shown that water could be taken from Kielder via a pipeline which might be laid in the sea along the coast to London and the southeast.[27] Such notions of Kielder Water serving a national water grid recur with each major drought.

Should severe water shortages elsewhere in the North East of England, or even in the London area, increase demand for water from the Kielder reservoir, vigorous use of the reservoir will produce a conflict of interest with its use as a recreational resource. If Kielder's water were to be fully used, then the level of the lake could be drawn down by 3 m or 5 m (Gibberd assumed an average annual drawdown of 3 m) and, for considerable periods during summer months, stretches of mud would become exposed around the shores beyond the Bakethin dam. Fumes laden with hydrogen sulphide and other organic products formed under reducing conditions below the water would be released as the mud and decaying vegetation along the shore dried out. The smell would be unpleasant and flies would breed. However, such drawdowns are unlikely, except for occasional maintenance purposes, because the need to retain head for hydroelectricity production would make lowering of the reservoir level more than 1.5 m below top water level costly with loss of generation income.[28] If the reservoir water continues to be little used – and Northumbrian Water Limited reports a decline in demand – then the appearance of the main reservoir, so important for tourism, will continue to look like a lake, and all the current shoreline features will bear their intended relationship with the water line.[29]

The dilemma of balancing release of water from the reservoir with tourism, hydroelectricity production and the need for consumption of the resource itself illustrates dynamic competition between economics and nature in management of the reservoir. Kielder is a city in the countryside, a place of industrial-scale production and recreation, where change is both rapid and continual.

Conclusion

The superficial appearance of stability of the Kielder landscape masks fears of climate change, known biological hazards presented by monocultures, the impoverished genetic inheritance of fish bred in hatcheries, dependence on foreign investment for the prosperity of the water utility, a market for hydroelectricity and dependence on cheap fuel to attract tourists. There is also the present, if remote, risk of dam break. The threat of terrorist action led to the dam's designation as an Economic Key Site, and thus subject to high security. The Irish Republican Army included Kielder on its list of potential bombing targets in the early 1990s.[30] Thus, a complex and dynamic web of financial relations, ecological considerations and security issues control the forest and reservoir.

No word expresses adequately the aesthetics of domination evoked by the spectacle of a large-scale landscape which has been radically and recently imposed by the ambition of a handful of politicians, engineers and scientists. The coming-to-earth, in Kielder, of technical plans, conceived elsewhere to meet national and global goals driven by political and economic forces for increased timber production and industrial water supply, raises anxieties about the sustainability of the changes and the lack of input from the local, affected people. Resilience may require diversity.

The Romantics, in analyzing their mixed emotions aroused by contemplation of dramatic and fearsome landscapes, used the word 'sublime' to capture their fear and admiration in distinction from a less disturbing view of beauty.[31] Contemporary landscape appreciation of megaprojects needs a new expression to encompass both feelings of disquiet over newly-introduced risks and admiration for the imposed order and scale of amendment of nature. This Kielder landscape of creative destruction is a disturbing spectacle to those concerned about the future of the planet during the Anthropocene.

Notes

1. Frederick Gibberd, *Proof of evidence submitted to the 1972 Kielder inquiry*, Unpublished (Newcastle upon Tyne: Northumberland Record Office, 1972), para.50.
2. J. M. Richards, 'Gibberd, Sir Frederick Ernest (1908–1984)', *Oxford Dictionary of National Biography* (Oxford: Oxford University Press, 2004); http://www.oxforddnb.com/view/article/31144 (accessed 23/11/14).
3. Christine S. McCulloch, 'The Kielder Water Scheme: The Last of its Kind', in Henry Hewlett (ed.), *Improvements in Reservoir Construction, Operation and Maintenance* (London: Thomas Telford, 2006), pp. 196–210; Christine S. McCulloch, *Dam Decisions and Pipe Dreams: The Political Ecology of Reservoir Schemes (Teesdale, Farndale and Kielder Water) in North East England* (Saarbrucken: VDM, 2008), chaps 9 and 10.
4. D. J. Coats and G. Rocke, 'The Kielder Headworks', Proceedings of the ICE 72/1 (1982), pp. 153–5.
5. Frederick Gibberd, 'The Landscape of Reservoirs', *Journal of the Institution of Water Engineers* 15 (1961), p. 88.
6. Gibberd, *Proof of evidence*, paragraph 123.
7. Information provided by David Hall, Northumbrian Water at the AHRC Kielder Workshop, March 2011.
8. Julie Black, E. J. Milner-Gulland, Nick Sotherton and Susanna Mourato, 'Valuing Complex Environmental Goods: Landscape and Biodiversity in the North Pennines, *Environmental Conservation* 37/2 (2010), pp. 136–46. See also chapter by Graham Gill in this volume, pp. 234–39.
9. Leona Jayne Skelton, *Kielder Oral History Report* http://www.environmentalhistories.net/?page_id=599 (accessed 01/06/13).
10. Independent Panel on Forestry https://www.gov.uk/government/publications/independent-panel-on-forestry-final-report (accessed 15/05/14); Department for Environment, Food & Rural Affairs, *Government Forestry Policy Statement*, 31 January 2013. See also chapter by Duncan Hutt in this volume, pp. 199–203.
11. Leona Jayne Skelton, 'The Uncomfortable Path from Forestry to Tourism at Kielder, Northumberland: A Socially Dichotomous Village?', *Oral History* 42/2 (Autumn 2014), p. 83.
12. Raymond Williams, *The Country and the City* (Oxford, London, New York: Oxford University Press, 1973), p. 290.
13. Kielder Water and Forest Park http://www.visitkielder.com/ (accessed 15/05/14).
14. The Kielder Observatory http://kielderobservatory.org/ (accessed 15/05/14).
15. Kielder Art and Architecture http://kielderartandarchitecture.com/home.html (accessed 15/05/14).
16. John Ruskin, *On Life and Art* (London and New York: Penguin, 2004 [1853]).
17. See Peter Sharpe's essay in this collection, pp. 143–48.
18. Gibberd, *Proof of evidence*, paragraphs 90, 123.
19. Kielder Water & Forest Park Development Trust 07424020 http://companycheck.co.uk/company/07424020/KIELDER-WATER--FOREST-PARK-DEVELOPMENT-TRUST/financial-accounts (accessed 14/12/14).

20. David Hall, Head of Leisure, Strategy and Transformation at Northumbrian Water, Presentation on Marketing the Park, AHRC Kielder Workshop, March, 2011.

21. See, for example, the chapters by Richard Oram and Matt Greenhall in this volume, pp. 53–55; pp. 224–25.

22. Cheung Kong Infrastructure http://www.cki.com.hk/english/about_CKI/cki_at_a_glance/index.htm (accessed 16/05/14).

23. Forestry Commission, England, *Establishment and Maintenance* (1995) http://www.forestry.gov.uk/forestry/INFD-6XJF34 (accessed 24/11/14).

24. M. Newson, 'Kielder Water, Kielder Forest and the North Tyne Valley', in M. C. Whitby (ed.), *Land Use Change: The Causes and Consequences*, ITE symposium, no. 27 (London: HMSO, 1992), p. 165.

25. Kielder Water and Forest Park http://www.visitkielder.com/ (accessed 15/05/14).

26. *The Economist*, 4 July 1992, p. 53.

27. See, for example http://www.theguardian.com/environment/2011/nov/08/water-supply-infrastructure (accessed 25/11/14).

28. J. A. Brady, J. M. Davis and E. W. Douglas, 'First Filling of Kielder Reservoir and Future Operational Considerations', *Journal of the Institution of Water Engineers and Scientists* 37/4 (August 1983), pp. 295–312.

29. Northumbrian Water Limited Financial Statement for the year ended 31 March 2012.

30. Kielder reservoir was included in a list of IRA potential bombing targets during the trial of Feilin O'Hadhmaill: *The Guardian* (London), 1 November 1994, p. 8.

31. Edmund Burke, *A Philosophical Enquiry into the Origin of our Ideas of the Sublime and Beauty* https://ebooks.adelaide.edu.au/b/burke/edmund/sublime, first published 1756 (accessed 14/12/14).

CHAPTER 30

Nature, Cultural Choice and History

T. C. Smout

Nature conservation is necessarily based both on science and on cultural choice. Britons have been among the world's pioneers, equally in the scientific and in the popular culture of conservation, as exemplified in studying, enjoying and setting aside sites like Wicken Fen to maximize species and habitat diversity. The detailed choices of which sites to use for nature conservation, and how to manage them once chosen, are themselves made on the basis of the objectivity of ecologists, which is why there is a Joint Nature Conservation Committee as statutory adviser to the British government and its devolved administrations and scientific staff in all three country conservation agencies (currently titled Natural England, Scottish Natural Heritage and Natural Resources Wales).

Additionally, as practised today, British nature conservation has come to have much in common with building conservation, in being based to no small degree on historical factors. When the National Trust (let us say) inherits an historic building, they have to decide what to do with it, the main alternatives being to conserve as found or to restore to some earlier condition, and to do this they have to know enough about the history of the building to decide what is valuable about it as it is, or what the earlier condition was. For managing a site for nature conservation, just as for building conservation, we also frequently need evidence from the past, whether we want to conserve as found, or to restore it to some earlier real or imagined state.

This historical turn is comparatively new, at least in emphasis. In Britain there are all manner of designations which confer a greater or lesser degree of legal protection on the biodiversity of a site: National Nature Reserves (NNR), Sites of Special Scientific Interest (SSSI), Special Areas of Conservation (SAC), Special Protection Areas for birds (SPA), Ramsar (wetland) sites, and so on. The most fundamental designation is the SSSI, as all the others have to start by being so designated. The first suite of SSSIs was selected between the 1950s and the 1970s, beginning under Max Nicholson's leadership of the Nature Conservancy and concluded when Derek Ratcliffe was chief scientist of its successor, the Nature Conservancy Council.[1] At this point, scientists were looking for a representative selection of ecological communities, nationally and regionally, of diverse species, normally within what they hoped were stable habitats. Hence the expression Sites of Special Scientific Interest. The history of the site really did not come into the selection process, though some of the sites, like Wicken Fen, might incidentally have had a very long and well-known history, not least of scientific study. Though the habitat there was very unstable, it was assumed that the National Trust would provide the resources and knowledge to stabilize it.

SSSIs came to be seen slightly differently in the accelerating countryside degradation of Britain between 1960 and the 1980s. By the time of the 1981 *Wildlife and Countryside* Act, they were regarded primarily, not as sites for scientific study and research, but as refuges for beleaguered nature. They were the main retreats of the rare and precious, remarkable for the presence within the site of one or more unusual species, or for the numbers and diversity of the species that inhabit or use them. Given their perceived value, management will now always at least try passively to sustain the habitat so that it can go on supporting the same species in the same way.

More proactively, ambitious management may seek next to bring about wanted change, but only to restore something lost in the past. The fashionable terms of the new millennium for any ambitious form of habitat restoration – one that will involve several similar or linked SSSIs and possibly affect also the wider countryside between them, as in the East Anglia Great Fen Project and Wicken Vision – is to bring about 'landscape-scale change' or to 'rewild'. And the change and the wildness in the conservationists' mind is always a change backwards, to something that once was, or is fancied once to have been.

Yet 'natural', the property of nature, in no way implies a given unchanging *state,* and no propensity, if disturbed, to return to a status quo. Rather, it involves great *processes,* which do not at all seek to maintain the static or even to maintain a balance, but which involve constant change and flux, and an element of chaos that ensures unpredictability. These natural processes involve plants using their chlorophyll to harness solar energy to grow and reproduce. The solar energy itself ebbs and flows both long term and short term, so that climate change and variation have been constantly present throughout history, and often rapid, affecting plant species and growth. Herbivores eat the plants and carnivores eat the herbivores. Death is the universal end of life. Recycling organisms, like fungi, feed on dead plants and animals alike, and so contribute to those processes. And natural processes involve adapting creatures to this continuously changing environment, the evolution by natural selection that has given us a worldwide biodiversity of 13 million species. Nature conservation can be considered in one sense to be an oxymoron, as nature equates with change and site-based conservation seeks to equate with stability.

But, you may say, these definitions of 'natural' and 'nature', in the context of conservation management, miss the point. What conservation is really trying to do is to mitigate the impact of humankind's constant degradation of the environment. Maybe so, but to do this, conservationists are compelled to use an implicitly historical approach in order to reverse or resist degradation, either seeking a baseline entirely before human influence, or choosing a time where human influence was less destructive than it is now.

It is very common and often convenient to use the word 'natural' to describe the world before any human influence was apparent. In woodland history, for instance, it was applied by the influential Dutch conservationist Frans Vera to describe what he thought Mesolithic Europe would have looked like after the end of the last Ice Age but before man made any impact through agriculture: others, in the same context, like George Peterken, have preferred the term 'original natural'.[2] According to Vera, the great work of European conservationists in the future should be the creation and 'rewilding' of reserves large enough to restore parts of the continent back to this 'natural' state of Eden, as well as to hold on to such remnants of Eden as remain. In North America, similar, though independently derived, visions of what is 'natural' invoke a pre-Columbian past, notably the project for the restoration of the Buffalo Commons, a rewilding on a vast scale of the grassland stretches of the Great Plains states, from Montana to Texas, to return them to a condition that existed until nineteenth-century railways and settlers with their cattle and crops violently replaced the bison and their Native American hunters.[3]

The most remarkable contemporary European exemplification of this new historical turn is in the Netherlands, with the rewilding of Oostvaardersplassen outside Amsterdam on the principles adumbrated by Vera.[4] Here, some 5,600 ha reclaimed from the sea have been populated by thousands of red deer, long-horned Heck cattle (standing in as proxies for the lost aurochs) and konik ponies (standing in for tarpan, the prehistoric horse). These roam the ground unfed, untended and unshot, except occasionally on welfare grounds, and the herbivores render the habitat around them 'natural', following the theory that originally the pattern of woodland was determined by such herds of large herbivores. Vera would say that the whole point of Ostvaardersplassen is to create a reserve large enough for natural forces now to operate. It does not matter if a patch of rare orchids is devoured or a bittern's nest is trampled underfoot by the animals, as the natural processes released by whole experiment will create the niches for more orchids and bitterns.

Vera would no doubt also argue that the allegation that nature conservation is an oxymoron does not apply to Oostvaardersplassen, as this reserve is big enough to accommodate the processes of natural change, while filtering out from it most of the degrading influences of humans, apart from air pollution and the effect of anthropogenic climate change. This is true, and that is what makes the reserve so remarkable. But there is probably not another site in western Europe big enough and so governed as to be comparable, except possibly the Coto Doñana in Spain and (with some reservations) the inner sanctuary of the forest of Białowieża in Poland. There are certainly no reserves on this scale yet in the United Kingdom, though the National Trust's ambition for wetland creation round Wicken will be almost as big as Oostvaardersplassen, at 5,500 ha, and the Great Fen project to the north of that plans an additional 3,700 ha of new reed-bed and mere.

To consider the condition of the Earth before farming to be the most natural, of course, adopts a definition of 'natural' that excludes humans from nature. This is a medieval Christian opinion endorsed and secularized by the Enlightenment, but overturned by Darwin, to whom man was but one twig on the tree of evolution, no more exceptional in being subject to nature and nature's laws than any other organism. And a definition that nature is the state of 'original natural' also, of course, underlines the contention that nature conservation is now inescapably about history, since it is the discovery of what was original natural that must lie at its root. In the USA, oral tradition, travellers' accounts and old newspapers will reveal much of what the prairie was like a century and a half ago. In Europe, though, such written history is not going to be of much help, as hunter-gatherers did not write. We necessarily turn to paleoarchaeology, but this is only another form of historical method. When English Nature (one of the bodies that succeeded the Nature Conservancy Council) wanted to consider the implications of Vera's work, the scientists under Keith Kirby tested his ideas by asking Philip Buckland and others about beetle assemblages 6,000–10,000 years ago, and a range of palynologists about pollen diagrams, to try to test if there really was as much open country then as he maintained.[5] It was entirely a historical question, and what actions they would recommend subsequently would depend on the historical evidence assembled to guide them.

Conclusions about the original natural state cannot be fixed, but must constantly be subject to historical revisionism. Should it be discovered that the hunter-gatherers made a considerable impact by the use of fire, using it to increase the degree of forest edge to gather berries and the area of open grass to attract grazing animals to hunt, which many archaeologists maintain, then no habitat is pristine in the sense of being exempt from human influence.[6] Then we would have to see that the great herds were themselves partly an artefact of human interference, and ask why we privilege the Mesolithic over other periods in our restorations, since, though more 'original', it would logically not be more 'natural'. In the USA we can see the implications of this, once it was theorized that the first Native Americans had hunted the original mega-fauna to extinction. Now, in order to get back to the true 'original natural', the Buffalo Commons proposal seems to the purist rather insufficient and historically shallow. Idealistic young scientists propose to introduce into stretches of the surviving prairie, lions and elephants, as proxy for the vanished mastodons and sabre-toothed tigers that the first humans slew, and set them to roam the grasslands or prey on the bison.[7]

So, inescapably, managing nature is not only about making an objective scientific choice, but also a subjective cultural choice. It is about what we value from the past, and which past, and historical expertise is needed to make an informed choice. Then, having decided on that, we enlist scientists to help us to keep the biodiversity associated with that past, or to re-create conditions for it to re-establish.

The problems that arise in Scotland over recreating extensive 'original natural' woodland cover illustrate the scholarly difficulties that can emerge in justifying ecological choices by history. The vision of a restored Great Wood of Caledon has great popular appeal, and rests on the idea that Scotland was originally clothed with an enormous forest in which wolves, lynx, bear and elk roamed, and that this survived in the Highlands until well into historic times, when the Romans, the Vikings, the English iron masters and the Scottish sheep masters successively assaulted it, until they had reduced the uplands to what the ecologist Frank Fraser Darling in 1956 famously termed 'a wet desert' of bog and moor.[8] This remains a compelling idea, and the notion of a Caledonian Forest is easily elided in popular imagination with that of a forest of Caledonian pine, though in fact the original tree cover of Scotland, when it reached its maximum extent 6,000 years ago, was dominated by Scots pine only in the Central Highlands.

But scientific and historical understanding of the woodland past of Scotland has moved on since Fraser Darling, though seldom acknowledged by the protagonists of a restored Great Wood of Caledon.[9] First of all, historians and archaeologists towards the close of the twentieth century began to appreciate that, by the time the Romans came, rather little wood was in fact left, and that the blame attached to Roman, Viking and English outsiders for its destruction was quite misplaced. It is now understood that the woodland maximum which peaked at the end of the Mesolithic was brought to an end not so much by human activity as by climate change, in which a relatively benign regime that had persisted up to the start of the Bronze Age was replaced by a modern regime of rising winds and rain, that made both growth and regeneration of trees more difficult. The spread of blanket bog that took place at this point is now seen by Richard Tipping as entirely natural, without trace of anthropogenic influence in its development.[10] James Fenton, more controversially, would go further to argue that even dry open heather moor would have developed naturally if young trees were not protected from grazing animals in winter by deep snow, to the degree that they were in Scandinavia or Russia. In this reading, the 'natural' environment of Scotland was exceptionally open by west European standards, and if you believe in the overriding justification of the 'original natural' as what evolved naturally without the influence of human intervention, then the task of future heritage management should be to keep it so.[11]

This has not stopped conservationists who favour tree planting from wanting to re-establish the Caledonian Forest, notably the charity Trees for Life, which (like the Royal Society for the Protection of Birds) complains that only 1% of the 'original' Caledonian Forest survives.[12] Such a statistic hardly seems relevant, when the original forest to which it refers existed in a different natural climatic regime. Both Trees for Life and RSPB are embarked on a planting campaign to redress the balance, sometimes in appropriate places adjacent to existing Scots pine woods that, for one reason or another, can no longer regenerate of their own accord. Often, however, charities do not take into account the fact that Scots pine has not grown on the selected site for thousands of years, or do not worry whether their intervention interferes with natural processes in woods like Abernethy Forest that actually can still regenerate without any assistance. Separately from this, the owner of the Glen Alladale estate in Sutherland hopes to create a fenced and restored Caledonian Forest reserve of at least 650 ha in an area already containing fragments of ancient pine wood, which will be expanded by planting up.[13] Within this, they had originally intended to reintroduce the full range of ancient native fauna – wolves, elk, wild boar, lynx and bear, but permission was refused for the predators, on the grounds that the introduction of predator and prey into the same enclosure was inhumane and illegal.

Both the intentions of the charities and those at Glen Alladale are interesting and innovative initiatives. Perhaps they deserve consideration on their own merits, rather than as appeals to the past, but there is no doubt that to advertise them as what they are – nothing more than countryside planning initiatives, analogous to eighteenth-century estate improvements reinterpreted to modern sensibilities – would be fatally to reduce their popular appeal. Apparently we cannot, in the twenty-first century, dare to say that we will plant Scots pine because we like it, rather than because we have some kind of moral debt to the past to do so.

Today, conservationists, even the official agencies like Natural England (which replaced English Nature in 2006) and Scottish Natural Heritage, consciously or otherwise, invariably seek to go back to some past time. Sometimes modern conservation does not even purport to defend the original natural, but just the historically interesting: of the wild plants prioritized for conservation in Britain, eight out of the ten species most at risk are archaeophytes, introductions made by humans before 1500, probably originally weeds accidentally brought in by Neolithic farmers.[14] One habitat that much exercises conservationists in upland Britain is heather moorland, extensive areas of which have (at least in recent times) depended on constant manipulation by domestic animals and humans. Scottish Natural Heritage offers advice on 'traditional' fire management of the moor to keep it like this.

Again and again, old sites of extractive industry dating from between the Middle Ages and the twentieth centuries (stone and lime quarries, gravel pits and so on) become nature reserves run nationally or by local Wildlife Trusts, as here alone are survivals of wetland fauna and of insects and plants otherwise wiped out by the drains, sprays and tidy-mindedness of modern farming. They are archaeological and anthropogenic sites rather than original natural ones, but often the nature within them can be presumed to be ancient in its presence in the area.

Let us take just two examples. Natural England runs Barnack Hills and Holes near Peterborough as an NNR, on the site of a medieval quarry that once provided stone for Norman and Gothic churches and cathedrals. The surface of the site was too rough and uneven to be transformed by herbicides and fertilizers into modern 'improved grassland', but with light grazing can be maintained for the biodiversity of flowers and invertebrates that have vanished from the surrounding countryside. Some miles to the south down the A1, part of Paxton Pits, created in the twentieth century to provide sand and gravel for East Anglia's burgeoning roads and houses, is run as a local nature reserve. Its uncleared scrub is a famous refuge for nightingales in summer and its waters shelter birds and plants that would have characterized the undrained fens and meres.

Most historic or anthropogenic sites of this sort can be managed by common sense and ecological knowledge. But sometimes conservation needed detailed historical evidence to manage some of the best sites, when it became clear (by the 1960s at the latest) that the ecological communities of SSSIs were frequently less stable than had been supposed when they were set up. The question was, then, what past practice had ensured stability?

At Wicken Fen, there was a constant puzzle about how to prevent natural processes taking over and wiping out the preferred and rarest species. The quest for the 'original natural', were it pursued there, would have been irrelevant, as the drainage of the surrounding fens has literally left it high and dry, and in any case today's National Trust is just as anxious to preserve and commemorate the cultural heritage of the fen dwellers as the natural heritage of the fen, believing here (as in so many places) that the two complement one another. The dilemma that management was originally faced with was explained by W. S. Farren in his recollections of 1926:

> When parts of Wicken Fen first came under the control of the National Trust there was a general idea, perhaps a natural one, that it should be allowed to run wild, and, to quote the expression often used, to return to its original state. This entirely ignored the question, what is the state most suitable to the ecology of the species of insects of all orders for which the Sedge Fen is famous.[15]

To return to the original natural state was manifestly impossible. But the 'natural conditions', which had made the Sedge Fen famous among Victorian entomologists for rare insects, depended on past human management. But exactly what had that management been? The answer to this question proved difficult and lengthy, but increasingly urgent as the fen progressively began to lose much of the biodiversity interest for which it had been acquired. Ultimately, it involved a detailed Cambridge doctoral thesis by Terence A. Rowell (finished in 1983) surveying the many historical records that survived concerning the fen's ancient management. The consequence of this was a series of modifications to how the Trust managed Wicken, including a critical change in the season at which the sedge harvest was cut from winter to summer, and also a resumption of turf cutting, management practices that go back to the Middle Ages. And the impact was considerable and successful.[16]

Both at Wicken and in the Great Fen Project what is sought is to extend, and to protect from modern farming and natural forces alike, the remnant heritage of the seventeenth century, complete with its sedge, reed and turf cutting, before the final onslaught of the drainage engineers, but still a world removed from the Mesolithic by several millennia.

Quite often, especially in bird conservation, the objective of conservation turns out to be an accidental outcome of relatively recent ways of farming, and has nothing remotely to do with the 'original natural'. The corncrake in the Hebrides is a refugee from twentieth-century farming elsewhere in Britain, and the RSPB pays crofters to mimic aspects of nineteenth-century agriculture in order to save it. Similarly, the attempts to save corn buntings in Fife and Angus involve providing winter seed and summer cover of a sort that would have belonged in the heyday of Victorian agriculture. The spectacular numbers of barnacle geese on Islay and on the Solway, on the other hand, take every advantage of the lavish fertilizers and rich grass of modern farming, originating in subsidy regimes after the Second World War. Conservationists exert every nerve, and spend large amounts of public money, compensating modern farmers not to reduce their numbers. If the RSPB in Tiree and Fife is trying to stop the historical clock for the corncrakes at about 1850, on Islay they are trying to maintain the benefits of a regime one hundred years younger. Neither could be more removed from 'original natural', but the basis is historical just the same.

Similarly, those concerned about the plants of semi-natural chalk grassland, whether archaeophytes or otherwise, are (whether they realise it or not) really looking for what was left of that habitat around 1940, not the full complexity of the countryside before 5,000 BC, and in this case, they have the opportunity of being able to use oral history from local communities to guide them in their practices, if they choose to call upon it. Perhaps too frequently, today's conservation management overlooks what is embedded in the richness of a community's recollection.

If we are willing to admit reliance on historical criteria and subjective cultural choice, we might also be prepared to admit that conservation practice relating to non-native species often has less to do with science than is claimed. Let us take the matter of *Impatiens glandulifera*, the Himalayan balsam, introduced as late as the nineteenth century, so not well regarded. Any plant introduced since 1500 is called a 'neophyte' and not entitled to protection (which this plant certainly does not need); if it is also invasive, which this plant is to a high degree, it is also considered a public nuisance. Neophyte and archaeophyte are historical terms, not scientific ones, and are an arbitrary division of time. Volunteers spend the day slashing and uprooting *Impatiens*, inside and outside nature reserves. The DEFRA (Department for Environment, Food and Rural Affairs) reckons it would take £200 million to eradicate it from the UK.

Does it actually do any harm? Would we attack it in this way if it were an archaeophyte or a native plant? It is a valuable source of pollen for bumblebees, honey bees and butterflies in a countryside often rendered bleak by pesticides or overgrazing. As Richard Mabey has observed, it is hard to find a case where native plant communities have been displaced by *Impatiens*, and although it is a common plant on the edges of wetlands where dredging has taken place, and also on disturbed ground, it does not invade reed-beds.[17] The worst argument against it, is that it is so good at providing nectar and pollen that bees might neglect native plants in their eagerness to use it, but this remains unproven, and as an argument has an air of desperation about it, overlooking the fact that plentiful supplies of nectar should strengthen the hive and make the bees more numerous, so more of them would be available to forage in native plants as well. That is not to say that *Impatiens* should never be eradicated, but that the ecological grounds for its eradication have to be balanced against the ecological costs of doing so. If they are equal, then we may still legitimately want to eradicate it on the aesthetic ground that we do not care to see it in a site like Wicken, historically free from it. In the same way, we might decide to take out Victorian glass from a medieval parish church because it reduces its authenticity. But we should be clear that it is done on these aesthetic and historical grounds, and not because it is an alien invader.

The well-rehearsed 'scientific' case for the eradication from Britain of the introduced American ruddy duck, and the many millions already spent on it in the interests of saving the white-headed duck from hybridization when British birds fly off to Spain, is another instance that can be questioned. Official conservation (as represented in this case by DEFRA) has been trying to prevent interbreeding between the two closely-related species, on the grounds that this would not have occurred had we not introduced the ruddy duck to the proximity of the white-headed duck in the first place. It is held to be unnatural, because (*contra* Darwin) man is not considered to be part of nature, so what we do is *ipso facto* unnatural. No-one imagines that the desire of the ruddy drake for the white-headed duck is unnatural. If it occurs and the hybrid is not well adapted to its surroundings, then nature will determine that the hybrid will die out anyway; if it is successful, by definition an organism better adapted to its environment will evolve. It is hard to see exactly what is wrong with that.

You could say that the planned extermination of the ruddy duck from Britain and continental Europe is a good thing because you do not care for alien species anyway. Roger Riddington, editor of the prestigious journal *British Birds*, takes this view, and would like to have done with the lot, the rose-ringed parakeet, the Canada goose and the red-legged partridge as well. This is based on a subjective preference for the historic avifauna of Britain. We should not imagine it is done by some scientific criteria above argument, reproach or cost-benefit analysis. We could also (while we are at it) ask which alien species deserve protection in Britain on the grounds of their endangered status in their native range, something which is not presently being done. Candidates are the Chinese water deer, at risk in China but doing well in its stronghold at Wood Walton Fen (and scientists say it is not another invasive munjac in waiting), and Lady Amherst's pheasant, barely clinging on in the wild, either in its native Asian forests or in Bedfordshire. The latest reports suggest that the pheasant has probably died out in Britain anyway. Neither has been shown to have any deleterious effects on other native species or habitats.

In sum, let us ask site-based and species-based nature conservation to recognize more explicitly the degree to which it has come to rest both upon history and upon cultural choices. Conservation will, of course, always be a partnership of scientific ecology and practical land management, where often the point of intervention is to stop the forces of nature from destroying what we value. But the point is 'value'. Humans are indeed part of nature, and it is absolutely legitimate for us to prefer some species above others. We may also decide that we want to protect some species because they have a historic value as representing survivors from a past that was also our own. Then let us indeed protect them as part of a cherished heritage – as part of the historical record. But if we are to do that authentically, as well as the very best science, we need the very best history to discover what that heritage actually was. My own preference always is for us to be informed by history but not to be dominated by it: there should always be room for making a new landscape and enjoying a new species, or an old one, within it.

Notes

1. In 1991, the Nature Conservancy Council was superseded by three bodies: English Nature, Scottish Natural Heritage and the Countryside Council for Wales.
2. George F. Peterken, *Natural Woodland: Ecology and Conservation in Northern Temperate Regions* (Cambridge: Cambridge University Press, 1996), p. 13; Franz W. M. Vera, *Grazing Ecology and Forest History* (Wallingford: CABI publishing, 2000).
3. Anne Matthews, *Where the Buffalo Roam: Restoring America's Great Plains* (Chicago: University of Chicago Press, 2002); Deborah E. Popper and Frank J. Popper, 'The Buffalo Commons as Regional Metaphor and Geographic Method' (Fort Worth: Great Plains Restoration Council, 2013).
4. Vincent Wigbels, *Oostvaardersplassen: New Nature below Sealevel*, (Zwolle: Statsbosbeheer, n.d.).
5. Kathy H. Hodder, James M. Bullock, Philip C. Buckland and Keith J. Kirby, 'Large Herbivores in the Wildwood and Modern Naturalistic Grazing Systems', *English Nature Research Reports* 648 (2005).
6. For example, Ian G. Simmons, *The Environmental Impact of Later Mesolithic Cultures*, (Edinburgh: Edinburgh University Press, 1996).
7. C. Josh Donlan and Harry W. Greene, 'NLIMBY: No Lions in my Backyard', in Marcus Hall (ed.), *Restoration and History: The Search for a Usable Environmental Past* (London: Routledge, 2010), pp. 293–305.
8. Frank Fraser Darling, *Pelican in the Wilderness* (London: Allen and Unwin, 1956), p. 180.
9. T. C. Smout, Alan R. MacDonald and Fiona Watson, *A History of the Native Woodlands of Scotland 1500–1920*, (Edinburgh: Edinburgh University Press, 2005), chap. 2.
10. Richard Tipping, 'Blanket Peat in the Scottish Highlands: Timing, Cause, Spread and the Myth of Environmental Determinism', *Biodiversity and Conservation* 17 (2008), pp. 2097–113.
11. James Fenton, 'Towards a New Paradigm for the Ecology of Northern and Western Scotland: a Synthesis of Issues' http://www.james-hc-fenton.eu/page19.html (accessed 28/05/13).
12. http://www.treesforlife.org.uk (accessed 28/05/13).
13. http://www.alladale.co.uk/wilderness-reserve (accessed 28/05/13).
14. C. D. Pearson, D. A. Pearman and T. D. Dines (eds), *New Atlas of the British and Irish Flora* (Oxford: Oxford University Press, 2002), pp. 37–8.
15. Cited in Laurie Friday (ed.), *Wicken Fen: The Making of a Wetland Nature Reserve* (Colchester: Harley Books, 1997), p. 216.
16. Friday (ed.), *Wicken Fen*, esp. chaps 10 and 11.
17. Richard Mabey, *Weeds: A Cultural History* (London: Profile Books, 2012).

CHAPTER 31

Concluding Reflections

David Moon, Peter Coates and Paul Warde

In the project that culminated in this book, a group of university-based environmental historians worked with a series of external partners who are involved in various ways in managing, exploiting, conserving and promoting the 'environments' of the local places we selected for the study. Of course spending time outdoors and visiting places is by no means the preserve of 'environmental' historians. An historian of religion can be expected to visit churches, mosques or temples, military historians tramp battlefields, and urban historians will walk the streets they study (*BBC History Magazine* carries regular features entitled 'Where History Happened' and 'Out and About'). Interaction with other specialists working outside the world of universities is also increasingly the norm for historians of all stripes, with museum curators, policymakers and, above all perhaps, the media. As university-based environmental historians we have all previously worked with conservationists, environmental managers and other practitioners.

But by and large this fieldwork and interaction are part of developing an individual hypothesis and the pursuit of a personal research agenda, not part of a conscious aim for mutual learning; and usually we are just trying to find out about a particular place. However in this project we have been consciously reflecting on ourselves as the latest instance in a continuing set of interactions between the local and the outside world. We have been aiming to see the environments – the local places – through the eyes of our partners, to understand their agendas and preoccupations, and in the process give us a new perspective for our work as environmental historians. In doing so we learned a great deal, and owe a considerable debt to our partners. While it might seem obvious or trite, it is still worth stating that we found a difference in approach between ourselves as academics and our partners. Our concerns were more abstract, scholarly and open-ended; those of our partners were essentially practical, immediate and rooted in the places they managed.

It would certainly be a mistake, however, to think that our partners were really interested only in the immediately relevant aspects of our discussions. It is true that one partner, generous with their time and insight, was heard to mutter good-naturedly during one on-site discussion that it must be wonderful to spend your days shooting the breeze about big stuff like the meaning of beauty, and why – and since when – we love mountains. Yet at the same time, we found that 'practitioners' valued the space and 'permission' we gave them to stand back from their everyday preoccupations and to think. What pass for commonplaces among academic historians were not always recognized or known, or perhaps they were known intuitively but had not received considered reflection. Historical practice itself provided our partners with an 'island in time' to de-familiarize utterly familiar places. 'I found it refreshing', reflected one partner, post-workshop, 'to have some challenging questions thrown at us about why and how we manage [our site]. All too often we are so busy with writing management plans and then delivering these that we do not look at the big questions and issues.' He finished off by quoting the lament of Welsh poet William Henry Davies that 'we have no time to stand and stare.' This is one of the most important services that an engagement with the humanities can provide. As Christof Mauch, co-director of the Munich-based Rachel Carson Center for Environment and Society, has emphasized, in the new academic configuration of the environmental humanities it is:

> the bigger ideas which are at stake. And these bigger ideas are linked by their common recognition of nature as a cultural challenge, focusing on the role played by human agents in the natural environment, the cultural consequences of natural change, and the way nature is portrayed.[1]

For our part, some of us cast an occasional longing glance at the muddy pick-up trucks that the rangers and forestry officials drove around in, imagining an alternative career: a working life made up of bat walks at dusk, checking on the osprey nests and konik ponies at dawn. But just as our partners did not see the more routine (usually desk and office-based) aspects of our jobs, we were inclined to overlook the comparable aspects of their more typical working lives. Regardless of whether it is timber sales figures, visitor numbers, squirrel sightings or the latest university research strategy document, we all spend too much of our working lives sitting at a computer screen: albeit those computers played a major enabling role in bringing us all together. We can consider the differences – and similarities – between ourselves and our partners under the three themes that ran through our project: the environment; environmental beauty; and environmental change.

The environment

Near the start of this book, Paul Warde analyzed the evolution of meanings of the word 'environment', or 'the environment'. His starting point was intellectual understandings of the term and how it has evolved over time. Working with our partners, we gained an understanding of what the term means to them.

For them, 'environment' is overlaid with statutory meanings as organizations involved in managing and exploiting 'the environment' are required by law, including international obligations, to protect it from harm and promote sustainable use. Northumbrian Water Limited, for instance, has a clear 'Environmental Policy', which states that the company is 'founded on water and environmental engineering and much of what we do influences the environment ... [W]e aim to protect and improve the environment for the benefit of all.' In practice, in addition to providing clean water to its customers and processing waste, the company states that it is committed to preventing pollution, reducing its carbon footprint and 'enhancing biodiversity' on its landholdings.[2] The company also acknowledges the existence of rare habitats, such as the upland limestone around its Cow Green reservoir in Teesdale, 'home to a rare snail and amazing plants like the Spring Gentian and Teesdale Violet'.[3]

This marks a shift in rhetoric since 1967, when the UK Parliament endorsed the decision by the then public water authorities to build the reservoir at Cow Green. In Chris Smout's words: 'the need to service ICI's projected new ammonia works [on Teesside] outweigh[ed] the united opposition of the Nature Conservancy, the British Ecological Society' and other bodies to the loss of the unique habitat.[4] A few years later, 'ecological' (not 'environmental') objections were raised to the plan to dam the North Tyne near Kielder.[5] The objections were overridden, also with the aim of providing water for the burgeoning industries on Teesside. Some concessions (such as the Bakethin dam) were made. But, as a plaque on the history of the reservoir on display in the water tower at Kielder today indicates, at the time, the fact that the Forestry Commission had already totally transformed the local area with its vast plantations weakened ecological objections to the main dam. Looking back a generation or so later at these past controversies, moreover, what is striking is that the word 'environment', which occurs frequently in literature produced by Northumbrian Water Ltd today, with a clearly understood meaning, was largely absent then.

Another partner, the Forestry Commission (FC), also makes liberal use of the term 'environment' in its literature, with a keen awareness of its statutory and international obligations to protect it. The FC acknowledges:

> The environment is one of the cornerstones of sustainable development, and a proper understanding of how woodlands and forests interact with it is vital. Our research on physical environmental issues aims to ensure that forestry policies and practice can support this objective for land management.[6]

Moreover, it commits itself to 'maintaining and enhancing the biodiversity of the nation's woodlands as laid out in the Helsinki Guidelines, the UK Forestry Standard, the UK Biodiversity Action Plan and Sustainable Forestry: the UK Programme'. It supports research that 'supports these objectives through the long-term monitoring of woodland condition and by identifying the underlying causes of any changes observed'.[7] These were the contexts in which Graham Gill, Forest Management Director for the Forestry Commission in the North East, used the term 'environment'. We might remember here that the word 'environment' was deliberately promoted as a policy tool to integrate a range of different issues. What this has meant in practice is the development of a sometimes bewildering array of metrics and instruments to manage the environment, overseen by layer upon layer of local and sometimes global institutions. We might then note that this is not some bureaucratic reduction of the term which seems strange to others; it reflects, in fact, the purposes to which it was intended to be put in the 1950s and 1960s. In a discussion with David Moon in July 2012 on the FC's use of the term 'environment' and environmental historians, Graham Gill responded: 'Ah hah, we probably use it differently in different contexts.'[8]

Duncan Hutt, Head of Land Management for the Northumberland Wildlife Trust, offered a definition of the term in an interview with Leona Jayne Skelton, as part of the Kielder Oral History Project:

> the environment is ... everything that surrounds us ..., it's where we inhabit, it's where wildlife inhabits, it's ... often used as ... an alternative word to ... nature, and but it doesn't necessarily mean that, it can be also about people who inhabit that area as well ... so ... it's more sort of habitat.[9]

The definition offered by Hutt, a professional nature conservationist, has more in common, perhaps, with those of environmental historians or indeed the wider public than those of Northumbrian Water and the Forestry Commission, whose understandings were overlaid with statutory obligations. 'Environment' is an idea laden with cultural expectations and channelled through disciplinary and professional training, and has been so from the start. A 'science policy briefing' that the European Science Foundation issued in 2010 distinguished sharply between 'environment' and 'landscape', giving the impression that 'environment' is a given, a non-negotiable material entity, beyond historical, cultural and perceptual construction, as well as a much narrower, more precise term: 'We all live not only in an environment, not only in a physical reality but also in our perception of it – in a landscape. Landscape includes the physical and the mental, the natural and the cultural.'[10] This appears to create a division of labour between the properly scientific 'environment' and 'landscape' as a term that is granted to the arts and humanities. In fact, this division is a matter of academic training and, indeed, history rather than any clear-cut facticity. It is, among other things, a convenience for allocating funding and privileging experts.

Perhaps ironically, having declared ourselves to be 'environmental' historians, we discover that some of our partners do not make great use of the term. 'Environment' is a word used sparingly within the most recent Quantock Hills Management Plan (2014–19) , which contains as many references to 'historic environment' as it does to 'natural environment'.[11] The preferred terms are place and nature, but above all, landscape. This should not, perhaps surprise us given that the institutional and managerial unity ascribed to the hills is as an 'Area of Outstanding Natural Beauty', unified above all by the eye and what pleases it.

Landscape, too, has its metrics and instruments of management: Landscape Character Assessment (LCA – as discussed elsewhere in this volume by Emma-Jane Preece). Though past usages have tended to emphasize visual engagement with place and its surface attributes, and have been almost reflexively linked to places of high scenic beauty, the use of the term has become more neutral, stripped of its origins as the name for a particular form of visual art. Today's aesthetic of landscape embraces the non-picturesque, the ordinary, the urban, the suburban and the industrial, often without prejudice. Moreover, it is a multi-sensory aesthetic that engages our faculties for hearing, smelling, tasting and feeling. And feeling is not just about touch in a literal sense; as Chris Townsend explained with reference to a range of hills in Scotland known as the Monadhliaths (threatened, in his view, by proposals for a large-scale wind farm):

> we're talking about … a subtly beautiful, quiet landscape. But it's not just about aesthetics. I think it's far deeper than that. It's about … the feeling of being in a wild, unspoiled area. It's not just about what it looks like – it's also about what it feels like.[12]

The case of Wicken Fen further demonstrates that, whereas landscape is more strongly associated with the arts and humanities (as well as the discipline of 'landscape history' which certainly has its technical aspects), the language of environment is first and foremost the language of science as well as the language of governance (perhaps even a different form of governance). While the Fen is certainly a kind of relict of a cultural landscape, as the National Trust which manages it certainly acknowledges, associated with a Fen 'way of life', Wicken Fen was preserved above all because of its role as a site of scientific endeavour. A collected volume from 1997 (and an excellent one) on 'the making of a wetland nature reserve' contains three chapters from twelve on 'the human dimension', including one on the Fen's history.[13] But the focus of 'the human dimension' is overwhelmingly on management by those trained in science (including 'the management of visitors'). This is not to say that such a balance is in error or regrettable; rather, that it reflects the kind of expertise that has been brought to bear on the place, and the aspirations for it, which also are expressed in narratives of place and change. Wicken Fen is a highly valued place because it is a highly valued 'environment', 'an exceptionally rich ecosystem' (showing the close relationship in some minds and readings between environment and ecosystem), containing high numbers of endangered species. This is at least in part a consequence of the Fen being studied, and in turn protected, and then studied again. It appears to be an unusually deep reservoir of environmental intensity, because, despite its small size, we have an awful lot of environmental knowledge about it, and this is itself a self-reinforcing process.

Our engagement with practitioners has assisted all of us in appreciating diversity of meaning, and helping to focus enquiry on the reasons for this. Should we accept the historical meanings and allocations of responsibility that this inheritance implies? What Stephen Daniels refers to as the 'creative range and depth of meaning' that the notion of landscape possesses, whether or not we introduce refinements such as riverscape, waterscape, mountainscape, animalscape, workscape or soundscape, lends it particular purchase for environmental historians and humanities scholars in general.[14] Should we then carve out a domain of 'landscape' that is more proper to the humanities? And yet we call ourselves *environmental* historians. These are not innocent terms, and there are gains and losses from focusing on each.

Environmental beauty

In his essay on 'beauty and aesthetics', Peter Coates examined the notion of aesthetic appreciation of the 'environment' in the contexts of protected areas such as AONBs and national parks and changing ideas about beauty over time and in different parts of the world.

In discussions with our partners, we were presented with the practical implications of the notion of beauty from the perspective of organizations that managed 'environments' to encourage tourism and recreation, that is, the need to conform to public expectations of what is pleasing as well as providing amenities for various forms of recreation.

Our places are promoted as tourist attractions but also projected through artists' engagements with place. We included artists and curators in our understanding of practitioners as well as managers. Nonetheless, there were differences in how art and artists featured from place to place. It is not a novel observation that aesthetics have played a considerable part in conservation in Britain, but it is perhaps a recent phenomenon that 'beauty' in various forms has been so widely proclaimed (not always with a broad consensus, of course) as a characteristic of many landscapes. With its designation as an AONB, the Quantocks landscape has received statutory protection, and it is perhaps no surprise to find artists active there. We had the fortune to hear from, view and discuss the work of landscape artist Jenny Graham. The flatlands of the Fens have received considerably less praise: it is big sky country rather than a charmed and charming landscape. Here we heard from Carry Akroyd, whose work in some regards embraces 'natures powers & spells' articulated by the Northamptonshire and Fenland poet John Clare, but does not shy away from documenting the ubiquitous presence of humanity: not just as shapers and makers of the landscape, but active with our vehicles, aircraft, satellites and spinning turbines.[15] Kielder represents a contrasting case both in its aesthetic history and the artworks brought into our project. Instead of representations of place and landscape and the physical presence of their creators, there were installations in the landscape. The manufactured nature of much of the most apparent aspects of the Kielder environment – lake and forest – seems to provide a creative latitude unavailable at Wicken and the Quantocks, where, surely, objections to large installations would be more vigorous. How would Friends of Quantock react to a proposal to site a fantastically carved wooden cabin that seemed to have leaped straight out of the pages of Brothers Grimm in a visually exposed spot on the hills they watch over?

Hence all three places have become 'places for art', but this takes on different institutional forms. At Wicken, it is a pastime or profession for visitors rather than a central consideration for managers; in the Quantocks, of course, beauty is inherent in its governance; at Kielder, art becomes part of reinvention (as with its regional metropolis, Newcastle) and perhaps a coming to terms with the artificial landscape we have created, providing a mythology for a place that has lost visual connection with its history. Beauty is supposedly, famously subjective, but in practice it seems to be strongly shaped by aesthetically powerful voices and representations. The ghost of a Wordsworth or a Coleridge bestows genuine political power on those who stake a claim to the conservation of a landscape (John Clare less so). Conservationists can rely on the expressive power of 'great art' to render somewhere more beautiful, because to do so means we are acknowledging the less controversial view that Coleridge is a great poet, rather than having to argue directly about the scenic merits of the land itself: that is self-evident.[16]

At Kielder, the art installations contribute to the sense of place, perhaps compensating, or overcompensating, for the lack of a major literary figure, artist or more obvious 'natural' beauty. Beauty is not an attribute traditionally associated with Kielder: the words beauty and beautiful are in fact conspicuous by their absence from the official literature of Kielder and in Natural England's National Character Area Profile (NCA) for the Border Moors and Forests region that includes Kielder. In a blog posted a few days in advance of our visit in late March 2011, David Moon wondered 'if the word "beauty" will cross our lips when we discuss Kielder'. The quality of the scenery most frequently mentioned instead in the Area Profile is 'dramatic'. In the case of Kielder, this attribute is closely related to scale, which explains why a number of workshop participants, on arrival at Kielder, were struck by its un-Englishness. As Peter Coates reflected post-workshop: 'As the car turned a corner, we passed out of the thoroughly northern English milieu of the Pennines (a far cry from the soft, picturesque Quantock Hills) and suddenly entered Oregon or British Columbia. A North American-sized lake opened up in front of us and a forest of equally North American proportions and connotations flanked the sides of the broad, characteristically North American parkway-style road.' Forestry and reservoir, largely for industry, have obliterated the appearance of the earlier landscape. Yet despite the absence of an admiring public, aesthetic concerns have not been absent: firstly in the design of the reservoir as documented by Christine McCulloch in this volume, and latterly in deliberate attempts to build artistry into the landscape through installations while also drawing in visitors to appreciate the splendour of its big dark skies, unmarred – not unbenighted, one might say – by light pollution.

Smallness and intimacy of scale are essential ingredients of Quantock charm and appeal. Size matters enormously at Kielder, too, but for the opposite reason. We knew before our visit about the record-breaking size of forest and lake. After all, those were among the reasons David Moon chose the site. Yet some of us were not prepared for the heavy emphasis on The Big in the promotional literature. Kielder's peerless status is spelled out loud and clear on a board at the Tower Knowe Visitor Centre: 'big facts' include not just the largest man-made lake in northern Europe and the largest forest in England; they also extend to more red squirrels than anywhere else in England (50% of the total population) and the darkest night skies in England. At Kielder, we confront the aesthetics of scale: 'Your Great Outdoors', to which you are welcomed by Northumbrian Water and the Forestry Commission. 'It's sheer scale, the breathtaking scenery and the pure, idyllic tranquillity makes it such a majestic and memorable place,' reflected Elisabeth Roward of the Kielder Water and Forest Park Development Trust, in an blog publicizing the impending thirtieth anniversary of the opening of the reservoir.[17] Nonetheless, the authorities at Kielder also seek to enhance the aesthetic appeal of the location. One aspect of the Kielder Development Trust's activities, as already mentioned, has been precisely the installation of a series of works of art and architecture around the park, as discussed elsewhere in this book, that become way stations and playgrounds for visitors. Thus, while the promotional literature might play on scale and wildness, there was felt a need to bring both to a human scale and provide local framings by which to navigate and view this – of course artificial – landscape. The artists and architects, however, took great care to locate them in 'the environment' to complement and interpret their surroundings.[18] In fact, the idea of making the artificial environment at Kielder 'beautiful' has a longer history, and utilitarian needs have never been entirely divorced from recreation in British public forestry. Indeed, in the 1930s, the Treasury feared that 'an agency intended by Parliament to plant trees was becoming an agency to promote hiking', and from the 1950s, social objectives were included in the national forest policy, with 'public recreation and amenity' seen as 'desirable functions'.[19]

The statutory purpose of AONB designation – reiterated by Section 85 of the Countryside and Rights of Way (CROW) Act of 2000 – is 'to conserve and enhance natural beauty'. The Quantock Hills are so explicitly and completely about beauty to a degree that is treated as self-evident. The beauty is there; hence any alteration must be assessed as to whether it somehow negates that beauty. One member of the AONB team reflected in a post-workshop e-mail that, despite enjoying a particular strand of discussion ('I know my colleagues and I found it very stimulating'): 'if I get asked for my opinion on "what is natural beauty?" one more time I may end up crying' (though I am sure he would agree that a 200-year-old hedgerow composed of a variety of native plants is more beautiful than one consisting entirely of (common) laurel, whether planted last year or 50 years ago).

Beauty may well enjoy undisputed pride of place in the literature of the AONB Service and other bodies such as Natural England that articulate the values and attractions of the Quantocks (the word appears four times in the chairman of the Quantock Joint Advisory Committee's foreword to the draft management plan for 2014–19). Yet it does not stand alone. It is frequently (and increasingly) allied to ideas of tranquillity, seclusion, spiritual refreshment and respite from the pace, noise and polluted air of everyday urban life, a place with an 'overtly rural character' that offers a counter-environment to both city and working life.[20] References to writers who are firmly part of the literary canon serve to confirm these expectations of place: like Coleridge and Wordsworth, you too can 'get away' to a place where you can get in touch with your own wilder side and express yourself without constraint, perhaps even generating a flow of your own creative juices.[21] It is treated as self-evident, again, that 'getting away from it all', that familiar trope of tourist boards promoting the outdoors, is easier in environmental settings distinguished by their beauty, making them implicitly polar opposites to our everyday environments and sheltering us temporarily from strife, disharmony and unhappiness, whether personal or related to local or global events.

'I remember once', recalled Wordsworth,

> when Coleridge, he [John Thelwall, the radical public lecturer] and I were seated … in the most beautiful part of the most beautiful glen of Alfoxden [the Wordsworths' Quantock residence, usually spelled Alfoxton], Coleridge exclaimed, "This is a place to reconcile one to all the jarrings and conflicts of the wide world." – "Nay", said Thelwall, "to make one forget them altogether".[22]

Today, the Quantocks AONB team and other groups that promote the area are ever alert to new ways of cementing the connection between the Quantocks and Coleridge. The 36-mile (58 km) Coleridge Way ('in the footsteps of the Romantic poets'), which runs from Nether Stowey through the Quantocks to the coast at Porlock, linking locations associated with the poet and his poems, opened in 2005. In May 2014, the official launch of a 15-mile (24 km) extension, from Porlock to Lynmouth, was attended by Rosemary Coleridge Middleton, great-great-great-granddaughter of Samuel Taylor Coleridge.

An important theme in Coates' essay on beauty and environmental aesthetics is the impact of ecological science on received notions of beauty in place, landscape and nature. This broadened sense – delivered by the rise of ecological understandings of place – of what 'beauty' (or non-beauty or anti-beauty) mean in an environment do also, of course, relate to natural processes. But this acceptance of natural processes only goes so far. It is not only health considerations which determine that visitors (or television viewers) do not want to see animal carcasses littering 'rewilded' spaces such as Oostvaardersplassen (discussed elsewhere in this book by Smout) or Wicken Fen as part of a programme to allow species populations to reach locally appropriate stocking levels.[23] It is notable that humans, who celebrate the natural world as a symbol of vitality and life, are rather less comfortable with visible processes of decay and death, though the public aesthetics of *human* mortality is highly developed in the settings of cemeteries, churches and war memorials, as well as in literature, film, music and visual arts. Instead, seasons of decay and winter emerged in English poetry, to take an example, as times of contemplation, of access to 'philosophic Melancholy'; as Raymond Williams wrote, nature becomes 'a substitute order; lonely, prophetic, bearing the love of humankind in just those places where men are not'.[24]

Nonetheless, notions of beauty have proved to be more resistant to change than our places themselves. In 1964, David Lowenthal, an American geographer who had recently moved to Britain, co-published an article with Hugh Prince, a British geographer, entitled 'The English Landscape'. The rural places that crop up in this long essay – and feature in the photographs – are the Lake District, Brecon Beacons [Wales], Surrey Weald, Dartmoor, Stourhead (Wiltshire) and the Cotswolds. Much of what Lowenthal and Prince had to say about tastes in landscape ('The English Taste in Landscape' would have been a more accurate title) 50 years ago is, and remains, directly relevant to our three places. Half a century ago, they argue, English people liked their landscapes to be orderly and neat; hedgerows and stone walls, for example, were essential ingredients. But they did not want them regimented; Lowenthal and Prince referred to an 'abhorrence of straight lines and uniform spaces'. At the same time, they did not like untidy elements in their landscapes, such as scrub: as such, 'scrubby' is a pejorative adjective in British English, and helps explain why the Quantocks AONB Service douses with chemicals the bracken that blankets open hillsides, and major scrub clearances have been undertaken at Wicken Fen to open up the sedge fields to the appearance they would have had when once intensively managed for fuel and thatch.[25]

What the English liked back in the early 1960s, according to Lowenthal and Prince, was the picturesque: a landscape that somehow looks less functional than the 'Sitka slums' of Kielder, yet also more finished. The qualities prized are density of feature and smallness of scale (the authors quote American novelist Henry James' statement that 'density of feature is the great characteristic of English scenery') and the feeling of intimacy this generates: 'soft green charm' was another American's generic description of the ideal English countryside.[26]

Nevertheless, opinions, like the natural world, are neither entirely consistent nor static. The skyscape, few would dispute, is an integral ingredient of the landscape. In their survey, Lowenthal and Prince reflected that the English particularly liked the union with the sky that rolling uplands supply – an asset, we can add, that flatlands such as Wicken also possess. These skyscapes can transform otherwise 'dismal' moors and 'bleak' Fens into something elevating and transcendent. Though they did not specify this, the skies of which Lowenthal and Prince wrote were, by default, daytime skies. Today, with almost inescapable levels of light pollution where most of us live, dark skies are a commodity that has moved much higher up the hierarchy of landscape values. Kielder's night time airy canopy is celebrated as one of the darkest skies in England, and their preservation above the Quantocks is identified as a priority in Natural England's recent National Character Area Profile for the area.[27]

Related to skyscapes is, of course, the weather. Light and shade are a critical part of this. The shifting dynamic of light and shade that Libby Robin notes in her essay in this volume, 'Light on Landscape: An Antipodean View', is arguably the great leveller that lords it over every English landscape and lends beauty to Quantocks, Kielder and Wicken alike (though beauty is a word that appears even less frequently in the National Trust's literature on this site than it does in that on Kielder). Landscape, it almost goes without saying, is always changing in appearance with different lights, weathers and the seasonal changes in vegetational cover and wildlife. Dorothy Wordsworth, for example, recorded in her journal that the first of March 1798 dawned mistily at Alfoxton, their rented home in the Quantocks: 'the shapes of the mist, slowly moving along, exquisitely beautiful. Passing over the sheep they almost seemed to have more of life than those quiet creatures.'[28] But these are not changes in the environment.

Environmental change

In their essay about local perspectives on global processes of environmental change, David Moon and Leona Jayne Skelton focused on one community over its residents' lifetimes. In other words, their timescale for considering environmental change was the life span of the oldest interviewees. On embarking on a project with partners concerned with managing their 'environments' at the present time, we anticipated that this engagement would draw us mainly towards present-day concerns. We could not have been more wrong. All the places had their own histories, histories of environmental change, that stretch back deep into the past, that our partners were well aware of, and which informed their decisions on managing the sites. If, as historians, we thought we had a near monopoly on the past, we were mistaken. It is perhaps a wider truth in environmental policy that the involvement of planners and managers with an historical interest, or indeed historians with an interest in environmental policy, has always been an important aspect driving policy, management and environmental history forward. Graham Gill, the Forestry Commission's managing director for the North East, commented himself at the presence of Chris Smout, who has written extensively on the history of woodlands in northern Britain, among the audience for his outdoor talk on planting policy, past, present and future.

At Kielder, many employees of the partners and other local residents, as well as Moon, who chose the location and organized the workshop, can remember the North Tyne valley before it was dammed in the 1970s. Only the oldest residents we met could remember the start of the forestry plantations in the 1920s and 1930s. Graham Gill was just as at home as historians in thinking across long time periods, and how what had happened in the past had an impact on the present. This is illustrated in a discussion between Graham Gill and environmental historians David Moon and Gideon Shapiro:[29]

GRAHAM: We're finding that ... before the forest was there the hills had been cleared of trees for certainly 2000 years and maybe 4000 years, so there'd been really no forest there and for the last ... 1000 years, pretty much managed on an extractive low intensity agricultural economy, so it would be sheep-grazing and ... grouse moor so the sheep were taken off, nothing was ever put back on and ... the site would be regularly burnt to get young grass to grow up.... [W]hen we started planting trees on these sites we had to create a raised planting spot for the trees to get them out of the wet, cold ground and onto a better drained mound and that was done initially with spades and later with ploughs, and now we use ... excavators to create mounds ... but it's the same principle, to get the tree onto a raised spot. On the first rotation, we found that they really need ... phosphate fertiliser and potassium fertiliser to get them to grow. Sometimes ... we would add nitrogen, but that was more on the heathery ground, but it was generally phosphate and potassium that was in short supply. On the second rotation, we're finding we don't need to add any fertiliser at all and partly that's because trees are good at filtering pollutants out of the atmosphere so sulphur pollutants come into the soil, nitrogen oxides pulled into the soil as well, ... but also we haven't been extracting nutrients any longer from the site so we're finding the fertility's increased by the second rotation, and provided on those nutrient poor sites if we're leaving the branches and the needles, we get a lot of the nutrients back ... cos the tree pushes the nutrients into its into its needles.

GIDEON: And is that to do with the modern method with those big machines that strip the branches off back to let you go on?

GRAHAM: Yeah, if we were ... chainsawing we would do the same, but there is a thought now, [at] some sites … we could actually harvest the whole tree, branches, needles, the whole lot and you would use the stem wood for sawing timber and the rest would go for a biofuel ... But we're concerned about loss on the nutrient poor sites we have ... [At] some places they were trying pulling up stumps as well, and they can burn them, but finding that where you do that you get so much soil disturbance that you lose carbon from the soil ... So here we wouldn't consider stump extraction.

This is one way that we use the past in connection with current debates about the environment and environmental change: to think about environmental dynamics, change and potential change. Another way to employ the past, though, is to validate the value of preserving the environment in its current form, to ensure that features such as archaeological sites remain intact. Conservation entails decisions about environmental change, either arresting it for purposes of protecting particular species, historic features or types of environment; seeking to change a location back to how it had once been, insofar as that can be inferred; or ensuring natural processes can occur. Geographers Caitlin DeSilvey, Simon Naylor and Colin Sackett have recently underscored environmental historians' emphasis on the constancy of change:

> Background assumptions about succession and stability (in animal and plant populations) and conservation and constancy (in landscapes, particularly those we value) often obscure the dynamism that shaped these places and their inhabitants.

They go on to argue that this approach to the past (that they term anticipatory history), which 'calls attention to process rather than permanence may therefore help us to be more prepared for future change; to respond thoughtfully and proactively, rather than in a mode of retreat or regret'.[30] Preserving archaeological remains, for example, can then become not so much an attempt to fossilize the past into the future, as a direct reminder of the inevitability that things become different. Historians, for whom change over time is meat and drink, can contribute to a better understanding of change and its consequences.

The change in the offing at Wicken Fen is not relinquishing a treasured local place or landscape feature such as the harbour at Mullion Cove in Cornwall that was the focus of DeSilvey's team's attention. Yet there is some common ground. For despite the scrupulousness with which Wicken has been studied, and the degree to which it is known intimately by science, it is perceived as a place 'under threat'. The aim of a study published in 1997 was 'to take the Fen backwards through time, to restore some of the biological diversity lost'.[31] Wicken was imagined as yet another exemplar of an 'environment' in decline and degraded by people. However, the 'thoughtful and proactive response' sought by the Fen's managers since that time has not been simply defensive, but has looked beyond the boundaries of the existing reserve to achieve a change in the surrounding agricultural landscape. Managers seek support for rewilding and re-naturalization, for the very idea of the process of change, not the retention of the status quo of an island amid reclaimed land, a landscape sanctioned by centuries of arable farming (from an ecological standpoint, small is not beautiful).

The National Trust at Wicken Fen do not themselves use the term 'rewilding'. As we discovered at a project workshop held at the site, the term is both controversial and interpreted in many different ways. If it is envisaged as a 'return' to a previous, more ecologically-desirable baseline, when was this time and what do we really know about it? Was it in the Palaeolithic, before any major anthropogenic impact on the landscape, in the more recent Mesolithic, or during one of the societies of the last few millennia which each exploited the changing environment in different ways? What level of managerial intervention would be required, now, to hold a 'rewilded' space to such a baseline? Consequently, the National Trust prefer to speak of unleashing ecological processes on a scale that could allow species relatively high up the food chain, such as wild cattle and horses, to subsist. While this implicitly evokes some scholar's interpretation of Mesolithic landscapes, it is not a specific goal. There is an acceptance of both the reality and the uncertainty of change.

We can also note that in the document setting out the 'Vision', this is reflected in a turn to speaking about 'nature' rather than the 'environment'. In this document, as we find elsewhere, 'environment' is used more frequently in referring to a passive object of study or regulation, especially when put at risk by human activity. In contrast, in the future, agency is conferred on 'nature' that will be free to act and self-determine. Although we have seen how Wicken Fen has been profoundly shaped over the past century by the aspirations and efforts of environmental scientists, it appears that when we confer some parity of esteem between people and other species we revert to speaking of 'nature'. The 'environment' can be restored to its proper functioning – at least according to the mandate of the people tasked with managing it.

Restoration is also part of the management agenda in the Quantocks AONB. This is evident in the bringing back into management of the signature beech hedge banks through Environmental Stewardship grants; many are overgrown and therefore vulnerable in storms. Further restoration projects include: husbanding more conventional hedgerows and hedgerow trees that delineate historic field patterns; diversification of planting within the older conifer plantations; efforts to encourage the replanting of traditional community orchards and preservation of local apple varieties; and the pursuit of energetic campaigns to reduce non-native rhododendron coverage in the interests of native flora.[32] But 'rewilding' in a grander sense, on a landscape scale, comparable to the Wicken Vision, is not an objective. In a place where 'character' is paramount, regulatory controls are concerned above all with meeting people's expectations, and both the attitude towards change, and language employed, reflect this. This is perhaps tied above all to the notion of 'outstanding beauty'. Perfection cannot be perfected. A few days after arriving at Alfoxton, Dorothy wrote to a friend (4 July 1797): 'There is everything here; sea, woods wild as fancy ever painted, brooks clear and pebbly as in Cumberland, villages so romantic.'[33] Not many would wager on the capacity of change, even natural change, to produce an even more beautiful place. Instead, they see change – which might take the form of planting highly visible crops such as the biofuel plant, miscanthus (elephant grass) and oilseed rape – as an inherent threat to a beauty that cannot be improved on, only impaired.

At Kielder and other Forestry Commission plantations, the term rewilding is not used. However, since the 1970s, by seeking to build in 'natural' elements, the Forestry Commission has taken an interest in designing its forests for aesthetic purposes and conservation as well as maximizing timber production.[34] Over the following years, regimented, geometric blocks of monoculture, often fast-growing Sitka spruce, of the same age, were gradually changed, especially in areas with large numbers of tourists. At Kielder Forest the shift began in the early 1980s. The new approach sought 'to integrate the requirement of efficient operational activity with a planned increase in visual and wildlife diversity'. The process aimed 'to change...even-aged plantations into ... diverse forests'.[35] Graham Gill explained to us (from a vantage point where we overlooked the forest) how the edges of planted areas were no longer straight lines, but were carefully designed to fit into the contours of the land. Account was taken of the perspective from particular view points. A wider variety of trees, including native species and more broad-leaved trees, are now planted to diversify the forest 'environment'. 'Forest design plans' for felling and restocking that take account of a variety of objectives are produced in consultation with 'statutory authorities like Natural England, National Park Authority, County Council ... and ... local businesses and [the] local community'.[36] Thus, plans for felling and restocking at Kielder Forest, and other

Forestry Commission forests, now take account of recreation, amenity, public access, conservation, landscape and aesthetic considerations as well as timber production. Kielder Forest is still artificial, but is being redesigned to appear somehow more 'natural', and an increasingly important objective is to protect and enhance its appeal to 'those seeking an escape from large urban centres'.[37] The success of the Forestry Commission in achieving its wider objectives can be seen in the outcry when the UK government announced it intended to sell off England's public forests in 2010. The decision was reversed.

Up to this point in our discussion, all the changes we have considered are local. Nonetheless, the managers of all our sites are cognizant of the pressing need to take account of changes at far larger scales that have local impacts, the most striking of which is the global dynamics of a changing climate. Yet it is not just climate change itself which is a global phenomenon; the understanding and public debate about it is profoundly shaped by global conversations that take place far from the places we have studied, and where local people experience them as recipients rather than participants. Indeed, there is a growing gap between scientific and popular knowledges of climate and climate change. According to Georgina Endfield and Erin Gill, members of the research network with particular expertise in climate history and communications strategies, this unsatisfactory situation is 'partly a function of the predominantly scientific discourse in which climate change debates have been couched, and partly the increasingly global-scale of climate thinking'. As a result:

> climate has, in effect, become decoupled from its local cultural significance. According to Duncan Hutt, head of land management for Northumberland Wildlife Trust, there is a mood of complacency among those he encounters. This is the attitude that says: "Desertification in Africa, flooding in Bangladesh, we don't have to worry. We're safe and cosy here in the North East."[38]

These gaps between the local and global generate two related ironies. Increasingly, as we have seen, it is viewed as desirable to conserve or introduce more 'natural' elements in the landscape. But what does this local 'rewilding' mean on a planet where global processes are increasingly anthropogenically steered? How will local management processes respond to the pressures of global anthropogenic processes? Secondly, environmental change is increasingly viewed as something distant, irreversible and perhaps catastrophic, when in fact it is ongoing, very much within people's lived experiences and conditioned by the choices they make.

While each of our case study areas faces a common challenge in climate change, their planning and scope for action are shaped by priorities set in statute, pursued by local managers and conditioned by the expectations of a wider public. This is revealed by an examination of climate change strategies.

Despite the long-standing and recently intensified interest from the Forestry Commission in a whole range of goals, the primary goal in Kielder Forest remains the production of timber. This shapes both short-term reaction and longer-term plans. More intense rainstorms, noted by Graham Gill, are already influencing policy, from the size of culverts installed under roads to the types of trees that will be planted in the future.[39] Climate scenarios for 2080 suggest that Sitka spruce, which has proved to be such a reliable performer since the 1920s, may no longer be fit for purpose: planting policy elsewhere in Northumberland, further east, is already adjusting to drier conditions by replacing Sitka with Douglas fir and larch. Species choice, Graham Gill stresses, is not taken lightly or imposed from on high. It is the subject of extensive public discussion and currently under trial are species such as Japanese red cedar and Macedonian pine.[40]

Experimentation with species and 'learning by doing' on particular sites is an established part of forestry practice over many decades, and such behaviour is nothing new. Indeed, such adaptability can also be seen in the Quantock Hills. The pressures of wartime timber demand that led to the foundation of the Forestry Commission in 1919 were felt in the southwest as well as the northeast. Between 1914 and 1918, in Somerset, 2,800 acres (1133 ha) of woodland was cut, mainly native oak – and much of it in the Quantocks. In 1922, the Forestry Commission secured several large tracts of land in the area amounting to over 2,000 acres (810 ha) in total. Two North American species, the Douglas fir and Sitka spruce, dominated afforestation, which, across the hills as a whole, extending to 2,800 (1133 ha) acres by 1960, the largest forestry plantation in southwest England.[41] Since the 1960s however, also paralleling the Kielder experience, native hardwood species have been introduced along the plantation perimeters, to 'soften the hard edges' of the softwoods.[42] The 'modern forester', Vincent Waite reflected half a century ago, 'is also a skilled landscapist who pays expert attention to the effects of the lay-out of the forest on the scenery'.[43] Forestry has also adapted to the 'global' or wider pressures of changing timber markets and subsidies (if not always as rapidly as some would like), seeking over the long-term a more resilient economic and ecological base.

The uncertainty engendered by climate change is, on the face of it, less of a problem for the ambitions of the Wicken Vision. As the aim of the strategy is to unleash ecological process towards no pre-determined end, a shifting climate simply becomes part of the mix. In a sense, the Vision and future uncertainties merely continue a pattern by which the Fen has almost in its entirety been restored to wetland from the arable land to which it had been converted in previous centuries, punctuated again in the twentieth century by some 'reversion' to crop-growing during wartime. Nevertheless, the National Trust plan is hedged by commitments to maintain biodiversity and the protected scientific interest of the site, as well as community participation and the provision of green space and access expected by a paying public. It thus remains to be seen how much future change will test the expectations and the tolerances of those who value the Fen, and whether demands will arise for greater levels of intervention. Other future uncertainties, such as the price of food and land, may affect the ability of the National Trust to obtain the real estate for the full implementation of the Vision.

The uncertainty that surrounds the impact of climate change is both problematic and already manifest at the local level in the Quantocks, a point emphasized by Iain Porter, development officer (and formerly acting manager) of the AONB service. The area's characteristic beech hedgebanks were expected to be an early casualty of more intense bouts of both wetter and drier weather, but this has not materialized and, instead of preparing to give them up, restoration and regeneration plans are afoot.[44] Another major current management issue is also directly associated with climate change: whether to continue to devote substantial effort and large amounts of funding to lowland heath management, which has become increasingly difficult logistically because a series of wet winters meant that the hills have been too wet to burn until late in the season (and the swaling season closes at the end of March). The rationale for swaling (controlled burning) to keep the scrub at bay is that this particular form of habitat is rare and because there is an aesthetic and recreational preference for open country. In other words, this is as much a question of beauty as an ecological matter.[45] A changing climate may add to the costs of meeting these preferences when the rural economy that created open country has disappeared. A pragmatic response, almost rewilding by default rather than design, might be letting the heath 'go back to woodland' because of the excessive cost of maintaining it.[46] But would that abandonment of its current character undermine the very rationale for the AONB designation?

Such changes are certainly not new to the Quantocks. The relics of past alterations in the land triggered by major climate change remain readily visible. In the fourteenth century, a series of catastrophically cold and wet summers, followed by the Black Death, spelled the end of upland arable farming and the subsequent predominance of grazing and woodland. Much of today's heathland and broadleaf woodland covers medieval field systems, whose ridges and furrows can still be easily detected. This was, in a certain sense, a 'market' response to the challenge, in that peasant cultivators adapted land use to the costs and climate they faced. In the future, global warming might lead to a longer growing season and capacity to cultivate new crop varieties: vineyards and lavender replacing orchards and livestock? Alternatively, the switch to a new energy infrastructure to avoid or mitigate climate change by encouraging greater use of renewable sources (according to the Draft Management Plan for 2014–19, the Quantocks 'provide good opportunities for renewable energy including hydro, solar, wind and biomass') might necessitate the appearance of new pylons, masts and wind turbines that 'change the landscape character from agricultural to industrial'.[47] Either way, the challenges may be profound, but they are perhaps no less than episodic major shifts in the form of the landscape that the region has previously experienced.

In a conclusion, it is perhaps appropriate to draw attention to the similarities between our places rather than to dwell, as we did at the beginning of the book (in the 'Three Places' chapter), on the differences. One quite simple thing to note is: change is normal, and while its causes may be different over time, the fact of change affected by a shifting global climate is also, in a certain sense, quite normal. This is not to trivialize the issue: that something is normal does not make it insignificant. Rather, it helps understand coming (and uncertain) changes as being *just as significant* as past ones about which history can serve to remind us. The transformations of the past have been deep, and those of the future will probably be no less so. History is also a lesson in unintended consequences and thwarted expectations. The water demand for which Kielder Water was constructed had disappeared before it was even in operation. But it may yet emerge again as a result of climate change as areas of southeast England are likely to experience more acute shortages of water and, at some point, it could become economically viable to transport it there.

In the meantime, the emergence of leisure activities in waters constructed for essentially infrastructural reasons is a common feature of all three of our places. Anglers enjoy the regularly replenished fish stocks of Kielder Water, just as they do at Durleigh Water in the Quantock foothills, constructed to supply the British Cellophane plant set up in the adjacent town of Bridgwater in 1937. Durleigh is also a space for dinghy sailing and windsurfing – as well as a sanctuary for birds and destination for birders – although production at the cellophane plant peaked in the late 1970s and the plant closed in 2005. Similarly, true to the long romantic tradition, the author of a guide to walks in Somerset, published in 1997, complained about the 'powerful lights' at Triscombe Quarry which, at night, 'rob this area of its sense of solitude'.[48] But Triscombe Quarry closed down in 1999, and the site is now in the process of being reclaimed 'by nature'; it might be surprising if it was not soon populated by rare species as has happened in numerous abandoned excavations around the country. Indeed, the 'Great Fen' project near Peterborough, in many ways a sibling re-wetting project to Wicken Fen's Vision, has been established in abandoned clay pits, and its managers continue to work with local extraction companies in planning landscape 'restoration' – not simply reverting to a re-establishing of the farmland present before quarrying began, the minimum requirement in law.

Ongoing processes of change of different scale, whether continuous or episodic in their impact, will shape places as they have done in the past. Equally, the role played by our project partners will continue to be significant, but may have to adapt to new challenges too – at times, challenges that call their original rationale into question. It seems to us, however, that these people will be crucial to ecologically and socially wise management of our landscapes, not just as experts and key institutional players, but as co-ordinators and mediators of all the knowledge that can be brought to bear on place, and helping to bridge gaps we can identify now. These may relate most importantly to local 'popular' participation and consultation (also mediated through bodies such as local government), but also the 'global' and outsiders. All of our places are to a degree 'de-localized' by conservation practice that is shaped nationally and internationally: the SSSI and National Nature Reserve are national designations, while the Quantocks, it bears repeating, are also part of Exmoor and Quantock Oakwoods Special Area of Conservation (SAC), which is a European designation under the EC Habitats and Species Directive that also covers Wicken, and the latter is also protected under the International Convention on Wetlands of International Importance (Ramsar Convention). Other global forces relate to the world of ideas and public debate, and in a very modest way, our own practice as historians.

In the case of climate, we can see how 'local, lay or "experiential" perspectives are assuming new importance as legitimate sources of climate knowledge.'[49] To this end, environmental managers have a role to 'tailor efforts to engage the public with climate change debates'. Rob Jarman, the National Trust's sustainability director, believes that the most effective responses to the impact of climate change address what has happened at the local level in the past, what local people have experienced, and how they have handled change; accordingly, the Trust's report, *Climate Change – Forecast? Changeable!*, examines the impact of climate change from the standpoint of local managers.[50] Adaptability – the fostering of appropriate skills, mindsets and attitudes – is the Trust's watchword, a flexible approach better equipped to cope with unpredictability than the search for security through adaptation to more precisely forecasted changes.

Environmental managers may collect directly, or assemble local knowledge such as that of nature conservationists at Kielder, both amateur and professional, who have in the past fifteen years noted, for example, an increase in the number of insect species associated with southern England, such as the speckled wood butterfly and broad bodied chaser dragonfly. This can help us see how global processes are articulated in local stories and experiences, and that while some of the challenges produced by a globalized industrial society are certainly novel, the experience of change in each place is nothing new. We may draw on the accumulated capacities and knowledge of place to make choices about our futures. Our contemporary concern about that future is not so 'present day' after all.

Notes

1. Christof Mauch, 'Notes from the Greenhouse: Making the Case for Environmental History', *Rachel Carson Center Perspectives* 6 (Rachel Carlson Center for Environment and Society, 2013), p. 9.
2. Northumbrian Water Limited, 2.2 Environment Policy http://www.nwl.co.uk/_assets/documents/Environment_Policy_New_2011.pdf (accessed 18/02/13).
3. Northumbrian Water, 'Living Water', Environment Policy Statement http://www.nwl.co.uk/your-home/for-the-environment.aspx (accessed 18/02/13).
4. T. C. Smout, *Nature Contested: Environmental History in Scotland and Northern England since 1600* (Edinburgh: Edinburgh University Press, 2000), p. 114.
5. David Archer, 'Kielder Water: White Elephant or White Knight?', in David Archer (ed.), *Tyne and Tide: A Celebration of the River Tyne* (Ovingham: Daryan Press, 2003), pp. 144–5.
6. Forest Research, Woodlands and the environment http://www.forestry.gov.uk/fr/infd-5suk4b (accessed 18/02/13).
7. Forest Research, Environmental Change Network http://www.forestry.gov.uk/fr/HCOU-4U4JA7 (accessed 18/02/13).

8. Interview held on 03/07/12 at the Forestry Commission District Office, Bellingham, Northumberland.

9. Interview held on 15/10/12 at the Northumberland Wildlife Trust, Gosforth, Newcastle upon Tyne.

10. Foreword, European Science Foundation, *Landscape in a Changing World: Bridging Divides, Integrating Disciplines, Serving Society* (Science Policy Briefing 41, October 2010).

11. Quantock Hills Area of Outstanding Natural Beauty, *Management Plan 2014–2019*, pp. 3, 7, 10, 13, 15, 22, 23, 25, 28, 29, 34, 35, 36, 45, 46, 52 http://www.quantockhills. com/resources/AONB_Managment_plan_searchable_pdf_nov_14.pdf (accessed 19/01/15).

12. Quoted in 'A Land Apart', *John Muir Trust Journal* 56 (Spring 2014), p. 10.

13. Laurie Friday (ed.), *Wicken Fen: The Making of a Wetland Nature Reserve* (Colchester: Harley Books, 1997).

14. Marianna Dudley and Peter Coates, *Cultural Ecosystem Services (CES): A Keywords Manual* (Cambridge: World Conservation Monitoring Centre/UK National Ecosystem Assessment Follow-On, June 2014), pp. 25–7; Stephen Daniels, 'What Landscape Means to Me', *Landscapes* 12/2 (2012), pp. 2, 92.

15. See Carry Akroyd, *Natures Powers & Spells: Landscape Change, John Clare and Me* (Peterborough: Langford Press, 2009).

16. In an interview in the Quantocks (at Fyne Court, Broomfield) on 6 July 2013, prior to an outdoor screening of *Pandaemonium* (2001), a 2-hour film set in 1797–98, the seminal year for English literature that Wordsworth and Coleridge spent in the Quantocks, director and local resident Julien Temple referred to the Quantocks themselves as the 'real star' of his film.

17. Visit Northumberland, 'Celebrating 30 Years of Kielder Reservoir', 15 May 2012 http://blog.visitnorthumberland.com/2012/05/15/celebrating-30-years-of-kielder-reservoir/ (accessed 20/01/15).

18. On art and the environment, see Nicholas Alfrey, Stephen Daniels and Joy Sleeman, 'To the Ends of the Earth: Art and Environment', 11 May 2012, Tate Papers Issue 17 http://www.tate.org.uk/research/publications/tate-papers/ends-earth-art-and-environment (accessed 16/01/15).

19. Smout, *Nature Contested*, p. 62.

20. Quantock Hills, *Draft Management Plan*, pp. 9–10, 12, 15, 17, 36 http://www. quantockhills.com/resources/FINAL_AONB_Management_Plan_18214.pdf (accessed 24/10/14).

21. Quantock Hills, *Draft Management Plan*, p. 10 http://www.quantockhills.com/ resources/FINAL_AONB_Management_Plan_18214.pdf (accessed 24/10/14).

22. William Wordsworth, *The Complete Poetical Works of William Wordsworth*, vol. 2 (Boston: Houghton Mifflin, 1911), notes to 'Anecdote for Fathers' (1798), p. 12.

23. Kathy Hodder and James Bullock, 'Toward a Multiple Vision of Ecological Restoration', in Marcus Hall (ed.), *Restoration and History: The Search for a Usable Environmental Past* (New York and Abingdon, Oxon: Routledge, 2010), pp. 226–7.

24. Raymond Williams, *The Country and the City* (London: Chatto & Windus, 1973), p. 71. Citation from the Scottish poet James Thomson's *The Seasons,* written between the 1720s and 1740s. We are indebted to Caitlin DeSilvey for the rich notion of the 'palliative curation' of environments.

25. David Lowenthal and Hugh Prince, 'The English Landscape', *Geographical Review* 54/3 (1964), pp. 317, 310.

26. Lowenthal and Prince, 'English Landscape', p. 310; Henry James, *English Hours*

(Boston: Houghton Mifflin, 1905), p. 141; Henry Adams, *The Education of Henry Adams: An Autobiography* (Boston: Houghton Miffin Co., 1918), p. 72.

27. Natural England, *National Character Area Profile 144: Quantock Hills* (2013), pp. 4, 33.

28. 'Dorothy Wordsworth's Journal, Written at Alfoxden in 1798' (1 March 1798), in William Angus Knight, *Coleridge and Wordsworth in the West Country: Their Friendship, Work, and Surroundings* (London: Elkin Mathews, 1914), p. 146.

29. Gideon Shapiro, 'Varieties of Value: Nature's Value and Variance at the Kielder Water and Forest Park', unpublished MA thesis, Department of Historical Studies, University of Bristol (2012).

30. Caitlin DeSilvey, Simon Naylor and Colin Sackett (eds), *Anticipatory History* (Axminster, Devon: Uniformbooks, 2011), p. 10.

31. Friday (ed.), *Wicken Fen*, especially p. 282.

32. Marianna Dudley, Nick Nourse and Peter Coates, 'Fallen Fruits and Orchard Roots: Historical Orchard Research in the Quantock Hills', *Somerset Archaeology and Natural History: Proceedings of the Somerset Archaeological and Natural History Society* 157 (2014), pp. 167–76; Natural England, *National Character Area Profile 144: Quantock Hills* (2013).

33. William and Dorothy Wordsworth, *Letters of the Wordsworth Family: From 1787 to 1855, Vol. I* (Boston: Ginn, 1907), p. 110.

34. See K. Jan Oosthoek, *Conquering the Highlands: A History of the Afforestation of the Scottish Highlands* (Canberra: Australian National University Press, 2013), p. 149.

35. 'Restructuring and Forest Design', materials prepared for the Visit of the Independent Panel on Forestry to Northumberland (including Kielder) on 26 July 2011.

36. Interview with Graham Gill, held on 3 July 2012.

37. Natural England, *National Character Area Profile 5: Border Moors and Forests* (2013), p. 58.

38. Georgina Endfield and Erin Gill, 'Local Co-Production and Reception of Climate Change Strategies: Conversations with Individuals Working in Nature Conservation and Land Management', unpublished report, University of Nottingham (September 2014), p. 4.

39. Endfield and Gill, 'Local Co-Production', p. 10.

40. Endfield and Gill, 'Local Co-Production', p. 10; *NCA Profile 5, Border Moors and Forests*, pp. 16, 33, 40, 43.

41. Peter Haggett, *The Quantocks: Biography of an English Region* (Chew Magna: The Point Walter Press, 2012), pp. 151–3; Vincent Waite, *Portrait of the Quantocks* (London: Robert Hale, 1969), p. 158.

42. Haggett, *The Quantocks*, p. 153.

43. Waite, *Portrait*, p. 160.

44. Natural England, *National Character Area Profile 144: Quantock Hills* (2013), pp. 8–9.

45. Natural England, *National Character Area Profile 144: Quantock Hills*, pp. 8–9

46. Iain Porter, quoted in Endfield and Gill, 'Local Co-Production', p. 9.

47. Quantock Hills, *Draft Management Plan*, pp. 18, 36. http://www.quantockhills.com/resources/FINAL_AONB_Management_Plan_18214.pdf (accessed 24/10/14).

48. James Roberts, *Walking in Somerset* (Milnthorpe, Cumbria: Cicerone Press, 1997), p. 56. According to unconfirmed reports, stone aggregate from Triscombe was used to build the runways at Heathrow.

49. Endfield and Gill, 'Local Co-Production', pp. 1, 13.

50. The National Trust, *Climate Change – Forecast? Changeable!* (London: National Trust, 2005).